BETWEEN THE TEXT AND THE CANVAS

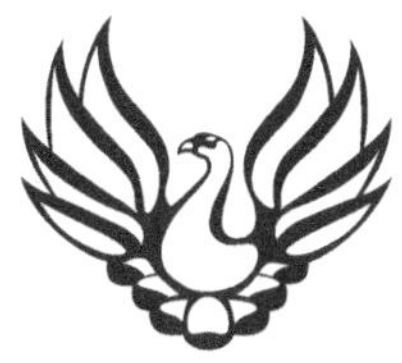

The Bible in the Modern World, 13

BETWEEN THE TEXT AND THE CANVAS

THE BIBLE AND ART IN DIALOGUE

edited by

J. Cheryl Exum

and

Ela Nutu

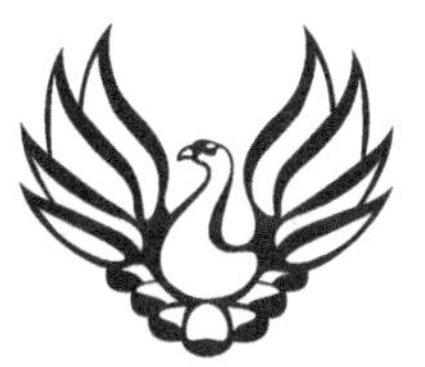

SHEFFIELD PHOENIX PRESS

2009

First published in hardback 2007
First published in paperback 2009

Published by Sheffield Phoenix Press
Department of Biblical Studies, University of Sheffield
Sheffield S10 2TN

www.sheffieldphoenix.com

A CIP catalogue record for this book
is available from the British Library

Typeset by Forthcoming Publications
Printed by Lightning Source

ISBN 978-1-906055-19-6 (hardback)
ISBN 978-1-906055-91-2 (paperback)

ISSN 1747-9630

CONTENTS

LIST OF CONTRIBUTORS

Kelly J. Baker is a doctoral candidate in Religion at Florida State University. Her Master's thesis explored the life and art of Henry Ossawa Tanner, and her current research interests include religion and material/print cultures, religion and the arts, and religious hatred. She is currently writing her dissertation on the interrelationships of religion, nationalism and material culture in the 1920s Ku Klux Klan.

Christina Bucher is Carl W. Zeigler Professor of Religion at Elizabethtown College, Elizabethtown, PA, where she is also Dean of Faculty. Her current research centres upon the interpretation of the Song of Songs in art, music and literature.

J. Cheryl Exum is Professor of Biblical Studies at the University of Sheffield. She is a Director of Sheffield Phoenix Press and Executive Editor of the journal *Biblical Interpretation*. Her books include *Tragedy and Biblical Narrative: Arrows of the Almighty* (1992), *Fragmented Women: Feminist (Sub)versions of Biblical Narratives* (1993), *Plotted, Shot, and Painted: Cultural Representations of Biblical Women* (1996) and, most recently, *Song of Songs, A Commentary* (2005). She is currently writing a book entitled *Cultural Industry: The Bible and the Arts*.

Heidi J. Hornik is Professor of Italian Renaissance and Baroque Art History at Baylor University in Texas. She received her degrees from Cornell University and the Pennsylvania State University. In addition to art-historical publications on Michele Tosini in *Artibus et historiae* and *Paragone*, Hornik has co-authored three interdisciplinary volumes on Italian Renaissance and Baroque painting and the Bible, under the title *Illuminating Luke* (*The Infancy Narrative* [2003], *The Public Ministry* [2005] and *The Death and Resurrection Narratives* [2007]), and co-edited one book, *Interpreting Christian Art* (2004), with Mikeal C. Parsons. Her current project is a book-length monograph, *Michele Tosini and the Ghirlandaio Workshop in Cinquecento Florence*, for Sussex Academic Press.

Christine E. Joynes is Associate Director of the Centre for Reception History of the Bible at the University of Oxford. One of her current research interests is the reception history of Mark's Gospel, and she is presently writing the Blackwell Bible Commentary, *Mark's Gospel through the Centuries*. She is also co-ordinating a project entitled *Biblical Women and Their Afterlives*. She has written a number of articles exploring the impact of the Bible on art, music and literature.

Sally E. Norris is a doctoral candidate in Theology at Oxford University (The Queen's College) and is currently writing her thesis on the reception history of the first chapter of Ezekiel. Her research interests include the study of *merkavah* mysticism and visionary literature, the reception history of biblical texts with particular emphasis on their interpretation in the arts, and the socio-political and theological import of vision and imagination in the contemporary church.

Ela Nutu is Research Associate in the Centre for the Study of the Bible in the Modern World at the University of Sheffield, and she also teaches in the Department of Biblical Studies. Her research interests focus on postmodern approaches to biblical interpretation (poststructuralist, psychoanalytical, cultural) and, more recently, on the Bible in art, music and literature. She is the author of *Incarnate Word, Inscribed Flesh: John's Prologue and the Postmodern* (2007) and a number of articles on the Bible, literary theory and film. She is currently working on a monograph on biblical women in art, entitled *Cuts: Violent Women in the Bible and Art*.

Martin O'Kane is Director of the Research Centre *The Bible and the Visual Imagination* at the University of Wales, Lampeter. His current research projects include *Imaging the Bible in Wales* and *The Bible and Art: Towards an Interdisciplinary Methodology*. His recent publications on Bible and art include *Painting the Text: The Artist as Biblical Interpreter* (2007). He is Chair of The Bible and Visual Culture Seminar of the European Association of Biblical Studies and co-chair of the Bible and Visual Culture section of the International Society of Biblical Literature.

Hugh S. Pyper is Professor and Head of Department in the Department of Biblical Studies, University of Sheffield. His books include *An Unsuitable Book: The Bible as Scandalous Text* (2006) and *David as Reader: 2 Samuel 12.1-5 and the Poetics of Fatherhood* (1996). He was assistant editor of the *Oxford Companion to Christian Thought* (2000). He is currently preparing a collection of his essays on Kierkegaard as a biblical reader, entitled *The Joy of Kierkegaard*, and is working on a commentary on Daniel and a study of the cultural effects of the concept of an 'old testament'.

Christopher Rowland is Dean Ireland's Professor of the Exegesis of Holy Scripture at the University of Oxford. He is Editor of the Blackwell Bible Commentary series on reception history and is co-director of the Centre for the Reception History of the Bible in Oxford. His books include *Revelation* (with Judith Kovacs, 2004) and *Radical Christian Writings: A Reader* (with Andrew Bradstock, 2002). He is currently writing a book on Blake and the Bible for Yale University Press.

ABBREVIATIONS

Ber. R.	*Bereshit Rabbah*
BibInt	*Biblical Interpretation: A Journal of Contemporary Approaches*
BWANT	Beiträge zur Wissenschaft vom Alten und Neuen Testament
BZ	*Biblische Zeitschrift*
CBQ	*Catholic Biblical Quarterly*
GKC	*Gesenius' Hebrew Grammar* (ed. E. Kautzsch, rev. and trans. A.E. Cowley; Oxford: Clarendon Press, 1910)
JAAR	*Journal of the American Academy of Religion*
JBL	*Journal of Biblical Literature*
JNES	*Journal of Near Eastern Studies*
JSOT	*Journal for the Study of the Old Testament*
KJV	King James Version
LCL	Loeb Classical Library
LXX	Septuagint
MT	Masoretic Text
NCAW	*Nineteenth-Century Art Worldwide*
NEB	New English Bible
NRSV	New Revised Standard Version
NTS	*New Testament Studies*
REB	Revised English Bible
RSV	Revised Standard Version
SJOT	*Scandinavian Journal of the Old Testament*
VTSup	*Vetus Testamentum*, Supplements
ZAW	*Zeitschrift für die alttestamentliche Wissenschaft*

List of Figures

(61 × 45.7 cm). Gift of Patrick and Beatrice Haggerty, 80.7.66. Haggerty Museum of Art, Marquette University, Milwaukee, Wisconsin. © ADAGP, Paris and DACS, London 2007

Fig. 4. Marc Chagall (1887–1985), *Paradise* from *Dessins pour la Bible* series, 1958–59. Lithograph, 14 × 10.5 in. Wake Forest University Print Collection, Winston-Salem, North Carolina. © ADAGP, Paris and DACS, London 2007

Christina Bucher, 'The Song of Songs and the Enclosed Garden'

Fig. 1. Martin Schongauer, *Madonna and Child in the Courtyard,* Kupferstichkabinett, Staatliche Museen zu Berlin. Photo: Bildarchiv Preussischer Kulturbesitz/Art Resource, NY

Fig. 2. Martin Schongauer, *Madonna on the Turfbench,* Kupferstichkabinett, Staatliche Museen zu Berlin. Photo: Bildarchiv Preussischer Kulturbesitz/Art Resource, NY

Fig. 3. Martin Schongauer, *Madonna in the Rose Garden*, Church of the Dominicans, Colmar. Photo: Snark/Art Resource, NY

Fig. 4. Stefan Lochner, *The Virgin in a Rose Bower,* Wallraf-Richartz-Museum, Cologne. Photo: Rheinisches Bildarchiv Köln

Fig. 5. Master of the Paradise Garden, *Little Paradise Garden*, Städelsches Kunstinstitut, Frankfurt. Photo: Foto Marburg/Art Resource, NY

Ela Nutu, 'Framing Judith'

Fig. 1. Lavinia Fontana, *Judith with the Head of Holofernes*, Musei Civici d'Arte Antica, Museo Davia Bargellini, Bologna

Fig. 2. Lavinia Fontana, *Judith with the Head of Holofernes*, Oratorio dei Pellegrini, Bologna. By kind permission of MiBAC—Archivio Fotografico Soprintendenza al Patrimonio Artistico, Storico e Demoetnoantropologico di Bologna

Fig. 3. Artemisia Gentileschi, *Judith Beheading Holofernes*, Museo Nazionale di Capodimonte, Naples. By kind permission of Fototeca delle Soprintendenza Speciale per il Polo Museale Napoletano

Fig. 4. Artemisia Gentileschi, *Judith Beheading Holofernes*, Galleria degli Uffizi, Florence. By kind permission of Ministero dei Beni e delle Attività Culturali

Fig. 5. Artemisia Gentileschi, *Judith and Her Maidservant*, Galleria Palatina (Palazzo Pitti), Florence. By kind permission of Ministero dei Beni e delle Attività Culturali

Fig. 6. Artemisia Gentileschi, *Judith and Her Maidservant with the Head of Holofernes*, c. 1623/1625. Gift of Mr Leslie H. Green. Photograph © 1984. The Detroit Institute of Arts

Fig. 7. Elisabetta Sirani, *Judith Showing the Head of Holofernes to the Israelites*, Burghley House, Stamford, Lincolnshire

Fig. 8. Fede Galizia, Italian, 1578–1630. *Judith with the Head of Holofernes*, 1596. Oil on canvas, 47.5 × 37 inches, SN684. Collection of the John and Mable Ringling Museum of Art, the State Art Museum of Florida

Fig. 9. Orazio Gentileschi, *Judith and Her Maidservant with the Head of Holofernes*, Wadsworth Atheneum Museum of Art, Hartford, CT. The Ella Gallup Sumner and Mary Catlin Sumner Collection Fund

INTRODUCTION

J. Cheryl Exum and Ela Nutu

The Bible has played an inspirational role in art for centuries, and art has, in turn, influenced the way the Bible is read. *Between the Text and the Canvas* aims, as its subtitle indicates, to create a dialogue between the biblical text and biblical art—a dialogue in which each plays a critical role in the process of interpreting the other. Analysing works of art based on biblical characters or stories is not a one-way conversation that looks at the text and then the visual representation and asks how the representation 'got it right' or 'got it wrong'. A painting of a biblical scene or story, as the contributions to this volume emphasize, is more than a simple transposition of a text onto a canvas. It is itself an interpretation of the text—visual exegesis, to use Paulo Berdini's term,[1] or visual narrative, as Heidi Hornik also refers to it in describing the work of Michele Tosini in her contribution to the present volume. Artists can be keen textual interpreters, intentionally or unintentionally drawing our attention to textual tensions or problems or possibilities or depths not immediately apparent to readers. In rendering a biblical scene visually, an artist must consider any number of questions, such as what the characters look like, how they should be dressed (in contemporary garb or however the artist imagined people in biblical times would have dressed), where the scene takes place and, most important, what to show, what aspects of the scene or story to emphasise and what to leave out. In analysing a visual representation of a biblical text we might, therefore, want to ask what specific textual clues an artist picks up on in order to present a particular interpretation and whether an artist's interpretation might help us see something in the text we might have missed. We might be interested in ways biblical art can help us appreciate the richness or complexity of the text, or we might want to use the work of art to help us interrogate the text and vice versa.

Among other questions a critic might profitably consider are: Is the artist's attitude to the subject the same as that of the biblical text? Does a painting attempt to represent the biblical story or to reshape it to fit certain interests,

1 Paolo Berdini, *The Religious Art of Jacopo Bassano: Painting as Visual Exegesis* (Cambridge: Cambridge University Press, 1997).

or does it reuse its themes in order to oppose it? What features of the biblical text does a visual representation draw our attention to? What aspects does it ignore or underplay? Does the artist respond to a perceived gap in the text or to questions unanswered by the text? Does the artist add something to the biblical text? Does she or he, for example, magnify something that is not very important in the biblical version? Does the visual representation illuminate dimensions of the biblical account in new and important ways, either positively or negatively? Whose point of view does the artist represent and how does this compare to the biblical story? Does the artist involve the viewer in the painting? If so, how? Is the viewer invited to identify with a particular character or see a scene through a particular character's eyes? How are our assumptions about biblical characters influenced, or even shaped, by our encounters with their visual counterparts, and how does this affect the way we read their stories?

Our knowledge of the biblical text will invariably influence the way we view a painting or other visual representation of a biblical scene. But it is also the case that our reading of the biblical text is likely to be shaped by our recollection of a painting or other visual representations of a particular biblical scene. Obviously the better one knows the biblical story the better equipped one is to analyse and to appreciate an artistic representation of it. If one does not know the Bible, one might not, for example, recognize a painting as a biblical painting, and in some cases even knowing the Bible is no help in identifying the topic of certain biblical paintings. Does Rembrandt's *The Jewish Bride* represent Isaac and Rebekah? Is his *David Sending Away Uriah* really David and Uriah, or are the two main figures Haman and Ahasuerus (and who is the third figure?). Sometimes, however, our 'knowledge' of the biblical story can inhibit our freedom in interpretation, so there are advantages in starting with the painting and interpreting it before reading the biblical story.[2]

Staging a meaningful dialogue between the text and the canvas is often a matter of identifying an interpretative crux—a conundrum, gap, ambiguity or difficulty in the text, a stumbling block for interpretation or question that crops up repeatedly in artistic representations of it—and following its thread as it knits the text and painting together in complex and often unexpected ways. Or we might begin by asking about the artist and what historical, social, economic or personal factors may have influenced the artist to paint a biblical scene in a certain way. What is the artist seeking to achieve? What kind of interpretation does the artist want to offer to viewers, and why? As is the case with texts and authors, the interpretation an artist wishes to present to the viewer may not be the interpretation an individual viewer discovers in

2. Well illustrated by Mieke Bal, *Reading 'Rembrandt': Beyond the Word–Image Opposition* (Cambridge: Cambridge University Press, 1991).

the image. Or, in the process of representing a biblical story, a painter may have difficulty maintaining a particular point of view over competing points of view, just as biblical narrators are sometimes at pains to promote a particular position at the expense of others (for example, a Canaanite perspective on Israel's claim to the 'promised' land). If a biblical narrator has to struggle to affirm a particular ideology, does the artist inadvertently reinscribe the difficulty, or recognise it or resolve it or treat it in an entirely different way?

Interpretation of texts and images is not disinterested; the answers we find in them are shaped by the questions we ask. Clearly there is no one 'correct' way to establish a dialogue between the Bible and biblical art, as the essays here demonstrate. Each of the contributors has her or his own distinct approach, her or his own way of relating the text to the canvas. Taken together these essays illustrate how varied, and how exciting, the interpretative possibilities are. We mentioned above that staging a dialogue between text and canvas is sometimes a matter of identifying an interpretative problem that the artist has inherited from the text, and considering how the artist's strategies for handling the problem relate to textual strategies. This kind of approach is especially evident in the first two articles in this collection, Cheryl Exum's study of the seventeenth-century Dutch master Solomon de Bray's painting *Jael, Deborah and Barak* and Hugh Pyper's examination of artistic representations of David and Jonathan. For Exum the problem is the unusual situation of role sharing in Judges 4–5, the only story in Judges in which the judge is a woman and the only time leadership is shared—a situation that is problematized in de Bray's painting, in which all three heroes appear together, though they never appear together in the text; for Pyper, it is the difficulty viewers have in distinguishing David from Jonathan in paintings of the famous biblical duo, which reflects the ambiguity in the text regarding the nature of their relationship—a much discussed question in biblical scholarship—and the difficulties artists consequently have in portraying it.

Jael, Deborah and Barak is not a dramatic painting, nor does it represent any scene from the story in Judges 4–5. The three heroes appear together as though they were posing for a group portrait. This painting would seem therefore to be an unlikely candidate for staging a dialogue between text and image. But, Exum argues, by choosing to represent something that has no textual basis, de Bray foregrounds a key issue that has occupied readers of the biblical story: who is the real hero of the story, Deborah, Barak or Jael? Exum explores the complexity of the text in relation to de Bray's painting, revealing its complexity too, even though de Bray partially answers the question of leadership for his viewers. He has arranged the sitters in what he sees as the order of their importance—Jael, Deborah, Barak—and in poses intended to represent for the viewer the roles they played in the victory. But what, exactly, do their poses suggest about the extent of their roles and, equally important, their relationship? And, another question that has much engaged readers: is Jael a *femme forte* or a *femme fatale*?

Pyper traces the iconography of the close relationship between David and Jonathan in visual representations of the two men by Giovanni Cima da Conegliano, Rembrandt, Julius Schnoor von Carolsfeld and Frederic, Lord Leighton. Each visual interpretation of the relationship between the men, he points out, reflects the artists' assumptions of what that relationship was—in much the same way that biblical scholars' assumptions colour their interpretations. Cima makes David and Jonathan two young men of similar age; Rembrandt portrays them as an older man and a younger man, father and son figures; for Carolsfeld they are soul mates, and either figure could be David or Jonathan. Rather than picturing David and Jonathan together, Leighton has Jonathan alone except for the company of a young boy, but, Pyper contends, although David appears to be beyond the frame, he is fully on display in the person of Jonathan.

In the biblical text, for David to replace Jonathan, David must in a sense become Jonathan. Just as their roles intersect and merge in the text, becoming confused, so their bodies become confused in artistic representations, making it difficult for viewers to be sure which figure is David and which is Jonathan. Pyper discusses how, in these four paintings, the artists try to express the relationship between David and Jonathan in terms of acceptable models of male–male relationships of their time—a 'solution' that points to ambiguity in the biblical text—but, in doing so, they reinscribe the problem (the queerness) of the relationship and make it more evident by the strategies they use to suppress it. 'Cima', Pyper concludes, 'avoids the obvious, but problematic, moments of dramatic encounter between his protagonists by leading them out of the story on an unbiblical journey and rendering the relationship a reversal of the master-servant trope. Rembrandt assimilates the relationship to father and son, thereby accentuating the impossible longing for procreation without female participation in the text. Carolsfeld leaves his characters frozen in an embrace from which it is impossible to predict which will carry forward the story. Leighton goes to the ultimate point of ostensibly excluding David from the picture while in another frame of reference placing him at its centre in a transgressive blending of the two male characters.'

Discussions of the Bible and art usually focus on easel paintings, mainly from the sixteenth century to the present, because it is primarily through painting, particularly of the sixteenth to nineteenth centuries, that certain ideas about the Bible have entered the public consciousness and influenced both cultural perception and scholarly interpretation of the Bible. Martin

O'Kane, in his study of the biblical Elijah and his visual afterlives, takes up a neglected subject of investigation, icons. O'Kane reads the icons in relationship to the text, noting, in particular, the tension in the Hebrew Bible between visualizing and concealing. 'What are we to make of this obsession with visibility and hiddenness that permeates biblical literature?', he asks. 'Why do its authors create stories evidently intended to stimulate and exercise the reader's visual imagination and yet appear to be so suspicious of the consequences?' Elijah on Mount Horeb provides an excellent example: 'The author presents the early and later incidents in the life of the prophet as a series of colourful vignettes (for example, the context with the prophets of Baal or the prophet's ascension in the fiery chariot) that are easy to visualize in the mind's eye but, on the other hand, presents the central episode, the prophet's experience on Mount Horeb, as an experience that is veiled and hidden both from the point of view of Elijah and the reader'.

O'Kane discusses three important aspects of the biblical story that have received little serious attention in the Western artistic tradition: concealment and revelation, the cave as sacred space, and Elijah's experience, in the cave on Mount Horeb, of the presence of God. These all figure importantly in the iconography of Elijah in the Orthodox traditions of the Eastern Church, due to the importance in the Eastern Church of the Transfiguration, where Elijah and Moses, from whom God's appearance is hidden in the Hebrew Bible, are granted a vision of the divine in the Transfiguration (Mt. 17.1-8). O'Kane draws our attention to an important aspect of much biblical art, its devotional character. Icons are intended to aid the faithful in their spiritual development. The icons showing Elijah in the cave offer the viewer two focal points: we see Elijah outside the cave and also from the perspective of God, inside the cave looking out, for the position of the cave in many icons is where the eye of God would have been drawn on the blank canvas before the icon was painted. The darkness of the cave points to the transcendence of God, and, for the icon maker, the viewer's ascent to the summit of the spiritual life ends not in light but in darkness. The darkness conceals and reveals the presence of God, an inspired visualization, as O'Kane interprets it, of the way, in the biblical text, God reveals himself to Elijah yet remains concealed.

Art and text are again brought into creative dialogue in Sally Norris's reading of Marc Chagall's striking engraving no. 104 from his *La Bible* series, which depicts Ezekiel's famous chariot (*merkavah*) vision, against the text of Ezek. 1.4-28. In Chagall's representation, Ezekiel appears to have a minor role, while the four living creatures of his vision dominate the canvas. These creatures, Norris observes, are still, and 'appear warm and friendly, quite unlike the grotesque creatures described by Ezekiel, who rapidly jet around in a seemingly haphazard manner', though other details in the engraving match the textual description. Of special interest to Norris is the figure on the right—a woman (in contrast to the human form, arguably male, Ezekiel attributes to the creatures). Who is she, and why does Chagall make this figure a woman? Knowledge of the artist's life is important, not only for identifying the woman, who is probably Bella, Chagall's first wife, who occupies many of his canvases, but also for appreciating the significance of the other figures as well. Norris shows how Chagall transforms Ezekiel's theological perspective into an anthropological hermeneutic 'through which the *merkevah* vision narrates his own text—his empathy for the struggles of his father in Vitebsk, his fondness for the whimsical animals of his childhood, and, most significantly, his enduring love for Bella'. But art like this is not constrained by the limits of autobiography, argues Norris, but offers a broader, universal vision that, like Ezekiel's, has a mystical quality.

Whereas the essays of Exum, Pyper, O'Kane and Norris are all, in their own ways, concerned with examining the 'story' a painting has to tell in relation to the biblical story, Christina Bucher's subject is devotional images that, rather than representing a particular biblical story, draw on a range of biblical themes and tropes. Bucher observes that the enclosed garden motif in Western art is often associated with the idea of Mary's virginity, but, as she shows in her study of the Song of Songs and the enclosed garden motif in fifteenth-century paintings and engravings of the Virgin Mary and the Christ-child, the garden symbolism is exceedingly rich and suggestive, reminding the viewer of the garden of Eden and the garden of the Song of Songs. Bucher focuses specifically on two engravings and a painting by Martin Schongauer (c. 1430–1491), a panel by Stefan Lochner (c. 1400–1451) and two paintings by anonymous masters. The enclosed garden motif is developed in different ways by these artists, for whom fruits and flowers, roses and apples point to spiritual realities. Mary herself is an enclosed garden, associated iconographically with Eve, the Song's female lover and the Church as the bride of Christ.

As Bucher's analysis makes clear, the viewer's understanding and appreciation of the images is enriched and expanded by a knowledge of the biblical text. The paintings and engravings she analyses, like the icons discussed by O'Kane, are devotional works; they 'invite Christian viewers to contemplate both the savior of the world and the woman who can intercede for the faithful in heaven, as they also remind viewers of the virtues of humility, purity, and love'. The rich symbolism in devotional images of Mary with the infant Jesus forges connections among texts, encouraging the viewer to find multiple biblical allusions, and consequently greater meaning, in the image. These visually stunning images draw the viewer into an enclosed garden like the garden of Eden or the garden of the Song of Songs, a protected, safe space away from the dangers of the world; thus in Stefan Lochner's and

Martin Schongauer's paintings of Mary and the Christ-child, Bucher observes, the viewer is 'invited to look in upon paradise itself'.

In her contribution to the volume, Ela Nutu examines portrayals of Judith in Italian Renaissance and Baroque art. Like Jael, discussed by Exum in her essay on the painting by de Bray, Judith brings victory to her people by slaying a man, and, like Jael, she has acquired an ambiguous reputation, appearing in later tradition as both a *femme forte* and a *femme fatale*.

Judith was a favourite subject for women painters, perhaps because figures from the Apocrypha were popular and thus lucrative subjects in the sixteenth and seventeenth centuries. Possibly women artists sought to appeal to male tastes by depicting a sexualized Judith as *femme fatale*, but perhaps also Judith as a *femme forte* had a particular appeal for these women painters. While recognizing that the choices artists make are inspired and limited by their social context, patrons and their own individual circumstances, Nutu asks whether men and women painters portrayed Judith differently. She analyses the ways in which both the text and its heroine are interpreted in paintings by Lavinia Fontana, Artemisia Gentileschi, Elisabetta Sirani and Fede Galizia as representatives of the female imagination, and paintings by Orazio Gentileschi, Caravaggio and Cristofano Allori as representing their male counterparts.

The women artists discussed by Nutu are drawn to Judith as a *femme forte*, with whom most of them wished to identify, whereas male artists of the time tend to depict her as either Virtue or Vice. Nutu shows how, despite the strong element of phallic power attributed to Judith in depictions by women painters, 'Judith remains feminine in them. She wears pretty dresses and jewellery, and her sexuality, while not emphasized, is nevertheless present. Whether by means of a thigh pushing through vulval folds of garment, or breasts surging with concentration, even allusions to Medusa, Judith's identity as a woman with sexual knowledge is betrayed in the work of all these female painters. Their Judiths are for most part natural, even when their feminine adornments strike a contrasting note with their actions. Judith emerges from the work of women painters as the prototype of female empowerment.' This proto-feminist ideal of Judith is not what we find in the biblical text, however. There, despite her portrayal as a devout, courageous widow who saves her people, Judith cannot escape the role of *femme fatale*, used by God to humiliate his adversary, her apparent power illusory.

Another potential biblical *femme fatale*, Salome (who hardly deserves this reputation), is examined by Christine Joynes in her study of visual representations of the beheading of John the Baptist (Mk 6.17-29; Mt. 14.3-12) by Hinrik Funhof, Caravaggio and Pablo Picasso. Like Judith, with whom, as Nutu notes, she is sometimes confused, Salome is a popular subject in art. Salome's dance, recorded by Mark and Matthew with different emphases, plays a small role in the biblical text but a large role in its reception history. Is Salome an innocent victim of her mother Herodias's ambitions? Is she a seductive temptress? The Gospel accounts are ambiguous and allow for both possibilities, and interpreters, both artists and biblical scholars, fill gaps to reflect both positions. Such gap filling is not new, Joynes reminds us; it can be found in interpretations of the text from the early Church onwards.

The paintings Joynes analyses illustrate three different moments in the story. Although only one of them is of the dance itself, Joynes shows how all three portrayals of Salome reveal the artist's understanding of the dance and its consequences. Picasso gives us a dancing Salome as a seductive temptress; there is no feast, just an erotic encounter between Salome and Herod. Caravaggio shows Salome receiving the head of John the Baptist; unlike Picasso's sensualized vision, his is a reluctant and somber Salome, an innocent victim of her mother's ambitions. Funhof depicts the delivery of John's head to Salome at Herod's birthday banquet. By omitting the dance altogether, he leaves the nature of the dance to the viewer's imagination; however, he offers a number of visual clues to suggest that he places the blame on Herodias, not Salome.

Funhof's is an altar painting, whose purpose is devotional. It thus makes an interesting contrast to Picasso's painting, which is not devotional but rather exemplifies the late nineteenth-century (male) fascination with Salome as the embodiment of female eroticism, perversity and danger, a *femme fatale* if there ever was one. In his devotional study, Funhof juxtaposes different features of the beheading with other Gospel passages, such as the birth of John the Baptist and his baptism of Jesus. As is the case with the devotional images discussed by Bucher, Funhof's altar painting creates a dialogue among narratives, drawing our attention to intertextual connections. Resonances and allusions created among texts prompt the viewer to reflect on the significance of such connections and challenge the viewer to find deeper meanings in both the work of art and the biblical texts. This, for Joynes, is a significant contribution that art can make to biblical exegesis.

Not surprisingly, the greatest attention given to artistic style and technique in this volume, as well as to the life and times of the artist, appears in the one contribution by a professional art historian. Heidi Hornik takes as her focus three biblical paintings by the sixteenth-century Florentine painter Michele Tosini: *Nativity*, *Way to Calvary* and *Crucifixion*. These paintings, representing different stages in the life of Christ, come from different periods of the artist's life and reveal his developing style. An innovator in sixteenth-century Florentine art, Tosini's contributions to artistic style and technique were considerable. Hornik gives us a sense of his importance in the world of art not only by describing the circumstances that led to the production of these works but, more specifically, by showing the stylistic progression in his work from the High Renaissance style in *Way to Calvary* to a more mature style in *Nativity* to Mannerism in *Crucifixion*. While discussing each painting in relation to the precise Gospel text that inspired it, making us aware of the scope of Tosini's biblical knowledge, Hornik reminds us that there is more to biblical art than an artist simply taking a text and visualizing it, a point also emphasized by Martin O'Kane in his essay. As Hornik's analysis of Tosini's paintings makes clear, Tosini drew on biblical and liturgical sources as well as on established artistic tradition for his inspiration.

The work of the African-American painter Henry Ossawa Tanner (1859–1937) as means of preaching the Gospel with the brush is the subject of Kelly Baker's essay. Like Hornik, Baker is very much concerned with the influences of the circumstances of the artist's life on his painting, while at the same time cautioning against explaining everything in terms of the artist's biography. She focuses on two of Tanner's paintings as expressions of the artist's deep faith in God and his active role in human life and of Tanner's wish to offer his viewers, through his visual biblical exegesis, an awareness that God is present in unexpected places. Tanner painted the world as he hoped it could be, presenting viewers with windows into a different, better world, in which all could pursue a relationship with God. In her detailed discussion of *The Annunciation* and *Nicodemus*, Baker shows how Tanner used domestic scenes and commonplace moments in human life to reveal how the divine can erupt into the everyday world. Tanner's preferred means of depicting the divine and divine messengers was in the form of light. In *The Annunciation*, the angel Gabriel appears as a bright light to an ordinary, 'awkwardly human' Mary. In *Nicodemus*, Nicodemus converses with a Jesus who is depicted as a human, universal figure, without a halo, yet luminous to show his divinity.

An introduction to William Blake's relationship to the Bible forms the background to Christopher Rowland's essay on Blake's biblical paintings—an essay that takes us into the world of Blake as a prophet and a visionary, an artist who could not only write about the Bible but who could also *see* the Bible. Blake, Rowland reminds us, was a critic of the Bible, often juxtaposing text and image in a way that problematizes them. 'Blake, seemingly deliberately, sets difficulties in his texts, most obviously in the ways in which pictures do not relate, and indeed sometimes bear no relationship, to the text', Rowland observes, a technique he finds reminiscent of 'what Origen describes as the *proskommata* placed in the text by the Holy Spirit to "trip up" and thereby enliven the readings and be an antidote to complacency'. Rowland emphasizes the way that Blake's work calls for the reader's involvement. Readers and viewers must participate in the exegetical task, using their own imaginations to make sense of the relationship between text and image, and sometimes the gap, between the two.

To illustrate Blake's extraordinary skill, and creativity, as a biblical interpreter, Rowland analyses a number of Blake's biblical paintings, beginning with Blake's Job engravings, moving on to a detailed discussion of possible interpretations of *The Nativity*, followed by discussion of other, mainly New Testament paintings (but also including a version of Ezekiel's chariot vision discussed by Norris), and concluding with *The Last Judgment*, about which Blake himself offered a commentary, as a guide to Blake's soteriology.

Having, we hope, given our readers a sense of the kind of approaches they can find here, we would like to conclude our brief introduction by observing that interest in the study of the Bible and the arts is rapidly growing among biblical scholars. As a sign of this interest we might note the increasing attention this area of inquiry has attracted in the Society of Biblical Literature. A number of the essays in this volume began as papers in sessions of the Bible and Visual Art Section at national meetings of the SBL and of the Bible and Visual Culture Section at international SBL meetings. Enthusiasm for the study of the Bible and art does not appear to be so widespread among art historians, a state of affairs reflected in the present collection. The field will surely continue to grow and attract practitioners, and more volumes like the present one will appear to explore new ways of bringing text and image into creative conversation. In our view, what is most exciting about this (and perhaps most consoling) is the fact that texts and their visual representations have a way of eluding our attempts to fit them into molds, of destabilizing our interpretations, maybe even of changing the way we look at things. They can surprise us.

SHARED GLORY: SALOMON DE BRAY'S *JAEL, DEBORAH AND BARAK*

J. Cheryl Exum

The book of Judges recounts Israel's struggles to occupy the land of Canaan as a series of episodes, most of which deal with the exploits of divinely inspired leaders who deliver their tribes from oppression by their enemies.[1] The only story in Judges in which the judge is a woman is also the only story in Judges in which the judge shares the limelight with other characters (besides God). In Judges 4–5 Deborah shares the glory with not one, but two other human heroes.[2] Israel owes its victory over the militarily superior Canaanites not only to Deborah, who is both a judge and a prophet, but also to Barak, who leads the Israelite troops in battle, and to a Kenite woman, Jael, who, in a surprise twist in the plot, kills the Canaanite general Sisera with a tent peg and a mallet. The unusual situation of role sharing in the text is interestingly problematized in a painting of all three characters by the seventeenth-century Dutch master Salomon de Bray. In what follows, I want to stage a dialogue between the biblical text and de Bray's artistic representation. The conversation involves, on the one hand, asking questions of the text such as, what sort of heroes are Deborah, Barak and Jael, what is their relationship, and how is fame apportioned among them, and, on the other hand, considering how de Bray, as a reader and visualizer of the text,[3] deals

Research for this article was funded by the Arts and Humanities Research Council, UK.

1. The so-called 'major judges' for whom Othniel (3.7-11) sets the pattern: Ehud (3.12-30), Deborah (4–5), Gideon (6–8), Jephthah (10.6–12.7), Samson (13–16).

2. God is the only character who appears in all the individual episodes in Judges, and he is credited for the successes of the judges. He is also implicated in their failures; see J. Cheryl Exum, 'The Centre Cannot Hold: Thematic and Textual Instabilities in Judges', *CBQ* 52 (1990), pp. 410-31. Deborah is not, as I observed in that article (p. 415), the only unsullied judge. The lack of clear leadership is problematic, her reputation is undermined by the tension hinted at in her relationship with Barak, and one could raise questions about her effectiveness (see below under 'Deborah: Judge, Prophet, Singer, Mother in Israel').

3. On the artist as exegete and visualization as interpretation, see Paolo Berdini, *The Religious Art of Jacopo Bassano: Painting as Visual Exegesis* (Cambridge: Cambridge

with these questions and how he thereby conveys something of the complexity of the biblical account to his viewers.

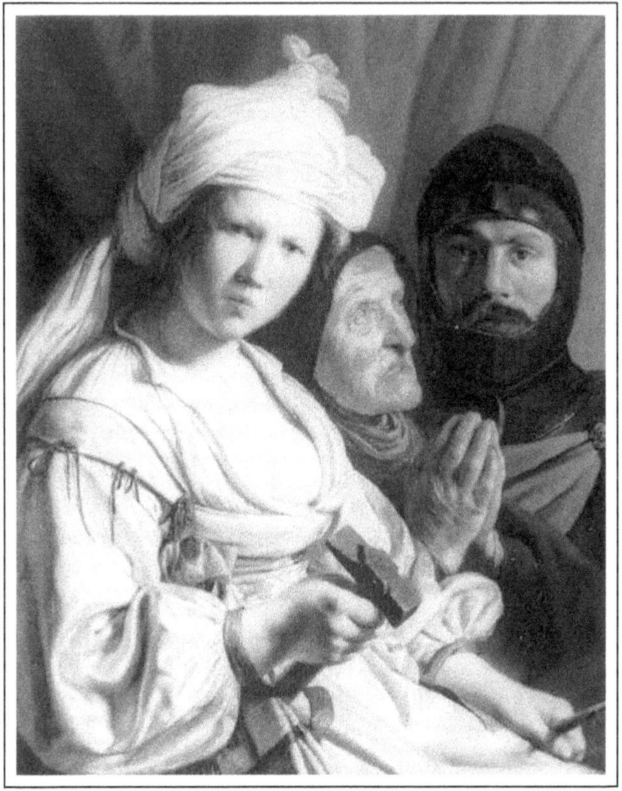

Figure 1. Salomon de Bray, *Jael, Deborah and Barak*
Rijksmuseum Het Catharijneconvent, Utrecht

De Bray's *Jael, Deborah and Barak*, painted in 1635, is not a dramatic painting, nor does it represent any scene from the story in Judges 4–5. It would seem therefore to be an unlikely candidate for staging a dialogue between text and image. Interestingly, however, by choosing to represent something that has no textual basis, de Bray foregrounds a striking and significant feature of the biblical story: the strange relationship—or lack of relationship—among the protagonists. As a static composition in which all

University Press, 1997), pp. 1-35; Martin O'Kane, *Painting the Text: The Artist as Biblical Interpreter* (Sheffield: Sheffield Phoenix Press, 2007). See also Athalya Brenner's brief comments on this painting in 'Afterword', in *A Feminist Companion to Judges* (ed. Athalya Brenner; Sheffield: Sheffield Academic Press, 1993), pp. 233-34, which came to my attention after I had completed this article.

three of the story's heroes appear as large half-figures against a featureless backdrop, the painting invites the viewer to consider the characters themselves, their respective roles and their relationship to one another.

The remarkable thing about de Bray's painting is that Jael, Deborah and Barak are pictured together, for all three characters never appear together in the biblical story. It is as if, the battle having been won (Judg. 4), and a victory song composed to celebrate it (Judg. 5), the three heroes of the day are now brought together to pose for a group portrait. The painter has asked Jael to bring her trusty hammer and nail with her for effect (or perhaps the idea that they would add a nice touch is hers, since she likes to pose with them). De Bray has arranged the sitters in poses intended to represent for the viewer the roles they played in the victory, as well as in what he sees as the order of their importance. In the foreground, illuminated from the right by a shaft of light that throws into stark relief her white-clad figure and full breasts, he places Jael, holding the hammer and tent peg with which she slew Sisera. In the middle is Deborah, whose pose alludes to her prophetic role, and who is either praying or reciting her victory song. Last, but not least—though partially in shadow—comes the military hero Barak, before whom the entire army of Sisera fell.

Jael appears to have dressed up for the portrait, for there is blood on the nail but not on her fine white dress. Barak wears his armor, which identifies him as a warrior. He too may have dressed especially for this occasion. He does not look as though he has just come from the battlefield, though de Bray gives him an expression that suggests his shock at seeing Sisera dead in Jael's tent. Only Deborah seems not to have donned her finest attire for the portrait, indicating to the viewer that, as a woman of God, she would not be concerned with such things.

Whereas in the biblical text God plays a major role, commanding Barak to go to war,[4] routing Sisera and his chariots before Barak's army (4.6-7, 14-15), and even fighting Sisera with the stars of heaven (5.20),[5] and the glory is ultimately God's (4.23), de Bray, in keeping with the widespread preference in the seventeenth century for realistic figures in art, interprets the story on human terms. Only Deborah's hands in prayer allude to the role of providence. De Bray shows all three characters at close range, in direct proximity to the viewer. Two of them look directly at the viewer: Jael seems to

4. Actually, we have only Deborah's word for it; see below.

5. Interpreters generally agree that God appears in Judg. 5 in his role as the divine warrior; see, e.g., Susan Ackerman, *Warrior, Dancer, Seductress, Queen: Women in Judges and Biblical Israel* (New York: Doubleday, 1998), pp. 37-46. Danna Nolan Fewell and David M. Gunn ('Controlling Perspectives: Women, Men, and the Authority of Violence in Judges 4 & 5', *JAAR* 58 [1990], pp. 400-402) draw attention to the countertheme of human accomplishment in the poem.

rebuff our gaze, whereas Barak stares vacantly at us, as though looking past us, his thoughts elsewhere. Deborah, in contrast, shows no interest in the viewer; her gaze is firmly fixed heavenward. The background consists solely of the folds of a dark curtain, suggesting perhaps Jael's tent, where Sisera met his foreordained end. The absence of any clearly defined setting further serves to focus the viewer's attention on the characters themselves and their roles, symbolized by their poses, physical appearance, dress and, in Jael's case, accoutrements.

Jael is the centre of attention in the painting, while Deborah, in the centre, seems crowded in between Jael and Barak. De Bray has placed Deborah in a position that corresponds to her role in the story, where her narrative importance is encroached upon by Jael and Barak. In spite of the fact that the painting's three subjects form a closely-knit group, they are not touching and no one is looking at anyone else. The absence of contact among them encourages the viewer to ponder the extent of their interaction in the biblical story. Although not a narrative painting, *Jael, Deborah and Barak* draws the viewer into the story of these three subjects, who appear not as types but rather as individuals so realistically portrayed that one wants to know more about them.[6] What kind of woman is Jael? She holds in her hands the domestic tools she would use for pitching a tent. How did she manage to overcome a warrior like Sisera with these as weapons? Why did she kill him, and how does she feel about it? Deborah seems less interesting: old, defeminized, pious. Her large hands in prayer are her most distinctive feature. Her deeply religious attitude invites the question, what is her connection to the cold-blooded assassin on one side of her and the soldier with the blood of countless adversaries on his hands, on the other? Barak, arrayed for battle, is in third place in the composition, overshadowed by the women. What does this say about his character?

Three Heroes, One Victory, Two Versions

Biblical scholars conventionally distinguish between the prose version of the story in Judges 4 and the poetic version in ch. 5. The poem, the so-called 'Song of Deborah', is widely thought to be older than the prose, which, as a later version of events, is interpreted in the light of the poem. In particular, where discrepancies occur between the two, the poem is privileged over the prose. Although reading the final form of the biblical text is now a widespread practice in biblical criticism, surprisingly, with the notable exception of Danna Fewell and David Gunn, few biblical critics attempt to interpret

6. A painting of all three heroes could be a narrative painting if the artist used compression to represent events unrelated in the narrative.

the prose and poem in the order in which they appear in the Bible, from beginning to end, as parts of a whole.[7]

Neither de Bray nor his intended audience, who would have been familiar with the biblical account,[8] would have thought of the story in terms of two different versions, nor, in fact, will most viewers of the painting or modern readers of the text who are not biblical scholars. Judges 4 and 5 can easily be read as a continuous story, in which a battle takes place and then a victory song is composed (on the spot, as it were) to celebrate it—a situation I envisioned above in order to construct a fanciful background for de Bray's group portrait. Thus what we have is, as Fewell and Gunn observe, an account told from the point of view of an omniscient narrator (Judg. 4), followed by a version of events told from the perspective of the characters Deborah and Barak (Judg. 5).[9] In the discussion that follows, I treat Judges 4–5 as a whole. Although questions of historical priority and the development of the tradition are not relevant for my discussion of the way de Bray has visualized the roles and relationships of the characters, some of the differences between the omniscient narrator's account and the characters' version are, and will be dealt with below. In visualizing the text and selecting what to allude to or to foreground and what to downplay or ignore, the artist has privileged certain aspects of the text over others. Like the omniscient narrator of ch. 4, de Bray is interested in the characters, and by the way he presents them he seeks to achieve similar results: to involve the viewer, as the narrator engages the reader, in the undercurrents of the plot. Deborah and Barak, in contrast, are more concerned with matters relating to the battle.[10]

7. Fewell and Gunn, 'Controlling Perspectives'.

8. Paintings of biblical scenes flourished in the seventeenth century, perhaps influenced by the large number of illustrated Bibles produced in the sixteenth century, which provided artists with a wealth of subject matter for inspiration. There was considerable interest in Old Testament themes in the United Provinces, where Israel's deliverance from Egypt was frequently compared with the struggles of the Dutch against Spain; see Richard Verdi, *Matthias Stom: Isaac Blessing Jacob* (Birmingham: The Trustees of the Barber Institute of Fine Arts, 1999), p. 23.

9. Fewell and Gunn. 'Controlling Perspectives', p. 390; cf. Yairah Amit, 'Judges 4: Its Contents and Form', *JSOT* 39 (1987), pp. 103-104. This being the case, a reader would be expected to privilege the narrator's version in ch. 4 over that of Deborah and Barak in ch. 5, which, as a limited point of view, is less reliable than that of the omniscient narrator. The omniscient narrator sets out to define the characters' roles, something de Bray does also in his painting, and, in particular, to set limits on Deborah's role and to problematize Jael's.

10. For a different view, see Fewell and Gunn, 'Controlling Perspectives', pp. 399-402. I would qualify my point above by noting that, although Deborah and Barak are primarily interested in the battle (the conditions leading to it, the participation of the deity, who came, who did not), their song concludes with a narrowed focus on Sisera's death and Sisera's mother's anxiety.

De Bray's static painting well suits the biblical story, in which the heroes are not well developed characters,[11] and the contact between them is minimal. The two female heroes, Jael and Deborah, act independently of each other; they never meet. Jael enters the narrative in Judg. 4.17, after Deborah disappears from it (v. 14). When the victory is celebrated in song, Deborah and Jael are mentioned together in a stanza that sets the background for the conflict by locating Deborah's rise to prominence as a 'mother in Israel' 'in the days of Shamgar, son of Anat' and 'in the days of Jael' (5.6-7). But nothing is said of any contact between the two women. The fact that Deborah predicts a woman's victory over Sisera (4.9), a victory that turns out to be Jael's, might suggest to some readers a connection between the women, for example, that Deborah knows who Jael is and what she will do,[12] but positing such a connection is simply gap filling, for the text gives us no insight into Deborah's consciousness.

Only two of the story's three heroes act in unison, Deborah and Barak. In fact, Barak will not lead his troops into battle unless Deborah goes too (4.8). Deborah goes with him (4.9, 10), but precisely what role she plays in the battle—and thus the extent of Deborah and Barak's partnership—is not entirely clear. From 4.14-16, it appears that, spurred on by the prophet Deborah, Barak alone leads the Israelite forces in battle. According to 5.15, Deborah and Barak jointly lead the tribe of Issachar to wage war against the Canaanites, but in what capacities? Do they both lead the troops into battle,[13] or, since the troops are described as entering the battle 'at his [Barak's] heels', does Barak alone lead the troops, while Deborah functions as no more *or less* than the prophet who instructs him? Deborah and Barak sing the victory song of ch. 5 in unison, if we accept the reading of the Masoretic text in 5.1, 'Then sang Deborah and Barak son of Abinoam on that day...' The verb here, however, is third person feminine singular ('she sang'), which leads some interpreters to posit that 'and Barak son of Abinoam' is a later addition and Deborah alone should be considered the singer.[14] The song begins with a

11. There is enough character development to give rise to numerous questions, as I discuss below. Nevertheless, their characters are less well developed than the other important judge-delivers, Ehud, and especially Gideon, Jephthah and Samson. Moreover, their lack of interiority contrasts sharply with the subtle development of Sisera's mother, at the end of the account (5.28-30).

12. See Gale A. Yee, 'By the Hand of a Woman: The Metaphor of the Woman Warrior in Judges 4', in *Women, War, and Metaphor: Language and Society in the Study of the Hebrew Bible* (ed. Claudia V. Camp and Carole R. Fontaine; Semeia, 61; Atlanta: Society of Biblical Literature, 1993), pp. 113-14.

13. So Ackerman, *Warrior, Dancer, Seductress, Queen*, pp. 31-32.

14. There is no textual evidence for omitting Barak, however, and a singular verb can be followed by more than one subject, in which case it often agrees with the first, as the one closest to it (see e.g. Exod. 15.1; Num. 12.1; GKC, § 146f-g).

declaration, 'to Yahweh I will sing, I will sing praise to Yahweh' (v. 3). Are these the words of one singer or both? In 5.12 Deborah is called upon to utter a song (the song that 5.1 represents her and Barak already in the act of singing?), and Barak to lead away his captives. These are not joint activities.[15]

Whereas the first half of ch. 4 is devoted to Deborah and Barak, in the second half of ch. 4 an encounter takes place between Barak and Jael. Just as she had met Sisera and invited him into her tent for what he assumed was shelter, so now Jael invites Barak to enter her tent to view Sisera's dead body. She seems to know who Barak is and what he is looking for: 'Come, and I will show you the man whom you are seeking' (4.22). Deborah and Barak do not mention this brief encounter in their song, but rather focus entirely on Jael's deed (perhaps Barak would rather forget the embarrassment of being so obviously upstaged by a woman).

Since Barak is not willing to accept Deborah's commission of him as it stands and imposes a condition, Deborah and Barak cooperate in a somewhat uneasy alliance. First one, then the other, is the subject of narrative attention, and the reader might well wonder who is destined to be the hero of the story.[16] When Deborah prophesies that the glory will not be Barak's but rather 'Yahweh will sell Sisera *into the hand of a woman*' (4.9), one might expect the glory to be Deborah's. Verse 14, where Deborah spurs Barak on with the prophecy, 'this is the day on which Yahweh has given Sisera *into your hand*', complicates matters, but not for long.[17] Jael soon enters the picture and acts independently, with no guidance or support from anyone. By killing Sisera, she steals the glory from both Barak and Deborah. As Meir Sternberg observes of the story's unfolding, 'Having so far divided interest and merit through the seesaw movement between Deborah and Barak, the narrative now diminishes both protagonists by shifting its focus to a third'.[18]

15. But cf. Ackerman (*Warrior, Dancer, Seductress, Queen*, pp. 44-45), who takes 'awake' as a call to battle, like the call to the divine warrior in Pss. 7.6 [Heb. 7.7] 44.23 [Heb. 24]; 59.4-5 [Heb. 5-6]; Isa. 51.9-10 (thus pairing Yahweh and Deborah as divine and human equivalents engaged in a 'holy war' against the Canaanites), and the 'song' Deborah is asked to utter here as 'the cry of reveille that will summon the Israelite troops into battle' (p. 31); see also Jo Ann Hackett, 'In the Days of Jael: Reclaiming the History of Women in Ancient Israel', in *Immaculate and Powerful: The Female in Sacred Image and Social Reality* (ed. Clarissa W. Atkinson, Constance H. Buchanan and Margaret R. Miles; Boston: Beacon Press, 1985), p. 27.

16. See the detailed analyses of Meir Sternberg, *The Poetics of Biblical Narrative: Ideological Literature and the Drama of Reading* (Bloomington: Indiana University Press, 1985), pp. 270-83; Amit, 'Judges 4', pp. 99-104.

17. 'Sisera' stands for the Canaanite army as well as the individual, just as the statement that Barak had gone up to Mount Tabor (v. 12) refers to all the Israelite troops. See Sternberg, *Poetics of Biblical Narrative*, pp. 278-80, on the way this double referencing contributes to the richness and ambiguity of the narrative.

18. Sternberg, *Poetics of Biblical Narrative*, p. 280.

De Bray manages to capture something of this narrative situation. By representing the three heroes together, he reminds the viewer that all three play an important role in the victory. At the same time, their lack of direct contact alludes to their separate spheres of action. Moreover, by placing Jael first, then Deborah, then Barak, de Bray instructs the viewer how to apportion the glory. Jael is the commanding figure in the painting, more fully represented than the others. She appears in radiant white, while the others, dressed in black, seem to blend into the background. De Bray presents her to the viewer in exquisite detail. She wears an elaborate dress, whose silken texture is almost tangible, and her intricately tied turban calls to mind a helmet, perhaps alluding to her contribution to military success (there is a balance between it and Barak's helmet). We see her head, her upper body, with exposed round breasts, her arms and sturdy hands, which look accustomed to wielding the implements she holds, and her lap, with the hand holding the bloody nail resting on her thigh. In contrast, Deborah, caught up in prayer, is mainly face and hands. Barak's face, as attentively rendered as that of the two women, is partially obscured by shadow, and, though he makes a strong impression, arrayed as he is in full military dress, little of his torso can be seen.

Jael: Femme Forte *or* Femme Fatale?

In the history of interpretation Jael has been viewed both as a *femme forte*, God's instrument and faithful servant, and also as a *femme fatale*, a dangerous woman who lured a man to his death.[19] The way the text presents her invites such speculation, and the painting allows both possibilities.

Clearly the text intends us to see Jael as the instrument by which God brings about Sisera's death. Deborah predicts that 'Yahweh will sell Sisera into the hand of a woman' (4.9), and this is what comes to pass. Jael kills the unsuspecting Sisera, to whom she has given refuge in her tent, by driving a tent peg into his head (4.21; 5.26-27). For this deed she is praised as 'most blessed of women...of tent-dwelling women most blessed' (5.24). But why does Jael, who belongs to a clan that has made peace with the Canaanite King Jabin (4.17), kill Sisera? Biblical interpreters have proposed various answers to the question. To vindicate her honour.[20] She was a hero who acted not only to defend her person but also to deliver Heber's household

19. See David M. Gunn, *Judges* (Blackwell Bible Commentaries; Oxford: Blackwell, 2005), pp. 61, 71-87.

20. John Gray, *Joshua, Judges, Ruth* (New Century Bible Commentary; Grand Rapids: Eerdmans, 1986), p. 259. Alternatively, says Gray, Jael could have been an older, discarded wife of Heber; see the critique of Mieke Bal, *Death and Dissymmetry: The Politics of Coherence in the Book of Judges* (Chicago: University of Chicago Press, 1988), pp. 211-13.

from the threat of slavery.[21] She was a loyal Yahwist.[22] The narrator gives her no motive in order to show that God was directing events and Jael was acting according to his plan.[23] She was a cultic functionary whose tent was regarded as a sacred space, and she killed Sisera, in spite of the fact that he came to her tent for sanctuary, because she recognized that it was God's will.[24] It was a tactical move to demonstrate her allegiance to the victorious Israelites.[25] Whereas the victory song, in typically elliptic poetic fashion, is simply not interested in Jael's motivation, the prose version, it seems to me, uses the withholding of motivation as a narrative technique to raise doubts about Jael's character.[26] The absence of a suitable explanation for Jael's behaviour and the brutality of the deed leave the deliverer's reputation somewhat tarnished. Critics frequently disapprove of Jael's blatant violation of hospitality, deceiving Sisera by making him think that he is safe and then brutally murdering him, but one suspects that what most bothers Jael's detractors is the fact that a vulnerable man is a victim of 'ignominious subjection to the effective power of a woman'.[27]

Jael's reputation is further cast into doubt by the sexual overtones in the account, by means of which the biblical narrator seeks to ridicule Sisera, making his humiliating death at the hand of a woman sound embarrassingly

21. Victor H. Matthews and Don C. Benjamin, *The Social World of Ancient Israel 1250–587* BCE (Peabody, MA: Hendrickson, 1993), pp. 87-95.

22. Robert G. Boling, *Judges: A New Translation with Introduction and Commentary* (Anchor Bible, 6A; Garden City, NY: Doubleday, 1975), pp. 97, 100, 119.

23. Amit, 'Judges 4', pp. 96-102.

24. Ackerman, *Warrior, Dancer, Seductress, Queen*, p. 102, following a suggestion by Benjamin Mazar, 'The Sanctuary of Arad and the Family of Hobab the Kenite', *JNES* 24 (1965), pp. 297-303.

25. Fewell and Gunn, 'Controlling Perspectives', pp. 396, 404.

26. On the withholding of motivation as a narrative device for undermining women characters, see Esther Fuchs, '"For I Have the Way of Women": Deception, Gender, and Ideology in Biblical Narrative', in *Reasoning with the Foxes: Female Wit in a World of Male Power* (ed. J. Cheryl Exum and Johanna W.H. Bos; Semeia, 42; Atlanta: Scholars Press, 1988), pp. 68-83.

27. D.F. Murray, 'Narrative Structure and Technique in the Deborah–Barak Story (Judges IV.4-22)', in *Studies in the Historical Books of the Old Testament* (ed. J.A. Emerton; VTSup, 30; Leiden: E.J. Brill, 1979), p. 173. Murray argues that this fate is shared by Barak and Sisera, but cf. the critique of this view, based on concepts of honour and shame, by Geoffrey P. Miller, 'A Riposte Form in the Song of Deborah', in *Gender and Law in the Hebrew Bible and the Ancient Near East* (ed. Victor H. Matthews, Bernard M. Levinson and Tikva Frymer-Kensky; JSOTSup, 262; Sheffield: Sheffield Academic Press, 1998), p. 126 and n. 35. Cf. also Mieke Bal, *Murder and Difference: Gender, Genre, and Scholarship on Sisera's Death* (Bloomington: Indiana University Press, 1988), p. 124: 'If "Jael's treachery" is unforgivable, the shame of the men becomes forgivable'. We might also compare the condemnation typically heaped upon Delilah for betraying Samson and the discomfort frequently expressed about Judith's assassination of Holofernes.

like a seduction and rape.[28] Jael invites Sisera into her tent, much as the wanton woman of Proverbs invites the young man to 'turn aside' to her (Prov. 9.16). While he sleeps there, she 'comes to him' (4.21). The expression 'come to/unto her' is often used of a man having sexual intercourse with a woman. She penetrates his body at a vulnerable point—the temple? the neck? the mouth?[29]—with a phallic tent peg. In a description rife with sexual innuendo, Sisera kneels over between Jael's legs, falls and lies there despoiled (5.27).[30]

De Bray was apparently familiar with Jael's dual reputation as a *femme forte* and a *femme fatale*, and though he foregrounds the former, he alludes to the latter.[31] The painting was conceived as a pendant, or companion piece, to *Judith with the Head of Holofernes*, a rather chaste portrayal of Judith, who holds the head like an offering, while her maid looks over her shoulder at it.[32] De Bray's association of Jael with Judith, who delivered her people from

28. For detailed discussion of this symbolism, see Susan Niditch, 'Eroticism and Death in the Tale of Jael', in *Gender and Difference in Ancient Israel* (ed. Peggy L. Day; Minneapolis: Fortress Press, 1989), pp. 43-57; Bal, *Murder and Difference*, pp. 100-134; Robert Alter, *The Art of Biblical Poetry* (New York: Basic Books, 1985), pp. 43-49; Fewell and Gunn, 'Controlling Perspectives', pp. 392-94. Some go so far as to suggest that Jael and Sisera had sexual intercourse (Pamela Tamarkin Reis, 'Uncovering Jael and Sisera: A New Reading', *SJOT* 19 [2005], pp. 24-47) or that this was the case in an earlier version of the story, which was subsequently censored (Yair Zakovitch, 'Sisseras Tod', *ZAW* 93 [1981], pp. 364-74).

29. All have been proposed; the precise meaning of the word *raqqa* is uncertain. It occurs elsewhere only in Song 4.3 and the parallel 6.7, where it could be the cheek, the temple, or the brow. The term may refer to a more extensive area of the face around the eyes. Ellen van Wolde ('Ya'el in Judges 4', *ZAW* 107 [1995], p. 245) understands it to be the throat and observes that, as a pun on Barak's name, 'into his throat' (*beraqqato*) alludes to the fact that, in piercing Sisera's throat, Jael is taking over Barak's task (this is one of a number of ways van Wolde discusses in which Jael contrasts positively with Barak).

30. Hebrew *raglayim*, 'legs' or 'feet', can be a euphemism for the genitals. The verb *kara'* ('to bend, kneel over') can suggest a sexual posture (cf. Job 31.10). The verb *shakav*, which means 'to lie', can also refer to sexual intercourse. Sisera falls 'violently destroyed' or 'despoiled' (*shadud*), which is suggestive of rape (cf. Jer. 4.30); see Niditch, 'Eroticism and Death', pp. 43-49.

31. Judith van Gent and Gabriël M. C. Pastoor, 'Die Zeit der Richter', in *Im Lichte Rembrandts: Das Alte Testament im Goldenen Zeitalter der niederländischen Kunst* (ed. Christian Tümpel; Zwolle: Waanders Verlag, n.d.), pp. 66-67.

32. *Judith with the Head of Holofernes*, like *Jael, Deborah and Barak*, is an after-the-fact portrayal, so to speak. Judith appears without her sword, the counterpart to Jael's domestic tools as weapons, which somewhat lessens her threatening aspect. She looks calmly and piously to heaven, and the grisly head appears almost out of place; indeed a later owner had the head altered into a pitcher. See Jacqueline Boonen, 'Die Geschichte von Israels Exil und Freiheitskampf', in Tümpel (ed.), *Im Lichte Rembrandts*, p. 117,

an evil oppressor, and his inclusion of Jael in the company of Deborah and Barak clearly locate her among the heroes of the faith. At the same time, even as Jael's implements direct the viewer's attention to her act of deliverance, her exposed breasts, on which the light falls, suggest the deadly allure of the *femme fatale*.

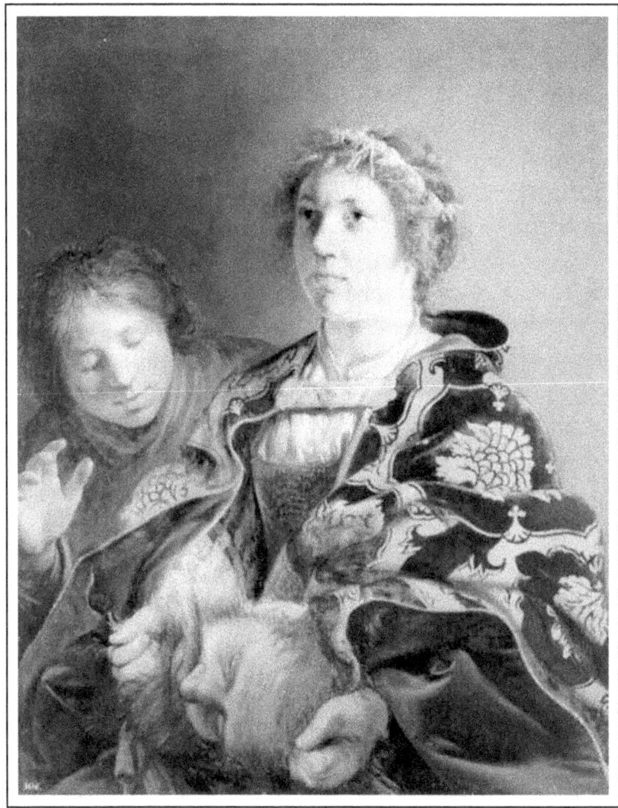

Figure 2. Salomon de Bray, *Judith with the Head of Holofernes*
Museo Nacional del Prado, Madrid

De Bray gives us a Jael whose expression seems to defy the viewer to ask questions about her motives. Who would venture to cross-examine a woman with a hammer and tent peg, who has only recently used them to dispatch an unwary victim? But just as readers stimulated by tantalizing textual gaps

where a version of the painting with the pitcher is reproduced. There is nothing of the *femme fatale* about this Judith. On the confusion of Jael and Judith in art and literature, see Margarita Stocker, *Judith, Sexual Warrior: Women and Power in Western Culture* (New Haven: Yale University Press, 1998), pp. 13-14, 120-72.

cannot resist filling them, viewers will likely find themselves captivated by Jael's enigmatic expression and unable to resist speculating about what lies behind it. Many meanings could be read into it: defiance, determination, resolution, tension, sensuality. She looks at the viewer in a way that seems to say both 'come hither' and 'don't you dare'. Her brow is wrinkled, her lips pursed. If it were not for the scowl, she could be offering a kiss. De Bray has skillfully captured on canvas the ambiguity surrounding Jael in the text.

The painting implies that the assassination was an on-the-spot decision, as does the text. The murder weapons, pictured here, are domestic tools, which suggests that the murder was not planned in advance. Jael, after all, could not have known that fate would lead Sisera to her tent, though the reader suspects it from the proleptic statement that Heber had separated from the rest of the Kenites and encamped near Kedesh, the site of the battle (4.11).

Do the fine clothes worn by Jael—the elegant billowy white dress, with full sleeves and décolleté, the flowery sash around her waist and the elaborate headdress—convey to the viewer something about her? Does her ornate attire defy the connection between the woman and the bloody deed? She wears white, which typically symbolizes purity. Is she, as God's instrument, above moral reproach, a *femme forte* 'most blessed of women'? Or is this part of the *femme fatale*'s guile? Is she not what she seems, which is precisely what the unsuspecting Sisera discovers about her?

Looking at this Jael, who gazes back unflinchingly, a viewer might well wonder how this woman, determined as she appears, could overpower a warrior like Sisera, even if he were exhausted from battle.[33] In the iconic tradition she is frequently pictured driving the tent peg through Sisera's temple while he sleeps, as, for example, in Artemisia Gentileschi's painting of the scene, which, like de Bray's painting, uses an indistinct background to draw attention to its protagonists (Fig. 3).[34] Gentileschi's Jael is less complex, less morally equivocal than de Bray's—a *femme forte*, not a *femme fatale*, calm and deliberative, almost contemplative as she raises her arm to hammer

33. That Sisera is exhausted is generally taken to be the sense of the Hebrew *wayya'ap*; some, following a suggestion of G.R. Driver ('Problems of Interpretation in the Heptateuch', in *Mélanges bibliques rédigés en l'honneur de André Robert* [Paris: Bloud & Gay, 1957], p. 74), take it to mean 'he twitched convulsively'. On the difficulties of the verse, see George F. Moore, *A Critical and Exegetical Commentary on Judges* (Edinburgh: T. & T. Clark, 1895), pp. 125-26; C.F. Burney, *The Book of Judges* (New York: Ktav, 1970 [1903]), pp. 93-94; Barnabas Lindars, *Judges 1–5: A New Translation and Commentary* (Edinburgh: T. & T. Clark, 1995), pp. 203-204.

34. There is a column in the background inscribed with the artist's name and date. Both paintings are moderately sized; Gentileschi's is 86 × 125 cm, de Bray's 86 × 71 cm. The absence of a clearly defined setting and the calmness of Jael's pose is in striking contrast to Gentileschi's violent Judiths.

the peg into Sisera's temple while he sleeps.[35] By portraying Jael after the murder has been accomplished, rather than in the act of performing it, de Bray hails the deed without indicating the manner in which it was carried out. Viewers who want to know the details are therefore led back to the text, where they will not find a straightforward answer. Does Jael kill Sisera by driving a tent peg into his temple with her hammer while he is sleeping, as the omniscient narrator's version in Judges 4 has it? Or is he awake and standing when Jael attacks him, since, according to Deborah and Barak's version in Judges 5, he sinks and falls at her feet?[36]

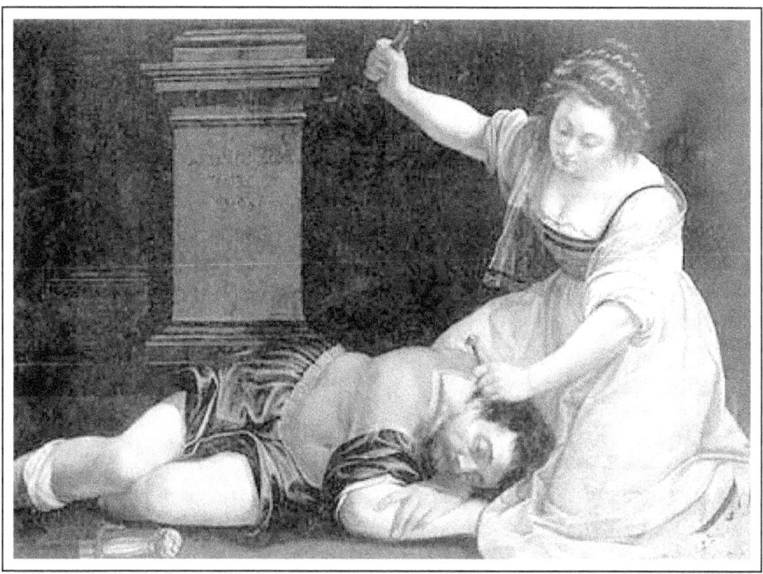

Figure 3. Artemisia Gentileschi, *Jael and Sisera*
Szepmuveszeti Museum, Budapest

35. For discussion of the artistic tradition of portraying Jael and of this painting as an uncharacteristically positive portrayal, see Babette Bohn, 'Death, Dispassion, and the Female Hero: Artemisia Gentileschi's *Jael and Sisera*', in *The Artemisia Files: Artemisia Gentileschi for Feminists and Other Thinking People* (ed. Mieke Bal; Chicago: University of Chicago Press, 2005), pp. 107-27.

36. Both the differences between the accounts and the details in both accounts are the subject of considerable discussion: Where does the murder take place, in the tent or outside, and under what circumstances? Is Sisera sleeping, or is he standing? Where does Jael strike him and does she use one weapon or two? See, *inter alia*, Moore, *Judges*, pp. 124-26, 163-66; Burney, *Judges*, pp. 79-80, 93-94, 152; Hans Wilhelm Hertzberg, *Die Bücher Josua, Richter, Ruth* (Göttingen: Vandenhoeck & Ruprecht, 1969), pp. 181-82; Lindars, *Judges 1–5*, pp. 200-201; van Wolde, 'Ya'el in Judges 4', pp. 244-45; Baruch Halpern, *The First Historians: The Hebrew Bible and History* (San Francisco: Harper & Row, 1988), pp. 82-84.

Deborah: Judge, Prophet, Singer, Mother in Israel

Deborah, in contrast to Jael who is famous for her one heroic act, holds an impressive number of roles in the text. She is a judge, and, in contrast to other judges who are 'raised up', commissioned or inspired by God to deliver Israel in a time of crisis, Deborah is already judging in Israel when the story of Israel's deliverance from oppression at the hand of King Jabin of Canaan begins.[37] In addition to being a judge, she is a prophet, and the only person, besides Samuel, to hold both these positions of authority. She is a singer of tales, called upon to 'utter a song' in 5.12, and one of the singers of the victory song according to 5.1. In addition, she is a 'mother in Israel' (5.7), a phrase that appears elsewhere only in 2 Sam. 20.19 in reference to a city, but which, applied to Deborah, would appear to mean that she ensures the welfare of her people through wise counsel.[38] In view of all her distinctions—judge, prophet, singer, mother in Israel—it is all the more remarkable that Deborah shares the glory with others. Or could it be that her exercise of these roles leaves something to be desired?

Judges 4.3 informs us that Jabin had oppressed Israel for twenty years. If Deborah was judging Israel 'at that time', why had she not acted sooner to deliver her people?[39] Even when she does take action, she does not act independently in leading Israel like the other judges. Although she is a prophet, the text does not represent God as speaking directly to her. We (and Barak) have only her word for it when she tells Barak that 'Yahweh, the God of Israel, commands you, "Go, take up position at Mount Tabor... I will draw out Sisera, the general of Jabin's army, to meet you by the Wadi Kishon with his chariots and his troops, and I will give him into your hand"' (4.6-7).[40] Like her leadership in the battle, which she shares with Barak, her

37. Again I refer to the so-called major judges. Othniel and Ehud are 'deliverers' 'raised up' by God (3.9, 15; cf. 2.18); God commissions Gideon to deliver Israel (6.14); Jephthah is appointed leader by the elders of Gilead to deal with a crisis, and inspired by the spirit of Yahweh (11.29); before his birth Samson is destined 'to begin to deliver Israel' (13.5).

38. See Claudia V. Camp, 'The Wise Women of 2 Samuel: A Role Model for Women in Early Israel?', *CBQ* 43 (1981), pp. 14-29; see also Ackerman, *Warrior, Dancer, Seductress, Queen*, pp. 40-43.

39. Perhaps the reader is to understand that it was twenty years before the Israelites 'cried out to Yahweh', and only then did God inspire Deborah to act.

40. Another comparison with the prophet Samuel can serve to illustrate this point. In 1 Sam. 13.8-15 Saul waits for Samuel at Gilgal for seven days, as instructed, and then, because circumstances are desperate, makes a burnt offering. Samuel then appears and accuses Saul of not keeping the commandment of God. But in 1 Sam. 10.8 the instructions to go to Gilgal and wait for Samuel are Samuel's, not God's; see, further, J. Cheryl Exum, *Tragedy and Biblical Narrative: Arrows of the Almighty* (Cambridge: Cambridge University Press, 1992), pp. 27-30.

role as singer of tales is also a shared one if, as mentioned above, we follow the MT in 5.1. But, curiously, the text seems to undermine the singers by casting doubts about their authorship of their song, for it is odd that, if Deborah and Barak are reciting the song, they would call on themselves to utter a song and lead away captives (5.12).

Is Deborah's description of herself as 'a mother in Israel' (5.7), a self-congratulatory boast?[41] As a mother in Israel, Deborah may be responsible for her people's welfare, but the question remains, what does Deborah actually accomplish as a leader?[42] Clearly she plays a decisive role in delivering Israel from oppression; she is the one who sets events in motion (4.6-7). Whereas other judges lead one tribe or, at the most, a coalition of two or three tribes against their enemies, Deborah and Barak muster six tribes to fight together under their leadership (Judg. 5.14-18). But her relationship with Barak is not a particularly harmonious one, and one could question the degree of mutual respect they display.

Given this surplus of textual information and ambiguity, what does de Bray choose to convey to the viewer about Deborah? For de Bray, Deborah is the religious inspiration for Israel's victory, whereas Barak is the military hero. I have already mentioned the way de Bray pictures Deborah hemmed in by the two figures who encroach upon her leadership role in the text, Barak, with whom she shares the limelight at the beginning of the story, and Jael, who snatches the glory from both of them at the end. In de Bray's painting, Deborah's position, in second place, indicates to viewers that her accomplishment is not so important as Jael's but more important than Barak's. She and Barak are overshadowed by Jael, and, in their dark clothing that blends in with the background, they form a unit that suggests their

41. A view expressed in the Talmud, *b. Pes*. 66a; cf. Fewell and Gunn ('Controlling Perspectives', p. 401), who speak of a 'tone of self-congratulation' in the song. The verb here, *qamti*, is a first person feminine form ('I arose'); most translations, however, take it as an archaic second person feminine form, 'you arose' (see, e.g., Michael David Coogan, 'A Structural and Literary Analysis of the Song of Deborah', *CBQ* 40 [1978], p. 147). In this case, we would have a situation similar to the one described above: why does Deborah, the singer, refer to herself as 'you'?

42. Unfortunately the text of Judg. 5.7 is difficult and proposals for translating it vary widely; cf. e.g. Coogan, 'Structural and Literary Analysis', p. 147: 'Warriors ceased, in Israel they ceased—until you arose, Deborah…'; Boling, *Judges*, p. 102: 'The warriors grew plump / In Israel they grew plump again / Because you arose…'; Ackerman, *Warrior, Dancer, Seductress, Queen*, p. 37: 'Settlements in unwalled hamlets ceased, In Israel they ceased, Until you arose…'; Renate Jost, *Gender, Sexualität und Macht in der Anthropologie des Richterbuches* (BWANT, 164; Stuttgart: Kohlhammer, 2006), pp. 356-57: 'Bewohner des freien Landes (Führende/Bauersleute/Kämpfende) gab es nicht mehr (Freigiebigkeit/Gastfreundschaft gab es nicht mehr) (Variante Kegler) / in Israel ruhten sie, bis ich aufstand…'

alliance in the battle against Sisera and his troops. But de Bray offers the viewer no indication that Deborah may have played a vital role in the battle other than influencing the outcome through prayer. Elsewhere in the iconographic tradition, she sometimes appears armed, engaging in the battle, or, more often, inspiring Barak and his army and spurring them on, as in this painting by Luca Giordano (1632–1705).[43] This highly dramatic composition offers a marked contrast to de Bray's static portrait, and Giordano's Deborah is nothing like de Bray's. Young and powerful, she directs events from a position of authority above, but not isolated from, the fray. Her role and her attitude mirror God's, and we can trace a clear chain of command from God to Deborah to Barak.[44]

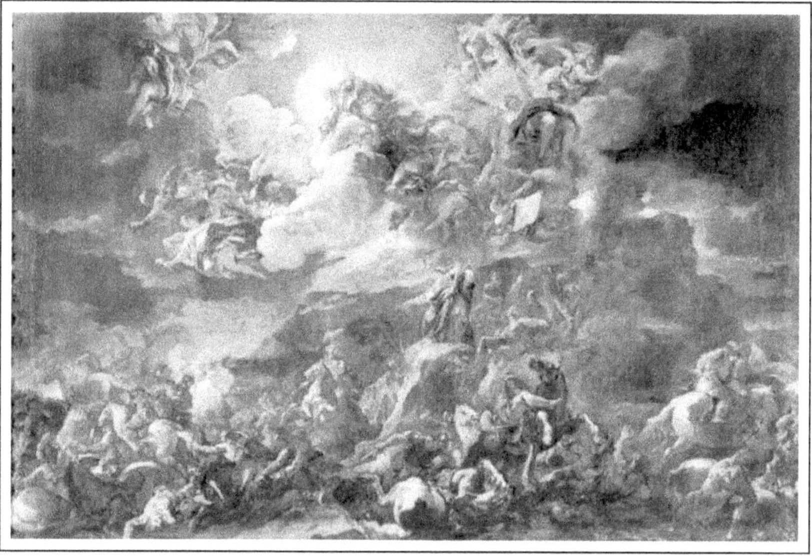

Figure 4. Luca Giordano, *The Victorious Fight of the Israelites*
Museo Nacional del Prado, Madrid

43. Some examples of Deborah going into battle, as well as Giordano's tumultuous battle scene reproduced here, can be found in Herbert Haag, Dorothée Sölle, Joe H. Kirchberger, Anne-Marie Schnieper-Müller, Emil Bührer, *Great Women of the Bible in Art and Literature* (Grand Rapids: Eerdmans, 1994), pp. 115-21; see also Gunn, *Judges*, pp. 66-68.

44. This is the kind of Deborah that Ackerman envisages in Judg. 5, the human counterpart to God above (*Warrior, Dancer, Seductress, Queen*, pp. 29-47). In Ackerman's view, Deborah and God are paired as human and divine equivalents (drawing on Canaanite traditions about Baal and Anat), and Deborah is unambiguously and emphatically 'Israel's chief military commander' with Barak her second in command (p. 31). Possibly ancient listeners to the song would have recognized allusions to the divine warrior Anat in the depiction of Deborah, but, as Ackerman admits, already Judg. 4 presents the reader with a Deborah whose leadership role is diminished.

The contrast between Deborah and Jael in de Bray's painting is dramatic. Jael is young and sexual, whereas Deborah is aged, wrinkled and not at all feminine. If there is a hint of the *femme fatale* in his Jael, de Bray assures his viewers that there is nothing of the *femme fatale* in Deborah, only the *femme forte*. Deborah's hands, pressed together in prayer, form a stark contrast to Jael's, which hold her weapons. They are large and illuminated against the dark background, emphasizing her intercessory role. De Bray thus directs the viewer to contemplate the role of God in guiding these three heroes to victory. The prophet looks up to heaven, her mouth open, perhaps offering a prayer of thanksgiving, perhaps reciting her victory song. Possibly in choosing to make Deborah old, de Bray alludes to her role as 'mother'. Who but an aged wise woman could merit such a distinction as 'mother in Israel'?

Barak: Out of the Shadows

When Deborah and Barak describe the battle in the song they sing for the benefit of their audience, all they tell us about Barak is that, together with Deborah, he led the Israelites to victory over the Canaanites. They mention Barak twice, both times in connection with Deborah:

> Rouse yourself, rouse yourself, Deborah!
> Rouse yourself, rouse yourself, sing a song!
> Rise up, Barak, capture your captives,
> son of Abinoam (5.12).

> The princes of Issachar were with Deborah,
> and Issachar loyal to Barak,
> into the valley they were sent at his heels (5.15).

Have they, like any good politicians after an outcome has been decided, suppressed their former differences and presented themselves as 'uniting in immediate, voluntary response to the cause'?[45] According to the omniscient narrator of Judges 4, they do not work so harmoniously together, though the precise nature of their relationship is not transparent.

Deborah summons Barak to her in order to give him instructions from God:

> Has not Yahweh, the God of Israel, commanded you, 'Go, march up[46] to Mount Tabor, and take with you ten thousand men of Naphtali and Zebulun. I will draw out to you, to the Wadi Kishon, Sisera, the commander of Jabin's army, and his chariots and his troops, and I will give him into your hand' (4.6).

45. Fewell and Gunn, 'Controlling Perspectives', pp. 399-400 (400).

46. Repetition of the Hebrew verb *mashak* produces a nice pun here, which my translation does not capture: Barak will 'lead out' or 'muster' the Israelite troops, while God will 'lead out' Sisera and the Canaanite troops against him.

Barak's response to this charge comes as something of a surprise: 'If you will go with me, I will go, but if you will not go with me, I will not go'. Why does he pose this condition? Does he lack confidence? Is his reluctance to do as Deborah commands a sign of cowardice? Most interpreters think so. Sternberg, for example, is particularly harsh in his criticism of Barak: 'Of the two leaders, it is he who plays the woman; and having been summoned to do a man's job, he refuses to act unless the woman who delegated it to him comes along to give him moral courage'.[47] Worse, has Barak been shirking his responsibility? The rhetorical question 'has Yahweh not commanded you' could be seen as providing a hint that Barak should already be aware of what God expects of him.[48]

Alternatively, could Barak be questioning Deborah's authority, as Fewell and Gunn propose? Does he wonder what a woman, even if she is a judge and prophet, knows about fighting? Can he be sure that what Deborah has commanded him is the word of God?

> Barak is being asked to risk his life as well as the lives of ten thousand men on the strength of this woman's unconfirmable word. Barak's conditional proposal, then, is a test: if Deborah is willing to stake her own life on this word, then he will believe and obey.[49]

If Barak's condition is a test of Deborah's authority, it is hard to see what it would prove. The narrator calls her a prophet (4.4). If Deborah believes that she is speaking on God's behalf, would she not be willing to stake her life on this word and go with Barak, thus passing his test even if she were wrong about her inspiration? Or do Fewell and Gunn think that Barak thinks that Deborah is deliberately deceiving him, only pretending to be a prophet? Rather than questioning her authority, could he be overly dependant on it?

The Septuagint has a longer reading in 4.8 in which Barak explains his hesitancy in terms of his reliance on prophetic guidance: 'For I do not know on which day the angel of the Lord will give me success'.[50] This justification

47. Sternberg, *Poetics of Biblical Narrative*, p. 274. Sternberg goes so far as to claim that 'the flat character [Barak] gains rotundity with a vengeance as soon as he betrays his lack of self-confidence' (p. 274), but surely this is to overstate the case, for none of the heroes in Judg. 4–5 is very well developed. On Barak as un-manned and shamed by the women in the story, see Yee, 'By the Hand of a Woman', pp. 115-16; Bal, *Murder and Difference*, pp. 115-24.

48. Cf. J. Alberto Soggin, *Judges*, *A Commentary* (trans. John Bowden; Philadelphia: Westminster Press, 1981), pp. 64-65, who acknowledges this as the normal sense of *halo'* but rejects it, primarily on the grounds that the text says nothing about Barak having already received but rejected a divine calling.

49. Fewell and Gunn, 'Controlling Perspectives', p. 398.

50. LXX reads literally, 'For I do not know on what day the Lord will help the angel on the way with me'. I follow Burney, *Judges*, p. 89, in assuming a Hebrew Vorlage that

suggests that he needs Deborah the prophet to go with him to confirm when the time is right to attack, which is, in fact, what happens in v. 14, when she says, 'Up, for *this is the day* on which Yahweh has given Sisera into your hand'. Was her initial commission, then, not sufficient?

Though not especially well developed, the uneasy relationship between Deborah and Barak invites comparison to that between another reluctant leader, Saul, and his nemesis Samuel, who, like Deborah, is both a judge and a prophet. Both Barak and Saul are, initially at least, reluctant commanders. Barak's reliance on Deborah is like Saul's dependence on Samuel, and Deborah's attitude to Barak resembles Samuel's impatience with Saul. Like Samuel, who, in the name of God, tells Saul what to do, Deborah instructs Barak. Samuel does not take up arms in Saul's military campaigns (another possible parallel with Deborah), but the presence and support of the prophet is important for the hesitant leader (1 Sam. 13.8-12; 15.13, 25-31; 28.15), just as Deborah's support is essential for Barak. Deborah seems to have the same sort of arrogant, or short-tempered, attitude to Barak that Samuel has to Saul. When Barak demurs at his commission, her rejoinder puts him in his place.[51] She takes back the promise she spoke in God's name, 'I will give [Sisera] *into your hand*' (4.7) and declares: 'I will indeed go with you; however, the road on which you are going will not lead to your glory, for Yahweh will sell Sisera *into the hand of a woman*' (4.9). The price Barak will pay for insisting that Deborah accompany him, whether it betrays a lack of manly courage or his over-dependence on the prophet or both, is that a woman will claim the glory that might have been his.

Unexpectedly, the prophet drops out of the story in Judges 4 after v. 14. God throws Sisera and his army into a panic before Barak (4.15), and Barak and his troops pursue them and kill them all except Sisera (4.16-17), who flees the battle on foot.[52] Still in pursuit of Sisera, Barak is met by Jael, who invites him into her tent to see the man he is seeking. Does Barak know who Jael is, and, more importantly, does he know about the alliance between the clan of Heber the Kenite and Jabin (4.17)? Why does he enter Jael's tent as trustingly as Sisera had done? It is necessary that Barak see for himself, with his own eyes, that God delivered Sisera into the hand of a woman, as

the LXX translator misunderstood, reading 'angel' (*mal'ak*) as the object of the verb, thus making *yhwh* the subject, and taking the accusative 'me' (*'ty*) as the preposition 'with me'.

51. Cf. Samuel's harsh rebukes of Saul, 1 Sam. 13.13-14; 15.17.

52. Judg. 5.12 mentions captives. Since, according to 4.16, Sisera's entire army was wiped out, the captives would be women, children and old men; cf. Fewell and Gunn, 'Controlling Perspectives', p. 408. Alternatively, we could allow Deborah and Barak's version of events to cast doubt on the reliability of the omniscient narrator of ch. 4.

Deborah foretold—and thus to get his comeuppance for responding the way he did to Deborah's instructions.[53]

In de Bray's painting, Barak's is a commanding presence, but he is overshadowed by the women, as he is in the text. De Bray celebrates Barak as a military hero, a strong man. If, in the text, Barak sounds like a little boy who needs his mother, Deborah, the 'mother in Israel' ('if you will go with me, I will go, but, if you will not go with me, I will not go'), there is nothing childish about the man with the moustache in the painting. Like the meaning of Barak's unexpected reply to his commission by Deborah in the text, the expression on Barak's face in the painting is open to interpretation. I read it as a look of shock, a shock of recognition, and thus as de Bray's way of conveying directly to the viewer what Barak must have felt at seeing Sisera dead in Jael's tent, dispatched by a woman's hand. The hands in the painting tell a story. Deborah's hands, pressed together in prayer, form a stark contrast to Jael's, which hold the murder weapons. Barak's hands, in contrast, are not visible. Thus de Bray reinforces the idea that God gave Sisera 'into the hand of a woman'.

Barak may be somewhat in the background here, but tradition brings him out of the shadows. In 1 Sam. 12.11 Jerubbaal, Barak,[54] Jephthah and Samuel are named as deliverers in the time of the judges, and Heb. 11.32 lists Barak along with the judges Gideon, Samson, Jephthah and Samuel as heroes who through faith conquered kingdoms. The judge Deborah is absent from both lists. Biblical commentators, too, bring Barak into the limelight. Soggin, for example, in his commentary, entitles the section on Judges 4–5 'Deborah and Barak as Judges' and speaks of 'the judgeship of Deborah and Barak'.[55] Boling gives his discussion of Judges 4 the title 'Deborah and Baraq', and, inexplicably, demotes Deborah to an 'honorary judge'.[56] Webb, in a literary reading, deals with Judges 4–5 under the title 'Barak', and considers Barak to be the intended 'deliverer', though admitting that the term *moshia*', used for other deliverer figures in Judges, is not applied to him.[57] Others use the title

53. Although I am more inclined to attribute Barak's insistence that Deborah accompany him to battle to over-dependence on the prophet rather than outright cowardice, I agree with Bal that the result is his narrative punishment: 'Barak is punished for his cowardice in soliciting the protection of Deborah on the battlefield, but his punishment is the shame of seeing his enemy killed by a woman—the shame of the other's shame' (*Murder and Difference*, p. 63).

54. The Hebrew reads 'Bedan', but since Bedan is unknown to us and 1 Sam. 12.9 mentions both Sisera and Jabin as enemies from whom Israel was delivered, most commentators emend 'Bedan' to 'Barak'.

55. Soggin, *Judges*, p. 60.

56. Boling, *Judges*, p. 94.

57. Barry G. Webb, *The Book of the Judges: An Integrated Reading* (JSOTSup, 46; Sheffield: JSOT Press, 1987), pp. 133-34.

'Deborah and Barak', letting Deborah and Barak share the glory, though not necessarily the same responsibilities.[58]

Visualizing Textual Oppositions

Jael, Deborah and Barak not only leads the viewer to contemplate the heroes as individuals and the roles they play, it also draws contrasts between them that resonate remarkably well with textual oppositions, demonstrating what a keen visual exegete de Bray is. An obvious opposition in both painting and text is that between male and female. Who is the deliverer, the real hero of the story, the female judge and prophet Deborah or the male military leader Barak, who, commissioned by her, destroys Sisera's entire army? Or is it Jael, the woman who kills Sisera? Is it a coincidence that the only female judge in the book of Judges shares the spotlight with others? Or, as seems to me more likely, is this surplus of heroes, vying, with divine assistance, for the glory, a literary device used by the biblical narrator in order not to allow a woman too much power?[59] A male leader is essential, since a woman could not lead an army in a major military campaign (and one need only recall how dubious Deborah's military role is).[60] Nor is the biblical narrator content for the glory to be shared between a woman and a man; a second woman is introduced to compete for the woman's portion of the glory.[61] Ironically Jael's victory not

58. See, e.g., Moore, *Judges*, p. 107 (who uses a longer title for Judg. 4, 'Deborah and Barak deliver Israel from the Canaanites; the defeat and death of Sisera'); Burney, *Judges*, p. 78; Hertzberg, *Josua, Richter, Ruth*, p. 169; Gray, *Joshua, Judges, Ruth*, p. 253; Lindars, *Judges 1–5*, p. 164.

59. If the victory over Sisera had been Deborah's alone, she might appear too powerful and threatening. Imagine, for example, if she, and not Jael, had slain Sisera, much as Samuel slaughtered Agag when Saul did not complete his mission to kill all the Amalekites (1 Sam. 15.32-33). Alternatively, if Deborah had overcome Sisera through deception like Jael's, replete with sexual innuendo, she would no longer be the non-sexual and thus unsullied mother figure she is. Perhaps any role in Sisera's death would have tarnished her reputation (a woman who kills—even Judith, for example—does not escape reproach).

60. But cf. Yee ('By the Hand of a Woman', pp. 110-17), who attributes to Deborah a military role, and argues that the representation of both Deborah and Jael as women warriors in Judg. 4 is the author's attempt 'to cope with the tension between the normative maleness of the military and the apparent involvement of women in war in pre-state Israel' (p. 114); see also Hackett, 'In the Days of Jael', p. 27; Ackerman, *Warrior, Dancer, Seductress, Queen*, pp. 31-45, 71; Jost, *Gender, Sexualität und Macht*, pp. 126-37.

61. Or, as Bal puts it, the two women function as 'a single *category* in which each has her predetermined place' (*Murder and Difference*, p. 215); cf. Murray, 'Narrative Structure', p. 173. On the splitting of woman's roles as a technique for diminishing a woman's power, see J. Cheryl Exum, *Plotted, Shot, and Painted: Cultural Representations of Biblical Women* (Sheffield: Sheffield Academic Press, 1996), pp. 96-97; Athalya

only detracts from Barak's glory, as Deborah had prophesied, but also from Deborah's, since 'the hand of a woman' that delivers Israel turns out to be not Deborah's but Jael's. Deborah, as prophet and judge, plays a crucial leadership role, but Jael's victory over Sisera, the climactic event in both the omniscient narrator's and the characters' accounts, is not a military victory.[62] '[S]he disarmed Sisera with a woman's weapons: soft words and strong drink.'[63]

The most visually arresting opposition the painting sets up is that between Jael and Deborah. I mentioned above the contrast between the non-sexual, hoary prophet Deborah and the sexual young assassin Jael. De Bray's portrayal of the two women virtually compels the viewer to compare them, to see them as vastly different and to overlook any similarities, similarities often overlooked in biblical commentary as well. The biblical text says nothing about Deborah's age, or anyone else's for that matter. It does, however, draw attention to Jael's sexuality in using language suggestive of seduction and rape to describe her murder of Sisera, language that might lead a reader to imagine Jael as young and seductive. I suggested above that, for de Bray, making Deborah old and nonsexual may be a way of affirming her role as an otherworldly servant of God, as well as alluding to her role as a wizened 'mother in Israel'. That, in the text, the erotic imagery applied to Jael does not extend to Deborah may reflect patriarchy's attempt to deny the mother's sexuality, especially in the case of a good 'mother', like Deborah.[64]

Interestingly, neither Deborah nor Jael is unambiguously identified as a wife. Deborah's epithet, *'eshet lappidot*, usually translated 'wife of Lappidot', could be translated 'fiery woman'.[65] Jael's epithet, 'wife of Heber the Kenite' (*'eshet heber haqqeni*) might be rendered 'a woman of the Kenite group'.[66]

Brenner, *The Israelite Woman: Social Role and Literary Type in Biblical Narrative* (Sheffield: JSOT Press, 1985), pp. 99-100.

62. For arguments that Jael, like Deborah, should be considered a military hero, see Hackett, 'In the Days of Jael', p. 28; Yee, 'By the Hand of a Woman', pp. 110-17; Ackerman, *Warrior, Dancer, Seductress, Queen*, pp. 59-72.

63. Sternberg, *Poetics of Biblical Narrative*, p. 282. Sternberg's patriarchal reading brings to the surface the patriarchal ideology implicit in the text.

64. One can see this clearly in the denial of the mother's sexuality in the story of another judge, Samson; see J. Cheryl Exum, *Fragmented Women: Feminist (Sub)versions of Biblical Narratives* (Valley Forge, PA: Trinity Press International; Sheffield: Sheffield Academic Press, 1993), pp. 61-93.

65. Cf. the NEB footnote, 'spirited woman'. Hebrew *lappid* is a masculine noun meaning 'torch'; *lappidot*, which looks like a feminine plural form, does not appear elsewhere. Van Wolde, reading 'woman of torches', suggests the feminine form appears because of the association with a woman ('Ya'el in Judges 4', p. 240 and n. 4).

66. Soggin, *Judges*, pp. 62, 65-66. The basic meaning of Hebrew *heber* is 'group', and in Soggin's view it refers here to an ethnic unit.

Whereas 'fiery woman' describes Deborah very well, in Jael's case 'wife of Heber' seems more likely, especially in 4.21, where Jael is described a second time simply as *'eshet heber*. It would not be unusual to find both women identified in terms of their husbands, just as Barak, son of Abinoam, is identified in relation to his father. Neither Lappidot nor Heber nor Abinoam plays a role in the story. Both women act independently of husbands or other male authority figures. But both are, symbolically at least, mothers.

Deborah is the good mother. She 'arose as a mother in Israel' (5.7) to deliver her children from danger and make their lives secure. She is the life-giving mother. Jael, on the other hand, is the death-dealing mother. Even stronger than the sexual imagery in the account of Jael and Sisera is the maternal imagery.[67] Jael behaves in a motherly fashion, offering Sisera security ('turn aside to me') and assurance ('have no fear', 4.18). The picture the text paints of her covering him and giving him milk to drink suggests a mother putting her son to bed. She even watches over him while he sleeps to protect him from harm ('Stand at the opening of the tent, and if any man comes and asks you, "Is there a man here?", say "There is not"', 4.20).[68] The maternal aspect of Jael is an important feature in the text that de Bray does not appear to represent at all in his visual exegesis of the story, unless Jael's full breasts allude to the nurturing mother of the text who gives Sisera milk to drink when he asks for water.[69]

As the biblical story shows, the nurturing, protective mother can suddenly, unexpectedly, turn deadly. She may attack her son in his sleep, when he is utterly defenseless (4.21). Or she may turn on him in the maternal act of feeding him (5.25-27). In Mieke Bal's reading of Judg. 5.27, Sisera drops between Jael's legs like an aborted fetus.[70] Thus it turns out that the nurturing

67. For discussion of the mixture of sexual and maternal imagery, see Bal, *Death and Dissymmetry*, pp. 211-17, 227-29; Bal, *Murder and Difference*, pp. 102-109, 121-34; Alter, *Art of Biblical Poetry*, pp. 43-49; Fewell and Gunn, 'Controlling Perspectives', pp, 392-94.

68. There is only a little boy, ironically about to become, as Johanna W.H. Bos observes, 'a dead man, "not there"' ('Out of the Shadows: Genesis 38; Judges 4.17-22; Ruth 3', in Exum and Bos [eds.], *Reasoning with the Foxes*, p. 54); cf. Bal, *Death and Dissymmetry*: 'he anticipates that his manliness may be questioned' (p. 213), 'his destruction is his unmanning' (p. 214).

69. Cf. the rabbinic tradition that the milk Jael gave Sisera came from her breasts (e.g. *b. Nid.* 55b); on rabbinic treatments of Jael and Deborah, see Leila Leah Bronner, 'Valorized or Vilified? The Women of Judges in Midrashic Sources', in Brenner (ed.), *A Feminist Companion to Judges*, pp. 78-91. Bronner observes that, whereas Jael receives a mixed reception, the rabbis consistently sought to diminish Deborah's role as judge and leader. Apparently Deborah posed more of a problem for rabbinic interpreters than Jael because the text did not already provide some support for undermining her role.

70. Bal, *Murder and Difference*, p. 131.

mother and the dangerous mother are one and the same, a characteristic of the mother well established in psychoanalytic theory, according to which the mother has a dual aspect as a source of security and protection but also of anxiety and frustration.[71] Although at first glance it may seem that Deborah is the good mother and Jael the terrifying one, the text in fact reveals that it is not possible to experience only one side of the mother and not the other.[72] Jael is both nurturing and deadly. Deborah is not only concerned for her people's security but also sends her 'sons' off to war, where many of them will die. So, to answer a question I posed at the beginning of this article, it would indeed seem that Deborah belongs, as de Bray presents her to us, in the company of a brutal assassin and a military hero who has shed much blood.

There is another opposition in the text, so fundamental that it is rarely discussed: the opposition between 'us' and 'them', between those on the 'right' side, those with God on their side—the heroes, Jael, Deborah, Barak and the Israelites—and those on the 'wrong' side, the oppressors, the enemy—the Canaanites, Jabin, Sisera and Sisera's mother. De Bray is interested only in the victors and, like the text, in commemorating their glorious victory. But, looking at this painting, a viewer might wonder about the defeated enemy, absent but hinted at in the bloody nail and the heroes' poses. The text, in contrast, draws attention to the forces opposing the Israelites at many points, but none so forceful as the final stanzas of Deborah and Barak's victory song. Here the focus is on two individuals as representative of the enemy: their leader Sisera, who, not unexpectedly, dies ignominiously (5.24-27), and, in an unanticipated *tour de force* of *Schadenfreude*, his mother, who grows increasingly apprehensive at his delay (vv. 28-30). 'So perish all your enemies, Yahweh!', exclaim the singers at the story's end (v. 31). *Schadenfreude*, however, is double-edged. The singers' delight in the enemy's false perceptions—Sisera's belief that he is secure, his mother's faltering assurance that finding and dividing the spoil has caused his delay—make it possible for the reader to consider the events from the perspective of those defeated.[73] Sisera's mother is given greater interiority than any other character in the story, and the finely crafted portrait of her is both moving and

71. Furthermore, according to psychoanalytic theory, the infant's desire for the mother's body has a sexual aspect, which helps explain the mixture of erotic imagery and maternal imagery in the account of Sisera's encounter with Jael.

72. The situation is thus more complex than that described by Fokkelien van Dijk-Hemmes, 'Mothers and a Mediator in the Song of Deborah', in Brenner (ed.), *A Feminist Companion to Judges*, pp. 110-14. My discussion of the mother above draws on J. Cheryl Exum, 'Feminist Criticism: Whose Interests Are Being Served?, in *Judges and Method: New Approaches in Biblical Studies* (ed. Gale A. Yee; Minneapolis: Fortress Press, 1995), pp. 71-75.

73. Witness the sympathy, albeit qualified, for Sisera and his mother in the commentaries.

chilling. Readers are likely both to sympathise with her anxiety and to be appalled by the vision of rape and pillage, realities of war, that she relies on to allay her fears.[74] In the picture of Sisera's mother peering through the window, hoping against hope that she will soon spy her son returning triumphantly, the text opens a window for its readers to look through the other's eyes, and to catch a glimpse of the horrors of war.

BIBLIOGRAPHY

Ackerman, Susan, *Warrior, Dancer, Seductress, Queen: Women in Judges and Biblical Israel* (New York: Doubleday, 1998).

Alter, Robert, *The Art of Biblical Poetry* (New York: Basic Books, 1985).

Amit, Yairah, 'Judges 4: Its Contents and Form', *JSOT* 39 (1987), pp. 89-111.

Bal, Mieke, *Death and Dissymmetry: The Politics of Coherence in the Book of Judges* (Chicago: University of Chicago Press, 1988).

—*Murder and Difference: Gender, Genre, and Scholarship on Sisera's Death* (Bloomington: Indiana University Press, 1988).

Berdini, Paolo, *The Religious Art of Jacopo Bassano: Painting as Visual Exegesis* (Cambridge: Cambridge University Press, 1997).

Bohn, Babette, 'Death, Dispassion, and the Female Hero: Artemisia Gentileschi's *Jael and Sisera*', in *The Artemisia Files: Artemisia Gentileschi for Feminists and Other Thinking People* (ed. Mieke Bal; Chicago: University of Chicago Press, 2005), pp. 107-27.

Boling, Robert G., *Judges: A New Translation with Introduction and Commentary* (Anchor Bible, 6A; Garden City, NY: Doubleday, 1975).

Boonen, Jacqueline, 'Die Geschichte von Israels Exil und Freiheitskampf', in Tümpel (ed.), *Im Lichte Rembrandts*, pp. 106-21.

Bos, Johanna W.H., 'Out of the Shadows: Genesis 38; Judges 4.17-22; Ruth 3', in Exum and Bos (eds.), *Reasoning with the Foxes*, pp. 37-67.

Brenner, Athalya, 'Afterword', in Brenner (ed.), *A Feminist Companion to Judges*, pp. 231-35.

— *The Israelite Woman: Social Role and Literary Type in Biblical Narrative* (Sheffield: JSOT Press, 1985).

Brenner, Athalya (ed.), *A Feminist Companion to Judges* (Sheffield: Sheffield Academic Press, 1993).

Bronner, Leila Leah, 'Valorized or Vilified? The Women of Judges in Midrashic Sources', in Brenner (ed.), *A Feminist Companion to Judges*, pp. 72-95.

Burney, C.F., *The Book of Judges* (New York: Ktav, 1970 [1903]).

Camp, Claudia V., 'The Wise Women of 2 Samuel: A Role Model for Women in Early Israel?', *CBQ* 43 (1981), pp. 14-29.

Coogan, Michael David, 'A Structural and Literary Analysis of the Song of Deborah', *CBQ* 40 (1978), pp. 143-66.

74. See further, Fewell and Gunn, 'Controlling Perspectives', pp. 406-409; Exum, 'Feminist Criticism', pp. 73-75. The text does not mention Israelite casualties, though it reports the whole scale slaughter of Sisera's army.

Dijk-Hemmes, Fokkelien van, 'Mothers and a Mediator in the Song of Deborah', in Brenner (ed.), *A Feminist Companion to Judges*, pp. 110-14.

Driver, G.R., 'Problems of Interpretation in the Heptateuch', in *Mélanges bibliques rédigés en l'honneur de André Robert* (Paris: Bloud & Gay, 1957), pp. 66-76.

Exum, J. Cheryl, 'The Centre Cannot Hold: Thematic and Textual Instabilities in Judges', *CBQ* 52 (1990), pp. 410-31.

—'Feminist Criticism: Whose Interests Are Being Served?', in *Judges and Method: New Approaches in Biblical Studies* (ed. Gale A. Yee; Minneapolis: Fortress Press, 1995), pp. 65-90.

—*Fragmented Women: Feminist (Sub)versions of Biblical Narratives* (Valley Forge, PA: Trinity Press International; Sheffield: Sheffield Academic Press, 1993).

—*Plotted, Shot, and Painted: Cultural Representations of Biblical Women* (Sheffield: Sheffield Academic Press, 1996).

—*Tragedy and Biblical Narrative: Arrows of the Almighty* (Cambridge: Cambridge University Press, 1992).

Exum, J. Cheryl, and Johanna W.H. Bos (eds.), *Reasoning with the Foxes: Female Wit in a World of Male Power* (Semeia, 42; Atlanta: Scholars Press, 1988).

Fewell, Danna Nolan, and David M. Gunn, 'Controlling Perspectives: Women, Men, and the Authority of Violence in Judges 4 & 5', *JAAR* 58 (1990), pp. 389-411.

Fuchs, Esther, '"For I Have the Way of Women": Deception, Gender, and Ideology in Biblical Narrative', in Exum and Bos (eds.), *Reasoning with the Foxes*, pp. 68-83.

Gent, Judith van, and Gabriël M. C. Pastoor, 'Die Zeit der Richter', in Tümpel (ed.), *Im Lichte Rembrandts*, pp. 66-87.

Gray, John, *Joshua, Judges, Ruth* (New Century Bible Commentary; Grand Rapids: Eerdmans, 1986).

Gunn, David M., *Judges* (Blackwell Bible Commentaries; Oxford: Blackwell, 2005).

Haag, Herbert, Dorothée Sölle, Joe H. Kirchberger, Anne-Marie Schnieper-Müller, and Emil Bührer, *Great Women of the Bible in Art and Literature* (Grand Rapids: Eerdmans, 1994).

Hackett, Jo Ann, 'In the Days of Jael: Reclaiming the History of Women in Ancient Israel', in *Immaculate and Powerful: The Female in Sacred Image and Social Reality* (ed. Clarissa W. Atkinson, Constance H. Buchanan and Margaret R. Miles; Boston: Beacon Press, 1985), pp. 15-37.

Halpern, Baruch, *The First Historians: The Hebrew Bible and History* (San Francisco: Harper & Row, 1988).

Hertzberg, Hans Wilhelm, *Die Bücher Josua, Richter, Ruth* (Göttingen: Vandenhoeck & Ruprecht, 1969).

Jost, Renate, *Gender, Sexualität und Macht in der Anthropologie des Richterbuches* (BWANT, 164; Stuttgart: Kohlhammer, 2006).

Lindars, Barnabas, *Judges 1–5: A New Translation and Commentary* (Edinburgh: T. & T. Clark, 1995).

Matthews, Victor H., and Don C. Benjamin, *The Social World of Ancient Israel 1250–587* BCE (Peabody, MA: Hendrickson, 1993).

Mazar, Benjamin, 'The Sanctuary of Arad and the Family of Hobab the Kenite', *JNES* 24 (1965), pp. 297-303.

Miller, Geoffrey P., 'A Riposte Form in the Song of Deborah', in Victor H. Matthews, Bernard M. Levinson and Tikva Frymer-Kensky (eds.), *Gender and Law in the Hebrew Bible and the Ancient Near East* (JSOTSup, 262; Sheffield: Sheffield Academic Press, 1998), pp. 113-27.

Moore, George F., *A Critical and Exegetical Commentary on Judges* (Edinburgh: T. & T. Clark, 1895).
Murray, D.F., 'Narrative Structure and Technique in the Deborah–Barak Story (Judges IV.4-22)', in *Studies in the Historical Books of the Old Testament* (ed. J.A. Emerton; VTSup, 30; Leiden: E.J. Brill, 1979), pp. 155-89.
Niditch, Susan, 'Eroticism and Death in the Tale of Jael', in *Gender and Difference in Ancient Israel* (ed. Peggy L. Day; Minneapolis: Fortress Press, 1989), pp. 43-57.
O'Kane, Martin, *Painting the Text: The Artist as Biblical Interpreter* (Sheffield: Sheffield Phoenix Press, 2007).
Reis, Pamela Tamarkin, 'Uncovering Jael and Sisera: A New Reading', *SJOT* 19 (2005), pp. 24-47.
Soggin, J. Alberto, *Judges, A Commentary* (trans. John Bowden; Philadelphia: Westminster Press, 1981).
Sternberg, Meir, *The Poetics of Biblical Narrative: Ideological Literature and the Drama of Reading* (Bloomington: Indiana University Press, 1985).
Stocker, Margarita, *Judith, Sexual Warrior: Women and Power in Western Culture* (New Haven: Yale University Press, 1998).
Tümpel, Christian (ed.), *Im Lichte Rembrandts: Das Alte Testament im Goldenen Zeitalter der niederländischen Kunst* (Zwolle: Waanders Verlag, n.d.).
Verdi, Richard, *Matthias Stom: Isaac Blessing Jacob* (Birmingham: The Trustees of the Barber Institute of Fine Arts, 1999).
Wolde, Ellen van, 'Ya'el in Judges 4', *ZAW* 107 (1995), pp. 240-46.
Webb, Barry G., *The Book of the Judges: An Integrated Reading* (JSOTSup, 46; Sheffield: JSOT Press, 1987).
Yee, Gale A., 'By the Hand of a Woman: The Metaphor of the Woman Warrior in Judges 4', in *Women, War, and Metaphor: Language and Society in the Study of the Hebrew Bible* (ed. Claudia V. Camp and Carole R. Fontaine; Semeia, 61; Atlanta: Society of Biblical Literature, 1993), pp. 99-132.
Zakovitch, Yair, 'Sisseras Tod', *ZAW* 93 (1981), pp. 364-74.

Love beyond Limits: The Debatable Body in Depictions of David and Jonathan

Hugh S. Pyper

'I am distressed for you, my brother Jonathan; very pleasant have you been to me; your love to me was wonderful, passing the love of women.' David's words of lament in 2 Sam. 1.26 for Jonathan, Saul's son, whose role David supplants when he becomes king of Israel, are justly famous—or notorious. This characterisation of the relationship between the two men as 'passing the love of women' still operates as a powerful but ambiguous icon. It is both an ideal and a threat that troubles boundaries when the limits of acceptable relationships between men under patriarchy are under discussion. For a man to be more than a woman may be an assertion of the distinction between male and female and the superiority of the former, but it also may blur that distinction by making woman the point of comparison. On the other hand, to be more than a woman might imply being more womanly than a woman. When the discourse involves loving relationships between men, the confusions are all the more possible and all the more threatening.

Because of its iconic status, the friendship between David and Jonathan has been the subject of a number of paintings in the Western tradition. On tracing the iconography of this image, I discovered that it is surprisingly common for the viewer to have difficulties with working out which of the two figures is which. There are analogies here with the difficulty of distinguishing between Naomi and Boaz in a painting by Philip Calderon which Cheryl Exum has discussed.[1] The interpretative choices and arguments made

1. See Chapter 5, 'Is this Naomi?', in J.C. Exum, *Plotted, Shot and Painted: Cultural Representations of Biblical Women* (Sheffield: Sheffield Academic Press, 1996), pp. 129-74. In her penetrating study of Calderon's painting *Ruth and Naomi*, Exum discusses how viewers interpret the ambiguous figure who is depicted embracing Ruth. Is her partner Naomi or Boaz? She explores how assumptions about the boundaries of allowable expression of affection between women colour the interpretations. The passionate nature of the embrace leads some to decide that this figure is Boaz, while others, perhaps more aware that normative assumptions of heterosexuality may be at work, interpret this figure as Naomi. The picture then becomes a celebration of the passionate bonding of

by various critics then become intriguing indications of their assumptions about relationships between men and allowable readings of the biblical texts.

My argument here is that this ambiguity in the artistic tradition arises from ambiguities in the text. These in turn reflect the price paid by the writers of the books of Samuel as they seek to deflect attention from the way in which David's succession to Saul flouts the expectations of dynastic succession at the founding moment of the Davidic kingship. By various gestures of textual sleight-of-hand, the writers of Samuel transform David from usurper to heir as he steps into Jonathan's role, eliding, but thereby paradoxically emphasising, the role of women in the process of succession. What is presented as a seamless transformation in the flow of the narrative, however, can be unmasked by taking a freeze-frame shot, so to speak, which is what the painterly tradition is always obliged to do. It is then fascinating to see how the dilemma this causes is worked out both in the work of the artists we shall examine and in the often divergent and sometimes surprisingly emotionally charged reactions of critics.

I shall argue that as the roles merge and cross so do the bodies of the two characters. Painting can deal only with the concreteness of bodies to express emotion, status and action. The boundaries of the autonomous male body are disrupted in a way that threatens the defining characteristics of the male in patriarchal society. The link between body and identity is troubled, creating what I have labelled here 'debatable' bodies. What is at stake is the threat to the hard-won autonomy and bodily integrity of the truly masculine man, which can be threatened by the potential feminization implied by the 'wrong' sort of loving relationship with another man. This iconic relationship takes the intrinsic ambivalence of patriarchy over femininity and thus of heterosexuality to its limit. In modern critical parlance, there is a queering of the assumptions of patriarchy where the effort to establish male supremacy and to differentiate the masculine and feminine roles by excluding the feminine paradoxically ends up by encompassing the feminine within the masculine, thereby undoing the very category it seeks to preserve.

Naomi and Ruth. Exum also considers the criteria by which artists and film makers have made decisions as to the relative ages of the characters, which are never specified in the biblical text. She sees the ambiguity in the painting as a pointer to ambiguities in the biblical text as to the role of the named characters. Specifically, she points out how Naomi occupies a number of roles which cross traditional gender barriers. She is not only Elimelech's wife and Mahlon's mother, but in relation to Ruth's child Obed she is spoken of in terms that are elsewhere only used of fathers and indeed acts like a surrogate husband to Ruth. In the end, Exum argues that there is a consistent destabilization of the gender roles in Ruth which invites readers to examine the gender distinctions with which they operate. The reader will be aware how many of these issues are addressed in the present paper, although my concern here is more directly with the inherent paradoxes of dynastic patriarchy than with gender politics per se.

In this article, my purpose is not to contribute to the continuing and ultimately inclusive debate about the precise nature of the bond between David and Jonathan and its implications for contemporary debates on the morality of homosexuality. Instead, the approach adopted is much in line with Ken Stone's conclusions on the matter in his treatment of 1 and 2 Samuel in *The Queer Bible Commentary*:

> In the end, then, it is neither necessary nor possible to reach a single, definitive conclusion about the nature of the relationship between David and Jonathan. Rather than insisting only upon a sexual interpretation of David's lament for Jonathan, a queer reading might call attention to multiple ways of understanding the text and use those multiple interpretations to raise questions about the reasons why particular readers tend to be drawn to certain conclusions rather than others.[2]

If we can expand readers to include artists and even the viewers of their art works, then this encapsulates my aims here.

I will argue that the decisions that these artists are obliged to make reveal the inherent instability of the ideology of patriarchy which the economy of biblical narrative may conceal. Just as any creation myth that derives humanity from a primal couple has to deal with the inescapable consequence that the second generation can only be propagated through incest, any myth of the pure origin of a hereditary dynasty that passes down the male line has to remove any suggestion of contamination from the female line and so must also deal with the consequences of incest and the impossible ideal of propagation from the male alone.[3]

2. K. Stone, '1 and 2 Samuel', in *The Queer Bible Commentary* (ed. D. Guest, R.E. Goss, M. West and T. Bohache; London: SCM Press, 2006), pp. 195-221 (208). Readers who are interested in the current state of the debate on these matters will also find that Stone gives an excellent short summary of the issues and the various positions adopted on pp. 205-208. My own understanding of queer commentary is in line with the definition that Stone gives in his earlier article, 'Queer Commentary and Biblical Interpretation: An Introduction', in *Queer Commentary and the Hebrew Bible* (ed. K. Stone; London: SCM Press, 2001), p. 33, where he describes it as 'a range of approaches to biblical interpretation that take as their point of departure a critical interrogation and active contestation of the many ways in which the Bible is and has been read to support heteronormative and normalizing configurations of sexual practices and sexual identities'.

3. Typically, this dilemma is most succinctly put by Shakespeare in *Cymbeline* (Act 2, Scene 5, lines 153-54), where Posthumus laments, 'Is there no way for men to be, but women / Must be half-workers?' He goes on to wish he could find out and remove the woman's part in himself which he sees as the seat of all his vices. The impossible male aspiration to pure masculinity, in both senses of unmixed and uncorrupted, which underlies *Cymbeline* is also at work in the biblical texts, as is what Jean Howard in the introduction to the Norton edition of the play calls 'the dream of androgenesis', i.e.

I want to proceed by concentrating on four depictions which represent this relationship. They show different stratagems for containing the inherent disruptiveness of this story, but also demonstrate that the disruption cannot be suppressed. In attempting to contain the queerness of the biblical text, the four artists in different ways queer the conventions of representative art, especially the cues to the recognition of characters. The four pictures in question are these:

1. a jolly picture in the National Gallery by the Venetian Giovanni Cima da Conegliano (1459/60–1517/18) which was painted around 1505–10;
2. an interestingly enigmatic picture by Rembrandt, now in the Hermitage;
3. a woodcut by Julius Schnoor von Carolsfeld (1794–1872) which is one of a set of illustrations for *Das Buch der Bücher in Bildern*;
4. a particularly disturbing and suggestive picture by the Victorian artist Frederic, Lord Leighton.

All of these, I will argue, reflect and shed light on some of the ways in which models of acceptable relationships between men have been applied to and challenged by this biblical story. Their differences and similarities demonstrate that this biblical passage has been assimilated to different ideals of relationship between men derived from the classical tradition. The first is the model of indulgent master and faithful servant. The second is the model of the friend as the other self exemplified by Cicero in his treatise *De Amicitia*. The third is the model of the pedagogical love between an older man and a younger boy of which Plato is the great exponent.

To apply any of these models to David and Jonathan, however, depends on making decisions about aspects of their relationship, particularly the relative age of the two, which are not specified in 1 Samuel. The biblical text can get away with a blithe disregard for the appearance and spatial arrangements of its characters in most circumstances. The visual artist has to make such decisions. What determines these choices is a complex interplay between audience expectations, social convention, and the pictorial tradition together with the artist's conscious and unconscious ideological commitments and personal experience. Works of art can thus throw an oblique light on the similar choices made by biblical commentators. Asking just the simple question of our artists, 'Which is David?', may throw up some surprising issues.

birth without the intervention of women (S. Greenblatt, W. Cohen, J.E. Howard and K.E. Maus [eds.], *The Norton Shakespeare* [New York: W.W. Norton, 1997], p. 2962). The prevalence of scenes of disguise and misidentification in this play makes it another prime example of the role of the debatable body in negotiating these paradoxes.

Cima da Conegliano: Master and Servant

So to begin, let us turn to Cima's painting, which introduces, in a relatively unproblematic way, some of the issues. In his picture, *David and Jonathan*, two young men are walking companionably along. Which is David and which is Jonathan? In this case, the question is relatively easily answered.

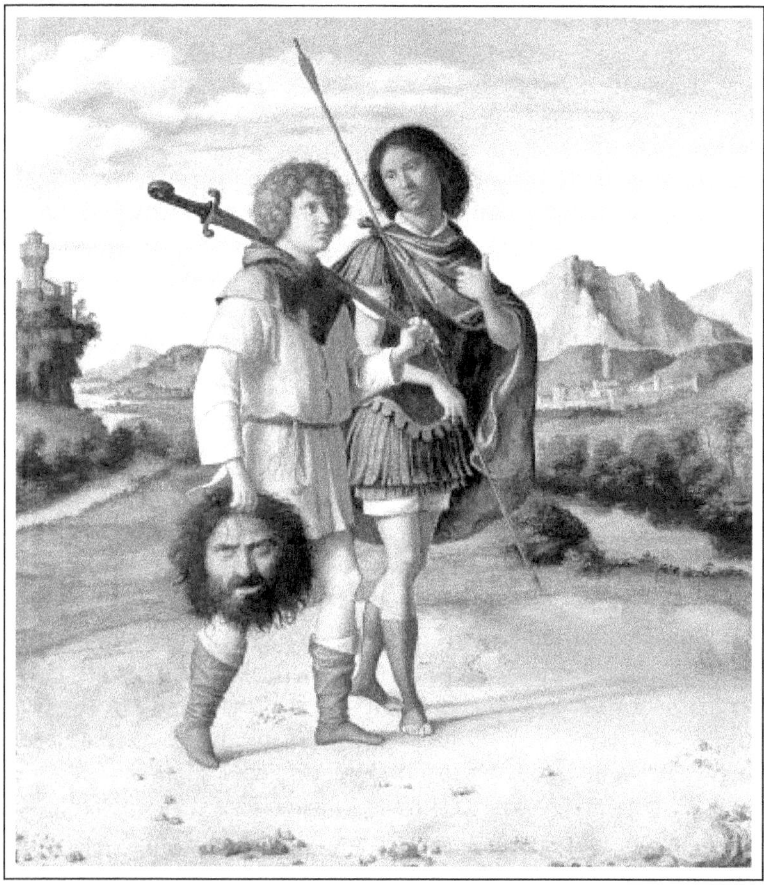

Figure 1. Giovanni Cima da Conegliano *David and Jonathan*
The National Gallery, London

Nearer the viewer is a stocky, curly-haired, ruddy-cheeked fellow, swinging a rather tell-tale attribute: a rather bemused and understandably grumpy-looking severed head which seems all the more incongruous in this otherwise innocuous scene. This seems to reflect 1 Sam. 17.54, which tells us that David, after slaying Goliath, 'took the head of the Philistine and brought it to Jerusalem'. This, together with the 'ruddiness' which is one of the very few elements of visual description in the biblical account of David (1 Sam. 16.12), makes the identification of this figure as David relatively easy.

This David is shorter and stockier, perhaps more of a peasant type, than his companion, now identifiable as Jonathan, One thing that is clear from the picture is that we are here dealing with a relationship between two young men of similar age. Nothing in the biblical text indicates how old either of them is, while any artistic depiction of their appearance cannot avoid making a decision as to the age of the character represented. Jonathan is taller, more slender and altogether more refined.[4] His finely made spear is held in an elegant pose, while David seems to be carrying his sword—or is it Goliath's?—in a very casual way, almost as a labourer might carry his pick-axe. Jonathan's clothing in particular seems more elaborate. Would it be wrong to see Jonathan's dress and comportment as somehow feminised in comparison to David, who looks like he could have just come off the football pitch?

When we turn to the Bible, however, we discover that the problem with this scene is that there is no mention of Jonathan in 1 Sam. 17.54. In fact, in the text of 1 Samuel there is no indication that David and Jonathan have yet met. The narrative sequence of this whole section of 1 Samuel 17 is very confusing, possibly due to the conflation of at least two stories of how David came into Saul's service, culminating in the strange final scene of ch. 17, where Saul appears not to recognize David and has to ask his name. It is only after this episode that, as the RSV has it,

> the soul of Jonathan was knit to the soul of David and Jonathan loved him as his own soul...then Jonathan made a covenant with David, because he loved him as his own soul. And Jonathan stripped himself of the robe that was upon him and gave it to David, and his armour, and even his sword and his bow and his girdle (1 Sam. 18.1, 3-4).

This is a crucial but puzzling passage for understanding this relationship. Words such as 'love' and 'soul' in the RSV translation come freighted with centuries of theological and philosophical weight which the Hebrew *'ahab* and *nephesh* may not necessarily imply. However we translate this, we have the king's son making a covenant and conferring his garments and weapons on a lad from nowhere, in a context where we might well ask who, if not the king's son, should have taken on the challenge from Goliath to the royal armies?

There is a weird blending, if not exchange, of identities here. Those who wish can also read some sexual tension into the disrobing of Jonathan. From

4. Does Jonathan's height reflect the emphasis that is placed on Saul's exceptional stature in 1 Sam. 9.2?

the painter's point of view, there is a particular problem in that clothes and weapons are essential props for the identification of a character, especially in the absence of an unambiguous title for the painting. Painting a disguised character raises complicated issues of recognition.

What in this case is interesting and typical of Cima's undramatic style is that he has side-stepped the problems of depicting any of emotionally and symbolically charged encounters between David and Jonathan by staging instead a rather prosaic journey *between* events. He seems to be picking up the beginning of 1 Sam. 18.6: 'as they were coming home, when David returned from killing the Philistine', taking 'they' to be Jonathan and David. The upshot of this second journey, which in the biblical narrative is a different one from the delivery of Goliath's head, will be the famous faux-pas by the women of Israel in their song which echoes in Saul's ears and the text of 1 Samuel thereafter: 'Saul has slain his thousands and David has slain his ten thousands' (1 Sam. 18.7).

Again, Cima has not chosen to depict this dramatic scene of welcome and celebration. Instead, by conflating two journeys, he has created a compound moment that gives a space where the relationship between the two men can be displayed by implication. In the terms that Susan Ackerman has used in her study of this relationship, it is a liminal space.[5] Cima has taken both his characters and his viewers on a journey literally outside the biblical narrative. This moment of travel together occurs, if I may be permitted the metaphor, at right-angles to the text. What appears to be a casual moment actually conflates and superimposes disparate narrative moments into a kind of virtual space that becomes a metaphor for the narrative destinies of the two characters. The relatively unproblematic quality that I remarked on earlier is, we begin to suspect, the result of a subtle strategy on Cima's part.

The main device for depicting their relationship is the difference in their gaze. David stares purposefully straight ahead of him, his eyes fixed on the goal of the journey, while Jonathan's attention is entirely on his companion. This asymmetry reflects the text of 1 Samuel 18, where, as has often been noted, all the initiative for their relationship comes from Jonathan. It is a truism that David throughout the books of Samuel is frequently the object, but never the subject, of the verb *'ahab*. Even in the famous funeral lament, it is Jonathan's love for him that David praises. We never hear explicitly of David's love for Jonathan, or for anyone else for that matter. In this picture, it is Jonathan whose gaze is deflected from his expected path to kingship, rapt in David, who does not seem to be paying him much attention. The only eyes engaging the viewer are those of Goliath, who almost seems to

5. S. Ackerman, *When Heroes Love: The Ambiguity of Eros in the Stories of Gilgamesh and David* (New York: Columbia University Press, 2005), especially pp. 200-36 *passim*.

be asking the age-old question of the bully: 'Who do you think you're looking at?'

Jonathan is also set back further from the viewer than David. By a cunning trick of perspective, although Jonathan is placed to the right of David in the picture and thus ahead of him in terms of the direction they are facing, the position of their feet indicates that they are walking side by side, and the relative postures make it clear that Jonathan is following David's lead, not the other way around. If the picture was to be run forward a few frames, from the viewer's perspective it would seem that David had overtaken Jonathan, another subtle indication of the forthcoming change in their respective fortunes and status.

Cima shows us a relationship where there is a tension between the subservience of Jonathan's gaze and the markers of his social status. One acceptable model of male interaction is the relationship between master and servant; Don Quixote and Sancho Panza or Mr Pickwick and Samuel Weller are classic literary examples. In this case, the relationship is unexpectedly reversed in a mismatch between the visual cues to social status encoded in the bodies, clothing and equipment of the two characters and the visual cues to the dynamic of the relationship. The stature and accoutrements that might mark Jonathan out as the master conflict with his gaze and his position, which are those of the servant. This fundamental social relationship in medieval and in ancient society is thus queered in the painting. The motivation for this mismatch is unstated, unless we read adoration into Jonathan's eyes. Cima's stratagem leaves this to the viewer to supply. At the end of this journey, however, the roles will reverse. Jonathan will give David his garments; David will take his kingship.[6] En route, Cima has provided an image where the underlying tensions are displayed in an outwardly untroubled setting which foreshadows the exchange of roles that will occur.

Rembrandt: Father and Son

The problem of identifying the two characters becomes more difficult in the case of a picture by Rembrandt now in the Hermitage. Unlike the carefree pastoral background in Cima's painting, it is a rather forbidding murk which frames the scene and this murkiness has extended to its interpretation. An older figure in turban and robes, certainly richly dressed, embraces a younger man with flowing golden hair, whose face is hidden in the other's bosom.

6. To stretch a point, in the end, perhaps, Jonathan's journey may take him to the position of Goliath in the painting, if we accept the implication in 1 Sam. 31.8-10 that his body is stripped, his head cut off and his body taken by the Philistines and displayed on the wall of Beth-shan along with his father's.

David's Farewell to Jonathan is the title under which Rembrandt himself referred to it in later catalogues. Here another construal is put on the friendship, which assimilates it to the platonic model of the older, more powerful and experienced friend who loves and encourages the beautiful and promising boy. Exegetically, one can argue for a reading of 1 Samuel which, rather than stressing the similarities between the two characters (the idea of 'one soul in two bodies'), emphasizes the difference in David and Jonathan's initial status, one a mere shepherd lad, the other a seasoned warrior and a king's son.

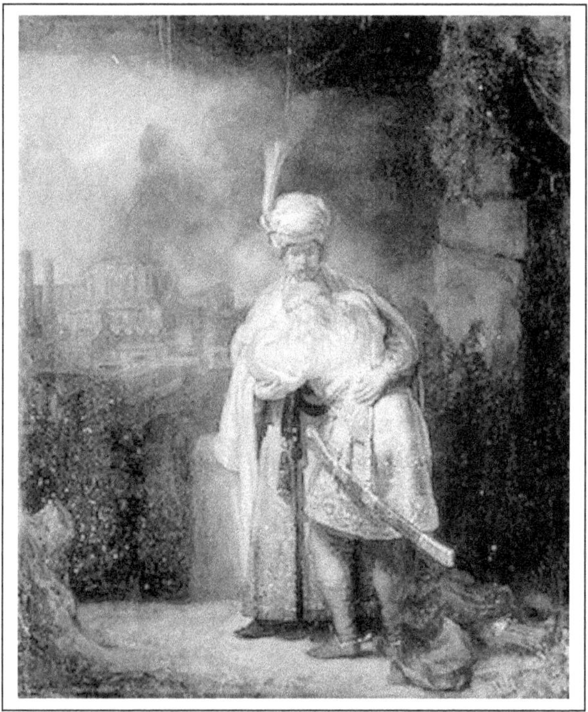

Figure 2. Rembrandt van Rijn, *David and Jonathan*
The Hermitage Museum, St Petersburg

Tellingly, however, the title of the painting has been disputed, precisely because it is so hard to identify the two figures. David and Absalom or David and Mephibosheth are alternative pairings which have been suggested.[7] The

7. The matter is discussed in G. Schwartz, *Rembrandt: His Life, His Paintings* (London: Guild Publishing, 1985), p. 224. Schwartz opts to read the painting as *The Reconciliation of David and Mephibosheth*, attributing Rembrandt's later identification of it as David and Jonathan to his 'blurred' memory.

rather odd posture of the figure with his back to us has been taken to strengthen the identification with Mephibosheth, who 2 Sam. 4.4 tells us was crippled in his feet. In this case, the picture is presumably related to the meeting between the two in 2 Sam. 9.5-8. Alternatively, the copious flowing hair of the younger figure could suggest Absalom, perhaps at the moment when David kisses his formerly exiled son in 2 Sam. 15.33. Interestingly, in both these recastings David remains the constant factor but shifts position in the painting. He is now read as the older figure, who offers his comfort to a younger supplicant. This may have seemed to some viewers a more appropriate role for the great ruler of Israel.

The identification of the older figure in the painting as Jonathan, however, is made more secure by the existence of drawings by Rembrandt of the scene of Jonathan's parting from David, where the difference in age and status between the figures is if anything more marked.[8] If the title is correct, then the scene being depicted comes at the end of 1 Samuel 20, a rather confused chapter, where Jonathan, again taking the initiative, has set up an elaborate scheme for communicating with David, who has been forced to flee the court. This involves a young boy shooting arrows and smacks of a rather adolescent love of intrigue, especially as at the end Jonathan and David do meet and take their leave.

The RSV translation of 1 Sam. 20.41 reads:

> And as soon as the lad had gone, David rose from behind the stone heap and fell on his face to the ground and bowed three times, and they kissed one another, and wept with one another, until David recovered himself.

The translation of the final phrase of v. 41, again from the RSV, is contested. The literal translation would be 'until David became' or 'made himself' 'great', or 'large' or 'strong'. Again, certain commentators have seen sexual connotations in this while to others such a thought has never occurred.[9] The most common, but antithetical, translations are either that David 'exceeded himself', which is taken to imply that he wept more than Jonathan (so the NRSV reads 'and David wept the more'), or that David 'steadied' or 'recovered' himself as in the RSV. Which version a translator or commentator chooses thus may reveal interesting things about an implied model of

8. One such drawing, now in the Louvre, is reproduced in H. Hoekstra, *Rembrandt and the Bible* (Utrecht: Magna Books, 1990), p. 117. Hoekstra also argues for the authenticity of Rembrandt's title for the Hermitage picture.

9. See here the discussion by Bruce Gerig in his online article, 'Jonathan and David: Their Companionship', part of his longer presentation on homosexuality and the Bible, accessible at http://epistle.us/hbarticles/jondave5.html (14 January 2007), where he invokes Arabic parallels to suggest that 'becoming great' implies that David experiences an erection.

manhood and of manly friendship. Is it more manly to weep, or is it more manly to retain self-control?[10] Once that is settled, is David or Jonathan the more favourably regarded? Hence, there is a pictorial ambiguity as well. In Rembrandt's depiction, there is a clear contrast in ages and also in manly self-control. If his title is accepted, here it is clearly David, the younger man, who weeps most copiously. Again, doubts about the appropriateness of this may have encouraged the retitling of the picture to preserve David's dignity.

It is evident that Rembrandt has read the biblical text with a different model of relationship in mind from that implied in Cima's painting, and has assimilated his picture to this model of the mentor and his beloved pupil rather than of equal friendship. Yet there are clues in the painting which suggest that it is gravitating towards an even more allowable intimacy between males, that of father and son. The face of the more kingly figure is strikingly similar to some of Rembrandt's self-portraits and his stance foreshadows the pose of the father in his well-known late picture of the return of the prodigal son.

Yet something oddly troubles later viewers, leading them to recast the roles in the painting. The vulnerability and emotionalism of the figure with his back to us is disconcerting as a depiction of David. The alternative titles of the painting seek to pre-empt the moment when the two figures will indeed exchange roles, as David supplants his friend as king and father to the dynasty. They read ahead of this moment of transition and parting. With these possibilities in mind, however, a further richness of allusion is added to the possibility that Rembrandt has cast Jonathan as the father figure who will transfer the legitimacy of his own succession to David rather than to his own son, Mephibosheth, who yet has a phantom life in the reception history of the painting, as he does in the subsequent story in 2 Samuel.[11]

Julius Schnoor von Carolsfeld: One Soul in Two Bodies

While Cima, then, contains the narrative by displacing it and assimilating it to a master-servant model and Rembrandt evokes the model of father and son, others read into the story the platonic model of 'one soul in bodies twain', to take up the title of Laurens Mill's classic study of Tudor

10. It is an interesting commentary on changing views of the appropriateness of male displays of emotion that the NRSV should opt to alter the RSV at this point.

11. Note that I am not here arguing that Rembrandt foresaw and therefore deliberately played off the misreading of his painting, but the fact that viewers are led into this misreading uncovers the implication of the paternal model within the painting. The invocation of Absalom also evokes the parallel in David's subsequent history of betrayal by a beloved son. That is certainly Saul's interpretation of the conduct of both Jonathan and David; both are sons turned traitor.

friendship.[12] David and Jonathan, as such ideal friends, demonstrate equality and the dedication to a common goal, together with a common dedication to divine love. It is their souls, not their bodies, which are united in a presage of the union of all souls with the divine. For this reading, it is precisely the reference in 1 Samuel 8 to the 'soul' that gives this relationship its ideal character.

The lengths to which proponents of this approach were prepared to go are exemplified in the unfinished epic poem *Davideis* by Abraham Cowley, published in 1656. A fair proportion of Book 2 of the existing four books is devoted to the relationship of David and Jonathan, which becomes the basis of a meditation on love founded on equality and a blending of identities:

> No weight of Birth did on one side prevaile,
> Two Twins less even lie in Nature's Scale.
> They mingled fates and both in each did share,
> They both were Servants, they both Princes were.[13]

For Cowley and others in this tradition, such male friendships, precisely because they are between people of the same sex, model true love in a way that marriage never can. In a striking passage, Cowley states,

> Never did Marriage such true Union find
> Or Men's Desires with so glad Violence bind;
> For there is still some Tincture left of Sin
> And still the Sex will needs be stealing in;
> Those Hoys are full of Dross, and thicker far
> These, without Matter, clear and liquid are.
> ...
> To this strange pitch their high Affections flew;
> Till Nature's Self scarce looked on them as two.[14]

The notion of a merged identity is here striking although Cowley's is an extreme version of this. Such a vision would account for the difficulty that arises in the later tradition in telling the two friends apart. For the visual artist, the soul can only be implied through depiction of the body. Paradoxically, perhaps, to depict two bodies that share one soul is most easily done by depicting two bodies that share physical features.

12. L.J. Mills, *One Soul in Bodies Twain: Friendship in Tudor Literature and Stuart Drama* (Bloomington: Principia Press, 1937). Mills' text gives a detailed history of the roots of this view of friendship and its blossoming in the courts of late mediaeval Europe.

13. A. Cowley, *Davideis*, Book 2 in *Poems* (ed. A.R. Waller; Cambridge: Cambridge University Press, 1905), p. 286. This aspect of the poem is discussed by T.-L. Pebworth in his essay, 'Cowley's *Davideis* and the Exaltation of Friendship', in *The David Myth in Western Literature* (ed. R.-J. Fontain and J. Wojcik; Lafayette, WI: Purdue University Press, 1980), pp. 96-104.

14. Cowley, *Poems*, pp. 286-87.

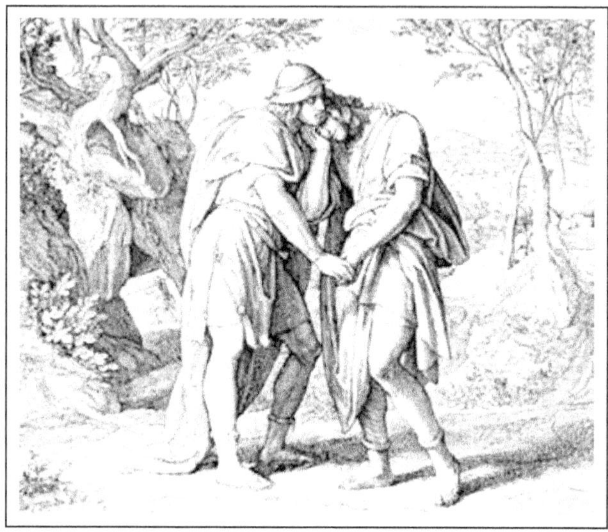

Figure 3. Julius Schnoor von Carolsfeld, *The Parting of David and Jonathan*, *Die Bibel in Bildern*. Leipzig: Georg Wigands Verlag, 1860

A case in point is one of Julius Schnoor von Carolsfeld's woodcuts for *Das Buch der Bücher in Bildern*.[15] It raises these questions in a way that may reveal the difference in sensibility characteristic of the mid-nineteenth century. Here two young men lean on one another in an embrace which combines tenderness and sadness. In an age of sensibility, the overt expression of emotion between two men does not seem to have troubled Carolsfeld. Again, however, we can ask which is Jonathan and which is David.

In this case, the two figures seem to be of the same age and similarly attractive in appearance. Neither shows any sign of being notably more regal than the other. The differences between them are slight. The right-hand figure is perhaps less well dressed and seems more emotionally dependent on his friend. Is this figure who seems to be weeping more thereby identified as David, more roughly dressed than his royal soul-mate, or is David the other figure, the one who weeps less and who has recovered himself? In the latter case, the difference in dress can be accounted for by his coming journey. The ambiguity of the biblical verse means that either figure could be acting out David's role. This seems genuinely undecidable.[16] Saul's son and the brash

15. This picture is used as the cover illustration for Ackerman's *When Heroes Love*.

16. In the discussion of this painting which followed a presentation of an earlier version of this paper at the meeting of the European Association for Biblical Studies in Dresden in July 2005, it was suggested that the figure wearing a hat is to be identified as David, after the model of Bernini's famous bronze. Further research might clarify

young upstart are here caught at a moment where they are indistinguishable and therefore where their roles blend. Either figure here could be the one who flees but will return as king while his partner dies valiantly beside his father. In contrast to Cima, Carolsfeld and his characters are stuck in a timeless moment of ambiguous identity.

Frederic, Lord Leighton: The Debatable Body

This blurring of identity between David and Jonathan reaches its furthest pitch in the fourth painting to be considered. The doyen of painters in Victorian Britain, Frederic, Lord Leighton, exhibited this picture, *Jonathan's Token to David*, to general acclaim at the Royal Academy in London in 1868. The poet Swinburne gave his reaction to it in his notes on the exhibition:

> The majestic figure and noble head of Jonathan are worthy of the warrior whose love was wonderful, passing the love of women; the features resolute, solicitous, heroic. The boy beside him is worthy to stand so near; his action has all the grace of mere nature, as he stoops slightly from the shoulders to sustain the heavy quiver.[17]

Tastes change, however, and in the introduction to the catalogue to the major retrospective exhibition of Leighton's work held in 1996 the editors reflect on what they regard as unprecedented critical abuse now directed at Leighton, once the most admired of British artists.[18] They record as a constant theme in this abuse a preoccupation with the femininity of his images. The present picture is a particular focus for this hostility. This critical ambivalence is linked, I contend, to the ambivalence we have seen at work in other paintings that deal with this relationship and ultimately to the ambivalence of the biblical text.

The scene Leighton has chosen to depict is described in 1 Sam. 20.35-39. In contrast to the other paintings we have looked at, Jonathan stands alone in this picture except for the company of a young boy. It seems to capture the moment when, faithful to his earlier pledge to David (1 Sam. 20.18-23), Jonathan and the boy have come out into the field where David is hiding. According to their pre-arranged sign, Jonathan is about to shoot three arrows near the rock where David is concealed. He will shout to the boy whom he

whether there is any consistent iconographic tradition, but preliminary investigations leave the question open.

17. A.G Swinburne, 'Notes on Some Pictures of 1868', in his *Essays and Studies* (London: Chatto & Windus, 3rd edn, 1888), pp. 358-80 (361-62).

18. R. Ormond, S. Jones, C. Newall, L. Ormond and B. Read, *Frederic Leighton 1830–1896* (New York: Harry N. Abrams, 1996).

sends to retrieve them that the arrows are beyond him to let David know that he should flee because Saul is resolved to kill him.

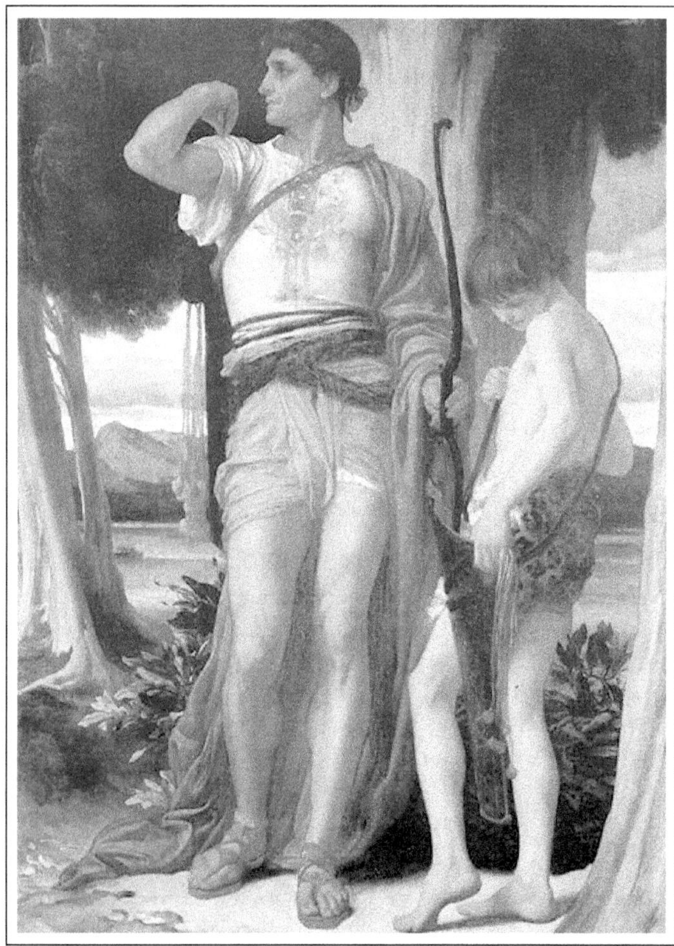

Figure 4. Frederic, Lord Leighton, *Jonathan's Token to David*
The Minneapolis Institute of Arts, Minneapolis

This seems an odd moment to choose, unless Leighton's point is the loneliness of Jonathan, rejected by his father who has just attempted to kill him (1 Sam. 20.33) and shortly to be separated from David, who is forced to flee into the wilderness. It might, however, be construed as another way to sidestep the problems inherent in depicting the two together in relation. Rather than depicting the two at the moment of parting, David here is already beyond the frame of the picture, in hiding, awaiting the sign. The asymmetry of the relationship and the inevitability of its rupture is graphically foregrounded here, without the artist being committed to any expression of intimacy.

Yet in another sense David is the dominating presence in the picture and the intimacy is absolute. In fact, the situation is rather like that of the notorious secret note of Edgar Allen Poe's story 'The Purloined Letter', which is hidden by being left visible and thus overlooked.[19] David here is hidden, but fully on display, in Jonathan.

Lene Østermark-Johansen in her essay, 'The Apotheosis of the Male Nude: Leighton and Michelangelo', lets us in on what she describes as a 'sophisticated intellectual joke' when she points out that the main figure is a dressed version of Michelangelo's famous statue of David.[20] A comparison of the figure here with Michelangelo's David makes the identification hard to resist: the profile, proportions and stance of the two figures are mirror-images of each other. The noble head of the warrior which so impressed Swinburne is David's head.

Østermark-Jensen remarks on doubleness of presence and absence in the painting, which is represented in the curious tension between movement and repose in the picture, carried over from the famous *contraposto* of Michelangelo's figure. The statue implies an absent Goliath, as the young David stares ahead, watching hawk-like for the moment when he will unleash the stone. In Leighton's version, it is David's absence which is implied by this glance and yet he is also fully present.

Østermark-Jensen sees this quotation of Michelangelo as an allusion on Leighton's part to 1 Sam. 18.4, where Jonathan is said to love David 'as his own soul'. Jonathan *is* David in this picture. She does not go on to make the further point that this Jonathan is more accurately a 'David' clad in Jonathan's garments. In this way we begin to enter an almost Shakespearean world of multiple disguised identities. This in turn recalls 1 Sam. 18.4, where Jonathan does give David his clothing.

As a matter of fact, the garments which Leighton bestows on Michelangelo's figure are, as Østermark-Jensen observes, themselves borrowed from another of Leighton's paintings, *The Shepherd and the Siren*. As she puts it, in both cases they serve to 'accentuate rather than hide the body which they so decently cover'.[21] Leighton's Jonathan, clad in his borrowed clothes, takes on a fin-de-siècle sensuality far from the frank nakedness of Michelangelo's

19. 'The Purloined Letter', in E.A. Poe, *Tales* (New York: Wiley & Puttnam, 1845), pp. 200-218.

20. L. Østermark-Johansen, 'The Apotheosis of the Male Nude: Leighton and Michelangelo', in *Frederic Leighton: Antiquity, Renaissance, Modernity* (ed. T. Barringer and E. Prettejohn; New Haven: Yale University Press, 1999), pp. 111-34. Her analysis of this painting is to be found on pp. 120-22.

21. Østermark-Jensen, 'Apotheosis', p. 122.

sculpture. Furthermore, Jonathan's clinging draperies, in their floating texture and rich colour, recall Leighton's most reproduced painting, *Flaming June*, where a buxom nymph sleeps, draped in the suggestive folds of her orange-gold gown which both conceal and reveal her naked form. We are certainly in the world of disguise and not far from the possibility of drag.

But what is the boy doing in this picture, a boy handling arrows, if not a bow, and who looks to me like a rather better-brought-up cousin of some of Caravaggio's scamps? An unnamed youth does figure in the biblical story as the innocent bearer, through the medium of arrows, of messages he does not understand between David and Jonathan. In most other contexts, however, the inclusion of a boy bearing arrows in a painting would instantly evoke a classical allusion to Eros, god of love. Why not here?

It is almost as if Leighton had read Mark George's article, 'The Body of the Heir Apparent', in which George argues that David's lament and its description of Jonathan's love as greater than a woman's reflect a textual response to a theological dilemma stemming from monotheism. If the king in some sense embodies God who has no consort, how is a new king to be created? George's account of the textual solution is as follows:

> In David's lament, and in the earlier conspiring of Jonathan and David, this theological problem is negotiated by male homosocial desire to complete a new royal body for David. Jonathan and David create this body across the bodies of men, excluding women's bodies. *Jonathan steps out of his skin, and David steps into it* [my emphasis]: they produce a body for David between themselves. By creating this body without the need for women, the theological concern to preserve monotheism is addressed; no women, and hence no consorts, are required. It is produced in the relationships between men, with one of the men becoming feminized in the relationship.[22]

Leighton's picture seems to come as close as is conceivable to depicting this body created from both David and Jonathan. Indeed, it is tempting to stretch Leighton's title for his picture and ask if this depicted body itself is not *Jonathan's Token to David.*

Leighton's picture could be seen as an analogous solution in painterly terms to the expression of a paradox. Where the philosophical and poetic tradition is able to speak of one soul in two bodies, the naturalistic painter can only depict the body. He expresses the same idea of union by the seeming reversal of transposing it to one ambiguous body that can be read as having two souls or identities. Leighton can bring off this trick only by visual quotation, which secures one identity for the body, juxtaposed with a plausible title, which asserts another. This depends on the viewer's familiarity with

22. M.K. George, 'The Body of the Heir Apparent: David's Lament', in *Reading Bibles, Writing Bodies: Identity and the Book* (ed. T.K. Beal and D.M. Gunn; London: Routledge, 1997), pp. 163-73 (172).

Michelangelo's David and therefore on the artist's judgment that he can rely on that image's cultural reach and recognizability. One debatable body evokes two identities.

David Becomes Jonathan

All four of the paintings we have looked at both reflect and resist the blurring of identities which George has pointed out. However, his explanation of this as a consequence of monotheism may not quite hit the point. The problem of succession here, which troubles these identities, is not a theological one over the production of an heir. That problem, presumably, would affect each king in the dynasty, not just Saul and David. The issue here is more deeply structural than that in that it concerns not simply the propagation but the origin of the monarchy. It comes down to the following paradoxical question: if the king in Jerusalem gains legitimacy because his father was of the Davidic line, what legitimates the first Davidic king? Conversely, if David can legitimately replace a king chosen by God, what is to stop a later usurper doing the same thing? Whatever the historical basis of the story, the books of Samuel manage to assert that David is both the originator of the divinely appointed dynasty and also the legitimate successor to the throne.[23]

In his study of the role of Jonathan in 1 Samuel 13–31, David Jobling suggests that Jonathan as a character, whatever the historical basis of this narrative may be, serves as a necessary intermediary device between Saul and David.[24] He becomes the agency of transfer of power from Saul to David. Saul cannot transfer power to David because part of the sign of his rejection is his lack of knowledge that he is rejected. Jonathan provides the missing link: 'Jonathan's identification with, his heirdom to, Saul provide him with the royal authority to abdicate; his identification with David enables the emptying of his own heirdom into David'.[25] In Jobling's account, Jonathan serves to mediate a fundamental paradox in Israel's story, which he sets out as follows:

1. Monarchy is intrinsically dynastic, but
2. Israel's monarchy is not traced from her [*sic*] first king.[26]

23. For further discussion of this point, see H.S. Pyper, *David as Reader: 2 Samuel 12.1-15 and the Poetics of Fatherhood* (Leiden: Brill, 1996), especially pp. 179-80.

24. D. Jobling, *The Sense of Biblical Narrative: Structural Analyses of the Hebrew Bible I* (Sheffield: Sheffield Academic Press, 1978), pp. 4-25.

25. Jobling, *Sense of Biblical Narrative*, p. 18.

26. Jobling, *Sense of Biblical Narrative*, p. 17.

This formulation of Jobling's, however, masks an even deeper problem in the consideration of the monarchy, which is this: if the monarchy is dynastic, how can there legitimately *be* a first king?

Jobling's formulation is predicated on an accident of history. In his view, what must be explained is the empirical fact that Israel's monarchy does not follow an uninterrupted dynastic line. However, this misses the point that this not simply a historical anomaly. There is an intrinsic difficulty in 'beginning' a monarchy. Just as there is an inherent problem with there being a first human being, so there is a problem with the first king. Jobling hypothesizes that Jonathan serves to mediate the dichotomy that has been set up. He is the heir who renounces his filiative claim to Saul's throne in favour of the affiliative claim of comradeship with David. Yet, another of Saul's children might at first sight be thought to be better placed to accomplish this feat. What about his daughter? Saul does wed his daughter Michal to David. David is thus tied into the royal household although, as the story is recounted in 1 Sam. 18.17-29, this is a calculated act of hostility on Saul's part.

Jonathan, however, performs a function that Michal cannot because of her sex. Though David can publicly be united with her through marriage in a way that the culture does not recognize with her brother, as a woman she does not stand in the direct line of succession. She cannot directly confer the throne on David. The very fact that Saul is able to give Michal to another man, Paltiel (1 Sam. 25.44), is paradoxically a by-product of the cultural conventions of marriage and divorce. Precisely because there is no formal, legal, culturally sanctioned relationship between David and Jonathan, Saul cannot intervene in their friendship in the same way.

Marriage to Michal also raises another problem. Any children produced from the union will not only perpetuate David's line, but will also be related to the line of Saul. A new dynasty may start, but its blood will always be mixed with that of Saul's line and any heir will perhaps become a focus for a resurgence of Saul's family once David is out of the way. As we saw above, the ideological commitment to the purity of David's line shies away from any suggestion that that line is tainted with Saulide blood.

David thus must not simply be the usurping son-in-law, bringing up grandchildren for Saul, but must take the place of Saul's son. While all these paintings suggest the possibility of interchange between these two characters, Leighton seems uniquely to catch the moment of transition where David supplants Jonathan through merging with him. The two become indistinguishable, generating between them the legitimate heir to Saul and the founder of a new dynasty in which Michal cannot participate.[27]

27. Here I would part company with the view of Ackerman, for instance, who sees the authors of Samuel as feminizing Jonathan in order to show his loss of status so that David is seen as legitimately moving into the higher status role of king (see Ackerman,

One painted body evokes two readings, as David and as Jonathan. Jonathan is evoked through the title of the painting and the viewer's knowledge of its biblical context. David is conjured up by the viewer's recognition of the visual echo of a classic work of art. The painting can only be read against these cultural intertexts but these are part of the common stock of knowledge among cultured Victorians, and remain recognizable to modern viewers.

This is not simply a conceit on the part of Leighton, however. It encodes in painterly conventions the fundamental queerness of any dynastic patriarchy. The dynasty must take its origin from the father alone and thus requires, but cannot bear to consider, a moment of begetting from the male through the male without the mediation of the female.

What Leighton has done here, not necessarily with full understanding, confirms a fundamental insight in the work of Judith Butler. She writes, 'The body posited as prior to the sign is always *posited* or *signified* as *prior*. This signification produces as an *effect* of its own procedure the very body that it nevertheless and simultaneously claims to discover as that which *precedes* its own action'.[28]

Although Butler's commitment to the constructedness of gender, even at the level of the body, may be questioned when applied to biological organisms, I would argue that the body as it is found in graphic art is a different matter and that her insights may be more easily applied. The body in painting is constituted from signs which themselves stand for signs in the painterly mimesis of the cues that we use to disambiguate what we read as a natural body. But, as Butler argues is the case for language, what appears to be mimetic may actually be constitutive. Painting offers a visual field containing the signs that can produce the effect of a singular body. Where it differs from the natural body is that it is not accessible to the other senses: it cannot be felt or heard or touched or smelt, as it is only visible. Hence, it brings to our attention the use of visual cues in sexing or ageing the body and in naming the body and therefore the conventions that underlie that identification. Set in two different but coincident frames of reference, the debatable body in this picture unmasks the constructedness and conventionality of any claim to recognize a body. The body of the king is sacred, as David is at pains to point out, but how is that body to be recognized? In one frame of reference,

When Heroes Love, pp. 226-27). While this responds to real clues in the text, which our artists have also detected, my hesitation is that it does not deal with the deeper structural issue of founding a dynastic patriarchy. The fundamental problem in these chapters of Samuel is not the legitimacy of David as against Saul or Jonathan, but the legitimacy of the monarchy as an institution. That feminization is part of the issue is clear and Cima and Rembrandt in particular may come close to illustrating Ackerman's reading, but, I would contend, as part of their strategy to reduce the queerness of the text.

28. J. Butler, *Bodies That Matter: On the Discursive Limits of 'Sex'* (London: Routledge, 1993), p. 30.

the sanctity of the body is a genetic quality, conferred ultimately at birth. In another, it is a quality conferred arbitrarily by divine gift and through anointing. In the superposition of both David and Jonathan, the painterly body signifies both forms of legitimacy, but makes both debatable.

While Cima, Rembrandt and Carolsfeld in their different ways all place a question mark over the visual conventions of identification of characters, Leighton's picture brings these hidden conventions too close to the surface for critical comfort, perhaps. It is hard to be sure how aware Leighton was of the implications of what he was doing. His other paintings do not show a notable subtlety of reading, although this story may have had particular significance for him. However it transpires, Leighton provides a remarkable limit case of the model of one soul in two bodies by depicting one body with two identities, thereby revealing, inadvertently or not, the queering of the heterosexual and patriarchal norm that is inevitable if the Davidic dynasty is to be legitimated.

What disturbs modern viewers of this picture is the particularly striking and unsettling way in which Leighton evokes the queerness of the biblical text. By queerness here I explicitly do not mean that either the picture or the biblical text make any direct or indirect statement on the modern notion of gay identity. What this word points to is how the picture unsettles binary notions of gender and sexuality and of sexual orientation. More fundamentally, it puts in question the relationship between the male body and male identity and the relationship between a private personality and a public role, interiority and exteriority.

All four of these paintings in different ways respond to the unsettling queerness of the text by assimilating the relationship between Jonathan and David to acceptable models. All four in different ways nevertheless participate in that queerness and make it all the more evident by the stratagems they employ to suppress it. Cima avoids the obvious, but problematic, moments of dramatic encounter between his protagonists by leading them out of the story on an unbiblical journey and rendering the relationship a reversal of the master-servant trope. Rembrandt assimilates the relationship to father and son, thereby accentuating the impossible longing for procreation without female participation in the text. Carolsfeld leaves his characters frozen in an embrace from which it is impossible to predict which will carry forward the story. Leighton goes to the ultimate point of ostensibly excluding David from the picture while in another frame of reference placing him at its centre in a transgressive blending of the two male characters.

In all these cases, the queerness of the biblical story of this relationship, which undercuts heterosexual patriarchy and hereditary monarchy at its founding moment, surfaces, whatever the artists' intentions may have been. The particular constraints and imaginative possibilities that arise from translating the story into a painting literally render visible the roots of this queerness in a way that other interpretations may miss. Reading the text back through the paintings inspired by it is therefore an illuminating exercise for biblical exegetes. The enduring fascination with this story, and the cultural significance of the Bible as a whole, depends on the way in which it embodies these tensions and provides the tools for subversion even as it seeks to justify the political and religious order of the day.

BIBLIOGRAPHY

Ackerman, S., *When Heroes Love: The Ambiguity of Eros in the Stories of Gilgamesh and David* (New York: Columbia University Press, 2005).

Barringer, T., and E. Prettejohn (eds.), *Frederic Leighton: Antiquity, Renaissance, Modernity* (New Haven: Yale University Press, 1999).

Beal, T.K., and D.M. Gunn (eds.), *Reading Bibles, Writing Bodies: Identity and the Book* (London: Routledge, 1997).

Butler, J., *Bodies That Matter: On the Discursive Limits of 'Sex'* (London: Routledge, 1993).

Cowley, A., *Poems* (ed. A.R. Waller; Cambridge: Cambridge University Press, 1905).

Exum, J.C., *Plotted, Shot and Painted: Cultural Representations of Biblical Women* (Sheffield: Sheffield Academic Press, 1996).

Fontain, R.-J., and J. Wojcik (eds.), *The David Myth in Western Literature* (Lafayette, WI: Purdue University Press, 1980).

Greenblatt, S., W. Cohen, J.E. Howard, and K.E. Maus (eds.), *The Norton Shakespeare* (New York: W.W. Norton, 1997).

Guest, D., R.E. Goss, M. West, and T. Bohache (eds.), *The Queer Bible Commentary* (London: SCM Press, 2006).

Hoekstra, H., *Rembrandt and the Bible* (Utrecht: Magna Books, 1990).

Jobling, D., *The Sense of Biblical Narrative: Structural Analyses of the Hebrew Bible I* (Sheffield: Sheffield Academic Press, 1978).

Mills, L.J., *One Soul in Bodies Twain: Friendship in Tudor Literature and Stuart Drama* (Bloomington: Principia Press, 1937).

Ormond, R., S. Jones, C. Newall, L. Ormond, and B. Read, *Frederic Leighton 1830–1896* (New York: Harry N. Abrams, 1996).

Østermark-Johansen, L. 'The Apotheosis of the Male Nude: Leighton and Michelangelo', in *Frederic Leighton: Antiquity, Renaissance, Modernity* (ed. T. Barringer and E. Prettejohn; New Haven: Yale University Press, 1999), pp. 11-34.

Pebworth, T.-L., 'Cowley's *Davideis* and the Exaltation of Friendship', in *The David Myth in Western Literature* (ed. R.-J. Fontain and J. Wojcik; Lafayette, WI: Purdue University Press, 1980), pp. 96-104.

Poe, E.A., *Tales* (New York: Wiley & Puttnam, 1845).

Pyper, H.S., *David as Reader: 2 Samuel 12.1-15 and the Poetics of Fatherhood* (Leiden: E.J. Brill, 1996).

Schwartz, G., *Rembrandt: His Life, His Paintings* (London: Guild Publishing, 1985).

Stone, K. '1 and 2 Samuel', in *The Queer Bible Commentary* (ed. D. Guest, R.E. Goss, M. West, and T. Bohuche; London: SCM Press, 2006), pp. 195-221.

Stone, K. (ed.), *Queer Commentary and the Hebrew Bible* (London: SCM Press, 2001).

Swinburne, A.G., *Essays and Studies* (London: Chatto & Windus, 3rd edn, 1888).

The Biblical Elijah and His Visual Afterlives

Martin O'Kane

Elijah: Tradition and Iconography

Surely no other narrative in the Hebrew Bible can have given rise to such a wide range and diversity of traditions as the dramatic story of the prophet Elijah in 1–2 Kings. What is perhaps so unique about the reception history of the Elian narrative[1] is the way faith traditions have explored and appropriated various episodes of the prophet's life along quite different and often unexpected lines, focusing on and then expanding specific details of the original narrative that the contemporary reader of 1–2 Kings might quickly pass over. The Koran, for example, dwells on Elijah's dramatic defeat of the prophets of Baal (Surah xxxvii, 123) while the New Testament focuses on the role of the prophet as precursor (Mt. 16.13-14). Imaginative interpretations of the Elijah story were facilitated particularly by the assertion that the prophet did not die at the end of his earthly life, since this allowed him to appear, again and again, outside of 1–2 Kings, in a variety of contexts and for quite different reasons: in Mal. 4.5, God will send him 'before the coming of the great and dreadful day of the Lord', in Mt. 16.13-14 he is identified both with John the Baptist and Jesus, while in Mt. 17.1-8 he reappears dramatically alongside Moses. In Judaism, it will be Elijah who announces the heralding of the messianic era: where the Talmud is unable to resolve certain questions of law or practice, the question will have to wait for Elijah, when, in the final era, he will resolve all those lingering quandaries. Until then, the cup of wine is reserved for him at each Seder. In the Christian tradition, the Elian narrative is important in that it is regarded as prefiguring several of the miracle stories of Jesus; for example, the raising of the widow's son anticipates three of Jesus' miracles: the raising of the widow's son at Naim, Jairus's daughter and Lazarus. Elijah's ascent by chariot to

1. Outside the English speaking world, Elijah is better known as Elias or a variant of this name. Following the ancient versions (Elias in the Septuagint, New Testament and Vulgate), he is known as Elias in Spanish and German, Elia in Italian and Elie in French. In iconography, both in the East and West, he invariably goes by the title Elias.

heaven is taken to prefigure the ascension of Jesus and the bodily assumption of the Virgin.

The figure of Elijah plays quite different and distinct roles in the respective traditions of the Eastern and Western churches, where the veneration accorded to him is justified on different grounds, based largely on which specific episodes from the prophet's life have been selected by each tradition as examples of piety for their faithful. Thus, Elijah can become a model of prayer and asceticism, symbolize the correct relationship of the believer to God or take on any number of other roles, depending on the time and place in which his patronage is invoked. An often overlooked but extremely important aspect of Elian tradition is the prophet's identification as founder and leader of the order of Carmelites, one of the oldest and most prestigious religious orders in the Catholic Church and a patron over many centuries of painting and music, art-forms used with great success to explore and celebrate the unique qualities of their illustrious founder. Given the range and diversity of traditions associated with Elijah, it is not surprising, then, that he should feature predominantly, and in many different guises, in the visual culture of those faiths that accord him such a privileged position.

One of the earliest depictions of the prophet can be found in a fresco of the synagogue at Dura-Europos (c. 245 CE) in which a flame consumes the offering on Elijah's altar while the priests of Baal display their deep dismay and desperation. The ascension of Elijah, with his cloak falling on Elisha (symbol of Christ's commissioning of his apostles) is the most frequently represented scene in early Christian art, the compositions often owing a great deal to the ancient classical world and specifically to the chariot of the sun god Helios or Apollo, as in the prophet's depiction in the cemetery of Domitilla, Rome (first century CE) and the catacombs of the Via Latina in Rome (fourth century CE). On the door of the church of San Sabina, Rome (fifth century CE), Elijah is raised up on a chariot of fire, his gaze turned towards the angel who bears him aloft, while a personified River Jordan lies on a river-bank. The episode of the massacre of the priests of Baal was a particularly popular subject in early Byzantine and Russian art. Gradually, however, the episodes from the Elian narrative that received most attention were those that were regarded as anticipating important aspects relating to the Eucharist. The depiction of these episodes was very popular during the periods of the Middle Ages and the Renaissance. In particular, artists frequently depicted the scene at the Wadi Cherith, where the raven brings Elijah bread from God (1 Kgs 17.5-6) and the later episode in which the angel brings him nourishing food and water in the desert (1 Kgs 19.6-9); frequently, they combined motifs taken from both texts. The choice of these episodes as popular subjects for visual expression lay in the Eucharistic overtones they could convey: the raven bringing the heavenly bread (in the distinctive round shape of the Eucharistic host) is depicted on a famous fresco at the Church of the Holy Trinity, Lublin, Poland (1428), and occurs on the decoration of the monastery of Lavra, Mount Athos (1502). The angel bearing food and water is traditionally taken to represent the bread and wine of the Eucharist and constitutes the subject matter of some of the most illustrious masterpieces of Renaissance and Flemish art: the fresco in the Duomo at Orvieto (fourteenth century), the panel on Bouts's *The Holy Sacrament Altarpiece* in the St. Pieterskerk in Leuven (1464–1468) and Tintoretto's painting in the Scuola di San Rocco, Venice (1577–1578).[2]

Of these three paintings, it is probably the representation by Dieric Bouts of Elijah in the wilderness, nourished with food and water by an angel, on the side panel of *The Holy Sacrament Altarpiece*, that best typifies how the episode was taken to prefigure the Eucharist in the Western church. Two professors of theology, Jan Varenecker and Aegidius Ballawel, were asked to provide the painter with precise instructions as to the subjects he should represent to accompany the central large panel depicting Christ's institution of the Eucharist at the last supper. They selected four episodes from the Old Testament that, according to tradition, prefigured the Eucharist. On the four surrounding side panels, they instructed Bouts to paint the biblical episodes of the meeting of Abraham and Melchizedek, the gathering of the manna in the desert, the feast of Passover and the feeding of Elijah by the angel in the desert. Of these, only the latter, where the angel bends over the prophet with his enormous wings, is painted on the same large scale and with the same grandeur as the last supper in the central panel; it was clearly intended by the theologians that it should stand out to the viewer as the principal Old Testament precedent for the miracle being enacted by Christ.

One of the more remarkable and original depictions of the Elijah narrative is to be found on the marble pavement of the Duomo in Siena. Described by the sixteenth-century biographer Giorgio Vasari as 'the most beautiful and magnificent pavement ever made',[3] its construction and development took place over many centuries; its subject matter is particularly famous for the sheer number of scenes inspired by the Old and New Testaments, juxtaposed in such a way as to suggest many original and insightful readings of the biblical stories depicted.[4] The most impressive images are

2. For a brief history of Elian iconography, see Peter and Linda Murray (eds.), *The Oxford Companion to Christian Art and Architecture* (Oxford: Oxford University Press, 1996), pp. 160-61, and G. Duchet-Suchaux and M. Pastoureau, *The Bible and the Saints* (Flammarion Iconographic Guides; Paris: Flammarion, 1994), pp. 133-35.

3. Cited by Bruno Santi in *The Marble Pavement of the Cathedral of Siena* (Florence: Scala, 1993), p. 5.

4. In the extensive literature dealing with the pavement, only one work, Friedrich Ohly, *Schriften zur mittelalterlichen Bedeutungsforschung* (Darmstadt: Wissenschaftliche

generally agreed to be those by Domenico Beccafumi that relate episodes in the life of Elijah, stories from the life of Moses and the sacrifice of Isaac in close proximity.[5] Beccafumi decorated the hexagon shape at the very centre of the cathedral directly under the dome with incidents in the life of Elijah taken from 1 Kgs 18 (1486–1551) and the cycle was completed by Alessandro Franchi with scenes from 1 Kgs 21.17-27 and 22.35-38 as well as from 2 Kgs 2.11 (1838–1914). Beccafumi's contribution to the hexagon consists of one of the most vivid portrayals ever made of the confrontation between Elijah and the prophets of Baal: Elijah's monumental figure points admonishingly at the useless sacrifice of the priests of Baal and is balanced by the erring flocks of priests who do not hesitate to wound themselves in order to move their god to compassion. At the centre of the hexagon, Beccafumi makes the pact between Ahab and Elijah, represented as two towering figures, the central and focal point of the narrative, but he also creates imaginative links between the stories of Elijah and Moses by depicting episodes from the life of the lawgiver—whom he obviously felt offered a parallel to the Elijah narrative—on the marble floor between the Elijah hexagon and the high altar. In a long rectangular frieze along the upper side of the hexagon, Beccafumi illustrated Moses bringing forth water from the rock at Horeb (Exod. 17.1-7). The entire length of the frieze is crowded with figures representing the tribes of Israel.

At the centre, Moses is shown as a monumental figure of authority smiting the rock and causing the water to gush forth. The figures are illustrated in an extraordinary variety of positions and attitudes and create a dynamic motif that animates the panel and counterbalances the monumental pose of Moses at the centre. What is striking to the viewer is the clear and intentional parallel that the artist draws between the power and authority of Elijah in drawing down fire from heaven (1 Kgs 18.38) and the figure of Moses as he brings forth water from the rock (Exod. 17.1-7). Beccafumi draws out other comparisons between prophet and lawgiver: for example, Moses is portrayed on a rock that symbolizes Mount Sinai as he receives the two tablets of the law, while the people of Israel try to convince Aaron to create a golden calf for them to worship. By means of this juxtaposition of images, it is clear that the artist intends to make a connection for the viewer between the incident of the worship of the Baals in 1 Kings 18 and the

Buchgesellschaft, 1977), contains a hermeneutical study of the design pattern system. It demonstrates how a vast, complex plan was creatively conceived and carried out through the centuries by the various artists involved in work on the floor.

5. For another interesting visual image that juxtaposes Jacob (Jacob's ladder in Gen. 28), Moses (his exhaustive prayer in Exod. 17) and Elijah (his prayer at the sacrifice in 1 Kgs 18), see the engraving by George Sanders (1845) in the collection of the Wellcome Trust and accessible through the Trust's website (http://medphoto.wellcome.ac.uk).

worship of the golden calf in Exodus 32. Commentators also point out how the tortured bodies of Elijah and Moses and the dramatic tension of their stories, so clearly delineated in the artist's depiction, anticipate the tortured figure of Isaac whose story is portrayed near the main steps to the high altar.[6]

Elijah and Carmelite Iconography

One of the frequently unacknowledged influences in the rich reception history and iconography of Elijah is the role played by the Carmelite Order. It is important, therefore, to include, if only briefly, some mention of the significance of the Carmelite contribution to the development of iconography associated with Elijah in western Europe. The Carmelite Order emerged and grew in Europe along with the Franciscans and Dominicans shortly after 1200 and its members were known as the Whitefriars. Its beginnings are lost in the mists of history but the earliest Carmelite writings (the *Rubrica Prima*) record that the order, then consisting merely of a band of mendicant monks, first came west when the Crusaders departed from the Holy Land in the 1230s. Jacques de Vitry, medieval bishop of Acres, describes their origins in terms of 'a group of hermits living in simplicity and contemplation on Mount Carmel'.[7] When they came to Europe and found the Franciscans and Dominicans already well established, they discovered that the lack of a charismatic founder such as a Francis or a Dominic was a serious handicap. While both the Franciscans and Dominicans could trace their roots to an authoritative and influential leader, the early band of Carmelite monks had never given much consideration to the details of their founding or the individual(s) who had founded them. They soon discovered that they too badly needed a founder, and Elijah, they concluded, was just the person to fill that role—someone who could command even more respect than Francis or Dominic ever could. As the Carmelite writer Patrick McMahon puts it, by choosing Elijah they were boastfully attributing to themselves a pedigree of unparalleled elegance among the religious families of the day.[8] It was unimportant to them who actually founded the order, but the choice of Elijah suited their purpose and mission and helped them focus

6. For detailed discussion of the images in their historical context, see Santi, *The Marble Pavement*, pp. 43-60.

7. Jacobus de Vitriaco, *Libri duo: quorum prior orientalis, siue Hierosolomitanae: alter occidentalis* (Douai, 1597), cited in Valerie Edden, 'The Mantle of Elijah: Carmelite Spirituality in England in the Fourteenth Century', in *The Medieval Mystical Tradition: Exeter Symposium IV* (ed. Marion Glasscoe; Cambridge: D.S. Brewer, 1999), pp. 67-84.

8. Patrick McMahon, 'Pater et Dux: Elijah in Medieval Mythology', in *Master of the Sacred Page: Essays and Articles in Honor of Roland E. Murphy on the Occasion of his Eightieth Birthday* (ed. K.J. Egan; Washington: Carmelite Institute, 1997), pp. 283-99 (285).

on possibilities for the future rather than merely concentrating on the past. More than any other patron, it was the Carmelites who were the most active in visualizing the prophet Elijah both for their own friars and for the laity at large: the role and reputation of their leader had to be promulgated as forcefully in the arts as in their doctrinal writings.[9]

At the end of the twelfth century, about fifty years before the Carmelites made their appearance in Europe, a monastic scriptorium had produced the *Biblia Pauperum* that subsequently became influential in Carmelite iconography. This book had illustrations from thirty-four episodes in the life of Christ from the Annunciation to the Last Judgment. Each of the thirty-four episodes was accompanied by two episodes from the Old Testament which paralleled the life and mission of Jesus. Elijah or his disciple Elisha or both are the focus of eight of these parallels. The *Biblia Pauperum* was instrumental in inspiring a wide variety of images of biblical figures, including Elijah, in the visual arts in the Middle Ages and beyond, most notably in stained glass and church sculpture. It was the inspiration for many early images associated with Elijah and constituted the beginning of an iconographic tradition that was to be rapidly developed with great enthusiasm within the Carmelite Order. Elijah thus became a central figure, due to his visual representation, in medieval consciousness and his frequent appearance in monastic garb reinforced the legend that he was the institutor of monastic life.[10]

An abundance and diversity of visual images associated with Elijah flourished throughout Europe under Carmelite patronage. In addition to the 'portrait' style depiction of the prophets Elijah and Elisha, there are many Carmelite monasteries where the cloisters are decorated with scenes from the prophets' lives. Best known among these are the frescoes in the Basilica of San Martino ai Monti in Rome (executed by Gaspare Dughet between 1640 and 1655), which depict the life of Elijah and present him as wearing the Carmelite habit, thus reminding the viewer that he was the first Carmelite, and Dughet's rare image of the emperor visiting a Carmelite priory in the Holy Land. Also well known is the depiction of some twenty scenes from the prophet's life in the Carmelite monastery in Barcelona. In the Church of Santa Maria del Carmine alle Tre Cannelle in Rome, the right side-altar has an altar painting of the prophet Elijah painted by Corrado Giaquinto (1703–1766). The reverse side shows *The Apparition of the Virgin to the Prophet Elijah on Mount Carmel* and bears witness to the importance of popular piety that linked the figure of Elijah with the iconography of the

9. The Carmelites also developed a rich musical tradition associated with Elijah. See James Boyce, 'The Feasts of Saints Elijah and Elisha in the Carmelite Rite: A Liturgico-Musical Study', in Egan (ed.), *Master of the Sacred Page*, pp. 155-88.

10. See McMahon, 'Pater et Dux', p. 293.

Virgin Mary, a practice encouraged by the Carmelites. Three of the most important artists of the fourteenth and fifteenth centuries, all of whom play a key role in the history of Western art, were very closely associated with the Carmelites: Lorenzetti, Sassetta and Masaccio, the latter having, by far, the closest association of all.

Creighton Gilbert, a specialist in Carmelite iconography, has shown how the desire for religious authenticity, characteristic of late medieval and Renaissance monasticism, which entailed the reinterpretation of the origins of religious orders and appeals to ancient traditions, can be traced very clearly in paintings and frescoes commissioned by the Carmelites.[11] Focussing on works of art created for Tuscan Carmelite communities over a hundred year period (1330–1430), Gilbert has demonstrated how the Carmelites, lacking any clearly defined historical founder, blended together their myths with contemporary events in their iconography, quite uniquely, for one purpose only: to persuade the viewer that their authentic founder really was Elijah, the biblical prophet. The special feature that remains the most familiar item of Carmelite iconography and in the work of the artists they sponsored is indeed Elijah. The chief subjects in the paintings of other religious orders were invariably the images and biographies of their founders (Ignatius, Dominic or Francis), since these were the most effective ways for these orders to approach their public visually; it was therefore equally if not more important for the Carmelites to identify themselves iconographically with Elijah.

One of the earliest Carmelite paintings in which Elijah features prominently is the great altarpiece of 1329, made up of many panels and painted for the Carmelite church in Siena by Pietro Lorenzetti.[12] Elijah is dressed in a Carmelite robe and holds a long scroll; its text is taken from 1 Kgs 18.19 in which the prophet calls on all Israel to gather at Mount Carmel. On this altarpiece, too, is depicted the story of Elijah's birth, an event not related in the biblical narrative where Elijah, of course, appears very suddenly and unexpectedly in 1 Kgs 17.1, but which becomes prominent in an apocryphal story of his birth widely circulated in Greek patristic writings of the fourth century. At the time of Elijah's birth, the legend goes, Sobach, the father of Elijah, saw men (or angels) wearing white, greeting the infant Elijah and offering him fire to eat. This story appealed to the Carmelites: there is a Carmelite text from 1337 citing the story but omitting the fire and specifying that Sobach's experience was in a dream by night. For the Carmelite writer, these men allude to Elijah's future disciples, the Whitefriars. In

11. Creighton Gilbert, 'Some Special Images for Carmelites, circa 1330–1430', in *Christianity and the Renaissance* (ed. Timothy Verdon and John Henderson; New York: Syracuse University Press, 1990), pp. 161-207.

12. Gilbert, 'Some Special Images for Carmelites', pp. 166-67.

Lorenzetti's panel, the men are not shown but are relegated to the words of a scroll above Sobach's head.

Another panel in the same altarpiece shows the disciples of Elijah living on Mount Carmel. It is intended as a visual expression of an important text found in the Constitutions of the Carmel Order, adopted in 1281:

> Certain brothers, new in the Order, do not know how to reply ...to those who ask from whom, or how, our order took its origin. We wish to indicate to them how to reply, in these terms. We therefore affirm, to witness the truth, that beginning with the prophets Elijah and Elisha, pious dwellers on Mount Carmel, the holy fathers of both the Old and New Testament, deeply in love with their solitude of the mountain, unquestionably lived there, in a manner deserving praise, near the spring of Elijah, in holy penitence, continued uninterruptedly in holy succession.[13]

In the image on the panel, the spring of Elijah is very prominent, as well as the brothers at their tasks living 'in a manner deserving praise'. Rarely is it possible, argues Creighton, in studying religious iconography, to point to such a direct illustration of a text that itself articulated the patron's most emphatic beliefs and concerns. The panel speaks to the viewer in just the way the new friar was instructed to relate to outsiders; it was later to become a model for the Counter-Reformation engraving by van Diepenbecke, which develops the same theme and depicts, in addition, the blood of Christ and the milk of Mary flowing down from the sky to fill the fountain, dispersing its liquid to the friars below. In Lorenzetti's panel, the monks wear striped Carmelite robes, the early habit adopted by the Carmelites and worn for a brief period in 1281.

The Carmelites were not the only order interested in iconography associated with the Elian narrative. When the thirteenth-century Cistercian abbot Joachim of Fiore forcefully denounced the monastic communities for having degenerated into moribund institutions, he announced that the Holy Spirit was about to renew the face of the earth using two new communities: a community of preachers in the spirit of Elijah and a community of hermits in the spirit of Moses. Within ten years of his death, Francis of Assisi began his mission and many identified Francis with Elijah. At his death, Francis was reported being seen ascending as a bright star into the heavens. Giotto interpreted this legend by painting Francis rising to heaven in a fiery chariot. This painting is part of the iconography commissioned for the basilica erected over the saint's tomb in Assisi, giving a very definite sanction to the identification of Francis with Elijah.[14]

The appropriation of Elijah as the Carmelite founder, then, ensured a very rich and unique iconographical tradition in the Western church over

13. Cited by Gilbert, 'Some Special Images for Carmelites', p. 169.

14. See McMahon, 'Pater et Dux', p. 293.

and above the artistic traditions that associated him with the Eucharist, with the miracles of Christ or with his ascension. But there is yet another strand of tradition, separate and distinct from those discussed so far, in which Elijah is given a visual afterlife that, uniquely, lays emphasis on one important episode in the biblical narrative, seemingly overlooked in Western iconography. The biblical text in question is 1 Kgs 19.8-13, Elijah's experience of God on Mount Horeb.

The Iconography of Elijah at Mount Horeb (1 Kgs 19.8-13)

Considering the range and diversity of visual expressions based on the life of Elijah, it is remarkable that so very few attempt to depict what is generally considered by commentators to be the most crucial and central element in the entire narrative, Elijah's intimate and personal experience of the divine presence on Mount Horeb in 1 Kings 19, confirming his prophetic mission.[15] Such representation seems to be singularly lacking in the western European artistic tradition—at least any meaningful expression of it.[16] The narrative is both mysterious and ambiguous: Elijah, having journeyed forty days and nights, reaches Horeb, spends the night in a cave and experiences what commentators describe as a theophany (the *showing*, the *revealing*, the *making visible* of God). His reaction to this experience is to cover his face with his mantle.

The episode is important because it is one of several enigmatic texts that convey a deep suspicion towards visual experience that persists throughout the Hebrew Bible. Despite the biblical authors' vivid and colourful descriptions of characters, places and events and the lengths to which they go in helping the reader visualize them, we are, at the same time, frequently reminded that what we can experience with our sight is quite restricted and limited. We are urged by the narrator to visualize events and explore different ways of seeing, yet the threat of blindness—the inability to see in the Bible's highly visual world, or seeing only dimly and obscurely—is forever present and forcefully articulated.[17] There are many areas of darkness,

15. The absence of a sustained iconographical tradition linking the figure of Elijah with John the Baptist is also surprising.

16. Interesting examples are few. They include Marc Chagall's *Elijah's Vision* (New York: Franklin Bowles Gallery, 1956) and Sieger Köder's *Elijah am Horeb* (contemporary artist, Germany).

17. Ambiguities and contradictions in relation to sight abound. No one can see God and live but the rule is often broken: he appears to, or lets himself be seen by, Abraham (Gen. 17.1; 18.1), Isaac (26.2, 24; 35.1), Jacob (35.9; 48.3) and Moses (Exod. 3.2,16; 4.1, 5; 6.3), while in Gen. 16.13-14, the climax of the story of Hagar's expulsion centres on how Hagar has survived the experience of seeing God whom she calls El-Roi (God who sees me) and how she names the well Beer-lahai-roi (well of the Living One who sees me).

obscurity and hiddenness in the Bible that the eye cannot penetrate. The God who is all-seeing prefers to remain out of sight and we are warned sternly against creating any visual likeness of him. He gives sight and yet makes people blind; he displays the skills of a craftsman and artist,[18] yet he is suspicious and distrustful of humans who mirror the same creativity.[19] What are we to make of this obsession with visibility and hiddenness that permeates biblical literature? Why do its authors create stories evidently intended to stimulate and exercise the reader's visual imagination and yet appear to be so suspicious of the consequences? The narrative of Elijah's experience on Horeb provides an excellent example of this ambiguity that runs throughout the Hebrew Bible: the author presents the early and later incidents in the life of the prophet as a series of colourful vignettes (for example, the contest with the prophets of Baal or the prophet's ascension in the fiery chariot) that are easy to visualize in the mind's eye but, on the other hand, presents the central episode, the prophet's experience on Mount Horeb, as an experience that is veiled and hidden both from the point of view of Elijah and the reader. Western art and iconography in general has followed the lead of the biblical authors, preferring to concentrate on the colourful vignettes related in 1 Kings 17–18 and 2 Kings 2 but largely ignoring Elijah's experience on Horeb in 1 Kgs 19.8-13.

I find the lack of visual representations of this passage in Western art surprising for three reasons. First, the obvious and intentional parallel between Elijah's experience here and Moses's on Sinai in Exodus 33 suggests that the author is exploring how a hidden God can somehow make his presence *visible*. In Exod. 33.17-23, Moses requests specifically *to see* God's glory, but when he passes by, Moses must hide in a cleft in the rock and can see only God's back and not his face. From Elijah's not dissimilar position in front of the cave, what exactly does the covering of his face with the mantle stop him from seeing? What visual aspect is the author denying us? Walter Houston suggests that we can never really explain theophanies—their visual descriptions are such that we can only picture them.[20] Calvin, too, argues

18. Many Christian theologians have described God as an artist. Bonaventure, commenting on the New Testament passage 'consider the lilies of the field', describes God as the supreme artist and nature as his opus. Von Balthasar interprets the verb יצר as 'modelling', 'creating' in Gen. 2.7-8, 19 and, from this, sees God as a craftsman. For a discussion of the way philosophers have seen God's creativity as the source of the artist's imagination, see Patrick Sherry, *Spirit and Beauty* (London: SCM Press, 2nd edn, 2002), pp. 130-31.

19. In Acts, too (17.29), we are warned against thinking 'that the deity is like gold, silver or stone, an image formed by the art and imagination of mortals'.

20. See Walter Houston, 'Exodus', in *The Oxford Bible Commentary* (ed. John Barton and John Muddiman; Oxford: Oxford University Press, 2001), pp. 67-91 (71). His comments relate specifically to Judg. 5.4-5; Pss. 18.7-15; 50.1-6 and Hab. 3.

that the whole point of this and other theophanies is precisely to conceal God and protect his essential invisibility.[21] The tension between concealment and disclosure in the episode on Mount Horeb is reflected throughout the narrative: Elijah appears very abruptly at the beginning (1 Kgs 17.1) and, at the end, disappears just as suddenly in a whirlwind (2 Kgs 2.11-12). He hides from Ahab (1 Kgs 17.3) only later to present himself (literally, 'make himself visible') to the king (1 Kgs 18.1-2); Obadiah hides the prophets out of sight in a cave (1 Kgs 18.4), an angel appears to Elijah in the desert (1 Kgs 19.5-7), but God remains stubbornly concealed in the theophany (1 Kgs 19.11-12). So, first, there is a clear and persistent preoccupation throughout the narrative with what we can see and what we cannot see.

Second, the notion of sacred space is carefully and subtly conveyed by the author: apart from the obvious sacredness of the location of Mount Horeb itself, the cave in which Elijah spends the night becomes highly significant. The first time it is mentioned in the Hebrew narrative in 1 Kgs 19.9, the definite article is used (המערה), suggesting that it is a place that should already be familiar to the reader. Indeed, Elijah's experience of the entire theophany must have been from within the cave, for later we are told in 1 Kgs 19.13:

> He wrapped his face in his mantle and *went out* and stood at the entrance to the cave.

Rashi, followed by other Jewish commentators,[22] and Gregory of Nyssa[23] see the cave as the very same cleft in the rock of Exod. 33.21-22 in which Moses hid as Yahweh passed by. The Jewish exegete Malbim claims that it was during Elijah's period in the cave that his mantle was invested with such miraculous powers.[24] The Orthodox ascetical tradition identifies the cave as the same place where Moses received the commandments and notes that 'the cave was not a place of retreat or repose but, as with Moses, the venue for a timeless moment of the most intimate encounter between Elijah and the Eternal'.[25] If the cave is of such importance, then, in the general reception history of the text, why is it not given more prominence in artistic tradition?

Third, what is this still small voice (קול דממה דקה) that is presented as the climax of the theophany? The phrase is so obscure that all the versions,

21. See David Brown, *Tradition and Imagination* (Oxford: Oxford University Press, 1999), p. 343.

22. A.J. Rosenberg, *The Book of Kings, 1. A New English Translation of the Text, Rashi and a Commentary Digest* (New York: Judaica Press, 4th edn, 1991), p. 198.

23. Isaias Simonopetritis, 'A Synoptic View of the Orthodox Ascetical Tradition of Mount Sinai', *The Orthodox Herald* (November–December 1998), pp. 122-23.

24. Rosenberg, *The Book of Kings 1*, p. 203.

25. Simonopetritis, 'A Synoptic View', p. 123.

rather than simply translate it, feel the need to interpret it.[26] Two examples show how it was associated with texts that report a *visual* experience that cannot be articulated. The Syriac version translates the phrase as 'a voice of gentle speaking'[27] in the light of Deut. 4.12:

> The Lord spoke to you from the midst of the fire and you heard a sound of words *but you did not see any form*, there was only a voice.

Rashi, followed by other Jewish commentators,[28] draws on Eliphaz's night vision in Job 4.16 to interpret the phrase:

> A spirit glided past my face: the hair of my flesh bristled; it stood still but I could not discern its appearance. *A form was before my eyes*. Then there was the silence.

Translators and commentators see the phrase as an attempt to convey the notion of a mysterious visual experience, ineffable, beyond words. As a climax to the theophany, the phrase puts the divine beyond all natural phenomena and also all human ability to comprehend it.

These three important aspects of the narrative (the preoccupation with concealment and revelation, the presentation of the cave as a sacred space, and Elijah's mysterious experience of the veiled presence of God) do not seem to me to be conveyed in any meaningful way in the Western visual tradition. But where they do feature very significantly, however, is in the iconography of Elijah in the Orthodox traditions of the Eastern Church.

The reason for such interest is clear: in Orthodox liturgy and iconography, one of the most important subjects is the Gospel narrative of the Transfiguration (Mt. 17.1-8), where Elijah and Moses look directly on the glory of Christ.[29] (This was not the case in the Western Church, where the institution of the Transfiguration as a feastday came only much later.) Elijah and Moses can gaze directly into the dazzling divine light and are even partly included in the divine mandorla; the three apostles, on the other hand, cannot bear to look up. There is no other place in the entire Bible where the curtain between the material and spiritual world is lifted so completely visually; Andrew Louth comments that the early fathers wrote as if they were basing their sermons on the icon of the Transfiguration rather than on the biblical text.[30] They explained that the two prophets whose

26. For a full discussion of the range of interpretations, see Craig E. Morrison, 'Handing on the Mantle: The Transmission of the Elijah Cycle in the Biblical Versions', in Egan (ed.), *Master of the Sacred Page*, pp. 109-29.

27. See Morrison, 'Handing on the Mantle', p. 113.

28. Rosenberg, *The Book of Kings 1*, p. 200.

29. For a full discussion of this, see Andreas Andreopoulos, *Metamorphosis: The Transfiguration in Byzantine Theology and Iconography* (New York: St. Vladimir's Seminary Press, 2005), pp. 37-60.

30. Andrew Louth, 'Foreword', in Andreopoulos, *Metamorphosis*, pp. 13-17 (13).

vision of God in the Old Testament was very partial and imperfect are now granted a perfected vision of God in the Transfiguration. That Elijah is able to gaze directly on the full glory of Christ in the New Testament is the reason for the sustained interest in and attention given to his experience in the cave on Mount Horeb in 1 Kings 19. Indeed, Elijah is quite unique in Orthodox tradition in that he is the only Old Testament figure to receive any detailed individual treatment on icons. Not even Moses is granted that distinction.

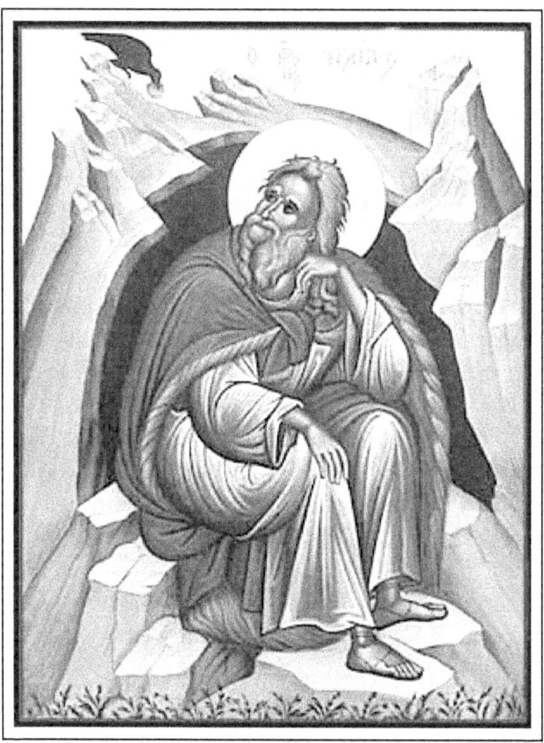

Figure 1. *Icon of the Prophet Elias*.
© Order of Carmelites

In Orthodox tradition, the figure of Elijah must be portrayed according to quite a strict iconographical canon, summed up by Dionysius of Fourna:

> Elijah should be presented as an old man with a white beard. There should be a cave with the prophet sitting inside it; he rests his chin on his hand and leans his elbow on his knee. Above the cave a raven watches him carrying bread in its beak.[31]

31. Dionysius of Fourna, *The Painter's Manual* (trans. Paul Hetherington; London: Sagittarius Press, 1974), p. 24.

Clearly, this iconography combines the episode of Elijah and the raven in 17.6-7 with Elijah in the cave on Horeb in 19.5-7, but the most distinctive and significant aspect of the iconography is not the obvious despondent pose of the prophet but rather the cave that is almost always associated with him. It is normally positioned at the very centre of the icon and encapsulates the prophet whose mantle touches its darkness on all sides.

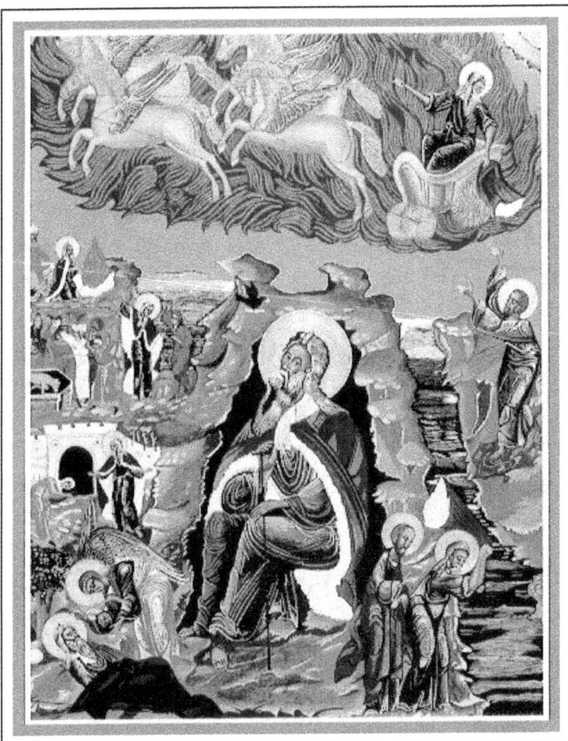

Figure 2. *Icon of the Prophet Elias.*
© Order of Carmelites

Where the figure of Elijah is surrounded by small miniatures depicting other episodes in the prophet's life, as is frequently the case, the experience of Elijah in the cave is still seen as central and pivotal to the way the entire narrative should be interpreted. This is evident from the icon illustrated in Fig. 2 where the various activities of Elijah that surround the prophet in his meditative pose in front of the cave are presented to the viewer in the light of his 'cave experience'.

Traditionally, before icon painters began their work, they were required to draw the great eye of God on the blank canvas and write the word 'God' underneath it to remind them that the icon, like a transparent membrane, is not only something for the viewer to look at but also something that looks at us through a window from another world.[32] The position of the cave in many icons is exactly where the eye of God would have been drawn. The intention is to create two focal points in the image: we can imagine that we are looking at Elijah from outside the cave or, from the perspective of God, we can choose to be in the cave looking outwards. A dual perspective is thus provided: how we see Elijah and how Elijah is seen by God. The cave thus becomes a site of recognition; it allows us to see and reflect on the figure of Elijah in the context of the biblical narrative of 1 Kings but it also suggests another Elijah, a timeless and unchanging figure as seen through the eyes of God, one who acts as a model to all generations.

The cave is not an unusual feature in icons. In several New Testament examples, such as the Nativity, the Baptism of Christ and the Resurrection, the symbolism of the cave and its position in the icon are very important. In the Nativity, the cave acts as a womb from which the Christ Child emerges—to parallel the womb of Mary. Gregory of Nyssa makes much of the importance of the cave in the Nativity story, drawing out an elaborate and complex comparison between it and Plato's parable of the cave, where a group of prisoners, representing humanity, mistake the shadows on the wall for reality.[33] John Chrysostom draws out the significance of the cave of Hades,[34] so important in icons of the Resurrection. In light of this tradition, we must treat the cave of Elijah as having a very special meaning; most significant of all is the way the aspect of the darkness of the cave is highlighted.

The cave's darkness contrasts with the blaze of colour of Elijah's cloak, his chariot of fire and the other episodes depicted in the surrounding panels on a Greek icon. The darkness touches the figure of Elijah on all sides; in many icons, he is almost engulfed by it. Greek Orthodox writers stress that the symbolism of the darkness reflects not so much the personal despair of Elijah but rather the notion of transcendence expressed through Gregory of Nyssa's theology of darkness.[35] The concept of divine darkness emerges from Gregory's *Life of Moses*, in which he concludes that Moses's ultimate and most intimate experience of God was not in the light of the burning bush but in his experience at the summit of Sinai in the cloud of darkness. On Exod. 20.18-21 (the text where, at Sinai, the people stand at a distance while Moses draws near to the thick darkness where God is present) Gregory comments:

32. Andreopoulos, *Metamorphosis*, p. 27.

33. See Anthony Meredith, 'Plato's Cave in Origen, Gregory of Nyssa and Plotinus', *Studia Patristica* 27 (1993), pp. 49-61.

34. A. Papageorgiou, 'The Paschal Catechetical Homily of St. John Chrysostom: A Rhetorical and Contextual Study', *Greek Orthodox Theological Review* 43 (1998), pp. 93-104 (100).

35. See Simonpetritis, 'A Synoptic View', p. 123.

> Since Moses was alone, he approached the very darkness itself and entered the invisible things where he was no longer seen by those watching. After he entered the sanctuary of the mystical divine doctrine, there, while not being seen, he was in company with the Universal. He teaches through this that the one who is going to associate intimately with God must go beyond all that is visible and—lifting up his own mind as to a mountain top to the invisible and incomprehensible—believe that the divine is here where the understanding does not reach.[36]

Similarly John Chrysostom notes that at the Transfiguration, the eyes of the apostles were *darkened* by excessive radiance.[37]

The image of the darkness is the capstone of Gregory's spiritual theology. At the peak of the mountain where all light has gone, Moses finds himself in the darkness of the cloud and Elijah finds himself in the darkness of the cave. According to Gregory, this represents the culmination of their experience of the divine. Both Moses and Elijah penetrate through all that is visible to reach the invisible and become intensely aware of their inability to grasp the transcendent and ineffable. Like Moses's and Elijah's ascent to Sinai, from the point of view of the icon-maker, the ascent to the summit of the spiritual life for the viewer, too, ends not in light but in darkness. The darkness depicted on the icon corresponds directly to Gregory's theology but also to the tendencies evident in several translations, as I have indicated above, that associate the 'still small voice', the climax of the theophany, with other biblical texts that express the essence of the divine presence as something that cannot be seen or articulated. There is a very real sense in which the icon-maker shares with the various translators the struggle to understand and express what exactly is in the mind of the Hebrew author of this biblical episode that seems so concerned with suggesting the presence of God but yet so keen to conceal his exact image.

A final point concerns the mandorla, the round or oval-shaped sacred space that frequently surrounds the person of Christ and that is associated particularly with the Transfiguration icon. It is interpreted in various ways: as a symbol of heaven, a symbol or sacred representation of the world or a symbol of the union of opposites such as the union of heaven and earth.[38] The bulk of scholarship on its origins concentrates on the mandorla as a solution to the problem of the visual representation of the Hebrew concept of *kabhod* (כבוד), a word that suggests the glory of God and the tabernacle of God. 'The mandorla is, in effect, the visual expression of *kabod* and represents', in the words of Andreas Andreopoulos, 'a metaphysical space, the

36. Gregory of Nyssa, *The Life of Moses* § 46, in *Gregory of Nyssa: The Life of Moses* (ed. A.J. Malherbe and E. Ferguson; Classics of Western Spirituality; New York: Paulist Press, 1978), p. 43.

37. Papageorgiou, 'The Pascal Catechetical Homily', p. 95.

38. Andreopoulos, *Metamorphosis*, p. 83.

portal to the divine dimension appropriate to Christian theophany'.[39] In the Targums and Talmud, *kabhod* (כבוד) is often translated as *shekinah* (שכנה) and refers to the majesty of the presence of God (frequently where more anthropomorphic expressions had to be avoided):

> The *Shekinah* is a name for God used only in statements having to do with God's nearness. It is therefore to be found in statements and ideas that reflect normal mystical experience and in statements and ideas about prayer.[40]

In *Targum Jonathan*'s interpretation and expansion of 1 Kgs 19.11-12, the term *shekinah* occurs several times: God's *shekinah* is not present in the first three manifestations of the theophany (the wind, the earthquake and the fire) but, with the fourth manifestation ('the still small voice' that *Targum Jonathan* translates as 'the voice of those praising in silence'), the *shekinah* has arrived and Elijah experiences the immanence and nearness of God.[41]

Since the mandorla is associated with the *kabhod* and *shekinah* of God, the sacred space of God's presence, is it possible that the oval-shaped entrance to the cave, so standard and consistent in Orthodox iconography of Elijah, could be conceived of in any sense as a mandorla, a visual expression of the concept of the *shekinah*, signifying a sacred portal or entrance into the world of the divine? Elsewhere, Elijah, with Moses, appears frequently within or touching the mandorla in icons of the Transfiguration, as in Fig. 3, suggesting that only they are worthy to enter the sacred divine space inhabited by Christ.

Greek Orthodox scholars have told me[42] that this would not have been the case intentionally (since the mandorla is normally reserved for Christ) but add that the informed viewer may subsequently have seen it as such since the cave depicted in the icon is obviously regarded as so sacred: it is when Elijah is in the cave that he experiences the 'still small voice' and it is at the cave's entrance, with his face wrapped in his mantle, that Elijah hears the voice of God. The cave is, therefore, at the very centre of Elijah's experience of the divine, and the outline of the cave around the figure of the prophet denotes the sacredness of that divine space and performs essentially the same role as the mandorla in other icons. From the viewer's point of view, the outline of the cave draws the eye into its centre where the *shekinah* resides but at the same time the intense darkness of the cave serves to protect and conceal the divine presence.

39. Andreopoulos, *Metamorphosis*, pp. 83-84.
40. Max Kadushin, *The Rabbinic Mind* (New York: Blaisdell, 1965), p. 228.
41. See Morrison, 'Handing on the Mantle', pp. 115-16.
42. In particular, I am grateful to Dr Andreas Andreopoulos for sharing his insights and opinions on a range of *Elias* icons with me.

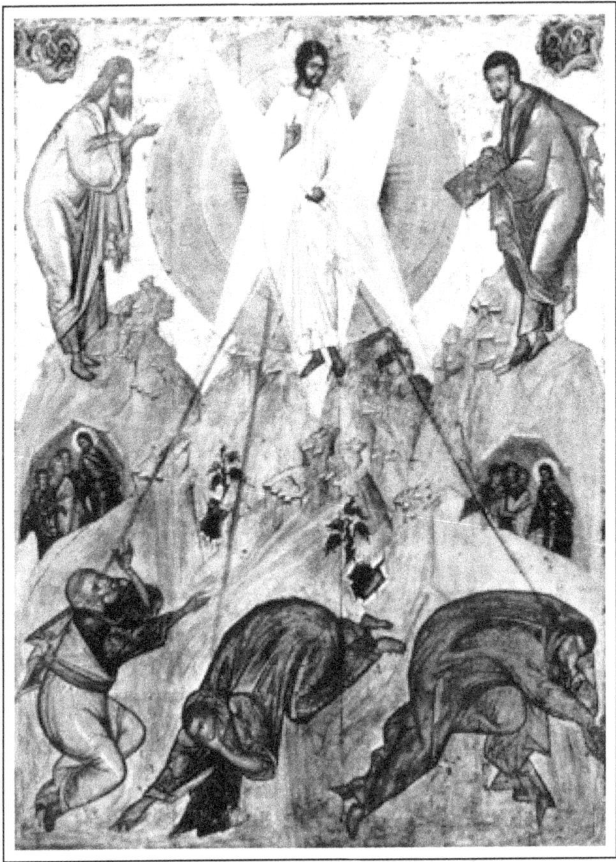

Figure 3. *Icon of the Transfiguration.*
© Tretyakov Museum, Moscow

Conclusion

The Elian narrative in 1 Kings conveys the picture of an intensely active prophet and the Western visual tradition relishes in portraying his feverish activity. Yet Elijah's moment of silence, his personal and intimate experience of God on Horeb in ch. 19, is much more influential in the reception history of the narrative. It is the reason why he is regarded as the founder of monasticism, the first desert father, why the Carmelites adopted him as their founder and why he is so important in Jewish mysticism. Yet, as far as I am aware, Orthodox iconography is the only visual tradition that attempts to depict this important moment in Elijah's life. In line with several translations, interpretations and expansions of the Hebrew narrative found in the different versions (Septuagint, Vulgate, Targum and Peshitta), it attempts to understand what Elijah sees or does not see in or outside his cave, how the passage is connected to Moses's experience of seeing God in the book of Exodus, and ultimately it tries to make some sense of the persistent ambiguity throughout the Hebrew Bible as to how and why God reveals himself in visible form or, alternatively, decides to conceal his presence.

Andrew Louth complains that far too little has been done to explore the parallels between the processes at work in the way we interpret icons and the way we interpret scripture, apart from the simple noting and cataloging of persons and themes from the Bible that have been portrayed on icons.[43] Little has been done on the hermeneutical level to explore the way in which the methods of exegesis found in the Church Fathers—that make use of symbol and allegory and expose a network of reference within the Bible—are transformed into painterly techniques by the icon painters. Symbolic or allegorical exegesis draws into its net more than the immediately obvious—something we need to be aware of when looking at an icon of a biblical scene.

In using different forms of visual media to help illuminate the subtleties and nuances of the biblical text, we should go beyond the narrow canon of biblical paintings scholars frequently limit themselves to. Icons, especially in relation to the Old Testament, are a much neglected area in this regard. In the controversy over iconoclasm in eighth- and ninth-century Byzantium, the defenders of the Orthodox veneration of icons made it clear that icons were a visual parallel to the scriptures. Theodore the Studite, too, made a famous comparison between scripture 'written in ink' and icons 'written in gold'.[44] The importance of including icons when we explore biblical texts through art is effectively underlined by Andreopoulos's summary of the functions that the icon performs: (a) it narrates biblical stories in a visual way; (b) it assists the faithful when they pray; (c) it suggests the presence of the depicted biblical person; (d) it unites the material and spiritual realms.[45] In the rich Orthodox iconography depicting Elijah's spiritual experience on Horeb, it is clear that the icon has fulfilled all four functions and has gone even further: the icon makers have also shed light on the puzzling nature of this episode and on the author's purpose in creating such an enigmatic narrative as 1 Kgs 19.8-14.

43. Louth, 'Foreword', p. 16.
44. Louth, 'Foreword', p. 15.
45. Andreopoulos, *Metamorphosis*, p. 26.

BIBLIOGRAPHY

Andreopoulos, A., *Metamorphosis: The Transfiguration in Byzantine Theology and Iconography* (New York: St. Vladimir's Seminary Press, 2005).

Boyce, J., 'The Feasts of Saints Elijah and Elisha in the Carmelite Rite: A Liturgico-Musical Study', in Egan (ed.), *Master of the Sacred Page*, pp. 155-88.

Brown, D., *Tradition and Imagination* (Oxford: Oxford University Press, 1999).

Bruno, S., *The Marble Pavement of the Cathedral of Siena* (Florence: Scala, 1993).

Dionysius of Fourna, *The Painter's Manual* (trans. Paul Hetherington; London: Sagittarius Press, 1974).

Duchet-Suchaux, G., and M. Pastoureau, *The Bible and the Saints* (Flammarion Iconographic Guides; Paris: Flammarion, 1994).

Edden, V., 'The Mantle of Elijah: Carmelite Spirituality in England in the Fourteenth Century', in *The Medieval Mystical Tradition: Exeter Symposium IV* (ed. M. Glasscoe; Cambridge: D.S. Brewer, 1999), pp. 67-84.

Egan, K.J. (ed.), *Master of the Sacred Page: Essays and Articles in Honor of Roland E. Murphy on the Occasion of His Eightieth Birthday* (Washington: Carmelite Institute, 1997).

Gilbert, C., 'Some Special Images for Carmelites, circa 1330–1430', in *Christianity and the Renaissance* (ed. T. Verdon and J. Henderson; New York: Syracuse University Press, 1990), pp. 161-207.

Houston, W., 'Exodus', in *The Oxford Bible Commentary* (ed. J. Barton and J. Muddiman; Oxford: Oxford University Press, 2001), pp. 67-91.

Kadushin, M., *The Rabbinic Mind* (New York: Blaisdell, 1965).

Louth, A., 'Foreword', in Andreopoulos, *Metamorphosis*, pp. 13-17.

Malherbe, A.J., and E. Ferguson (eds.), *Gregory of Nyssa: The Life of Moses* (Classics of Western Spirituality; New York: Paulist Press, 1978).

McMahon, P., 'Pater et Dux: Elijah in Medieval Mythology', in Egan (ed.), *Master of the Sacred Page*, pp. 283-99.

Meredith, A., 'Plato's Cave in Origen, Gregory of Nyssa and Plotinus', *Studia Patristica* 27 (1993), pp. 49-61.

Morrison, C.E., 'Handing on the Mantle: The Transmission of the Elijah Cycle in the Biblical Versions', in Egan (ed.), *Master of the Sacred Page*, pp. 109-29.

Murray, P., and L. Murray (eds.), *The Oxford Companion to Christian Art and Architecture* (Oxford: Oxford University Press, 1996).

Ohly, F., *Schriften zur mittelalterlichen Bedeutungsforschung* (Darmstadt: Wissenschaftliche Buchgesellschaft, 1977).

Papageorgiou, A., 'The Paschal Catechetical Homily of St. John Chrysostom: A Rhetorical and Contextual Study', *Greek Orthodox Theological Review* 43 (1998), pp. 93-104.

Rosenberg, A.J., *The Book of Kings I. A New English Translation of the Text, Rashi and a Commentary Digest* (New York: Judaica Press, 4th edn, 1991).

Santi, B., *The Marble Pavement of the Cathedral of Siena* (Florence: Scala, 1993).

Sherry, P., *Spirit and Beauty* (London: SCM Press, 2nd edn, 2002).

Simonopetritis, I., 'A Synoptic View of the Orthodox Ascetical Tradition of Mount Sinai', *The Orthodox Herald* (November–December 1998), pp. 122-23.

THE IMAGINATIVE EFFECTS OF EZEKIEL'S *MERKAVAH* VISION: CHAGALL AND EZEKIEL IN CREATIVE DISCOURSE

Sally E. Norris

Introductory Remarks

In his commentary on Ezekiel, the reformer John Calvin professes bewilderment at the text of the first chapter, which depicts strange creatures, interlocking wheels covered with eyes, cosmic flashes of light, and a grand heavenly throne:

> Now, if any one asks whether the vision is lucid, I confess its obscurity, and that I can scarcely understand it: but yet into what God has set before us, it is not only lawful and useful, but necessary to enquire. Base indeed would be our sloth should we willingly close our eyes and not attend to the vision.[1]

Calvin is refreshingly honest in acknowledging how the text of Ezekiel's *merkavah* vision *affected* him—he was perplexed, if not confounded, by it. Yet, as his commentary proceeds, he discards his puzzlement in favour of an explanatory discourse upon what he deems the original, and thus divinely appointed, meaning of the text and its images. Indeed, despite his stated reserve, Calvin approaches this task with long-winded earnestness, explaining the meaning of each detail of the vision and clearly noting the errors of interpretation which preceded him.

The spirit of Calvin's zeal tends to propel our own biblical enquiries, in particular when we encounter a text such as Ezekiel's *merkavah* vision, whose spiritual, moral, or ethical message initially appears opaque, if not mysterious. Our resistance to imaginative prose compels us to impose a systematic analysis upon the text, persuaded that if we can discover the original meaning of its components, the primary intent of the writer, or the psychological state of the visionary, then we can neatly reduce the vision to a comfortable formula guaranteed not to disturb accepted traditions and beliefs. But Ezekiel's vision beckons quite a different response. It reaches deeply into the realm of our imagination, inviting us to suspend preconceived notions of the

1. John Calvin, *Commentaries on the First Twenty Chapters of the Book of the Prophet Ezekiel* (trans. Thomas Myers; Grand Rapids: Eerdmans, 1948), p. 62.

divine and of the created order, and to travel with the visionary to a place where spiritual reflections and intellectual musings upon God and humanity are stretched, challenged, and re-formed. Texts such as Ezekiel's vision have the power both to confuse and inspire and hence become potent examples of *Wirkungsgeschichte*—a consideration of the *effects* of the text upon communities and individuals as they engage with it.

Given the visual nature of the narrative, artistic interpretation over the centuries has provided fertile ground for discovering new or unexpected meaning hidden in the text's words and images. A particularly compelling example appears in the portrayal of the vision by the artist Marc Chagall. The following discussion will consider the hermeneutical implications arising when text meets image in the art of Chagall and the *merkavah* vision of Ezekiel. It will be demonstrated how Chagall's particular hermeneutic re-orients the reading of Ezekiel's vision from the *theological* to the *anthropological*. In so doing, Chagall circumvents the iconoclasm inherent in religious tradition and re-directs the text away from the actual *merkavah* encounter to a commentary upon his own life as mirrored in the person and experience of Ezekiel himself—an example of the *Wirkungsgeschichte* of Ezekiel's vision in the twentieth century.

Chagall and La Bible: *Engraving 104, Ezekiel's* Merkavah *Vision*

The Hebrew Bible, and even the figure of Jesus in the Christian Scriptures,[2] traversed Chagall's canvas. He was fascinated by the pathos of the dramatic narratives of Genesis and Exodus; he delighted in the sensuous eroticism of the Song of Songs; he was inspired by the visions of hope announced by the prophets. Indeed, this life-long discourse between his art and the biblical text suggests a *romance* with the scriptural writings in which the stories and personages provided the locus for the exploration of his life and love, angst and fear, ideals and yearnings. For Chagall the Bible transcended the boundaries of Jewish and Christian belief, becoming less of a sacred tome and more of a humanist one to be used to interpret and re-imagine both the particulars and universals of the human condition. The Bible served as a *textual muse* for which Chagall held admiring gratitude and affection. Such were the sentiments expressed in his remarks at the 1973 opening of the *Musée National Message Biblique Marc Chagall* in Nice, spoken in his adopted language with the wisdom of his then 86 years:

2. E.g. *The White Crucifixion* (1938), Art Institute of Chicago, www.artic.edu/aic/collections; and *The Crucifixion* (1940), Philadelphia Museum of Art, www.philamuseum.org/collections/permanent/57439.html.

> Depuis ma première jeunesse, j'ai été captivé par la Bible. Il m'a toujours semblé et me semble encore que c'est le plus grande source de poésie de tous les temps. Depuis lors, j'ai cherché ce reflet dans la vie et dans l'Art. La Bible est comme une resonance de la nature et ce secret j'ai essayé de le transmettre. (Ever since my early childhood, I have been captivated by the Bible. It has always seemed to me and still seems that it is the greatest source of poetry of all time. Since then I have searched for its reflection in life and in Art. The Bible is like an echo of nature and this secret I have tried to convey.)[3]

It was, then, not surprising that in 1930 Chagall enthusiastically accepted a commission from the art publisher Ambroise Vollard to illustrate the Bible,[4] a project which occupied his artistic imagination from 1932 to 1939 and inspired his initial visit to Palestine in 1931. The series *La Bible* consists of 105 engravings, originally gouaches, illustrating narratives from the first twelve books of the Jewish Bible—Genesis through Ezekiel. Engravings 104 (Ezek. 1.4-28) and 105 (Ezek. 2.9-10) respectively conclude the work. The publication of the series was delayed due to Vollard's death in 1939 and Chagall's subsequent exile to New York in 1941, at the time of the Nazi invasion in Paris. By that time Chagall had only transposed 66 of the original 105 gouaches into engravings. It was not until Chagall resettled in France after the war that he completed work on the remaining 39 engravings and the series was subsequently published by another Parisian art dealer, E. Tériade, in 1956.[5] Of particular significance is the medium of the published images in *La Bible*. Chagall wrote of the media of engraving and lithography with great passion, suggesting that the tactile labour of these methods enabled him to enter more fully into the emotion of the text:

> When I held in my hand a lithographic stone, or a copper plate, I believed I was touching a talisman. It seemed to me that I could entrust them with all my joys, all my sorrows… Everything that has crossed my path, throughout the years: births, deaths, marriages, flowers, animals, birds, poor working people, my parents, lovers at night, the Prophets from the Bible, on the street, in my home, in the Temple, in the sky.[6]

3. Marc Chagall, 'Message', in *Musée National Message Biblique Marc Chagall: Catalogue des collections* (ed. J.-M. Foray and S. Forestier; Paris: Éditions de la Réunion des Musées Nationaux, 2001), pp. 9-11 (9).

4. *La Bible* was the third in a series of illustrated books commissioned for Chagall by Vollard, preceded by Nikolai Gogol's *Les Âmes mortes* (1923–27) and Jean de la Fontaine's *Fables* (1927–30).

5. The series was published in the art journal *Verve* 33/34 (1956). A reproduction of the series appears in Marc Chagall, *Illustrations for the Bible: Text by Jean Wahl, with an Appreciation by Meyer Schapiro* (New York: Harcourt Brace, 1956).

6. Marc Chagall, 'On Engraving and Lithography, 1960', in *Chagall: A Retrospective* (ed. Jacob Baal-Teshuva; New York: Hugh Lauter Levin, 1995), pp. 223-24 (223).

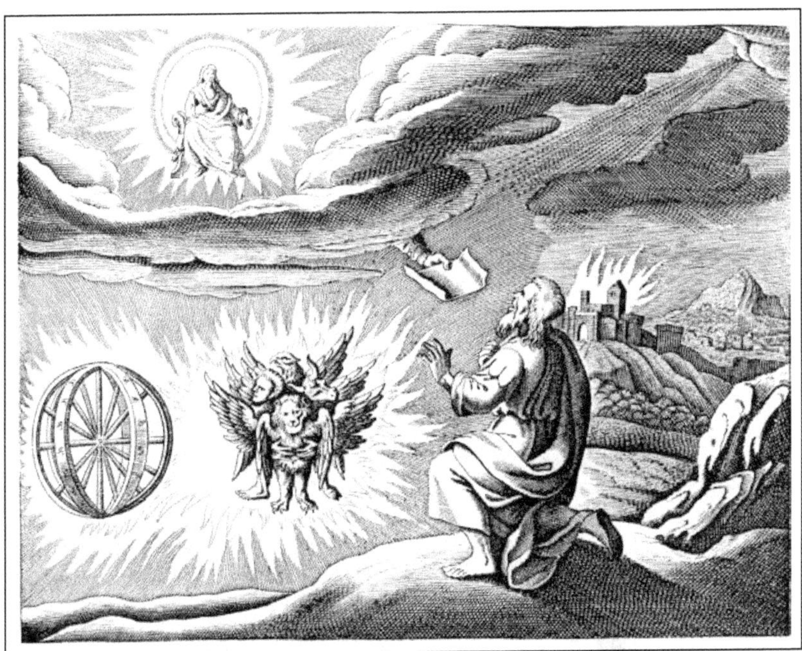

Figure 1. Artist unknown, *Ezekiel's Vision* (after image by Matthaeus Merrian, 1625) in Nicholas Fontaine (1625–1709), *L'histoire dv Vieux et dv Nouveau Testament* (Paris: Chez Pierre Le Petit, 1670). Courtesy of the Pitts Theology Library, Candler School of Theology, Emory University

Chagall's engraving of Ezekiel's *merkavah* vision is indeed an unusual work, suggesting both a spiritual depth and a light-hearted whimsy. Unlike portrayals of the vision which convey terror, chaos, or confusion, such as the image from Fontaine's illustrated Bible (Fig. 1) as well as those of Raphael, Blake, and Kiefer,[7] engraving 104 invites placid, yet rapt, reflection (Fig. 2). In the lower portion of the image, shrouded in darkness, Ezekiel lies prostrate and coiled as if mirroring a serpent's pose. The subtle light cast upon him illumines his opened, up-turned hands, and his down-turned face with its vacant eyes. He appears at once distraught and resigned, alive and paralyzed, detached and prayerful. Upon initial reflection, this depiction of Ezekiel

7. Cf. Raphael, *The Vision of Ezekiel* (1518), image after Raphael at Museum of Fine Arts Boston, www.mfa.org (original in Galleria Palatina, Firenze); William Blake, *The Whirlwind: Ezekiel's Vision of the Cherubim and Eyed Wheels* (1803-05), Museum of Fine Arts Boston, www.mfa.org; and Anselm Kiefer, *Die Himmelspaläste: Merkaba* (1990) reproduced in *Anselm Kiefer: The Heavenly Palaces, Merkabah* (ed. Peter Nisbet; Cambridge, MA: Harvard University Art Museums, 2003), pp. 26-54.

should present little surprise. Chagall would appear to be literally following the text, which reads in 1.28 that, upon seeing the 'likeness of the appearance of the glory of YHWH', Ezekiel 'fell on his face'.

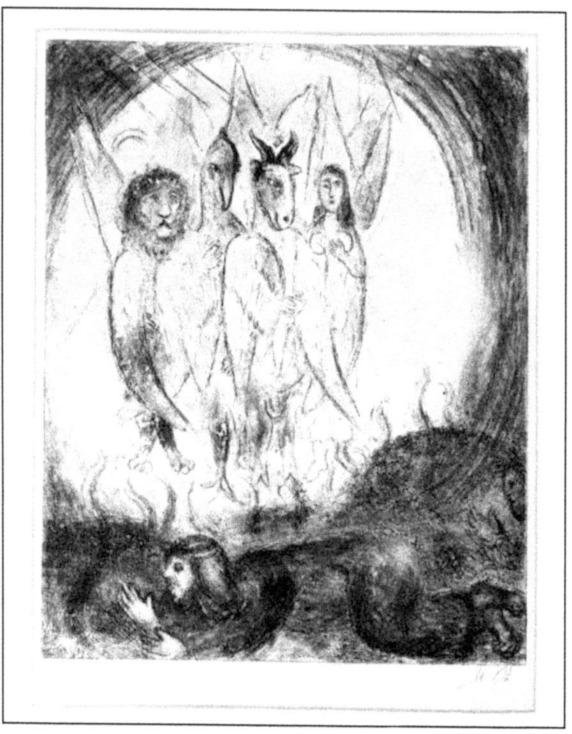

Figure 2. Marc Chagall (1887–1985), *The Vision of Ezekiel* (no. 104) from *La Bible* series, 1956. Hand-colored engraving, 24 × 18 in. (61 × 45.7 cm). Gift of Patrick and Beatrice Haggerty, 80.7.4. Haggerty Museum of Art, Marquette University, Milwaukee, Wisconsin. © ADAGP, Paris and DACS, London 2007

Given that Chagall's artistic expression always was mediated through the lens of his imagination and life experience, particularly his idealized and fantastical childhood memories from Vitebsk, Russia,[8] where he was born in 1887, it seems likely that the figure of Ezekiel depicts something greater than the prophet himself. This is evident in images of Chagall's father, as well as a rabbi in Vitebsk, who bear similar pensive, down-trodden guises to the Ezekiel of engraving 104.[9] Life in Vitebsk was difficult, if not oppressive,

8. Vitebsk is located in what is today Belarus.

9. Cf. *The Artist's Father* (1914), www.auburn.edu/academic/liberal_arts/ foreign/russian/art/chagall-father.html; and *Solitude* (1933), The Tel Aviv Museum, www.tamuseum.com/museum/modern.htm.

particularly for labourers living in the Jewish *shtetl*. Chagall writes of his father in his early autobiography, *My Life*:

> He lifted barrels and my heart used to twist like a Turkish pretzel as I watched him carrying those loads and stirring the little herrings with frozen hands. His fat employer stood by like a stuffed animal... Everything about my father seemed sad and full of enigma. An inaccessible image. Always tired, always worried... I was the only one who knew him—that simple heart, poetical and blunted with silence.[10]

In the figure of Ezekiel we see not only the prophet, awe-struck by the power of his vision, but also the Jewish *Jedermann* in Vitebsk, whose despairing life seems so distant from the divine. In ascribing this dual significance to Ezekiel's portrait, Chagall visually articulates a social comment that is at once time-bound and eternal: the despondent worker in turn-of-century Vitebsk is also the persecuted Jew in Nazi Europe, as well as any human being dwelling in troubled circumstances in any place and any time.

The depth of Chagall's commentary notwithstanding, Ezekiel actually seems to be assigned merely a supporting-cast role in the image. The viewer's eyes are primarily drawn to the halo-like light-filled centre in which the four living creatures (*hayyot*) are encircled. The contrast between light and dark in the image is indeed dramatic, although the engraving itself is composed of subdued brownish-black lines surrounded by a soft, yet brilliant, cream-coloured centre. The *hayyot* convey a peaceful aura. In their stillness they appear warm and friendly, quite unlike the grotesque creatures described by Ezekiel, who rapidly jet around in a seemingly haphazard manner (Ezek. 1.12-14). Yet, in other details Chagall adheres to the text faithfully: the *hayyot* assume a quasi-human form (1.5); their legs are straight (1.7) though not calf-like; the discernable hands suggest a human shape (1.8); they face straight forward (1.9); and, while the number of wings appears rather uncertain, the wings do touch one another above and cover their bodies (1.9, 11).

The most striking feature concerns the figure of the *hayyah* on the right: it is a woman. In his vision Ezekiel reports that each of the *hayyot* had four faces, resembling those of a lion, an ox, an eagle, and a human being (1.10), with the human face at the centre, the lion on the right, the ox on the left, and the eagle facing backwards, or possibly upwards. Not surprisingly, the human being has commonly been identified as a man in many translations,[11]

10. Marc Chagall, *My Life* (trans. D. Williams; Oxford: Oxford University Press, 2nd edn, 1989), p. 12. Chagall completed his autobiography, a work of imaginative poetic flair, in 1922 and hence it describes just the first 35 years of his life. Originally written in Russian, Bella Chagall translated it into French in 1930; the English translation by Dorothy Williams first appeared in 1965, published by Peter Owen.

11. For instance the following English translations: KJV, NEB, REB and RSV. The NRSV is an exception.

in artistic renderings such as Fig. 1 and the Raphael and Blake images, and in tradition. Jerome's identification of the four Gospels with the four creatures of Ezekiel persists even today: Matthew as a man, Mark as a lion, Luke as an ox, and John as an eagle. Rabbinic tradition identified the human *hayyah* as Jacob in a fascinating midrash on his dream of angels ascending and descending the ladder between heaven and earth (Gen. 28.12). In *Gen. R.* 68.12, the angels enquire of Jacob:

> 'Are you the one whose visage is incised above?' They would then go up and look at his features and go down and examine his features.[12]

Commenting on this tradition, R. Eliezer is reported to have remarked:

> And the ministering angels were ascending and descending thereon and they beheld the face of Jacob, and they said: This is the face like the face of the Chayyah, which is on the Throne of Glory. Such (angels) who were (on earth) below were ascending to see the face of Jacob among the faces of the Chayyah, (for it was) like the face of the Chayyah, which is on the Throne of Glory.[13]

Given the predominance of masculine interpretations of the *hayyot*, why, then, does Chagall take such dramatic poetic license with the text—or does he really? Who is this woman, the female *hayyah*? Is she merely the product of a sophisticated artistic imagination or does she command a particular significance for Chagall?

Chagall and Ezekiel's Merkavah *Vision: The Feminine Defined*

It would be tempting to dismiss any further discussion of this female figure by suggesting that Chagall was not exclusively depicting the narrative from Ezekiel 1, but rather an amalgam of the text with ch. 10 in which Ezekiel revisits his *merkavah* vision with substantial interpretive editing. In Ezekiel 10 the *hayyot* become the *kerubim*, the angelic beings who sit upon their chariot and protect the ark of the covenant (1 Chron. 28.18).[14] The faces of these *kerubim* (10.14) form a different quartet from that which Ezekiel witnesses in ch. 1: a cherub (i.e. an angelic being), a human being, a lion, and an eagle. The ox of ch.1 has been replaced by the cherub in ch. 10. It could be argued, then, that the woman in engraving 104 is simply an angel—one of the *kerubim*. There are several reasons why this explanation is unlikely.

12. *Gen. R.* 68.12.6 in Jacob Neusner, *Genesis Rabbah: The Judaic Commentary to the Book of Genesis, A New American Translation* (3 vols.; Atlanta: Scholars Press, 1985), III, pp. 11-14 (13).

13. *Pirkê de Rabbi Eliezer* (trans. Gerald Friedlander; New York: Hermon Press, 1965), pp. 261-67 (265).

14. See also Exod. 25.19-20.

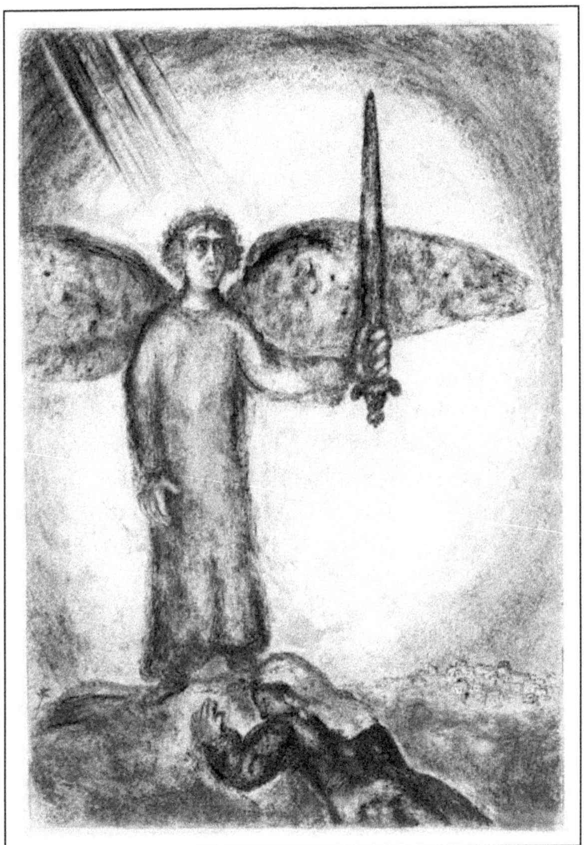

Figure 3. Marc Chagall (1887–1985), *Joshua before the Angel with the Sword* (no. 45), from *La Bible* series, 1956. Hand-coloured engraving, 24 × 18 in. (61 × 45.7 cm). Gift of Patrick and Beatrice Haggerty, 80.7.66. Haggerty Museum of Art, Marquette University, Milwaukee, Wisconsin. © ADAGP, Paris and DACS, London 2007

First, in engraving 104 Chagall's creatures are clearly portrayed as a lion, a bird (hence, eagle), a pastoral animal (hence, ox) and a woman (hence, human being), firmly in accord with the description found in the text of Ezekiel 1. And, although the lion in Chagall's image may suggest some masculine human characteristics, it bears a close facial resemblance to other lions in Chagall's repertoire, such as the animal being slaughtered by Samson in engraving 54 (Judg. 14.5-16), and the lion in engraving 62, which David boasts of killing because it is attempting to devour the sheep in his care (1 Sam. 17.34-36). With typical Chagallian whimsy, the young David and the lion appear to be happily dancing together rather than engaged in brutal conflict. Secondly, Chagall typically portrays the angels in *La Bible* as male, as is evident for instance in Fig. 3, as well as in engraving 16, which depicts Jacob wrestling with an angel (Gen. 32.24-28), engraving 53, which illustrates Manoah's encounter with an angel who foretells the birth of Samson (Judg. 13.2-21), and engraving 87, which shows an angel ministering in the desert to a fearful and exhausted Elijah (1 Kgs 19.4-8). Thirdly, and decisively, the images of *La Bible* appear in chronological order beginning with Genesis 1. There is no deviation. Engraving 104 of the *merkavah* vision precedes the concluding image of *La Bible*, engraving 105 representing Ezek. 2.9-10 in which Ezekiel sees a hand from heaven offering him a scroll that he is subsequently commanded to eat.

The question, then, demands further enquiry: who is this woman, or *why* a woman among Chagall's portrayal of the *hayyot* of Ezekiel's vision? A survey of Chagall's biblical art suggests that she is a frequent visitor to his canvas. She finds, for instance, a particularly prominent place among his images from his second biblical series, *Dessins pour la Bible*,[15] such as Fig. 4, as well as his multiple images from the Song of Songs, one of the biblical writings that most enchanted Chagall and one that found expression in a range of media.[16] This woman is not confined to the biblical corpus. A woman of similar affect accompanies Chagall as he journeys through myriad themes and genres.[17] Does she have particular meaning?

Every Chagall image requires consideration of the multi-textured confluence of sources that define the artist himself. This complex 'polyphony'[18] of voices provides the heuristic matrix through which text, image, and the artist converse. The theme of love, in particular the effusive love for his first wife Bella, permeates Chagall's art as an especially pronounced vocal line. She appears, for instance, in his 1915 painting *Birthday*,[19] the year of their

15. *Dessins pour la Bible*, consisting of 120 lithographs (24 colour and 96 black and white), was published by Tériade in *Verve* 37/38 (1960). The series was also reproduced in Marc Chagall, *Drawings for the Bible* (New York: Dover, 1995). In contrast to *La Bible*, the series depicts most particularly the women of the Hebrew Bible, such as Hagar, Rebekah, Rachel, Zilpah, Miriam, Rahab, Deborah, Ruth, Esther, and the female beloved from the Song of Songs. Chagall also includes images from Job, Qohelet, the Psalms and the twelve minor prophets. The woman in Fig. 4 in the lithograph 'Paradise' not only resembles the woman in engraving 104, but also the woman in the lithographs illustrating the Song of Songs.

16. See, for example, the Song of Songs murals at Musée National Message Biblique Marc Chagall, www.musees-nationaux-alpesmaritimes.fr/pages/page_id18013_u1l2.htm.

17. See, for example, Marc Chagall, *The Triumph of Music* (1966), a mural designed for the Metropolitan Opera House in New York, www.metoperafamily.org/metopera/news/photos/40thAnniversary.aspx.

18. Following the terminology in Benjamin Harshav, *Marc Chagall and His Times: A Documentary Narrative* (Stanford: Stanford University Press, 2004), pp. 2, 8.

19. Marc Chagall, *Birthday* (1915), Museum of Modern Art, New York, www.moma.org/collection/search.php.

wedding, and as the bride in such canvases as *The Betrothed* (1911).[20] He writes of her in *My Life*, when she was yet his fiancée and posed for sketches:

> Bella knocks at the door, knocks timidly with her thin, slender little finger. In her arms, clutched to her breast, she holds a big bunch of mountain ash, cloudy green splashed with red. 'Thank you', I say, 'thank you'. That wasn't the right word. It's dark. I kiss her. A still life magically takes shape in my mind. She poses for me. Reclining, a rounded white nude shape... Although she was practically my fiancée I was still afraid of approaching her, of going any nearer, of touching all that loveliness. As if a feast were spread before your eyes, I did a study of her and hung it on the walls...my fiancée is purer than Raphael's Madonna and I'm an angel.[21]

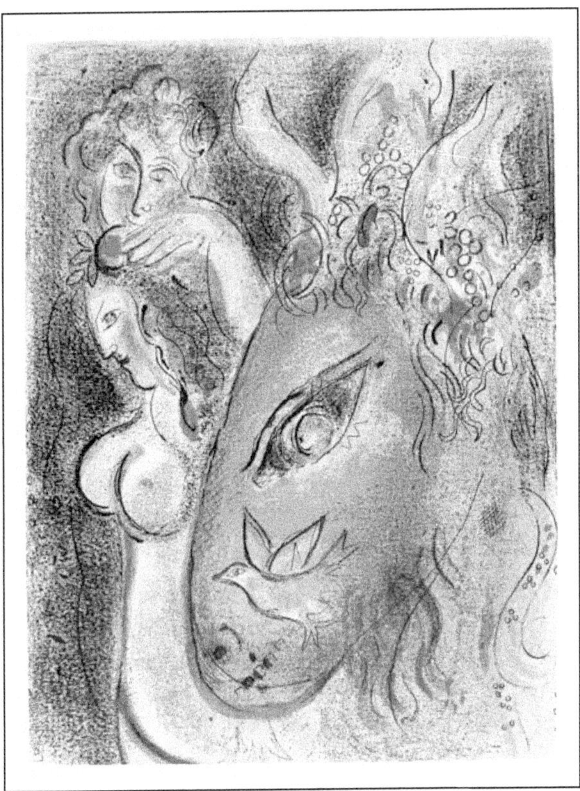

Figure 4. Marc Chagall (1887–1985), *Paradise* from *Dessins pour la Bible* series, 1958–59. Lithograph, 14 × 10.5 in. Wake Forest University Print Collection, Winston-Salem, North Carolina. © ADAGP, Paris and DACS, London 2007

20. Marc Chagall, *The Betrothed* (1911), Metropolitan Museum of Art, New York, www.metmuseum.org/special/Matisse/3.r.htm.

21. Chagall, *My Life*, pp. 79-80.

Chagall's disarming tendency for hyperbolic or imaginative self-description notwithstanding, his self-identification as an angel does indeed convey a kinship with the heavenly realm as another childhood remembrance suggests:

> There are many stars, my sweet stars; they accompany me to school and wait for me in the street till I return. Poor things, forgive me. I have left you alone up there at such a dizzying height.[22]

Hence his striking self-portrait as the sword-bearing angel of Josh. 5.13-15 in Fig. 3 and as the abstract male figure warmly gazing at the woman in Fig. 4 is perhaps as much yearning as artistic whimsy.

Bella's death in 1944, during the family's wartime exile in New York, devastated Chagall. He refrained from any artistic production for nearly a year, devoting his grief-filled attention instead on compiling Bella's letters and papers. And although Chagall eventually re-married, the spirit of Bella remained with him, infusing his heart and soul and art until his own death more than forty years later in 1985 at the age of ninety-seven. His life-long love for Bella and the predominance in his artistic corpus of a common female figure with Bella's dark hair and an abstract bodily shape, resembling his description of her when she posed prior to their marriage, suggest that Bella, or a Bella archetype, defined the ideal female representation for him. Bella's beauty and spiritual purity adorned his canvas while she was alive and in the years after she died, as is expressed in a letter from Chagall to the Yiddish poet Abraham Sutzkever in 1949, on the fifth anniversary of Bella's death:

> I sent you two books by Bella.[23] I am glad that, with your great sensibility and talent, you will take care of the text. She was my Muse. The embodiment of Jewish art, beauty, and love. If not for her, my pictures would not be as they are.[24]

I would argue, therefore, that as well as the woman amorously inhabiting Chagall's repertoire of biblical images illustrating the creation and the Song of Songs, Bella is the *hayyah* tenderly gracing the canvas of Ezekiel's *merkavah* vision. In a sense, Chagall re-imagines rabbinic tradition, composing his own midrash in which Bella becomes the new Jacob. The identification of Bella with the female figure is especially poignant, considering the span of years over which the composition took shape, rendering the image both prescient

22. Chagall, *My Life*, pp. 10-11.

23. Bella Chagall had written two memoirs, *Brenendike likht (Burning Lights)* and *Di ershte bagegenish* (*First Encounter*), both published posthumously in 1945 and 1947 respectively. Marc Chagall illustrated both books.

24. 'Marc Chagall in Orgeval to Abraham Sutzkever in Tel Aviv, June 14, 1949', in Harshav, *Chagall and His Times*, p. 679. Translation from the Yiddish by Benjamin and Barbara Harshav.

and reflective. The original gouache was painted in the 1930s, prior to the Chagall's American exile and thus preceding Bella's illness and death. The corresponding engraving was completed following Chagall's return to France in 1948, with Bella now gone.[25] Thus, Bella in the form of the female *hayyah* becomes simultaneously a tribute to, and a memory of, Chagall's cherished love for her and his perception of her idealized beauty, a beauty that reaches beyond the bounds of their mutual love, to symbolize comfort for the suffering and hope for universal peace.

Of course, the woman is not the sole *hayyah* in engraving 104. She is accompanied by three additional characters, or caricatures: the ox, the bird, and the lion. The animals Chagall encountered as a child in Vitebsk befriended his imagination, appearing frequently in the recollections of *My Life*:

> On market day, the little church was choked, crammed with people… wagons, baskets, all sorts of wares pressed in on it so closely that it seemed as though God Himself had been driven out. All around people were bustling, shouting… Cats were meowing. Roosters for sale were cackling, tied up inside their baskets. Pigs were grunting. Mares were whinging. Brilliant colours were rioting in the sky. But everything fell quiet towards evening. The icons came to life, the lamps shone again. The cows fell asleep in their sheds, snoring… and so did the hens on their rafters, blinking maliciously.[26]

Having permanently imprinted the text of his life, these animals repeatedly find a whimsical home on Chagall's artistic page. Whereas in most images they are simply earthly, if not anthropomorphic, beasts who mysteriously defy gravity to fly across the canvas, in engraving 104 they become stationary angelic creatures who mediate between the sacred and the mundane. They do not assume an identical celestial nature to the remote creatures in the *merkavah* narrative, who journey upwards through the heavens to the divine gleaming throne. Rather, in the stillness of their company with the idealized Bella, they transmit an endearing guise of compassionate love to humanity below.

The uniqueness of Chagall's hermeneutic resides in the intermingling of text, canvas, and autobiography, yielding a reading of the narrative that transcends the conventional and invites a renewed consideration of the vision through fresh eyes. Chagall and his art become, in essence, a provocative heuristic paradigm though which the modern reader may approach Ezekiel's words and redirect them in ways previously unimagined. The twenty-eight verses of the narrative contain over sixty contiguous forms, colours, and movements of both feminine and masculine genders, all of

25. Chagall completed work on the 39 images of the *La Bible*, which had not yet been translated into engravings, in 1952–56.

26. Chagall, *My Life*, p. 46.

which acquire a sense of the surreal as they inhabit mystical terrain. Chagall chose to portray only a few select images. He omits, for instance, the ominous wheels covered with eyes, which give the vision its identity—*merkavah* (chariot). He disregards the climactic jewel-like heavenly throne and the gleaming male figure who sits upon it. Chagall depicts only those images from the text that intersect with the text of his life—the *hayyot* and the prophet himself. The biblical narrative and Chagall's life experience coalesce to form a subtext of Ezekiel's *merkavah* vision: the love of Bella in idealized form and her leonine, bovine, and feathered companions from Vitebsk, contrasted with the pondering angst of Chagall's father in the guise of the prostrate Ezekiel. Light revealed in opposition to darkness.

Concluding Remarks: Theology, Anthropology, and Mysticism

In summary, Chagall's portrayal of Ezekiel's *merkavah* vision in engraving 104 of *La Bible* reorients the reading of the text. In the biblical narrative Ezekiel describes a theophany in which he participates in a mystical seeing (chs. 1–3) and travelling to (chs. 8–10) the heavenly realm and all that dwells therein. His perspective is *theological*. The purpose of his *merkavah* journey lies not in communicating deeper insight into the travails of human existence, but rather in attaining a revelatory glimpse into the ways of a distant, powerful God, who resides atop a complex celestial sphere harbouring living creatures and wheels. The feminine and masculine intermingle, with both contributing to the discovery of hidden mystical knowledge contained within the divine. Ezekiel's language is always restrained by an 'appearance' and a 'likeness'. To suggest a vision of the actual—a portrait of God with detailed boldness—would transgress the iconoclasm of his tradition. And yet, Ezekiel's account of the *merkavah* vision was sufficient to challenge norms of belief, practice and ways of seeing, as Daniel Berrigan observes with incisive poetic insight:

> He (Ezekiel) was granted access to a Mystery. But then he fell from grace. He dared tell or write or allow to be written of 'a Being, a Someone, a Glory, a brilliant human Silhouette'... This was accounted excessive, outrageous. He played with fire; he broke a taboo. And the question: Would not the violation encourage others in a like direction, making him the father of a renegade tradition of 'see and tell'?[27]

Chagall saw and told, only differently. In Chagall's discourse the theocentrism of Ezekiel is replaced by an *anthropological* hermeneutic through which the *merkavah* vision narrates his own text—his empathy for the struggles of

27. Daniel Berrigan, *Ezekiel: Vision in the Dust* (Maryknoll, NY: Orbis Books, 1997), p. 3.

his father in Vitebsk, his fondness for the whimsical animals of his childhood, and most significantly, his enduring love for Bella. Yet his narrative does not remain constrained by the limits of his autobiography. It assumes a broader purpose, conveying the pathos and potential of human life, as Chagall so poignantly expressed at the unveiling of his Metropolitan Opera murals in 1966:

> ...all the questions and their answers can be seen in the paintings themselves. Everyone can see them his own way, interpret what he sees, and how he sees. Often there are hidden in paintings more utterances of silence, of doubt than words can express. These utterances pronounced often diminish the essential and lead away to other roads.
>
> ...I thought that only love and uncalculating devotion towards others will lead to the greatest harmony in life and art of which humanity has been dreaming so long. And this must, of course, be included in each utterance, in each brush stroke, and in each colour.[28]

Given this distinct bifurcation of theological and anthropological perspective, it would be tempting to conclude that Chagall was neither a mystic nor a visionary in the manner of Ezekiel, and to a significant degree this would be true. Although he comments in 1944 that 'dozens of years flying around in the sky convinced me about what is happening on earth',[29] such a reflection does not suggest that Chagall ever embarked on a *merkavah* experience. And yet, Chagall embraced a passionate affinity for the mystical as a necessary component of the anthropological if it is to properly seek love and justice. Hence he wrote at the conclusion of the war:

> Some people are wrongly afraid of the word 'mystical', to which they give a meaning that is too religiously orthodox. We must strip this term of its obsolete and musty exterior and understand it in its pure form, exalted and untouched.
>
> 'Mystic!' How often have people hurled this word at me—just as they had accused me earlier of being 'literary'. But without a mystical element is there a single great picture, a single great poem, or—even—a single great social movement in the world? Does not any organism (individual or social) wither and die if it is deprived of the power of the mystical, of feeling, of reason? Sadly I answer myself. It is unjust to set upon mysticism, when it is precisely the lack of mysticism which almost destroyed France. But we should distinguish between different kinds of mysticism, and this war through which we

28. Marc Chagall, 'At the Unveiling of the Murals at the Metropolitan Opera, September 8, 1966', in Baal-Teshuva (ed.), *Chagall*, pp. 208-17 (208).

29. Marc Chagall, 'Speech at the Chagall-Fefer Celebration, New York, April 30, 1944', in *Marc Chagall on Art and Culture* (ed. Benjamin Harshav; Stanford: Stanford University Press, 2003), pp. 95-100 (99). Translation from the Yiddish by Benjamin and Barbara Harshav.

> have just passed should have the final purpose of insuring victory over a misconceived mysticism...[30]

Chagall's anthropological reading of Ezekiel's theological text becomes mysticism in its highest form for Chagall. The text is no longer the *merkavah*, but rather the mirror of his life, a mirror which extends beyond autobiography to a yearning for universal love. Such is the outcome when Ezekiel's text meets Chagall's canvas—a creative discourse seeking to uncover the mysteries embedded in the human and the divine.

BIBLIOGRAPHY

Baal-Teshuva, Jacob (ed.), *Chagall: A Retrospective* (New York: Hugh Lauter Levin, 1960).

Berrigan, Daniel, *Ezekiel: Vision in the Dust* (Maryknoll, NY: Orbis Books, 1997).

Calvin, John, *Commentaries on the First Twenty Chapters of the Book of the Prophet Ezekiel* (trans. Thomas Myers; Grand Rapids: Eerdmans, 1948).

Chagall, Marc, 'Some Impressions regarding French Painting: Address at Mount Holyoke, August 1943/March 1946', in Harshav (ed.), *Chagall on Art*, pp. 66-79.

—'At the Unveiling of the Murals at the Metropolitan Opera, September 8, 1966', in Baal-Teshuva (ed.), *Chagall*, pp. 208-17.

—*Drawings for the Bible* (New York: Dover, 1995).

—*Illustrations for the Bible: Text by Jean Wahl, with an Appreciation by Meyer Schapiro* (New York: Harcourt Brace, 1956).

—'Marc Chagall in Orgeval to Abraham Sutzkever in Tel Aviv, June 14, 1949', in Harshav, *Chagall and His Times*, p. 679.

—'Message', in *Musée National Message Biblique Marc Chagall: Catalogue des collections* (ed. J.-M. Foray and S. Forestier; Paris: Éditions de la Réunion des Musées Nationaux, 2001), pp. 9-11.

—*My Life* (trans. Dorothy Williams; Oxford: Oxford University Press, 2nd edn, 1989).

—'On Engraving and Lithography', in Baal-Teshuva (ed.), *Chagall*, pp. 223-24.

—'Speech at the Chagall-Fefer Celebration, New York, April 30, 1944', in Harshav (ed.), *Chagall on Art*, pp. 95-100.

Friedlander, Gerald (trans.), *Pirkê de Rabbi Eliezer* (New York: Hermon Press, 1965).

Harshav, Benjamin, *Marc Chagall and His Times: A Documentary Narrative* (Stanford: Stanford University Press, 2004).

Harshav, Benjamin (ed.), *Marc Chagall on Art and Culture* (Stanford: Stanford University Press, 2003).

Neusner, Jacob, *Genesis Rabbah: The Judaic Commentary to the Book of Genesis, A New American Translation* (3 vols.; Atlanta: Scholars Press, 1985).

Nisbet, Peter (ed.), *Anselm Kiefer: The Heavenly Palaces, Merkabah* (Cambridge, MA: Harvard University Art Museums, 2003).

30. Marc Chagall, 'Some Impressions regarding French Painting: Address at Mount Holyoke, August 1943/March 1946', in Harshav (ed.), *Chagall on Art*, pp. 66-79 (75).

THE SONG OF SONGS AND THE ENCLOSED GARDEN IN FIFTEENTH-CENTURY PAINTINGS AND ENGRAVINGS OF THE VIRGIN MARY AND THE CHRIST-CHILD

Christina Bucher

In European art of the fifteenth century, the Virgin Mary is frequently portrayed seated in an enclosed garden (*hortus conclusus*). Often in these settings, the Virgin holds the Christ-child; however, the Christ-child may also be near to Mary, but not seated in her lap. The garden may be illustrated in a variety of ways. The enclosure is usually suggested, rather than literally portrayed. It may be implied by two walls meeting in a corner, but it may also be indicated by Mary sitting on a bench or on the ground in front of a wall or a trellis. The garden that is enclosed may be filled with lush vegetation or represented by a single tree and a few tufts of grass.[1]

Art historians frequently suggest the enclosed garden symbolizes Mary's purity, or virginity;[2] however, this interpretation of the symbolism is too narrow. It is the goal of this essay to develop a fuller understanding of the

1. James Hall, *Dictionary of Subjects and Symbols in Art* (London: John Murray, 1974), s.v. 'Garden', identifies as the basic elements of an enclosed garden a walled or fenced enclosure within which is located 'fruitfulness'. Peter Murray and Linda Murray, *Oxford Dictionary of Christian Art* (London: Oxford University Press, 1996), s.v. 'Hortus Conclusus', define the enclosed garden as a 'walled garden with a well or fountain, and usually with several female saints'. I do not consider a well or fountain essential to the enclosed garden, although it does appear in early manuscript illustrations of the enclosed garden. Similarly, the Virgin and Child with Saints is one subtype of the enclosed garden type, but is not essential to the type.

2. Murray and Murray, *Oxford Dictionary of Christian Art*, s.v. 'Hortus Conclusus', claim that the enclosed garden refers to Mary's virginity. Hall, *Dictionary of Subjects and Symbols*, s.v. 'Garden' associates the enclosed garden with Mary's virginity when it is made the setting for the Annunciation, the Virgin with the unicorn, or the Virgin and Child. According to Hall, the enclosed garden can also symbolize the Immaculate Conception. Gertrud Schiller (*Iconography of Christian Art* [Greenwich, CT: New York Graphic Society, 1971], I, p. 53), observes that the enclosed garden 'signifies the virginity of Mary and her state of immunity to the attacks of Satan'. I agree with Schiller that the enclosed garden symbolizes both Mary's virginity and her immunity to temptation.

symbolism by looking first at the biblical background in Song 4.12; second, at the ancient and medieval interpretation of this verse; and third, at several fifteenth-century paintings and engravings that make use of the enclosed garden motif.

The Biblical Text

The symbol originates in the Song 4.12: 'A garden locked is my sister bride, a pool locked, a fountain sealed'. The Hebrew word *gan*, here translated 'garden', occurs six times in the Song of Songs, always in reference to the female lover of the poems. In 4.12, the garden is described as being 'locked' or 'enclosed'. The Hebrew term translated 'locked', *na'ul*, can be used to describe the bolting of a door from the inside. How should we understand this metaphor in the context of the Song of Songs? What does it mean for the man to say that his lover is a 'garden locked'? Several interpretations of this metaphor have been proposed. Marvin Pope argues that the metaphor refers to the woman's virginity.[3] Roland Murphy, Ariel and Chana Bloch, Diane Bergant, and Cheryl Exum all read the metaphor as a reference to the man's exclusive rights of ownership to his beloved (that is, she is locked or closed to all men save her lover).[4] Othmar Keel argues that the metaphor of the locked garden refers to the woman's inaccessibility, and that it belongs to a series of metaphors of inaccessibility in this book, a series that includes the dove in the cleft of the rock (2.14) and the bride on the peak of Mount Hermon (4.8). Furthermore, Keel asserts that this imagery symbolizes neither the woman's chastity nor the man's exclusive ownership of the woman.[5] Elizabeth Huwiler expresses a similar view, although she suggests the verse 'may be something of a

3. Marvin H. Pope, *Song of Songs: A New Translation with Introduction and Commentary* (Anchor Bible, 7C; Garden City, NY: Doubleday, 1977), p. 488.

4. Roland E. Murphy, *The Song of Songs: A Commentary on the Book of Canticles or the Song of Songs* (Hermeneia; Minneapolis: Fortress Press, 1990), p. 161; Ariel Bloch and Chana Bloch, *The Song of Songs: A New Translation* (Berkeley: University of California Press, 1995), p. 176; Diane Bergant, *The Song of Songs* (Berit Olam; Collegeville, MN: Liturgical Press, 2001), p. 54; J. Cheryl Exum, *Song of Songs, A Commentary* (Old Testament Library; Louisville, KY: Westminster John Knox Press, 2005), p. 176.

5. Othmar Keel, *The Song of Songs: A Continental Commentary* (trans. Frederick J. Gaiser; Minneapolis: Fortress Press, 1994), p. 174: 'Contrary to frequent claims, the locking and sealing have nothing to do with chastity or with exclusive rights of usage and ownership, under which the "garden" would not be locked to the rightful owner. This image is simply about the inaccessible loved one, whose charms are all the more wonderful, mysterious, and exotic the tighter the doors that lead to them are locked.'

taunt'.[6] Thus, biblical scholars suggest a range of possible meanings in their exegesis of this verse: virginity, exclusivity of ownership or of relationship, and inaccessibility. This last idea of 'inaccessibility' has the broadest range of meanings and can incorporate within it the notions of virginity and exclusivity. Inaccessibility can have both positive and negative implications. In the exegetical context, Keel suggests a negative implication—the man finds it difficult to reach his beloved. Inaccessibility can have positive implications as well. The idea that the man has an exclusive relationship with his beloved can be taken positively to mean that she is inaccessible to others. In cultures or contexts in which a woman's virginity is valued, her physical inaccessibility to all men serves to preserve her chastity and, thus, may be viewed positively.

Ancient and Medieval Texts

> My sister bride is a closed garden, a garden[7] closed, a sealed spring (Song 4.12, Vulgate).

If we are to understand the background to fifteenth-century European art, we must also look at early and medieval Christian interpretations of the verse. Ancient and medieval Christian interpreters treat the love poetry of the Song of Songs allegorically. Earliest Christian exegesis of the Song of Songs understands the male lover of the Song to represent Christ and the female lover to represent the Church. This ecclesiological approach to the book dominated Christian interpretation for some time; in the Middle Ages, however, Christian liturgy and later Christian commentary came to understand the female lover of the Song as a representation of the Virgin Mary. In this Marian interpretation of the Song, Mary 'becomes the normative exemplar of the faithful souls that, taken collectively, constitute the Church'.[8] A few examples may serve to illustrate the range of interpretations.

In the fourth century, Ambrose reads the imagery as relating to virginity; however, he does not specifically connect the imagery of the Song of Songs to the Virgin Mary.

6. Elizabeth Huwiler, 'The Song of Songs', in Roland E. Murphy and Elizabeth Huwiler, *Proverbs, Ecclesiastes, Song of Songs* (New International Biblical Commentary; Peabody, MA: Hendrickson, 1999), p. 272: 'The verse intimates wasted potential and may be something of a taunt'.

7. The Septuagint and Vulgate translate 'garden', rather than 'pool'.

8. Richard A. Norris (ed. and trans.), *The Song of Songs Interpreted by Early Christian and Medieval Commentators* (Grand Rapids: Eerdmans, 2003), p. xix.

> 'A garden enclosed' [is virginity] because it is shut in on all sides by the wall of chastity. 'A fountain sealed up' is virginity, for it is the fount and wellspring of modesty that keeps the seal of purity inviolate, in whose source there may shine the image of God, since the pureness of simplicity coincides with the chastity of the body.[9]

Also in the fourth century, Gregory of Nyssa explains that the enclosed garden refers to 'purity of mind', rather than bodily chastity.

> Because a seal protects the inviolability of whatever it guards, it scares off thieves; everything not stolen remains unharmed for the master. Praise of the bride in the Song would then testify to her excellence in virtue because her mind remains safe from enemies and is guarded for her Lord in purity and tranquility.[10]

In the fifth century, Peter Chrysologus takes the imagery to refer to Mary's virginity when he writes, 'He so departed from the abode of the womb that the virginal door did not open, and what is sung in the Canticle of Canticles was fulfilled: "My sister, my spouse, is a garden enclosed, a garden enclosed, a fountain sealed up"'.[11]

In the twelfth century, Honorius of Autun interprets the verse allegorically to refer to the Church.

> In the garden herbal medicines grow, as well as a variety of flowers. The garden is the Church, in which there are the manifold virtues of the saints —the different sorts of herbs that provide cures for the different wounds of sinners. In this garden are a variety of flowers, which represent the different orders of the elect: martyrs, like roses; confessors, like violets; virgins, like lilies; and other believers, like other flowers. The gardener in this garden is Christ. He is also the Bridegroom, who when he plants by grace also irrigates by teaching. This garden is closed for the benefit of contemplatives—which means fortified against the attack of demons by an angelic guard. It is also closed for the benefit of those who lead the active life, for it is walled about by the defense that its teachers provide against heretics. In this garden the herbs and flowers are the individual believers, blooming with faith and good works.[12]

9. Ambrose, Letter 5, 'To Priests', in J. Robert Wright (ed.), *Ancient Christian Commentary on Scripture*. IX. *Proverbs, Ecclesiastes, Song of Solomon* (Downers Grove, IL: InterVarsity Press, 2005), p. 338.

10. Gregory of Nyssa, 'Homilies on the Song of Songs 9', in Wright (ed.), *Ancient Christian Commentary*, p. 338.

11. Peter Chrysologus, 'Sermon 145', in Wright (ed.), *Ancient Christian Commentary*, p. 339.

12. Honorius of Autun, *Expositio 2*, in Norris (trans. and ed.), *The Song of Songs*, p. 183.

For Honorius, imagery of the Church as an enclosed garden suggests that the Church is protected from the dangers of the larger world, just as, in a walled garden, the plants are protected from predators. In the language of Keel, the Church is 'inaccessible' to the temptations and dangers of the world. Other twelfth-century writers, however, equate the enclosed garden with the Virgin Mary. According to Ann Matter,

> A logical consequence of medieval fascination with the Song of Songs was an association of the Bride with a human, a woman, although a highly idealized figure, the Virgin Mary. This form of personification begins early in the Latin liturgical tradition, and gradually becomes a part of Song of Songs commentary.[13]

Already in the ninth-century pseudepigraphical work *Cogitis me*, attributed to Paschasius Radbertus, we see that the monk equates the Virgin Mary and the woman of the Song in a way that sets forth Mary as a spiritual model for the religious women to whom he is writing.

> Whence it is sung about her in those same Canticles: 'A garden enclosed, a fountain sealed, your shoots a paradise'. Truly a garden of delights, in which are planted all kinds of flowers, and the good scents of virtues; and so enclosed that it cannot be violated or corrupted by any trick of deceit.[14]

Thus, although some medieval interpreters begin to identify the woman of the Song with Mary, the mother of Jesus, they do so in such a way as to make Mary a model for other Christians. As Matter observes, 'the image of the Virgin Mary has no one fixed form, but changes shape from liturgy to commentary, from verse to verse. Mary is seen as at once the Church and the soul, the Bride, mother, and child of God'.[15]

One final medieval text sheds light upon the enclosed garden motif in Christian art. The *Speculum humanae salvationis*, a fourteenth-century compilation of events in the lives of Mary and Jesus, typologically connects Mary and the Song's enclosed garden. The *Speculum humanae salvationis*, often translated into English as *The Mirror of Salvation*,[16] is an anonymous medieval work that uses typology to relate people, stories, and objects from the Old Testament to the Christian story of salvation.[17]

13. E. Ann Matter, The *Voice of My Beloved: The Song of Songs in Western Medieval Christianity* (Philadelphia: University of Pennsylvania Press, 1990), p. 151.

14. Quoted in Matter, *The Voice of My Beloved*, p. 154.

15. Matter, *The Voice of My Beloved*, p. 168.

16. Or, 'The Mirror of Man's Salvation', or 'The Mirror of Human Salvation'.

17. This work was produced under the following titles, in addition to the Latin title, *Speculum humanae salvationis*: *Spieghel der menscheliker behoudenisse*, *Spiegel menschlicher Behältnis*, *Miroir de la Salvation humaine*, *Mirouer de la Redemption*, *Miroure of Mans Salucacienne*. See Adrian Wilson and Joyce Lancaster Wilson, *A Medieval*

Written in the first quarter of the fourteenth century, this work was widely disseminated in the late Middle Ages.[18] By the end of the fifteenth century, several hundred copies of the *Speculum* had been made, with some copies translated from the original Latin into German, Dutch, Czech, French, and English. Nearly all of these editions are illuminated.[19] Although the styles of visual interpretation differ, the illuminated manuscripts of the *Speculum* follow the same pattern of the original manuscript and interpret the text using the same iconographical subjects.[20] Today, more than three hundred fifty manuscripts exist, including both the original Latin and the various translations (although the autograph is not extant).[21] Editions of the *Speculum* consist of three different types: manuscripts, blockbooks, and incunabula (i.e. books printed before 1501).

It is commonly accepted that the *Speculum* was written for the use of monks and clerics in the education of the laity.[22] The *Speculum* itself draws upon older sources, including Josephus's *Antiquities of the Jews*, the twelfth-century *Historia scholastica* of Petrus Comestor (d. c. 1179), the thirteenth-century *Golden Legend* (c. 1260–1270) of Jacobus de Voragine, and the works of Thomas Aquinas (c. 1225–1274).[23]

Both the text and the illustrations of the *Speculum* offer a typological interpretation of the Bible, an approach that was common in the Middle Ages. Blockbook editions of the *Speculum* have twenty-nine chapters.[24] Each chapter has four illustrations. In all but the first two chapters and the last chapter, the first illustration is taken from the New Testament (or from a Christian apocryphal story) and the remaining three images are taken from the history of Israel found in the Old Testament (including the Apocrypha) and in other ancient and medieval sources. The Old Testament illustrations are interpreted as types of the Christian story of salvation. In the first two chapters, all eight illustrations are from the Old

Mirror: Speculum humanae salvationis, 1324–1500 (Berkeley: University of California Press, 1984), p. 9.

18. Wilson and Wilson, *A Medieval Mirror*, p. 216, note that the *Speculum* was the source for medieval tapestries at La Chaise-Dieu in the Auvergne; stained glass at Mulhouse, Colmar, and other towns in the Alsace; and sculptures at Vienne, near Lyon. Emile Mâle discusses the influence of the *Speculum* on French art in *Religious Art in France* (Princeton, NJ: Princeton University Press, 1986), pp. 220-30.

19. Wilson and Wilson, *A Medieval Mirror*, p. 10.

20. Wilson and Wilson, *A Medieval Mirror*, p. 10.

21. Wilson and Wilson, *A Medieval Mirror*, p. 24.

22. Wilson and Wilson, *A Medieval Mirror*, p. 24.

23. Wilson and Wilson, *A Medieval Mirror*, p. 25.

24. Older editions of the *Speculum* contain an additional sixteen chapters not included in the blockbook editions. See Wilson and Wilson, *A Medieval Mirror*, pp. 200-205.

Testament. The text and illustrations set the stage for the story of salvation by telling of the events that led to the human condition that necessitates the salvation offered through Christ. The eight illustrations are: the casting out of Lucifer from heaven, the creation of Eve from the side of Adam, God's admonition not to eat the fruit of the tree of knowledge of good and evil,[25] the temptation of Eve by the serpent, the eating of the fruit by Adam and Eve, the expulsion of Adam and Eve from the garden, life for Adam and Eve outside Eden, and, finally, Noah's ark.

For the author of the *Speculum*, as for many medieval authors and theologians, the Virgin Mary plays an important role in the history of Christian salvation. Thus, chapters 3–7 of the *Speculum* illustrate events in the life of Mary and the Old Testament events or subjects that prefigure Mary. Each chapter has four illustrations: the first illustration is taken from the life of Mary and the following three from the history of Israel. Chapter 3 illustrates the annunciation of the birth of Mary; chapter 4 illustrates the birth of Mary; chapter 5 portrays the presentation of Mary in the Temple; chapter 6, the marriage of Mary and Joseph; and chapter 7, which serves as a transition to the rest of the book, illustrates the annunciation to Mary of the birth of Jesus Christ.

In chapter 3 of the *Speculum*, we find the enclosed garden of the Song of Songs associated typologically with the annunciation of the birth of Mary. In illustrated editions of the *Speculum*, the first illustration of chapter 3 is that of the annunciation of Mary's birth to her parents. The second illustration is of the dream of King Astyages, whose daughter gave birth to the Persian King Cyrus, a story that can be found in the twelfth-century *Historia Scholastica* by Petrus Comestor. The image draws a typological connection between the two women who give birth to saviors. The third illustration of the chapter is of an enclosed garden, in which is located a sealed fountain. The text accompanying this illustration associates the enclosed garden and the annunciation of Mary's birth.

> Most assuredly, Solomon had foretold the coming of this daughter who was hallowed before birth; he called her an enclosed garden and a fountain sealed in the Canticle of Canticles (4.12). While her mother Anna bore her, the Holy Spirit pours grace into her soul and signs her with the seal of the Holy Trinity so that no sin ever defiles her. Truly, Mary, you are the garden of happiness and the unfailing fountain for the thirsting souls.[26]

25. This illustration is sometimes interpreted as the marriage of Adam and Eve. God appears to be officiating at the marriage of the first couple.

26. Albert C. Labriola and John W. Smeltz (trans.), *The Mirror of Salvation [Speculum humanae salvationis]: An Edition of British Library Blockbook G. 11784* (Pittsburgh, PA: Duquesne University Press, 2002), p. 23.

The chapter concludes with a fourth Old Testament type, the prophecy of Balaam in the book of Numbers. As do all the chapters in this work, this chapter concludes with a petition directed to Jesus: 'O good Jesus, give us this star [from Balaam's prophecy] to contemplate so we may merit to escape every peril'. Thus, the Virgin Mary, an enclosed garden, serves as a source of inspiration for the Christian who seeks to live a righteous life. In this way, the *Speculum* combines allegorical and tropological interpretations to portray the Virgin Mary as both the model for Christians to follow and the spiritual source for Christians who strive to live a Christian life.

What we see, then, in ancient and medieval commentary on the Song, is the interpretation of the woman as either the Church or Mary. Interpretation of the metaphor of the enclosed garden appears as purity of body, or more specifically, virginity, but also purity of mind, or moral character, and, even more broadly, as invulnerability to the temptations of the world.

The Enclosed Garden in Visual Art

Martin Schongauer (b. c. 1430, Colmar; d. 1491, Breisach)

The upper-Rhine artist Martin Schongauer portrays Mary and the Christ-child seated in an enclosed garden in several paintings and engravings.[27] Two engravings and a painting offer examples of the variation that occurs within the enclosed garden artistic tradition. In a 1490 engraving, *Madonna and Child in the Courtyard*, the Virgin Mary sits on the ground in an open courtyard that is empty except for one bare tree that is, perhaps, budding (Fig. 1).[28] On Mary's lap is the infant Christ. Behind her can be seen an expanse of wall that ends in a corner gate. The right angle formed at the gate suggests that the courtyard is enclosed, although we cannot see that it is actually walled in on four sides. The wall appears high, given the relative height of the gate in the corner. Mary and the Child are the central focus of the engraving, as is suggested by their relative size. Because the vegetation in this courtyard is minimal—all we can see are some tufts

27. The enclosed garden motif can be found in other artistic settings, including that of Mary and a unicorn in an enclosed garden, some annunciation representations, and some visual art portraying the assumption of Mary and the Immaculate Conception. In this essay, I discuss only examples of the Virgin Mary and the Christ-child in an enclosed garden.

28. James Snyder, *Northern Renaissance Art* (Upper Saddle River, NJ: Prentice–Hall, 2005), p. 259, describes the tree as 'dry' and 'leafless' and suggests that 'the dry tree reminds us that from its sterile roots new sap will soon flow now that the humble giver of life, Mary, sits beneath its branches'. It might also be argued that the tree is in bud, thus hinting at the future life made possibly by the Incarnation. Cheryl Exum (personal communication) suggests it may allude to Song 7.12: 'Let us go out early to the vineyards, and see whether the vines have budded'.

of grass and a tree—it might be argued that this engraving is not an example of an enclosed garden. Nevertheless, the scene contains the basic elements of the enclosed garden tradition: Mary and the Christ-child seated within an enclosed outdoor space that contains vegetation.[29] Schongauer has another engraving that locates Mary and the Christ-child in an enclosed garden, *Madonna on the Turfbench* (Fig. 2). Although the enclosed garden is portrayed quite differently in this engraving, the basic elements remain. Mary and Child are seated—here, Mary sits on a type of turfbench. Behind her is a fence. Not far behind the fence is a leafless tree. In the distance we see a building, perhaps a church, and boats on a river or lake. In this engraving, the Christ-child reaches out to an apple Mary holds in her hand.

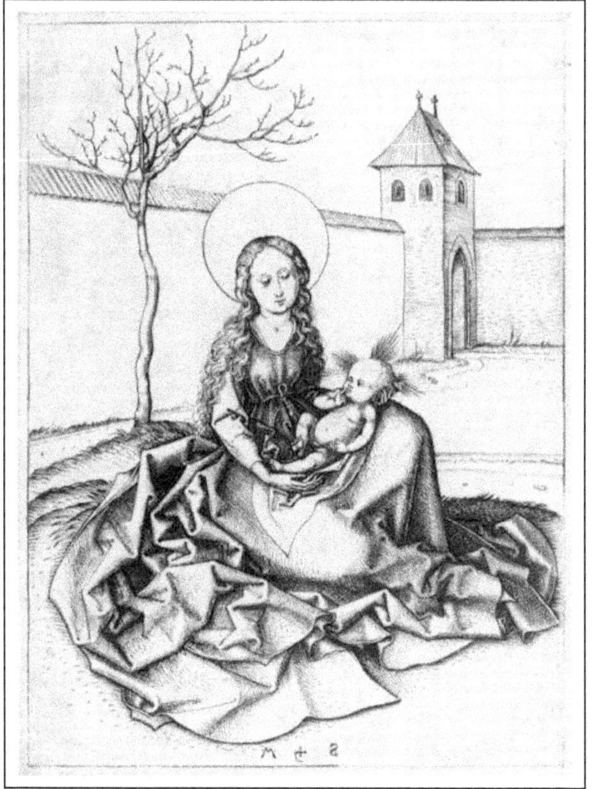

Figure 1. Martin Schongauer, *Madonna and Child in the Courtyard*, Kupferstichkabinett, Staatliche Museen zu Berlin. Photo: Bildarchiv Preussischer Kulturbesitz/Art Resource, NY

29. Snyder (*Northern Renaissance Art*, p. 259) considers this engraving an example of an enclosed garden.

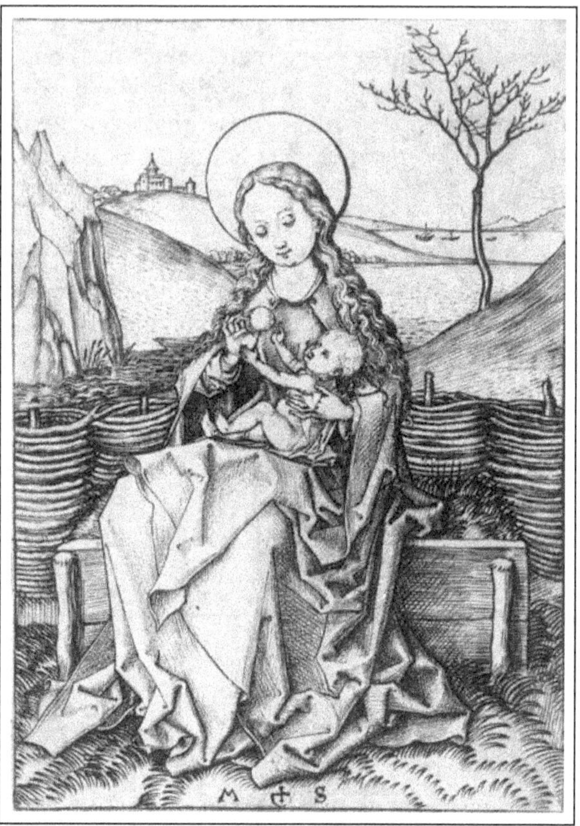

Figure 2. Martin Schongauer, *Madonna on the Turfbench*, Kupferstichkabinett, Staatliche Museen zu Berlin. Photo: Bildarchiv Preussischer Kulturbesitz/Art Resource, NY

Schongauer is perhaps better known for his painting *Madonna in the Rose Garden* (Fig. 3).[30] Like the engravings of Mary and the Christ-child, the painting portrays mother and child in an enclosed garden. Mary is again seated on a turfbench with the infant Christ in her arms, as in the second of the two engravings discussed above. The painting is otherwise quite different. Behind Mary and the Christ-child is a trellis of red and white roses. Next to Mary, we see a red peony. Other smaller flowers can be seen growing from the bench, and birds perch on the trellis and among the branches of the rosebush.

30. The original panel, now in the Eglise de Saint-Martin, in Colmar, France, is thought to have been cut down to its present form. A copy of the original painting can be seen in the Isabella Stewart Gardner Museum in Boston and may reflect the original form of Schongauer's work.

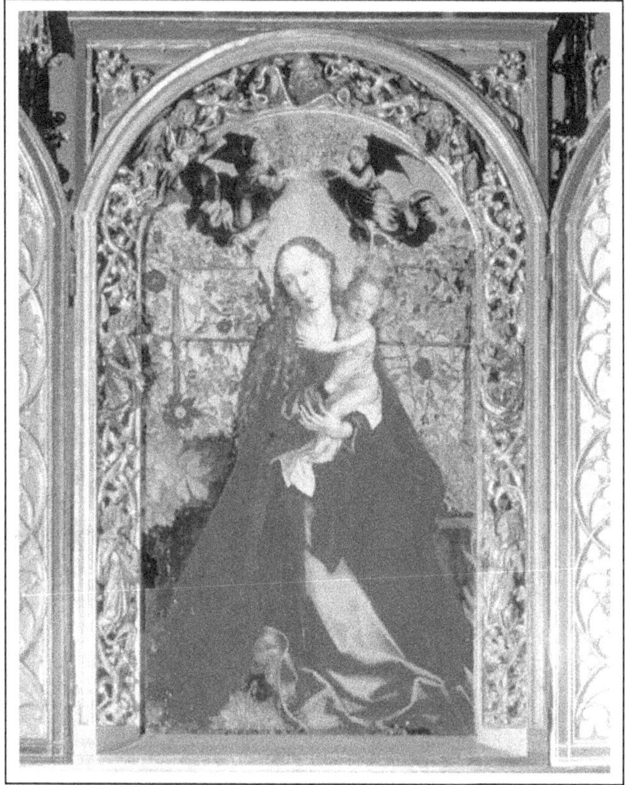

Figure 3. Martin Schongauer, *Madonna in the Rose Garden*,
Church of the Dominicans, Colmar. Photo: Snark/Art Resource, NY

In Schongauer's painting, two angels hold a crown above Mary's head, which is already framed by a gold halo. On the halo is inscribed *Me carpes genito tu qu(oque) o s(an)ctissi(m)a V(irgo)* ('Pick me also as your child, most blessed Virgin'), an element that establishes a relationship between the viewer and the subject.[31] The painting thus provides an opportunity for the viewer to reflect upon the relationship of the Virgin and Child and the redemptive possibilities offered by Mary, the mother of Jesus. The setting of this devotional painting in an enclosed garden contributes to the idea that it is desirable to establish such a personal relationship with Mary and the Christ-child. Mary, simultaneously the Savior's mother and the Church, offers to the viewer who reads this painting devotionally a safe space in a luxurious rose bower that offers protection from the dangers of the world.

31. Christian Heck, *The Virgin in the Rose Bush by Martin Schongauer* (Colmar: n.p., 1990), p. 12.

Stefan Lochner (c. 1400–1451), The Virgin in a Rose Bower

In this small devotional panel by the fifteenth-century northern-Rhine painter Stefan Lochner, Mary, the mother of Jesus, is seated low to the ground, on a red cushion (Fig. 4). Mary's facial features—her small mouth, straight nose, hooded eyes, and strong forehead—are typical of the Cologne school. The low wall behind Mary and the simple rose trellis together suggest that this scene is an enclosed garden. The gold background and the curtained frame also contribute to the viewers' sense that this scene is set apart from the rest of the world in a protected and enclosed space.

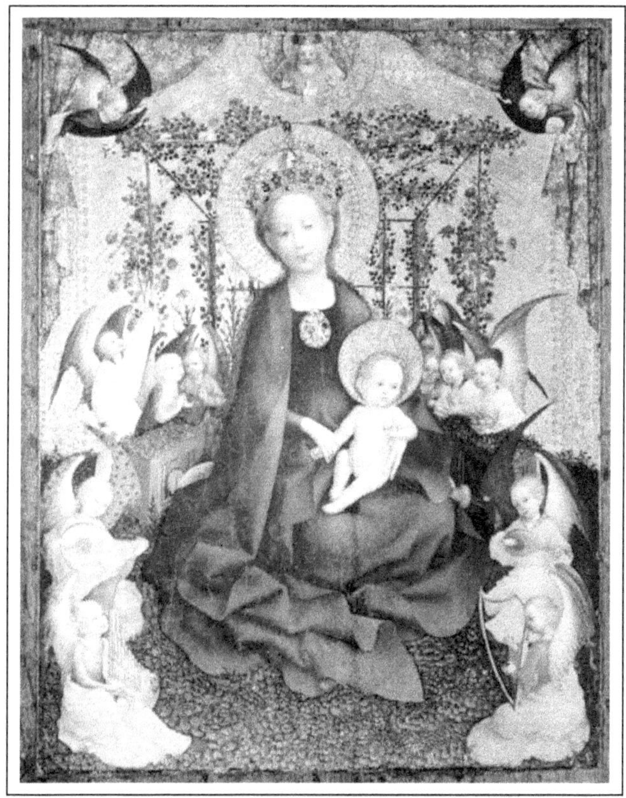

Figure 4. Stefan Lochner, *The Virgin in a Rose Bower*
Wallraf-Richartz-Museum, Cologne. Photo: Rheinisches Bildarchiv Köln

Like the painting by Schongauer, this panel is a devotional painting, rather than a narrative painting of a scene from the New Testament. Two angels pull open red brocade curtains, as if they are revealing a sacred scene to profane eyes. Julien Chapuis suggests the angels offer us a glimpse into paradise.[32] At the center of the painting is Mary, holding the Christ-child. Directly above Mary is God the Father, who looks down upon the scene as if peering out from heaven. We also see a dove, representing the Holy Spirit. Thus, at the center of this painting is the Trinity—Father, Son, and Spirit. Given Mary's centrality to the painting, however, it is almost as if the second member of the Trinity comprises both Mother and Son. Eleven angels encircle Mary and the Child, suggesting that this is a heavenly scene, rather than an earthly one. Four angels play musical instruments (perhaps to suggest the music of the heavenly spheres). Five kneel in adoration. One angel picks roses and one holds a basket of apples and offers an apple to the infant. The white and red roses on a trellis frame the woman's figure and give depth to the picture.

Lochner's painting is filled with symbolism.[33] Roses are Mary's flower. In general, red roses in Christian art symbolize martyrdom, white roses, purity. Mary's exemption from the consequences of original sin may be symbolized by thornless roses. A legend told by Ambrose reports that in the garden of Eden, roses grew without thorns. Red roses may symbolize the Passion, the adult Christ's blood shed for humanity, but also Mary's passion, which is her love for her son, who is also her Bridegroom.[34] The white roses of the trellis along with the lilies at the base of the trellis remind us of Mary's purity. Roses and lilies may remind modern viewers of the words of Song 2.1: 'I am a rose of Sharon, a lily of the valleys'.[35] Together, the violets and strawberry plants that cover the ground and the turfbench symbolize Mary's humility. A few daisies can also be seen, symbolizing the innocence of the Christ-child. Apples in the painting remind us of the garden of Eden and the fall from grace associated with the eating of the fruit of the tree of the knowledge of good and evil; however, when apples appear in association with Christ or with the Virgin Mary, they symbolize salvation. Thus, we are simultaneously reminded of the fall from grace in Eden and the redemption that is offered by the Christ-child.

Lochner's painting draws together two other seemingly disparate qualities or characteristics. Mary is seated low to the ground in front of the turfbench. Just visible are two corners of the red cushion on which she

32. Julien Chapuis, *Stefan Lochner: Image Making in Fifteenth-Century Cologne* (Turnhout: Brepols, 2004), p. 88.

33. On symbolism in Christian art, see George Ferguson, *Signs and Symbols in Christian Art* (New York: Oxford University Press, 1959); James Hall, *Dictionary of Subjects and Symbols in Art*; Gertrude Grace Sill, *A Handbook of Symbols in Christian Art* (New York: Simon & Schuster, 1975). On flowers and fruit in Western painting, see Celia Fisher, *Flowers and Fruit* (London: National Gallery Publications, 1998).

34. Chapuis, *Stefan Lochner*, p. 88.

35. The Vulgate makes no specific reference to a rose: *Ego flos campi, et lilium convallium* ('I am a flower of the field and a lily of the valleys').

sits. Along with the violets and strawberries on the ground, Mary's seated position low to the ground contributes to the notion of her humility. Other features of the painting, however, highlight the worthiness of this humble woman to bear the son of God and also suggest her status as Queen of Heaven. Although seated low on the ground, rather than on a throne, this woman wears a crown of diamonds, sapphires, rubies, emeralds, and pearls. Similarly, the gold of the background contributes to the impression that we are viewing royalty. Additionally, the scale of Mary's figure in this painting also counters the humility of her seated position: if she were to stand up, she would not fit within the picture.[36]

An interesting feature of Mary's adornment is her brooch, which portrays a seated maiden holding a unicorn, a medieval symbol of the Incarnation.[37] In some visual images of this scene, the maiden and unicorn are located in an enclosed garden.[38] Thus we have a typical enclosed garden scene encapsulated in the brooch worn by the Virgin, who is herself seated in an enclosed garden.

Four angels play musical instruments. Two play lutes, one plays a harp, and the fourth plays a portative organ. These instruments can symbolize love, but in the hands of angels, they are often featured in angelic concerts. From the fifteenth-century onward, artists portray angels playing instruments in celestial orchestras, usually in paintings that portray the Virgin Mary or the Virgin and Christ-child. Music often symbolizes love, so that in Lochner's painting the angelic orchestra both glorifies the Virgin Mary and acknowledges the love of Mother and Child, Bride and Bridegroom.[39]

In Stefan Lochner's *Virgin in the Rose Bower*, we have an image for devotion and meditation. The enclosed garden symbolizes purity, love, and protection, while calling to mind both the garden of Eden and the garden of the Song of Songs. This garden is located not in Eden, not in some earthly locale where two lovers meet, but in a heavenly realm, where this woman dwells, bound throughout time in a loving embrace with her infant son, who is both child and savior, just as she is both virgin and mother, humble young woman and Queen of Heaven.

36. Chapuis (*Stefan Lochner*, p. 88) makes this point.

37. Chapuis (*Stefan Lochner*, p. 89) has a close-up of the brooch.

38. See, for example, the second panel of the fifteenth-century altarpiece attributed to Martin Schongauer's workshop, which portrays the Virgin Mary seated within an enclosed garden. A unicorn stands with its front legs in Mary's lap. She touches the horn with her right hand and holds the unicorn's front legs in her left hand. To her right are Marian symbols, including a sealed fountain (*fons signatus*) and an angel with a horn at his lips from which unfurls a banderole announcing *Ave, Maria* ('Hail, Mary').

39. See Erika Langmuir, *Angels* (London: National Gallery Publications, 1999), pp. 15-17.

Master of the Paradise Garden
Little Paradise Garden (*Paradiesgärtlein*) is attributed to an artist who worked in southern Germany in the early fifteenth century and may have influenced the young Stefan Lochner (Fig. 5). It is thought to have been painted sometime in the second decade of the fifteenth century (c. 1410–20). In this painting, the space in which Mary and the Child are located is sharply defined by a crenellated wall. Although we see only two walls meeting at a right angle, we imagine that the garden pictured on the panel is completely enclosed by the wall. The greater realism of this painting may at first suggest a more naturalistic scene; however, we soon notice an angel seated among the people in the garden and, near him, a monkey and a small dragon.

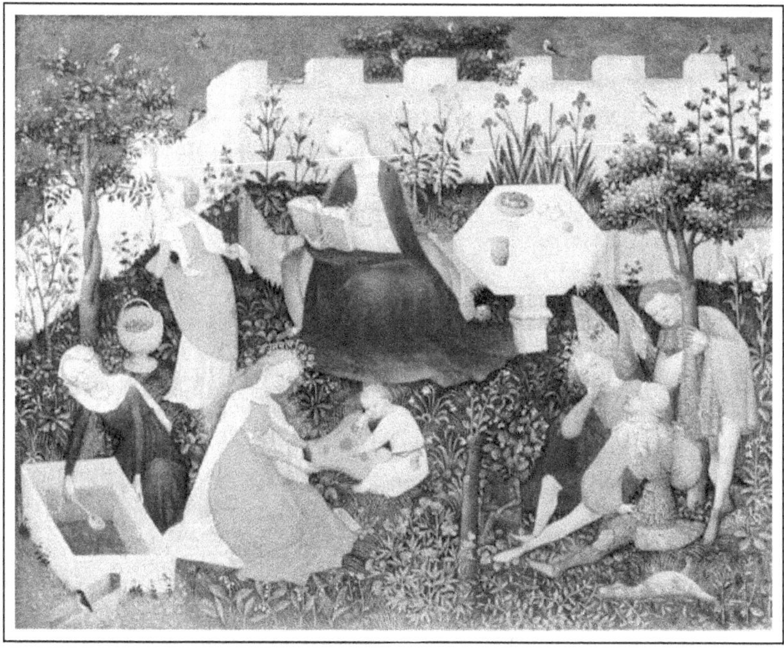

Figure 5. Master of the Paradise Garden, *Little Paradise Garden*, Städelsches Kunstinstitut, Frankfurt.
Photo: Foto Marburg/Art Resource, NY

The elements of this painting include eight people, two animals, a quantity of small birds, flowers, trees, a musical instrument, a basket, a table with food and drink set upon it, and a rectangular well, or container, of water. At the center of the painting is Mary, seated on a red cushion on the ground. Near her sits the Christ-child, strumming a stringed instrument held by a woman in a red dress. Mary sits quietly, reading. She is dressed in a gold-trimmed dress and a deep blue mantle and she wears a gold crown. To the right of Mary, we see a six-sided table, on which sit a basket of apples, a glass, and slices of a cut apple. The cup reminds us of the chalice. Six is the number of creation and may suggest that we are viewing 'new Eden', a paradise regained. The apples on the table call to mind the garden of Eden in Genesis, but also the garden of the Song of Songs.

> As an apple tree among the trees of the wood,
>   so is my beloved among young men.
> With great delight I sat in his shadow,
>   and his fruit was sweet to my taste (Song 2.3).

This garden is filled with an even greater variety of flowers than we saw in Lochner's rose bower.[40] In addition to roses, lilies, and daisies, we see other flowers that have symbolic meanings in Christian paintings. Along the back wall stand irises. In Latin and German the name for this flower means 'sword lily', an allusion to the Passion of Christ and the sorrows of Mary. In the foreground, we see lilies of the valley, often associated with Mary and, more specifically, the Immaculate Conception. Also in the foreground is a clump of peonies. The peony bloom resembles a rose, but the plant has no thorns. Thus, the peony can symbolize Mary, who is the 'rose without thorns'.

Although not a prominent feature of the painting, birds are perched on the wall and in the trees and can be seen in flight in the background. In Christian art, birds symbolize the spiritual, as Christian artists have retained antiquity's association of birds and the human soul or spirit. Some birds carry even more specific symbolic meanings. The goldfinch, for example, symbolizes the Passion, because of its fondness for eating thorns and thistles.

Fruit and fruit trees also play an important symbolic role in this painting. The artist has included two trees and a tree stump in this garden. The fruit tree on the left, with the twisted trunk, appears to be a cherry tree. In Christian symbolism, this sweet fruit symbolizes the rewards of heaven and is often referred to as the 'fruit of paradise'. The red color of the fruit may allude to the blood of Christ that brought the possibility of paradise to the world. The twisted trunk of the tree likely has symbolic import. It may suggest the two trees of Eden, which in paradise are conjoined as both knowledge and eternal life become possibilities for humans. The

40. In the museum catalogue, Bodo Brinkman states that there are twenty-four kinds of flowers and twelve species of birds in the painting (*Städelsches Kunstinstitut and Städtische Galerie Frankfurt*/M. [Prestel Museum Guide; Munich: Prestel, n.d.], p. 25).

intertwining of the trunks also calls to mind the artistic tradition in which the snake is portrayed wrapped around the trunk of the tree of knowledge in a similar way. In this paradise garden, however, there is no snake, and the dragon in the right foreground has been vanquished. If the figure clasping the trunk of the second tree is Saint Sebastian (see below), the second tree may allude to the cross, the tree on which Christ defeated evil. The tree stump in the foreground appears to have fresh growth sprouting from it and, thus, may symbolize the tree of Jesse, and the prophecy in Isa. 11.1-3 that a messiah will emerge from the line of Jesse, David's father. Hall observes that 'the prefigurative significance of the passage "a shoot shall grow from the stock of Jesse" ("*Egredietur virga de radice Jesse*") was plain to the medieval exegete because of the similarity of *virga*, a shoot, and *virgo*, a virgin'.[41]

As noted above, Mary and the Christ-child are located in the center of the painting. To their left are three male figures, clustered around a tree. To their right, are three women, each occupied with a particular task. James Snyder identifies the men as three militant saints: George, wearing chain mail and sitting near his slain dragon; Michael, located near the monkey, a symbol of human lust; and, possibly, Sebastian, standing by a tree.[42] The men appear relaxed, as if the dangers represented by the monkey and the dragon no longer require their militancy. If the standing male saint is, indeed, Sebastian, the wounds inflicted by arrows upon his body as he was bound to a tree are not visible, although the dotted red scarf he wears may allude to those wounds.

The female figures can also be identified as saints. St Dorothy picks fruit from the tree with a twisted trunk. Dorothy, a third-century Christian martyr, was mocked on her way to her execution by a scribe named Theophilus, who asked her to send flowers and fruit from the garden of Christ, her heavenly bridegroom. After Dorothy's death, a child delivered a basket of roses and apples to Theophilus, who then converted to Christianity (and was himself later martyred).[43] The saint with the musical instrument (a zither or psaltery) is thought to be St Cecilia (or St Catherine of Alexandria by some), who, beginning in the fifteenth century, is the patron saint of music. According to legend, Cecilia told her husband shortly after their wedding that she had taken a vow of chastity. Her husband, Valerian, asked to see the angel who watched over Cecilia. The angel later appeared, bearing two crowns of flowers, a crown of lilies for

41. Hall, *Dictionary of Subjects and Symbols in Art*, s.v. 'Jesse, Tree of'.

42. Snyder, *Northern Renaissance Art*, p. 65.

43. Hall, *Dictionary of Subjects and Symbols in Art*, s.v. 'Dorothea'; Ferguson, *Signs and Symbols in Christian Art*, p. 69.

Cecilia and a crown of roses for Valerian.[44] In Christian art, Cecilia may be shown listening to music, singing, or playing a musical instrument. In the *Little Paradise Garden*, she holds out a musical instrument to the Christ-child.

The identity of the third female saint seems less apparent, although she is usually identified as St Barbara, perhaps because the woman in the painting dips water from a well and St Barbara is associated with the chalice. Derek Pearsall and Elizabeth Salter identify her as St Martha, which is also possible, given that Martha is often pictured holding a ladle.[45] Like Mary, this woman is dressed in white and dark blue and the two women's facial features, hair color, and the tilt of their heads are nearly identical.

Although this garden is peopled by saints, the Virgin Mary, and the Christ-child, it portrays these figures as if they are relaxing in a pleasurable garden setting. The garden in this painting may reflect the actual practice of pleasure gardens and the courtly world of medieval Europe, and the enclosed garden tradition in visual art may have been influenced at least in part by the style of pleasure gardens of the artist's time.[46] Nevertheless, nearly every element of this scene is highly symbolic. The enclosed garden recalls both the garden of the Song of Songs and the garden of Eden.[47] It envisions paradise as a garden of great beauty, in which we may relax, read, and enjoy such pleasures as music and refreshments. The *Little Paradise Garden* draws upon traditional devotional themes and motifs—in addition to the enclosed garden motif, we see the traditional motif of Mary seated and reading combined with the tradition of the 'holy conversation', in which saints accompany the Virgin and Child. The unknown artist of this little work has, however, assembled these traditional motifs and themes in a charming and distinctive new way.

44. In the painting, this female figure wears a floral crown.

45. 'St. Martha draws water from a flowing well, as grace and truth is "drawn" from the Virgin, the "fountain of living waters" (Cant. 4.15)' (Derek Pearsall and Elizabeth Salter, *Landscapes and Seasons of the Medieval World* [London: Paul Elek, 1973], p. 109).

46. Brian E. Daley, 'The "Closed Garden" and the "Sealed Fountain": Song of Songs 4.12 in the Late Medieval Iconography of Mary', in *Medieval Gardens* (ed. Elisabeth B. MacDougall; Washington, DC: Dumbarton Oaks Research Library and Collection, 1986), pp. 255-78.

47. Helen Phillips ('Gardens of Love and the Garden of the Fall', in *A Walk in the Garden: Biblical, Iconographical and Literary Images of Eden* (ed. Paul Morris and Deborah Sawyer; JSOTSup, 136; Sheffield: Sheffield Academic Press, 1992], p. 209), suggests that the dead dragon in this painting symbolizes the garden of the Fall inverted.

Master of the House-Book (Active 1475–90 in Mainz)
A drypoint by a Rhenish artist known as the 'Housebook Master' offers another example of the enclosed garden motif.[48] In *The Holy Family in a Graden*, Joseph joins Mary and the Christ-child in the enclosed garden. Mary is seated on a low bench, of a type known as a 'turfbench'. The wall behind the family creates an enclosed garden, but the only plants we see, other than the tufts of grass on the bench and the ground, are a rosebush and an apple tree, just barely visible in the upper right corner of the picture. The Christ-child stands awkwardly, reaching down towards an apple on the ground, while at the same time, leaning against his mother's legs. Mary reaches both arms around her child as if to offer support. Joseph appears somewhat comically to be crouched by the bench, perhaps playing with the young child. Behind Mary there appears to be an opening into a building. In the background, we can see a tower, a harbor, and a church.

By contrast with the paintings by Schongauer and Lochner and with the *Little Paradise Garden*, this scene appears more natural; however, despite this more natural setting, this scene retains much of the same symbolism found in the works by Schongauer, Lochner, and the Master of the Paradise Garden. We see Mary and the Christ-child seated in an enclosed garden amid highly symbolic apples and roses. In this engraving, Mary's turfbench symbolizes her humility. There are naturalistic-looking buildings and a harbor in the background, which also have symbolic meanings.[49] A circular tower behind Mary may allude to the tower of David (*turris Davidica*), a Marian symbol that derives from Song 4.4, in which the man praises his lover by describing the beauty of her physical body:

> Your neck is like the tower of David,
> built in courses;
> on it hang a thousand bucklers,
> all of them shields of warriors.

As a Marian symbol, the tower of David symbolizes Mary's purity, virginity, and her strength to resist temptation. The harbor suggests that Mary is a safe haven for believers,[50] and an open door on the left may suggest

48. See Snyder, *Northern Renaissance Art*, p. 259, Fig. 12.28, for the visual image. It can also be reviewed at the Web Gallery of Art (www.wga.hu), where it is titled *The Holy Family with the Rose-Bush.*

49. Jane C. Hutchison (*The Master of the Housebook* [New York: Collectors Editions, 1972], p. 36), believes this work reflects the Marian iconographic tradition, but Snyder (*Northern Renaissance Art*, p. 259) questions this assumption.

50. Hutchison, *The Master of the Housebook*, p. 36: 'The Housebook Master's more explicitly harbor-like setting with its small fishing craft may well represent the Virgin in her role as *portus naufragantium*, as listed in the earliest recorded Marian litany, which was set down in Mainz in the twelfth century'.

that the Virgin and her son provide an open way into heaven (a *porta coeli*). In the upper right in the background, a church reminds us of Mary's role as *Maria ecclesia*. Even the way in which the artist portrays the three family members may contain symbolic elements. According to Hutchison, 'it must be remarked that the relative roles of Joseph and his spouse are still the medieval ones of court jester and Queen of Heaven'.[51] In the late fifteenth century, the view of Joseph was changing. Whereas earlier he was viewed as a buffoon, he later will be revered by the Church. This engraving reflects the older view.

This, too, is a devotional piece. Although the viewer may find it easier to identify with this scene of family harmony in a familiar outdoor setting, the traditional Marian symbols call to mind the idea that the beautiful young maiden portrayed in the picture brought into this world an innocent, young child who became the savior of the world. We see both the 'new Eve' and the 'new Adam', as the apples bring to mind Eden and the first Eve and Adam. Interestingly, in this engraving, only Mary has a halo.[52] Her relative size and the space that she occupies in this picture suggest that she is the central figure in this family portrait, even though her eyes direct our gaze downward to the child reaching for an apple. Joseph's gaze similarly focuses the viewer's attention upon the child.

Conclusion

The enclosed garden motif in Western art is often associated with the idea of Mary's virginity. There is, however, more going on in these paintings and engravings than simply that. The enclosed garden scenes are serene. Mary sits quietly, holding the Christ-child or, as in the *Little Paradise Garden*, reading, while the Child plays contentedly nearby. Flower symbols are Marian symbols, but they also remind us of two other gardens: the garden of Eden and the garden of the Song of Songs, whose garden is described in richer botanical detail than the garden of the book of Genesis. In the Song's garden, we find roses, lilies, and other exotic vegetation, unlike Eden's garden. The apples in these fifteenth-century paintings and

51. Hutchison, *The Master of the Housebook*, p. 36: 'There is still a slight aftertaste of mystery play buffoonery here despite the artist's gentler and more modern sense of humor'.

52. Hutchison (*The Master of the Housebook*, p. 35) comments on the seeming carelessness of the artist: 'With the insouciance typical of his latest period, the artist has permitted his Madonna to appear here in a halo that would have caused the meticulous Martin Schongauer to die of embarrassment—its rings are neither circular nor concentric… After Schongauer's machine-like precision, there is something quite appealing about a man who could turn out such a blatantly incompetent halo—who could forget, moreover, to provide one for the Christ Child.'

engravings remind us of both Eden and the Song's garden, where the woman describes her beloved as an apple tree. Thus, the enclosed garden offers new possibilities for the viewer who reads this visual art devotionally. As Helen Phillips points out, the typological association of Mary and Eve means that 'since Mary reverses Eve's action ("death by Eve, life by Mary"), she can be presented as an earthly garden transformed, Eden restored'.[53]

In Lochner's and Schongauer's paintings of Mary and the Christ-child in a rose garden and in the *Little Paradise Garden*, we are invited to look in upon paradise itself. In the *Little Paradise Garden*, we see a group of saints enjoying an afternoon in a beautiful garden, filled with all types of flowers and birds. In both of the rose garden paintings, angels pull open the curtains so that we mortals can look upon the beautiful Mary, who is both mother of God and bride of Christ. In Lochner's rose garden, Mary is seated low to the ground to represent her humility, but she is also crowned, wearing jewels, as befits a Queen of Heaven. In Schongauer's painting, Mary sits on a simple turfbench and the words above her head and below the crown being lowered by angels invite comment on how we are to read this painting. Thus, these devotional paintings and engraving invite Christian viewers to contemplate both the savior of the world and the woman who can intercede for the faithful in heaven, as they also remind viewers of the virtues of humility, purity, and love. As in Marian textual interpretations of the Song of Songs, these paintings comment on Mary's identity as both mother of God and bride of Christ and at the same time promote Mary's virtues of humility, chastity, and purity of mind. These paintings lure viewers into an enclosed garden, a sacred space that offers protection from the dangers of the world, a glimpse of paradise regained.

BIBLIOGRAPHY

Bergant, Diane, *The Song of Songs* (Berit Olam; Collegeville, MN: Liturgical Press, 2001).

Bloch, Ariel, and Chana Bloch, *The Song of Songs: A New Translation* (Berkeley: University of California Press, 1995).

Brinkman, Bodo, *Städelsches Kunstinstitut und Städtische Galerie Frankfurt/M.* (Prestel Museum Guide; Munich, Germany: Prestel, n.d.).

Chapuis, Julien, *Stefan Lochner: Image Making in Fifteenth-Century Cologne* (Turnhout: Brepols, 2004).

Daley, Brian E., 'The "Closed Garden" and the "Sealed Fountain": Song of Songs 4.12 in the Late Medieval Iconography of Mary', in *Medieval Gardens* (ed. Elizabeth

53. Phillips, 'Gardens of Love', p. 207.

MacDougall; Washington, DC: Dumbarton Oaks Research Library and Collection, 1986), pp. 255-78.

Exum, J. Cheryl, *Song of Songs, A Commentary* (Old Testament Library; Louisville, KY: Westminster / John Knox Press, 2005).

Ferguson, George, *Signs and Symbols in Christian Art* (New York: Oxford University Press, 1959).

Fisher, Celia, *Flowers and Fruit* (London: National Gallery Publications, 1998).

Hall, James, *Dictionary of Subjects and Symbols in Art* (London: John Murray, 1974).

Heck, Christian, *The Virgin in the Rose Bush by Martin Schongauer* (Colmar: n.p., 1990).

Hutchison, Jane C., *The Master of the Housebook* (New York: Collectors Editions, 1972).

Huwiler, Elizabeth, 'Song of Songs', in Murphy and Huwiler, *Proverbs, Ecclesiastes, Song of Songs*, pp. 219-90.

Keel, Othmar, *The Song of Songs: A Continental Commentary* (trans. Frederick J. Gaiser; Minneapolis: Fortress Press, 1994).

Labriola, Albert C., and John W. Smeltz (trans.), *The Mirror of Salvation [Speculum humanae salvationis]: An Edition of British Library Blockbook* G. *11784* (Pittsburgh, PA: Duquesne University Press, 2002).

Langmuir, Erika, *Angels* (London: National Gallery Publications, 1999).

Mâle, Emile, *Religious Art in France* (Princeton, NJ: Princeton University Press, 1986).

Matter, E. Ann, *The Voice of My Beloved: The Song of Songs in Western Medieval Christianity* (Philadelphia, PA: University of Pennsylvania Press, 1990).

Murphy, Roland E., *The Song of Songs: A Commentary on the Book of Canticles or the Song of Songs* (Hermeneia; Minneapolis: Fortress Press, 1990).

Murphy, Roland E., and Elizabeth Huwiler, *Proverbs, Ecclesiastes, Song of Songs* (New International Biblical Commentary; Peabody, MA: Hendrickson, 1999).

Murray, Peter, and Linda Murray, *Oxford Dictionary of Christian Art* (London: Oxford University Press, 1996).

Norris, Richard A. (trans. and ed.), *The Song of Songs: Interpreted by Early Christian and Medieval Commentators* (Grand Rapids: Eerdmans, 2003).

Pearsall, Derek, and Elizabeth Salter, *Landscapes and Seasons of the Medieval World* (London: Paul Elek, 1973).

Phillips, Helen, 'Gardens of Love and the Garden of the Fall', in *A Walk in the Garden: Biblical, Iconographical and Literary Images of Eden* (ed. Paul Morris and Deborah Sawyer; JSOTSup, 136; Sheffield: Sheffield Academic Press, 1992), pp. 205-19.

Pope, Marvin, *Song of Songs: A New Translation with Introduction and Commentary* (Anchor Bible, 7C; Garden City, NY: Doubleday, 1977).

Schiller, Gertrud, *Iconography of Christian Art*, I (Greenwich, CT: New York Graphic Society, 1971).

Sill, Gertrude Grace, *A Handbook of Symbols in Christian Art* (New York: Simon & Schuster, 1975).

Snyder, James, *Northern Renaissance Art: Painting, Sculpture, the Graphic Arts from 1350 to 1575* (Upper Saddle River, NJ: Prentice–Hall, 2005).

Wilson, Adrian, and Joyce Lancaster Wilson, *A Medieval Mirror: Speculum humanae salvationis, 1324–1500* (Berkeley: University of California Press, 1984).

Wright, J. Robert (ed.), *Ancient Christian Commentary on Scripture.* X. *Proverbs, Ecclesiastes, Song of Solomon* (Downers Grove, IL: InterVarsity Press, 2005).

FRAMING JUDITH: WHOSE TEXT, WHOSE GAZE, WHOSE LANGUAGE?

Ela Nutu

The apocryphal book of Judith presents us with an idealized female character. She is beautiful, wise, devout, loyal, generous and courageous, and she saves the Israelites from, at best, colonialization, at worst, annihilation at the hands of the Assyrian armies led by Holofernes. Judith saves her people by killing Holofernes, indeed decapitating him with his own sword. In the text, Judith is left alone with Holofernes in his tent after an evening of celebrations. In ch. 13 we read that he was 'stretched out on his bed, for he was overcome with wine' (Jdt. 13.2). Taking hold of Holofernes' sword, which was hanging from the bedpost near his head, Judith 'came close to his bed and took hold of the hair of his head and said, "Give me strength this day, O Lord of Israel!" Then she struck his neck twice with all her might and thus cut off his head' (vv. 6-8). Judith's maidservant had been waiting outside the bedchamber all this time, and when Judith comes out with the head of Holofernes, the servant places it in her food bag (vv. 9-10). They make it back to Bethulia safely, and Judith becomes a revered figure among the Israelites.

The Christian Church developed the character of Judith by associating her metaphorically and iconographically with Esther, Jael and, most importantly, with Mary the mother of Jesus. With Esther, because she too delivers her people from annihilation.[1] Without going too much into it, I would suggest that, when compared with Judith, Esther occupies a position that is culturally unchallenging. In order to achieve her goal, which in itself was not of her own creation but rather Mordecai's, she relies on her husband's power and authority. Some might say that so does Judith, for she is spiritually 'married' to God, and her deed is presented as performed under the auspices of God. Yet Judith's character is more complex than Esther's and one cannot escape the fact that Judith kills, and she does so sword in hand.

1. See in particular Alice Bach, *Women, Seduction, and Betrayal in Biblical Narrative* (Cambridge: Cambridge University Press, 1997).

Because of this direct killing, Judith has been paired also with Jael. While not in the leading female role (which is reserved for Deborah), Jael performs a murder similar to Judith's 'bedroom killing'. While Sisera, the Canaanite general, is asleep in her tent, Jael kills him by driving a tent peg through his temple (Judg. 4.22). Like Esther, Jael's character is limited when compared to Judith. Not only is Sisera already defeated, and thus Jael's violent act becomes less important in its political consequences than that of Judith, but Jael's choice of murder weapon, the tent peg, is intrinsically domestic, womanly. Judith's weapon, the sword of her enemy, is both male and political.

Judith's association with Mary is primarily due to her preferred and prolonged widowed status, which acts as reinstated virginity. Like Mary, Judith is seen to birth salvation; her celibate status becomes closely connected to the safety of her people, and the text reassures us that 'no one ever again spread terror among the Israelites during the lifetime of Judith, or for a long time after her death' (Jdt. 16.25). Furthermore, Uzziah praises Judith upon her return to Bethulia, and his words echo Mary's song, the Magnificat, in Lk. 1.46-55. Uzziah declares, 'O daughter, you are blessed by the Most High God above all other women on earth' (Jdt. 13.18). Judith is sold as a virtuous heroine, and an asexual one at that. Jerome declares, 'I see her hand armed with the sword and stained with blood. I recognise the head of Holofernes which she has carried away...Here a woman vanquishes men and chastity beheads lust'.[2] Decapitating the sin of lust is only another way of saying that Judith castrated Holofernes; the association between decapitation and castration is a generally established psychoanalytical motif.

Visually Judith became in the middle ages the personification of Virtue, Chastity and Humility.[3] In the twelfth-century manuscript *Speculum virginum*, the illumination 'Humilitas and Virtuous Women' shows Judith and Jael together, stepping on Holofernes and Sisera respectively (much like Christ on death in representations of his resurrection), while in the centre *Humilitas* puts a sword through *Superbia*. In another manuscript, dated from the late tenth, early eleventh century, which provides illustrations for the *Psychomachia of Prudentius* (a Latin poem, dated c. 348 CE), *Humilitas* is shown holding the severed, disproportionately large head of *Superbia* in a composition that becomes typical of representations of Judith with the head of Holofernes. In this tradition, Judith had become *Humilitas*.

2. Jerome, 'Letter LIV', *Patrologia latina* (Paris, 1864), XII, par. 16.

3. For more on the treatment of Judith in literary sources, see Mary D. Garrard, *Artemisia Gentileschi: The Image of the Female Hero in Italian Baroque Art* (Princeton, NJ: Princeton University Press, 1989), pp. 278-95.

Yet Judith is a complex character, and she may be more credible as the embodiment of a number of biblical women, namely Esther, Jael and Deborah. She is beautiful like Esther, wise and strong like Deborah and murderous like Jael. By the nature of her deed, she may resemble other characters, too, like Salome, with whom she is sometimes artistically confused[4]—they both make men's heads roll—perhaps even Delilah, for she also cuts—if not Samson's head, then his hair and his power, so his phallic credentials. Judith is certainly not simply *Humilitas*. Or *Fides*. Or *Sobrietas*. She is all these, and she also kills. She cuts a man's throat in cold blood. How is this different from the deeds of biblical women like Salome and Delilah, who are instead demonised? Judith's means of infiltrating the Assyrian camp rely heavily on her looks, for the text informs us that she had 'special beauty' (Jdt. 11.21). She was knowingly alluring, and she uses the power this gives her to subject and destroy Holofernes. She may not perform a 'dance of death' like Salome, but she does adorn herself to the same purpose. Perhaps she only uses what God gave her. Did God make her a *femme fatale*, a deadly woman?[5] Is this the reason why no one gets to marry her in the end, despite her many suitors? Is she that dangerous? Perhaps the only difference between Judith, Salome and Delilah is, as Alice Bach would declare, that the latter simply 'kill the wrong men'.[6] Delilah and Salome destroy biblical heroes, and so they become associated with the enemies of the people of the Book.

Judith's multiple identity seems too complex for her own skin. On the one hand, she emerges as the prototype of female empowerment, the *femme forte*, who demonstrates that looks and brains, as well as a strong arm, can go together. Perhaps for that reason women painters (and I concentrate here on Italian Renaissance, Baroque and Mannerist painters) have shown a certain taste for the book of Judith; among them Lavinia Fontana, Artemisia Gentileschi, Elisabetta Sirani and Fede Galizia, who turn to Judith for inspiration. What interests me in this brief study is whether their representations are any different from those of their male contemporaries also painting Judith. Are they perhaps manifestations of

4. See in particular the work of Gustav Klimt, whose Judith paintings have been the subject of confusion. Klimt's *Judith I* (1901) was first exhibited as *Salome*, while Klimt was still alive and despite its being framed in the original golden frame embossed with 'Judith and Holofernes' (*Judith I* is currently in the Österreichische Galerie Belvedere, Vienna). Klimt's second Judith painting, *Judith II/Salome* (1909), is even now catalogued under both titles (currently in the Galleria Internazionale d'Arte Moderna Ca'Pesaro, Venice).

5. A propos Margarita Stoker's brilliant treatment of the narrative; M. Stocker, *Judith, Sexual Warrior: Women and Power in Western Culture* (New Haven: Yale University Press, 1998), p. 3.

6. Bach, *Women, Seduction, and Betrayal*, p. 186.

feminist proclivity,[7] examples of *écriture féminine*, or are these women's voices shut inside the Language of the Father, the 'spurious phallocentric performing theatre' of a male-dominated industry?[8]

The Female 'I'/Eye

Lavinia Fontana (1552–1614), born and raised in Bologna (a major Renaissance art centre), is considered the first woman artist to become a successful professional painter. Taught by her father, Prospero Fontana (1512–1597), a renowned Bolognese fresco painter, Lavinia received some of the most prestigious commissions while in Bologna and then, because of her reputation, she moved to Rome in 1604 at the invitation of Pope Clement VIII, where she became an established portraitist at the Vatican. As an only child, she supported her parents later in life, and as wife and mother she supported her husband and their eleven children.[9] In his 1568 volume of the *Lives of the Artists*, Giorgio Vasari identified Lavinia as a highly educated woman, having studied at the University of Bologna, where she became a 'dottoressa', or doctor of letters, in 1580.[10]

Lavinia's two Judith paintings date from before her move to Rome. The first, *Judith with the Head of Holofernes* (1600), was commissioned by a widowed noblewoman from Bologna, Constanza Bianchetti Bargellini (Fig. 1).[11] It is possible that for Lavinia's patron, Judith was meant to exemplify virtuous widowhood. Adorned in lavish attire and splendid jewels (in keeping with the text, which tells us that she had abandoned her widow's clothes for the banquet; Jdt. 10.3-4), Judith stands triumphant, holding the head of Holofernes by the hair with her left hand and his sword with her right. She looks straight at the viewer, with no distinct emotion. Her face is resolute yet calm and distinguished. All the while, her left thigh emerges suggestively from the vulval folds of her red garment, in direct line with the erect sword. In the background, Judith's maidservant (here young and attractive, generally a rather unusual

7. As Griselda Pollock might suggest; see her *Visions and Difference: Femininity, Feminism and Histories of Art* (London: Routledge, 1988).

8. The expression belongs to Hélène Cixous, 'The Newly Born Woman', in *The Hélène Cixous Reader* (ed. Susan Sellers; London: Routledge, 1994), pp. 36-55 (41).

9. Katherine A. McIver, 'Lavinia Fontana's "Self-Portrait Making Music"', *Woman's Art Journal* 19 (1998), pp. 3-8 (3).

10. Giorgio Vasari, *The Lives of the Most Eminent Painters, Sculptors, and Architects* (trans. Gaston du Vere; New York: Knopf, 2nd edn, 1996), p. 918; McIver, 'Lavinia Fontana', p. 3.

11. Caroline P. Murphy, *Lavinia Fontana: A Painter and Her Patrons in Sixteenth-century Bologna* (New Haven: Yale University Press, 2003), pp. 41-43.

occurrence) smiles knowingly—if not seductively—while holding a basket ready for the head dangling in front of her.[12] The rather big, disproportionate head of Holofernes looks ordinary, somewhat remote in its peaceful demeanour. There is no blood in this picture.

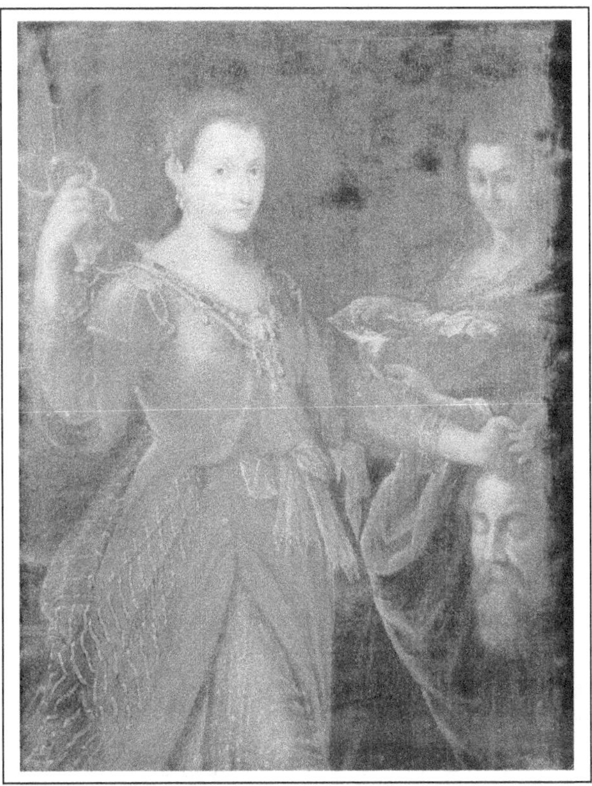

Figure 1. Lavinia Fontana, *Judith with the Head of Holofernes*, Musei Civici d'Arte Antica, Museo Davia Bargellini, Bologna

12. Among art historians, the maid is known as 'Abra'. This is an unfounded tradition, for the text does not name Judith's servant. The only way this tradition could have been established is by mistaking for a name the common noun ἅβρα (*habra*) used by the LXX translation of the book of Judith, meaning 'favourite/faithful servant/slave'. I will not perpetuate this tradition, even though it is tempting to personalize the maid by giving her a name. The same LXX term, ἅβρα, is used in Gen. 24.61 of Rebekah's maidservants whom she takes with her upon her betrothal, in Exod. 2.5 of the female slave whom Pharaoh's daughter sends to collect Moses' basket from among the reeds, and in Est. 2.9 and 4.4 of Esther's slaves, who served her while in the king's harem and after she became queen.

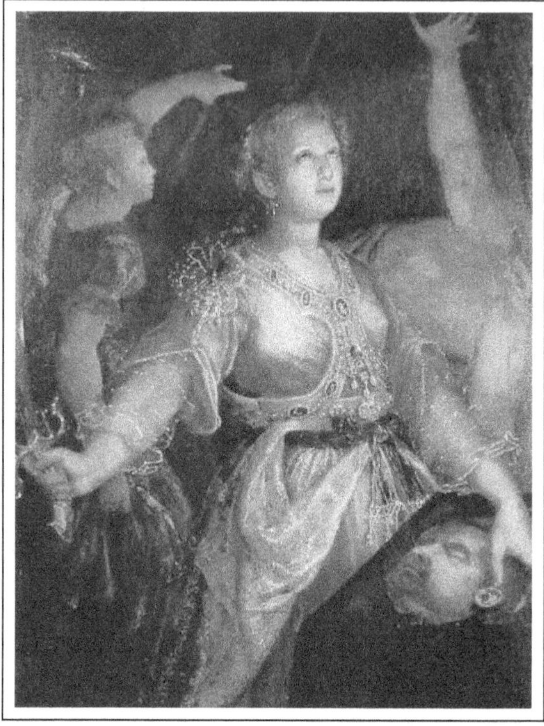

Figure 2. Lavinia Fontana, *Judith with the Head of Holofernes*, Oratorio dei Pellegrini, Bologna. By kind permission of MiBAC-Archivio Fotografico Soprintendenza al Patrimonio Artistico, Storio e Demoetnoantropologico di Bologna

The other of Lavinia Fontana's Judith paintings (c. 1600) is quite different (Fig. 2). This Judith is captured in a moment of thanksgiving. She lifts her eyes up to heaven, and it appears that God responds to her call. She is bathed in divine light, indicating the presence or the blessing of the divine. Judith holds Holofernes' sword—which is here identical in its design to the sword in the Bargellini painting—in her right hand and his head in her left. What is rather unique to this painting is that Holofernes' head rests on what looks like a makeshift altar, covered in black cloth. Judith's fingers are entangled in Holofernes' hair, but not in a possessive gesture. She appears to make a sacrifice to God; the head is her offering. Behind Judith, her maidservant (also young here) seems to be engaged in a post-mortem dance with Holofernes' headless torso. They face each other, and their arms are in the air, in a somewhat mimicking gesture, almost closing in towards a touch. Yet their hands clutch not at each other. Holofernes seems to be frozen in a defensive gesture, macabre in its timing, for his head already lies away from his body. This gesture is angry and threatening at the same time, aimed at Judith's God, Holofernes' arm paralleling the trajectory of Judith's gaze. Meanwhile the maidservant pulls down Holofernes' canopy, a further symbol of his status, his authority. In the text, it is Judith who tears the canopy, and it is that which she presents to God as a 'votive offering' along with the spoil in ch. 16 (v. 19).

Lavinia Fontana's Judiths are women of both beauty and strength, whom she empowers further by allowing them to look straight into the eyes of either the viewer—and thus reverse the power of the possessive, subjecting gaze—or God himself—and thus appropriate a superior spiritual status. Interestingly, it is believed that Lavinia modelled the Bargellini Judith on herself at a younger age.[13] An earlier self-portrait, *Self-Portrait at the Keyboard with a Maidservant* (1577), now in the Galleria dell'Accademia Nazionale di San Luca, Rome, shows a striking resemblance between Lavinia and Judith.

The Baroque painter Artemisia Gentileschi (1593–1653) is also said to have modelled her Judiths on herself, evident when one compares the paintings depicting the biblical heroine with her *Self-Portrait as the Allegory of Painting* (c. 1630), now in the Royal Collection, Windsor Castle. The daughter of a successful artist, like Lavinia Fontana—and indeed the majority of Italian women painters of the sixteenth and seventeenth century: Barbara Longhi (1552–1638) was the daughter of the painter Luca Longhi of Ravena; Marietta Tintoretto (1554–1590), daughter of Jacopo Tintoretto; Fede Galizia (1578–1630) of Milan, born to Nunzio Galizia—Artemisia asserts herself as a professional painter despite the fact that her training was meant to assist her entry into a convent (this way she could be accepted with a smaller dowry).[14] She worked in Naples, Florence, Rome, Genoa, even London for a period. Like Lavinia, Artemisia also turned repeatedly to the book of Judith for inspiration.

Artemisia's first interpretation of the narrative, *Judith Beheading Holofernes* (Fig. 3), painted around 1611/1612 and now in Naples, at the Museo Nazionale di Capodimonte, depicts its protagonist as a strong woman. She holds both Holofernes' head and his sword very tightly while performing the killing without a flicker. Her face is calm, and she seems unperturbed by the blood flowing from the neck of her victim, caking the bed sheets. Yet her fetching dress bears no spot. There is not one drop of blood on Judith, and this is meant to mark her 'innocence'. Like Lavinia's second Judith (Fig. 2), this Judith has God on her side, and, though her deed is evil in isolation, its end justifies it: the Israelites are saved. Judith's killing is divine retribution.

13. Murphy, *Lavinia Fontana*, pp. 154-55.
14. Murphy, *Lavinia Fontana*, pp. 14-15.

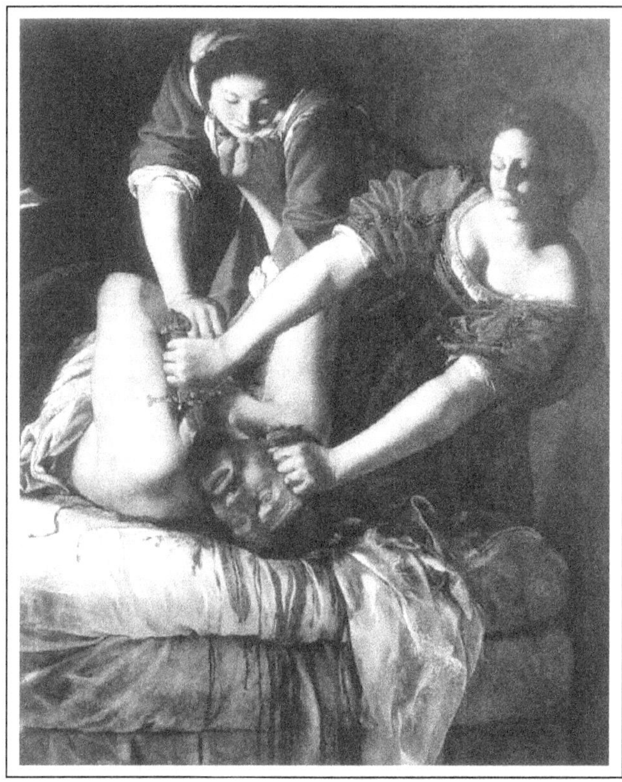

Fig. 3. Artemisia Gentileschi, *Judith Beheading Holofernes*, Museo Nazionale di Capodimonte, Naples. By kind permission of Fototeca della Soprintendenza Speciale per il Polo Museale Napoletano

Artemisia goes further in regards to the maid than Lavinia, whose maid either pulls down Holofernes' canopy (in the second painting) or stands happily by, keeping the food basket ready for the head (in the Bargellini painting). Artemisia has the maid help out in the murder. The servant holds Holofernes down while Judith cuts off his head. The presence of the maid detracts from Judith's crime by confusing the balance of guilt in the work. Holofernes' dying struggles are directed at the maid, and his right hand is clasping at the maid's neck and not Judith's. The maid's red dress even mirrors the blood of the dying man. By contrast, Judith holds Holofernes at arm's length literally, and she looks down at him with disdain. Furthermore—and this is an intriguing choice for Artemisia—Holofernes lies on his bed naked under the sheets, a detail which would compromise Judith if she were alone. The text does indicate that Judith lies down at Holofernes' feet in his tent, something which makes the

Assyrian rather giddy and so he drinks 'a great quantity of wine, much more than he had ever drunk in any one day since he was born' and becomes, as the text puts it, 'dead drunk' (12.15-20; 13.2). However, even though feet and genitals have been closely associated in Hebrew Bible tradition, at no point in the text are we led to believe that Holofernes gets undressed, or that there is some heavy petting going on before Judith kills him (as implied by other depictions of the narrative). In the text Judith declares her innocence openly, upon her return to Bethulia: 'As the Lord lives, who has protected me in the way I went, I swear that it was my face that seduced him to his destruction, and that he committed no sin with me, to defile and shame me' (Jdt. 13.6). Artemisia is very careful to protect Judith's reputation, her marked virtue.

And yet, in the later, revised version of this painting (between 1612–1621) now at the Ufizzi (Fig. 4), which is quite similar despite Artemisia's protestations in letters to her patrons that she never repeated 'the same design...not even one hand',[15] the blood spatter is more pronounced, and one can see the blood gushing towards Judith. A few drops end up on the maid's arm and Judith's breast and light dress. Why does Artemisia allow the blood to taint her heroine? Is it merely due to her Baroque, indeed Caravaggesque, commitment to realistic depiction? (Not that this is necessarily realistic; we're only talking about a few, miniscule blood drops here.)

In the Ufizzi version the collaboration between the two women seems more evident. The maidservant is closer to her mistress, the triangulation with Holofernes more balanced (almost equilateral), and so their partnership seems more synchronised here. Furthermore, their clothes are painted in similar—if not identical—colours, and their forearms are exposed to the same degree. It is as if we are looking at one woman with two torsos, a phantasmatic woman with the strength of two. Yet class distinction is also clearer in this painting. While in the Naples version Judith wears no jewellery, and her blue dress is only slightly more refined than the red dress of her servant, in the Ufizzi version she is rather undoubtedly the mistress. Judith's hair is tidier, her coiffure more elaborate, and her left arm is adorned by a bracelet. The maid's head is bound in a more evident turban, emphasising her inferior status. Why does Artemisia include these changes? Only to please her patron, the Grand Duke Cosimo II de' Medici? Or are we meant to witness an attempt to add femininity to the composition? What of Judith's frown, not present in the Naples version?

15. In her letter to Don Antonio Ruffo dated 7 August, 1649, cited in Ann Sutherland Harris and Linda Nochlin, *Women Artists: 1550–1950* (Los Angeles: Los Angeles County Museum of Art, 1976), p. 119.

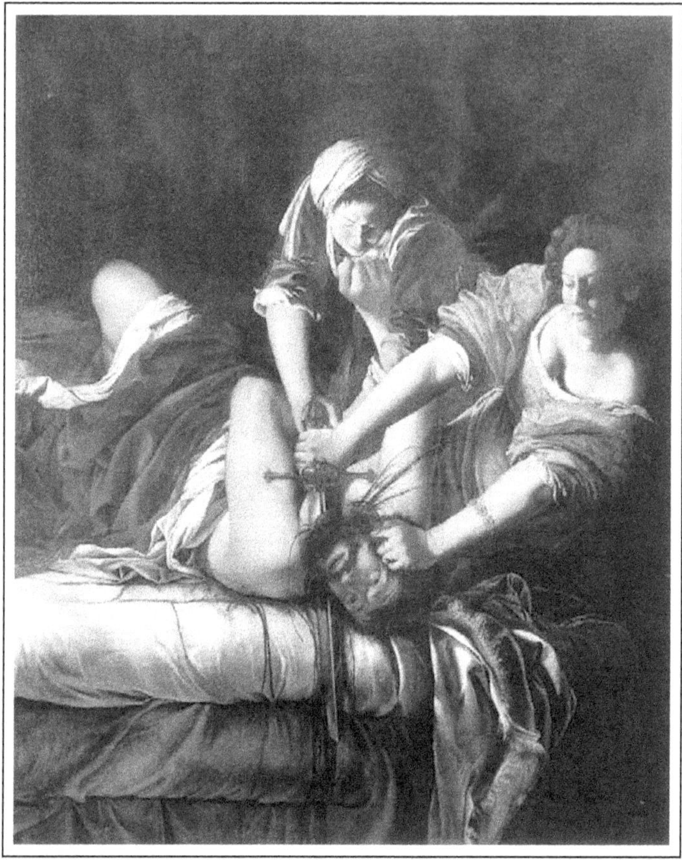

Figure 4. Artemisia Gentileschi, *Judith Beheading Holofernes*, Galleria degli Uffizi, Florence. By kind permission of Ministero dei Beni e delle Attività Culturali

One of the most disturbing elements of the painted narrative, present in both compositions, is the depiction of Holofernes' naked arms. They have been said to pose like thighs, here forced open by the maid in order for Judith to perform the castration violently. Is this a cathartic, subverted re-enactment of Artemisia's alleged rape by her art teacher, Agostino Tassi? Tassi had been a partner of Artemisia's father, Orazio, on a number of commissions. He was a violent man, who had already been convicted of arranging his wife's murder. He was alleged to have raped Artemisia and then promised to marry her, which he did not. Orazio took Tassi to court over the 'sverginamento' of his daughter and the theft of a number of paintings. The trial lasted five months, during which Artemisia was tortured with the thumb-screw, a contemporary method for lie detection.

She insisted that she had been raped, a fact that Tassi denied. A month after the trial Artemisia was married to a Florentine, Pietro Antonio di Vicenzo Stiattesi, and moved to Florence. Tassi spent eight months in prison but was finally acquitted, which had a damaging effect on Artemisia's reputation.[16]

It seems inevitable for many critics to include Artemisia's private life in the making of her art.[17] And with good reason. Is it reasonable to expect that an artist's genius be created in a vacuum? It is probable to assume, therefore, that Artemisia allowed some of her emotions to be expressed through her work, more notably her desire to establish her artistic identity as separate from her identity as a woman with a troubled past. It is telling that she chose a number of female heroic characters for her subjects. She painted not only Judith but also *Susanna and the Elders* (collection of Graf von Schönborn-Wiesentheid, Pommersfelden), *Minerva* (Soprintendenza alle Gallerie, Florence), *The Penitent Magdalen* (Palazzo Pitti, Florence), *Lucretia* (Palazzo Cattaneo-Adorno, Genoa) and *Cleopatra* (Amadeo Morandotti, Milan), all women who excelled in some way. Although Artemisia's women have been deemed by critics as 'gory', 'animalistic', 'buxom' and 'sullen',[18] I must confess that my opinion differs considerably. What is refreshing about Artemisia's women is that they are not idealized to the point of caricature, as is so common.

Returning to her Judith paintings, I find fascinating Artemisia's attitude towards Judith's virtue. A few drops of blood in the Uffizi painting, then a turned look. In *Judith and Her Maidservant* (c. 1612/1613), also in Florence but at Palazzo Pitti, Artemisia moves away from the tent of Holofernes and captures the two women during their flight back to Bethulia (Fig. 5). Artemisia holds Holofernes' sword casually on her shoulder, while the maidservant is burdened with his head, which she carries in the food basket. Both women seem to have been startled (by a noise?), and so look back towards the Assyrian camp to check whether their deed has been discovered, whether Assyrian soldiers are closing in. Judith holds the servant by the shoulder with her left hand, in an intimate, supportive gesture. With her right hand, Judith holds Holofernes' sword on her shoulder. This beautiful painting, masterfully executed, depicts Judith in a moment of vulnerability, of brief yet real panic, a moment of frozen breath. Artemisia further develops the idea of danger by

16. Harris and Nochlin, *Women Artists*, p. 118.

17. Griselda Pollock, 'Feminist Dilemmas with the Art/Life Problem', in *The Artemisia Files: Artemisia Gentileschi for Feminists and Other Thinking People* (ed. Mieke Bal; London: University of Chicago Press, 2005), pp. 169-206.

18. Rozsika Parker and Griselda Pollock, *Old Mistresses: Women, Art and Ideology* (London: Pandora, 1981), p. 21.

allowing the dark metal of the sword to be so close to Judith's own neck, which is open, unprotected. Holofernes' head is unveiled only for the sake of the viewer, not merely as an aid for the identification of the two characters but also as a signifier of death, a *memento mori* hanging between the two women, directly connected to the sword, here acting more like the sword of Damocles.

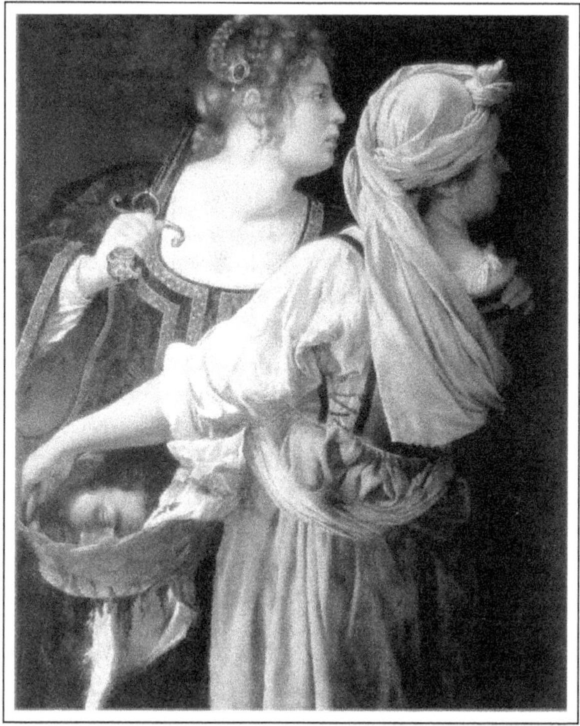

Figure 5. Artemisia Gentileschi, *Judith and Her Maidservant*, Galleria Palatina (Palazzo Pitti), Florence. By kind permission of Ministero dei Beni e delle Attività Culturali

This sword is different from the cross-like (and thus righteous) sword in the Naples and Uffizi paintings, and is rather more adorned. The sword's pommel is sculpted in the shape of a screaming Gorgon, perhaps Medusa, an interesting choice for Artemisia. Mary Garrard suggests that on this occasion, Artemisia uses the Medusa head as a positive talisman, representative of Medusa as a powerful yet benevolent mother image, which is meant to support the concept of Judith as androgynous hero.[19] I am not convinced. Why should Artemisia wish to dispense of Judith's feminine

19. Garrard, *Artemisia Gentileschi*, p. 319.

identity? After all, she adorns her character with jewels (pearl earrings and a hair cameo pin) and gives her an elaborate coiffure (despite the few locks by her face, which seem to have escaped the rigid turns of her braids). Why should Judith not be allowed to use the head of Medusa as a weapon against her enemies, as Perseus did after slaying her? Although the sword belongs to Holofernes and is not part of Judith's adornments, my impression is that Artemisia may have employed the screaming Gorgon as yet another sign of vulnerability on the part of her heroine. Faced with the challenge to defeat the Assyrian general, Judith feels the need to invoke extra help, the mythic power of Medusa to stun her enemy, emphasized perhaps further by Judith's coiled braids, reminiscent of Medusa's snake-covered head. Is this Judith, the fearful woman who thwarts a man's plans for annihilation, meant to represent a surviving Medusa? Are her rather pronounced eyes meant to have the power to turn their possible pursuers into stone? Is there power in Judith's gaze?

Judith and the Medusa had been thrown together by political changes in Renaissance Florence. During the fifteenth century, the powers of the Florentine patrician-dominated government, formed by *il signori*, diminished in favour of one family in particular, the Medici, who slowly became the autocratic rulers of the city. However, after the death of Lorenzo de' Medici (known as 'the Magnificent' because of his lavish support of the arts) in 1492, the family was overthrown, and Florence came under a broadly republican government. The new rulers of the city confiscated much of the Medici property, and in 1495 they displayed Donatello's bronze statue *Judith Decapitating Holofernes*—which had once graced the Medici gardens—in front of Palazzo Vecchio, on its ceremonial platform (known as the *ringhiera*) in Piazza della Signoria. The Medici had commissioned the work as an allegory of virtue conquering vice, and Donatello gave Judith a rather Marian look, to accompany its inscription declaring, *Regna cadunt luxu, surgunt virtutibus urbes; caesa vides humili colla superba manu.*[20] The new republican government replaced the first inscription with a new one, *Salus Publica*...[21] Donatello's statue was now meant to take on a political hue, and thus represent anti-Medicean sentiment, the victory of republicanism against autocratic tyranny.[22]

20. Latin, 'Kingdoms fall through luxury, cities rise through virtues; behold the neck of pride severed by a humble hand'.

21. Latin, 'The salvation of the state'. The new inscription continues, *Petrus Medices. Cos. Fi. Libertati simul et fortitudini hanc mulieris statuam, quo cives invicto constantique animo ad rem publicam redderent, dedicavit* ('Piero de' Medici, son of Cosimo, dedicated this statue of a woman both to liberty and to fortitude, whereby the citizens with unvanquished and constant heart might return to the republic').

22. Geraldine A. Johnson, *Renaissance: A Very Short Introduction* (Oxford: Oxford University Press, 2005), pp. 112-19.

Less than a decade later, however, the statue was replaced with Michelangelo's *David* (the original marble sculpture is now in the Galleria della Accademia). The new government had decided, 'Judith is a deadly sign and inappropriate in this place because our [Florence's] symbol is the cross as well as the lily, and it is not fitting that the woman should slay the man'.[23] Because Michelangelo's sculpture had little narrative power (though more than enough visual appeal), a new sculpture was introduced in the Piazza della Signoria in 1554: Cellini's *Perseus Holding the Head of the Medusa*, which, more palatable to the patriarchal regime of the day, was meant to challenge Donatello's *Judith* more successfully. While Michelangelo chose not to depict Goliath's decapitated head, Cellini had Perseus stand on top of a decapitated female body while holding Medusa's head demonstratively in his right hand and a sword in his left. In ancient Greek culture, the death of Medusa at the hands of Perseus, much like that of Chimaera at the hands of Bellerophon, represented the death of matriarchy. The decapitation of Medusa, which later evolved into the Freudian symbol for the defeat of the phallic woman, became in Piazza della Signoria, 'the expression of the required subordination of wives and mothers in patrilineage'.[24] Power and politics change, however, and the Medici returned to rule in 1512. A hundred years later the Grand Duke Cosimo II de' Medici commissioned from Artemisia Gentileschi one or two Judith paintings. Alluding to the Medusa, Artemisia's Judith lives on in Palazzo Pitti, once the residence of the Medici family.

With the power of the Medusa, Judith's turned look motivates the viewer to shift his or her gaze away from the protagonist in search of the unseen danger lurking out of the dark side of the painting. Perhaps that is the power of Judith's gaze: redirection. She looks neither at her enemy nor at the viewer, and she emerges as somewhat less possessed in this painting. Whether or not the painter herself was aware of the political connotations of the terrifying Gorgon in Florentine history may be insignificant. What is clear is that Artemisia's attitude towards Judith is changed. Away from the tent and the actual killing, this Judith is both vulnerable—her head could fall at any time—and the paragon of strength—she has already defeated Holofernes, for his head is in the basket. Although blood is scarce in this painting (there is a little blood on the white cloth meant to cover the head and some at the bottom of the basket), Artemisia chooses the colour of blood for the lining of Judith's sleeve. From it her right hand emerges, tainted by association, to hold the murder weapon.

23. In the words of Francesco di Lorenzo Filarete, January 1504, cited in Johnson, *Renaissance*, p. 115; his full name is given in Yael Even, 'The Loggia dei Lanzi: A Showcase of Female Subjugation', *Woman's Art Journal* 12 (1991), pp. 10-14 (10).

24. Marina Warner, *Monuments and Maidens: The Allegory of the Female Form* (New York: Atheneum, 1985), p. 111.

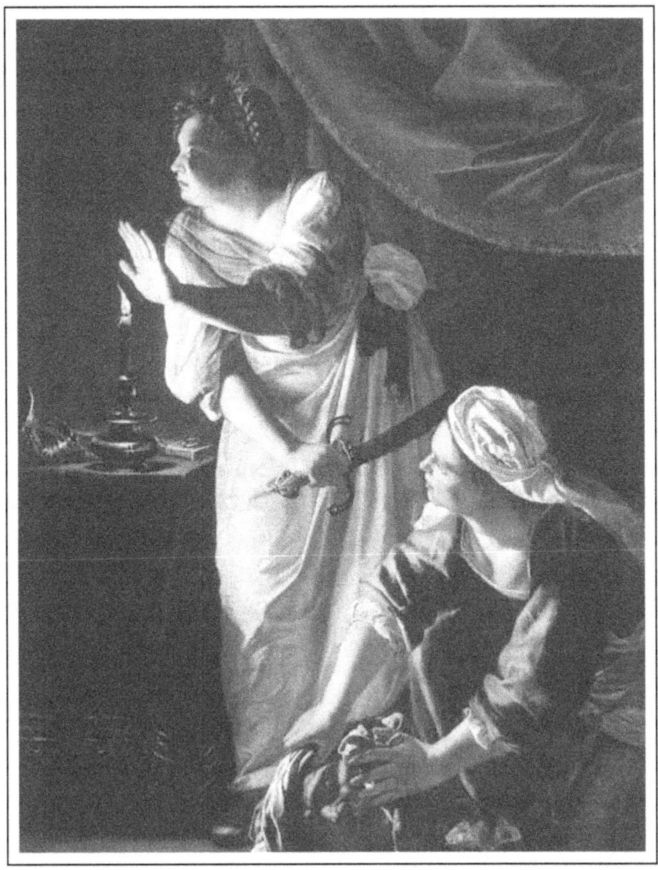

Figure 6. Artemisia Gentileschi, *Judith and Her Maidservant with the Head of Holofernes*, c. 1623/1625. Gift of Mr Leslie H. Green. Photograph © 1984. The Detroit Institute of Arts

This attitude towards Judith is made even clearer in a yet later painting (c. 1623/1625), *Judith and Her Maidservant with the Head of Holofernes* (Fig. 6), considered by critics as Artemisia's 'finest work',[25] now at the Detroit Institute of Arts. It is here that Artemisia allows Judith the ambiguity of character present in the text. In their rush to leave Holofernes' tent, Judith turns somewhat fearfully into the light, checking that they have not been discovered, while her maid is hurriedly placing the head in the food bag. Judith still holds the sword tightly in her right hand, blood

25. Keith Christiansen and Judith Mann (eds.), *Orazio and Artemisia Gentileschi* (Exhibition Catalogue, Metropolitan Museum of Art; New Haven: Yale University Press, 2001), p. 368.

dripping off its end, yet her left goes up to the candle and thus casts a shadow on her face. Alerted by either movement or noise from outside the tent, the two women stand still for a moment, in perfect tandem, even though they no longer share a physical bond. Artemisia manages to capture their complete immobility and their silence. If Judith's mouth is somewhat parted in the Pitti painting, as though she is either about to speak or has just stopped speaking, this Judith's lips are completely shut. There is still not one drop of blood on her, and the red drape behind her might represent the presence of God and thus his warrant, yet this Judith's apparel is no longer completely brilliant and 'innocent'.

Judith is slightly older here, and her features are neither the most elegant nor the most attractive. Again Artemisia does not idealize her heroine. The moment she chooses here is after the killing (depicted in the Naples and Uffizi paintings) and before the flight back to Bethulia (the Pitti painting). Judith has just killed Holofernes, and this act of murder stops her from looking directly into the searching light of the candle, as the maidservant does. The shadow on Judith's face signifies a change within her that cannot be undone. Even performed under the righteous banner of God, the shedding of blood confers upon its perpetrator knowledge of evil. The decapitated head of Holofernes looks monstrous in shades of grey and green, large and ill defined, heavy, almost dragging the painting down with it, and the blood from it taints the hands of Judith's servant, particularly her left. This is the first time that Artemisia allows for anyone's hands to be bloodied in her Judith paintings. While they are not Judith's hands, but rather her servant's, they invoke the text, 'The Lord has struck him [Holofernes] down by the hand of a woman' (Jdt. 13.15). Judith's right hand still holds the bloody sword, but her left is brightly lit by the candle. It is clean. Spotless. Righteous. Perhaps an acceptable trade in Artemisia's understanding of the biblical woman: a shadowed face for a bright hand, a tenebrous soul for a righteous deed.

The text does not explore the suspense between the kill and Judith's return to Bethulia. In fact, we are told that all of Holofernes' servants go to bed after the banquet, for it had lasted quite a long time and they were all exhausted (Jdt. 13.1). Yet Artemisia fills the gaps of the story with extraordinary talent, for most attentive readers would wonder about the moments following the kill, about the reaction of the two characters to Judith's deed, about the two women's night journey back to the safety of their city while holding a bloody head in a food bag.

The moment of Judith's safe arrival back in Bethulia, the denoument of the narrative, is depicted by Elisabetta Sirani (1638–1665) in her *Judith Showing the Head of Holofernes to the Israelites* (1658), now at Burghley House (Fig. 7). Sirani was, like Lavinia Fontana, from progressive Bologna

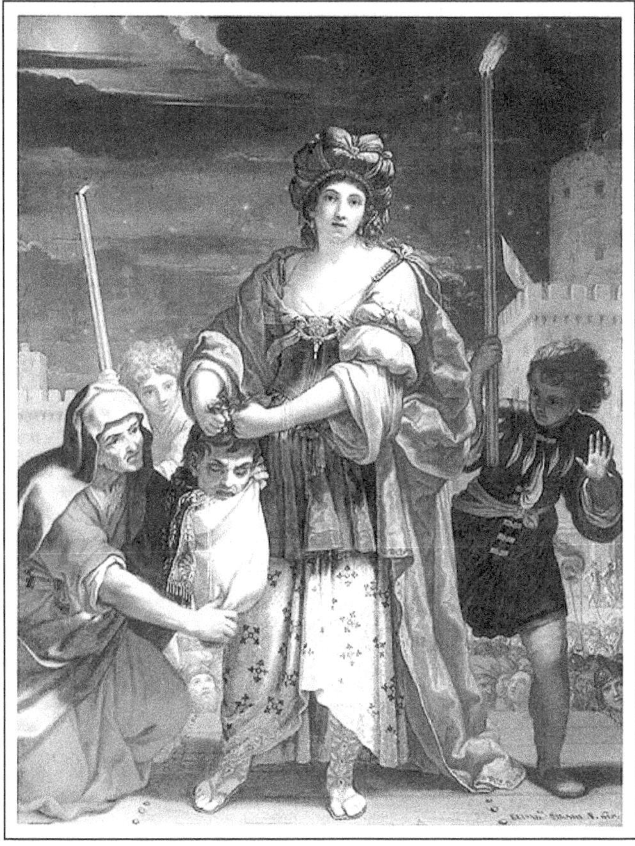

Figure 7. Elisabetta Sirani, *Judith Showing the Head of Holofernes to the Israelites*, Burghley House, Stamford, Lincolnshire

and thus a representative of a strong community of women artists. Sirani has the privilege of being referred to by her surname, since her reputation outshone that of her father, Giovanni Andrea. However, the tendency is to catalogue her as a follower of Guido Reni—she was even buried in the same tomb as Reni, so that they could be together in death as they were in life. However, Reni died in 1642, when Sirani was only four years old and therefore too young to be his pupil or assistant.[26] She was a prolific artist, and by her twenty-seventh birthday—which was to be her last—Sirani had completed over two hundred paintings (most of them signed and dated), ten etchings, and a number of drawings. Furthermore, she had

26. Babette Bohn, 'The Antique Heroines of Elisabetta Sirani', *Renaissance Studies* 16 (2002), pp. 52-79 (55).

established the first school of painting for women outside a convent in Europe, where she trained not only daughters of painters, like herself, but also women without an artistic background.[27]

Sirani chooses to depict Judith at her most triumphant, when her victory is openly declared to her nation, who in turn praise God, for he has 'humiliated the enemies of [his] people' (Jdt. 13.17).[28] Flanked by two young light-bearers, whose expressions betray great respect and amazement, Judith gets ready to show the proof of her victory (or rather God's victory): the head of the Assyrian general. With both hands in Holofernes' hair, she pulls the severed head from the bag presented to her by her servant (quite old here), who kneels at her side. Judith's apparel is an odd mix of feminine delicacy—jewels and luxurious fabrics—and soldierly rigidity—roman sandals, blue *lorica* and red toga fastened with shoulder plates. The elaborate turban gives her head an exaggerated appearance, which couples with the Medusa brooch on Judith's chest to create an unsettling, Gorgon effect. With no sign of speaking and a calm, understated expression, Judith looks straight at the viewer, holding his or her gaze. It is only when one takes a step back that the other, eerily disembodied heads become apparent. Small and pale, like victims of this Judith-Gorgon hybrid, they line the back of the raised platform from which Judith makes her muted address. If the heads belong to Judith's rapt audience, the Israelites of Bethulia, then why are they at the back, while the viewer occupies the front row? Sirani's Judith takes on mythical proportions, while the rest of the Israelites are reduced to a diminutive presence. Behind them, fragments of the city walls break the night sky, perhaps reminding the viewer of the totemic value of the decapitated head, which in the text is hoisted and displayed on the parapet (Jdt. 14.1).

Despite the strong element of phallic power attributed to Judith in depictions by Lavinia Fontana, Artemisia Gentileschi and Elisabetta Sirani, Judith remains feminine in them. She wears pretty dresses and jewellery, and her sexuality, while not emphasized, is nevertheless present. Whether by means of a thigh pushing through vulval folds of garment, or breasts surging with concentration, even allusions to Medusa,

27. Bohn, 'The Antique Heroines of Elisabetta Sirani', p. 59.

28. A rather different, more traditional painting of Judith has been attributed to Elisabetta Sirani, now in the Walters Art Gallery, Baltimore. In it Judith and her servant are in the tent of Holofernes. Judith stands by the bed holding Holofernes' decapitated head. The attribution of this painting to Elisabetta is questionable. Firstly, the painting is not signed by her (and, as a rule, she signed all her paintings). Secondly, the painting is a replica of an etching attributed to Elisabetta's father, Giovani Andrea Sirani, which bears the inscription 'G.R.I.', 'Guido Reni invenit'. Elisabetta is not known to have done any reproductive prints.

Judith's identity as a woman with sexual knowledge is betrayed in the work of all these female painters. Their Judiths are for most part natural, even when their feminine adornments strike a contrasting note with their actions. Judith emerges from the work of women painters as the prototype of female empowerment, the *femme forte*, with whom most of the artists wish to identify.

As a female heroic character, Judith seems a favourite among women painters. Yet this preference may have had something to do with the fact that apocryphal subjects were lucrative choices in late sixteenth- and early seventeenth-century Europe. Artemisia's father, Orazio Gentileschi, as well as other contemporaries, most famously Caravaggio, Reni and Allori, also produced Judith paintings. Is there a marked difference between the ways in which female and male painters interpreted Judith? Women painters were trained by men, and the art industry was dominated by men. Do these female painters bow to the taste *du jour*, dishing out Judiths? Some male critics may think so. In his 1999 book on Artemisia Gentileschi, Ward Bissell argues that, under the pretence of developing mythical and historical stories, the painter chose to paint female subjects—often in the nude (like her Cleopatra and Lucretia)—precisely in order to cater to the salacious tastes of her male patrons and a larger male audience.[29] Mary Garrard and Babette Bohn would insist that works by women artists, especially Artemisia, Lavinia and Sirani, are far less titillating than those of their male counterparts, that in fact the women painters downplay the sensuality of their heroines. Margarita Stocker, on the other hand, shows that Judith had indeed been appropriated by the sex industry of Renaissance and Baroque Europe as an 'advertising gimmick'.[30] Like the other courtesans, Judith would hang in bawdy galleries, her portrait showing her particular skills, sado-masochistic techniques.[31]

As an example of bordello décor painted by a woman, but one that she is quick to point out should not be interpreted in the same way as depictions by Artemisia and other women painters, Stocker names Fede Galizia's *Judith with the Head of Holofernes* (1596), now at the John and Mable Ringling Museum, Florida State University (Fig. 8).

29. R. Ward Bissell, *Artemisia Gentileschi and the Authority of Art: Critical Reading and Catalogue Raisonné* (University Park: Pennsylvania State University Press, 1999), pp. 43, 51-54.

30. Stocker, *Judith, Sexual Warrior*, pp. 24-45 (35).

31. Cf. appropriation of Judith as sado-masochistic icon, particularly in the works of Gustav Klimt.

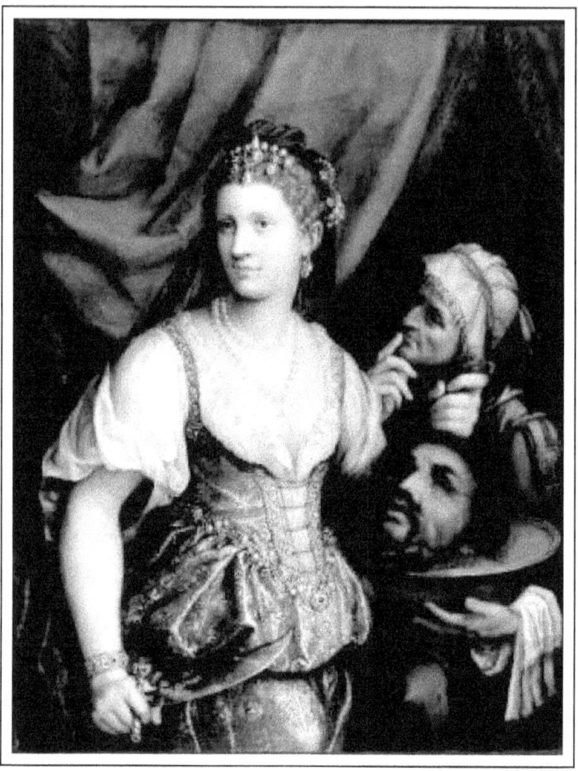

Figure 8. Fede Galizia, Italian, 1578–1630. *Judith with the Head of Holofernes*, 1596. Oil on canvas, 47.5 × 37 inches, SN684. Collection of the John and Mable Ringling Museum of Art, the State Art Museum of Florida

Standing in front of a lush red canopy (possibly Holofernes' tent), dressed in beautiful, delicate, luxurious garments that expose the flesh of her breasts, and adorned with many pearls and other jewels, Judith looks out of the painting with an enigmatic smile, while holding a clean dagger at groin level in her right hand and Holofernes' head by the hair in her left. Behind her, the maid (old here) holds up with her left hand the platter on which Holofernes' head rests, while with her right she lifts a finger to her mouth conspiratorially, while looking at Judith. The decapitated head is large and putrid-looking, the slightly open mouth a terrifying detail. Why would this Judith be a *femme fatale*, an embodiment of *Vanitas*? Is it her phallic dagger? The inviting, vulval opening of the tent, perhaps? The discretion promised by the maid, who is here a 'madame'? Stocker draws attention to Judith's many pearls. In a pious context, they would represent either chastity, or tears of joy, repentance or compassion. In a bordello, they represent instead the willingness of the courtesan to take pity on a client and thus oblige his fantasies.[32] This is certainly not femininity as 'masquerade', the guise from under which an androgynous hero can act out. It is rather femininity as currency, with no superior (read spiritual) goal. Is Fede Galizia's interpretation not what Judith-as-lucrative-subject is all about, however? Is it not about selling Judith?

The Male Perspective

Having looked at the ways in which some women painters interpreted Judith, we should look briefly at the work of some of their male contemporaries.

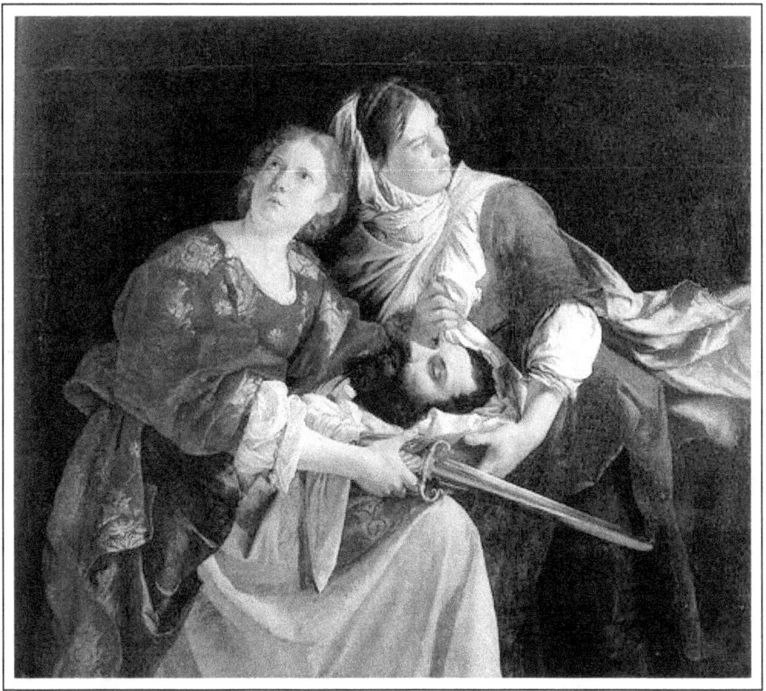

Figure 9. Orazio Gentileschi, *Judith and Her Maidservant with the Head of Holofernes*, Wadsworth Atheneum Museum of Art, Hartford, CT. The Ella Gallup Sumner and Mary Catlin Sumner Collection Fund

Orazio Gentileschi (1563–1639), whose Judith painting is dated later than his daughter's first works on the same subject, paints the Jewish heroine and her young maidservant as very close collaborators. While in Artemisia's version Judith and the maid are joined at the hip, borrowing

32. Stocker, *Judith, Sexual Warrior*, pp. 36-37.

from each other's physical strength, in his *Judith and Her Maidservant with the Head of Holofernes* (c. 1621/1624), Orazio chooses to depict the two women in a pose resembling conjoined twins, joined at the head (Fig. 9). Judith and her servant have plotted together against men, and now, in the aftermath, they huddle up close, cradling the decapitated head with what looks like misplaced tenderness. The head, which by its size is meant to be monstrous, is rather peaceful, if not handsome. There is no blood on the two women, and there is no blood around the head either. Nor is there blood on the sword, which Judith holds in a rather maladroit manner, her hand wrapped around both it and the basket in a double claim of ownership that in fact sabotages her hold on either. Why do the two women gaze in different, indeed opposite, directions, despite their close link? If the illusion is meant to reinforce the ambiguous, dual nature of Judith as both Virtue and Vice, that effect is not quite achieved here. There is simply not sufficient difference between Judith and her maid.

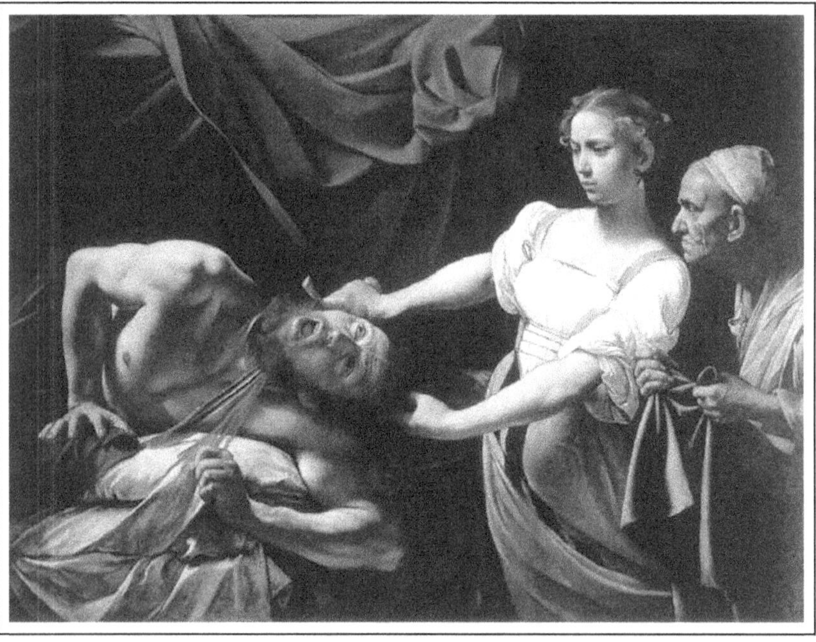

Figure 10. Michelangelo Merisi da Caravaggio, *Judith Beheading Holofernes*, Galleria Nazionale d'Arte Antica a Palazzo Barberini, Rome.
By kind permission of Archivio Fotografico Soprintendenza Speciale per il Polo Museale Romano

The two could not be more different for Caravaggio (1573–1610), however. In Caravaggio's *Judith Beheading Holofernes* (c. 1600), now at Palazzo Barberini, in Rome, the Jewish heroine is more beautiful than she is strong (contrary to Artemisia's later renderings), perhaps betraying the focus of the male gaze (Fig. 10). Judith is slender and very pretty, and she holds both Holofernes' head and his sword a bit too gently for credibility. Holofernes' grimace does not convince, for his muscular torso betrays strength far superior to that of his slender attacker. The killing scene seems rather staged. It is as if the viewer is invited to the dress-rehearsal of a Judith play, and the actor playing Holofernes (here Caravaggio, who models the Assyrian on himself) is trying his best to create the horror of the moment and rather overdoing it in the process. (Interestingly, Holofernes' expression in Artemisia's paintings is remarkably similar to the one here, but she manages to produce a convincing, indeed terrifying vision of the killing.) Caravaggio's Judith seems quite perturbed by her supposedly violent act. Her gaze is focused on her victim, and her face shows sorrow and remorse. She is clearly pained by her deed. Her apparel is proper (not a hair out of place), and Caravaggio chooses to dress Judith in a fetching and immaculate white blouse, which matches her pearl earrings. Not only is there not one drop of blood on Judith, but the spurt of blood is actually directed away from her. The blood-red canopy flowing down between Judith and Holofernes again signifies God's presence, indeed his warrant, and so this Judith is the epitome of Virtue.

And yet, this Judith is unconvincing. Indeed, it is the maid's face that bears the determination that in the text belongs to its protagonist. Peering over Judith's shoulder, the old crone shows no sympathy for the man dying before her but instead holds up her apron impatiently, if not excitedly, her hands viciously gripping its corners, ready to receive his severed head. She seems to be spurring Judith on, her eyes wide open, in keen anticipation of death. If Judith here is Virtue, the maid is certainly Vice. They are indeed opposing sides of woman, the virgin and the bawd, innocence and experience.

Caravaggio is said to have modelled his Judith on Beatrice Cenci, a beautiful young girl who in 1599 was tried and beheaded for the crime of patricide.[33] The case attracted a lot of public attention, for the girl's father, whom she killed, had been proved to be a tyrannical, sadistic person, who treated his family very cruelly. Because of her youth and beauty, as well as her tragic execution, the public sided with Beatrice. Caravaggio exalts Beatrice to the role of Judith in a rather political gesture, and her story becomes the legend of the 'virgin martyr'. Like Judith's, Beatrice's murderous deed is thus interpreted not only as righteous, but also necessary, part of Caravaggio's eroticised imaginings of trapped virtue.

33. Maurizio Marini, *Michelangelo Merisi da Caravaggio, 'pictor praestantissimus': La tragica esistenza, la raffinata cultura* (Rome: Newton Compton, 1987), p. 418.

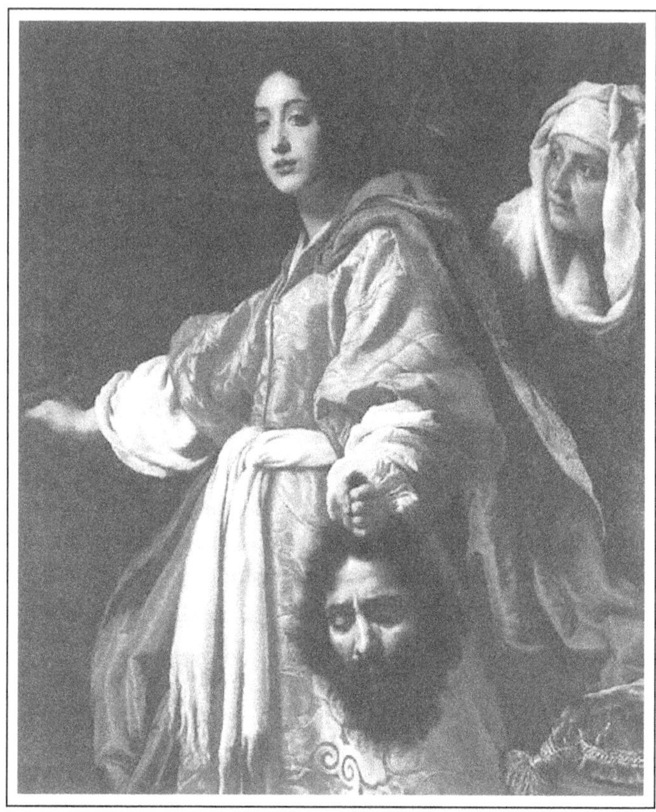

Figure 11. Cristofano Allori, *Judith with the Head of Holofernes*, Galleria Palatina (Palazzo Pitti), Florence. By kind permission of Ministero dei Beni e delle Attività Culturali

Cristofano Allori (1535–1607) decided on a different kind of muse for his Judith paintings, the best known *Judith with the Head of Holofernes* (1613), now at Palazzo Pitti, in Florence (Fig. 11).[34] Allori modelled his Judith on a former mistress who rejected him, the maid on her mother, and the head of Holoferenes on Allori himself—much like Caravaggio, in fact, who does it twice. Caravaggio is not only Holofernes; the decapitated head of Goliath in his *David with the Head of Goliath* (1606) is also a fragmented self-portrait.[35] Allori's Judith is not Virtue (not even eroti-

34. One other Judith painting by Allori is an almost identical replica of the Pitti painting and is now in the Royal Collection, at Windsor Castle, England.

35. By modelling the decapitated heads of Holofernes and Goliath on himself, Caravaggio is said to have wished to express his open remorse for having killed a man, and to request a pardon from the Pope, so he could return to Rome from his exile.

cised Virtue) but rather Vice, the woman empowered not by God but by experience, her prowess not spiritual but rather sexual. The maid appears as a kind, wise old woman, who looks up to Judith, with either fear or respect. Like Caravaggio's maid, she is behind Judith, yet here she seems to act as the voice of reason. Allori engages the maid to his own purpose, to act out his fantasy that his mistress could be persuaded to take him back. This beautiful Judith looks down at the viewer, and her demeanour betrays not a sense of justice, but rather haughtiness, Vanity. Judith's luxurious garments leave very little of her body exposed, which makes her the most dangerous of *femmes fatales*, for she cannot be subjugated by the gaze of the viewer; she cannot be objectified. The head of Holofernes is dark yet pitiful, bearing a sorrowful expression while dangling in the strong grip of Judith, in front of her womb. It serves as a warning to all men who allow themselves to be overpowered by the allure of the feminine. For Allori, Judith is the independent woman who dares to reject man's attentions, the phallic woman who escapes subjugation but instead subjects and thus emasculates, dephallicizes, man.

Judith: Femme Fatale *or* Femme Forte?

In the text, Judith and Holofernes play hybrid gender roles. The woman, despite using her beauty as bait, is powerful and calculated, while the man, despite holding the cultural and political power as the colonizer general, acts out his emotions and loses his head. While some women painters wish to interpret, indeed identify with, Judith as the *femme forte* (not true across the board—Fede Galizia's Judith may be yet another '*déshabillée* harlot'[36]), Judith as phallic woman is inevitably a challenge. As such, she seems to be interpreted by male painters as either Virtue or Vice.

As a virtuous, asexual heroine Judith is grouped with Mary the mother of Jesus in Christian tradition. Jerome declares her to be 'chastity behead[ing] lust'.[37] As a vicious, experienced woman Judith is hated and rejected as abject, for, by acquiring and using the phallic sword against a man, she disrupts and destabilises the Law of the Father. (Judith already lives on the margins, as an apocryphal character, despite her loftier associations with Mary.) The metaphorical emasculation of Holofernes is anticipated in the narrative, for Bagoas, Holoferenes' representative and mouth-piece (or Holofernes' 'pimp', as Stocker muses),[38] is a eunuch. The concept is further moralized by Achior's conversion to Judaism, which brings about his circumcision and thus his subjugation to a greater, more

36. Stocker, *Judith, Sexual Warrior*, p. 39.
37. Jerome, 'Letter LIV', par. 16.
38. Stocker, *Judith, Sexual Warrior*, p. 7.

virile male, God. The characters take on nationalistic hues, and in the end we are dealing with the Israelites, as God's people, and their enemies, who become impotent when pitched against the power of God. Judith might be seen as the ultimate phallic woman (for she subverts even the authority of the male leaders of Bethulia by accusing them of hubris), but she is only an instrument in God's hands. The fact that she remains a widow despite many marriage proposals (Jdt. 16.22) emphasizes the trade-off imposed on her: she can escape her gender limitations for a little while, as long as she renounces her sexuate identity henceforth. Judith becomes the personification of Bethulia, indeed the Jewish nation. As such, she can only be committed, or married to, God, who is a notoriously jealous husband. Ironically, Judith accepts ownership of Holofernes' bed after the Assyrian camp is plundered by the Israelites (Jdt. 15.11), a memento of her deed and a further symbol of what is denied her. She signs the contract offered by God with the blood of the man who dares to desire what is God's.

We may want to read Judith as the *femme forte*, for there are so few examples of strong biblical women who offer desirable models for identification to female readers. Yet Judith cannot escape the role of the *femme fatale*, for it is precisely the part that God himself designs for her. He gives her special beauty, he gives her special strength, and he uses them both to his gains. God uses Judith to humiliate his challenger, here Holofernes. By freeing her maidservant (Jdt. 16.23), Judith gives her slave the freedom that she herself may desire but cannot have. Judith's perceived power is illusory, and her image of 'a woman with a borrowed sword' serves only to shame the Israelites' enemies even further. It is God who holds the ultimate authority, the ultimate phallic power in the narrative. The book of Judith was perhaps written with the purpose of reminding its readers of this uncircumventable fact.

Engaging with visual interpretations of Judith is a complex business. Not least because one is torn between the mixed and colourful re-workings of the narrative, the works of art as individual texts, and the painters and their cultural and socio-historical contexts. Without the knowledge of the text, these paintings could produce, what Mary Garrard calls, 'naïve readings'.[39] Rather than witnessing the salvation of an entire nation through the killing of one general, some viewers might think they were witnessing, in Germaine Greer's words, 'two female cut-throats, a prostitute and her maid slaughtering her client',[40] proof perhaps that paintings

39. Garrard, *Artemisia Gentileschi*, p. 321.

40. Germaine Greer, *The Obstacle Race: The Fortunes of Women Painters and Their Work* (New York: Farrar, Straus & Giroux, 1979), p. 189.

do create their own visual rhetoric and legislate their own semiotics.[41] Of course, it would be naïve to suppose that there is only one way of reading Judith, even if the text had provided more details about her. Readers themselves—be they artists, scholars, or other—are works in progress, *sujets en procès*. It is precisely this fact that makes reading worth re-reading.

BIBLIOGRAPHY

Bach, Alice, *Women, Seduction, and Betrayal in Biblical Narrative* (Cambridge: Cambridge University Press, 1997).

Bissell, R. Ward, *Artemisia Gentileschi and the Authority of Art: Critical Reading and Catalogue Raisonné* (University Park: Pennsylvania State University Press, 1999).

Bohn, Babette, 'The Antique Heroines of Elisabetta Sirani', *Renaissance Studies* 16 (2002), pp. 52-79.

Christiansen, Keith, and Judith Mann (eds.), *Orazio and Artemisia Gentileschi* (Exhibition Catalogue, Metropolitan Museum of Art; New Haven: Yale University Press, 2001).

Cixous, Hélène, 'The Newly Born Woman', in *The Hélène Cixous Reader* (ed. Susan Sellers; London: Routledge, 1994), pp. 36-55.

Even, Yael, 'The Loggia dei Lanzi: A Showcase of Female Subjugation', *Woman's Art Journal* 12 (1991), pp. 10-14.

Garrard, Mary D., *Artemisia Gentileschi: The Image of the Female Hero in Italian Baroque Art* (Princeton, NJ: Princeton University Press, 1989).

Greer, Germaine, *The Obstacle Race: The Fortunes of Women Painters and Their Work* (New York: Farrar, Straus & Giroux, 1979).

Harris, Ann Sutherland, and Linda Nochlin, *Women Artists: 1550–1950* (Los Angeles: Los Angeles County Museum of Art, 1976).

Holly, Michael Ann, 'Past Looking', *Critical Inquiry* 16 (1990), pp. 371-96.

Johnson, Geraldine A., *Renaissance: A Very Short Introduction* (Oxford: Oxford University Press, 2005).

Marini, Maurizio, *Michelangelo Merisi da Caravaggio, 'pictor praestantissimus': La tragica esistenza, la raffinata cultura* (Rome: Newton Compton, 1987).

McIver, Katherine A., 'Lavinia Fontana's 'Self-Portrait Making Music'', *Woman's Art Journal* 19 (1998), pp. 3-8.

Murphy, Caroline P., *Lavinia Fontana: A Painter and Her Patrons in Sixteenth-century Bologna* (New Haven: Yale University Press, 2003).

Parker, Rozsika, and Griselda Pollock, *Old Mistresses: Women, Art and Ideology* (London: Pandora, 1981).

Pollock, Griselda, *Visions and Difference: Femininity, Feminism and Histories of Art* (London: Routledge, 1988).

— 'Feminist Dilemmas with the Art/Life Problem', in *The Artemisia Files: Artemisia Gentileschi for Feminists and Other Thinking People* (ed. Mieke Bal; London: University of Chicago Press, 2005), pp. 169-206.

41. A propos the work of Michael Ann Holly, 'Past Looking', *Critical Inquiry* 16 (1990), pp. 371-96.

Prudentius, *Psychomachia* (London: British Library MS Cotton Cleopatra c. VIII, Canterbury, Christ Church).

Stocker, Margarita, *Judith, Sexual Warrior: Women and Power in Western Culture* (New Haven: Yale University Press, 1998).

Vasari, Giorgio, *The Lives of the Most Eminent Painters, Sculptors, and Architects* (trans. Gaston du Vere; New York: Knopf, 2nd edn, 1996).

Warner, Marina, *Monuments and Maidens: The Allegory of the Female Form* (New York: Atheneum, 1985).

VISUALIZING SALOME'S DANCE OF DEATH: THE CONTRIBUTION OF ART TO BIBLICAL EXEGESIS

Christine E. Joynes

The present burgeoning interest in *Wirkungsgeschichte*, or reception history of the Bible,[1] has brought with it fresh appreciation of the significant role that artists play as biblical interpreters.[2] In contrast to the focus of historical criticism upon the original meaning of the biblical text, reception history highlights the afterlives of these texts, suggesting that 'how people have interpreted and been influenced by a sacred text like the Bible is often as interesting and historically important as what it originally meant'.[3]

Exploring the afterlives of biblical texts is a risky business, for it prompts the exegete to trespass on areas outside of the traditional field of theology. I comment as a biblical scholar, not as a trained art historian.[4] Nevertheless, in spite of the dangers, fruitful dialogue can emerge when theology converses with the arts, aiding better understanding on both sides.

1. The new Blackwell Bible Commentary series, edited by John Sawyer, Christopher Rowland, Judith Kovacs and David Gunn, illustrates this interest in reception history. For a helpful discussion of the difference between reception history and history of interpretation see Mary Callaway, 'What's the Use of Reception History?', at www.bbibcomm.net/news/latest.html (accessed 27 February 2005).

2. See for example, Christopher Rowland, 'Imagining the Apocalypse', *NTS* 51 (2005), pp. 303-27.

3. Judith Kovacs and Christopher Rowland, *Revelation: The Apocalypse of Jesus Christ* (Oxford: Blackwell, 2004), p. xi. There is not space here to discuss the relationship between historical criticism and reception history, but it is worth noting that though they are contrasting methodologies they are not necessarily mutually exclusive.

4. See Robin M. Jensen, 'Giving Texts Vision and Images Voice: The Promise and Problems of Interdisciplinary Scholarship', in *Common Life in the Early Church: Essays Honoring Graydon F. Snyder* (ed. Julian V. Hills; Harrisburg, PA: Trinity Press International, 1998), pp. 344-56, for a detailed discussion of the risks involved in such interdisciplinary dialogue.

In an attempt to illustrate the rich contribution of art to biblical exegesis I will focus here upon some representations of John the Baptist's beheading (Mk 6.17-29; Mt. 14.3-12).[5] This episode has had an immense impact on art, both inside and outside of the church, across the centuries.[6] Whereas it is frequently associated in the popular imagination with the figure of the dancing girl who became known as Salome,[7] we shall see that this is not always the dominant concern of artists, who sometimes omit the dance and focus upon other aspects of the story. Irrespective of the narrative moment represented, such visualizations of the biblical text all prompt the viewer to reflect upon features which are often implicit, ambiguous or unspecified in the Gospels.

Salome's Dance of Death in the Gospels

John the Baptist's beheading is described only by the Gospel writers Matthew and Mark. The historian Josephus mentions the Baptist's death in his *Jewish Antiquities*, but does not specify details concerning his demise.[8] We are therefore reliant on the two evangelists for information pertaining to Herod's birthday banquet and the dance which leads to the Baptist's death. Matthew abbreviates the lengthier Markan narrative, and by omitting much of Mark's detail he heightens the emphasis upon the dancing girl, who plays a crucial role in the Baptist's murder according to both

5. For analysis of the reception history of this passage in music and literature, see Christine E. Joynes, 'John the Baptist's Death', in *Mark, Gospel of Action: Personal and Community Responses* (ed. John Vincent; London: SPCK, 2006), pp. 143-53.

6. Surveys of the story's influence include H.G. Zagona, *The Legend of Salome and the Principle of Art for Art's Sake* (Paris: Librairie Minard, 1960); E. Kuryluk, *Salome and Judas in the Cave of Sex: The Grotesque: Origins, Iconography, Techniques* (Evanston, IL: Northwestern University Press, 1987); Janice Capel Anderson, 'Feminist Criticism: The Dancing Daughter', in *Mark and Method: New Approaches in Biblical Studies* (ed. Janice Capel Anderson and Stephen D. Moore; Minneapolis: Fortress Press, 1992), pp. 103-34; Alice Bach, *Women, Seduction and Betrayal in Biblical Narrative* (Cambridge: Cambridge University Press, 1997), pp. 210-62; Caroline Vander Stichele, 'Capital Re-Visions: The Head of John the Baptist as Object of Art', in *Missing Links: Arts, Religion, Reality* (ed. Jonneke Bekkenkamp; Münster: LIT Verlag, 2000), pp. 71-87.

7. The identification of the girl as Salome originates from Josephus, *Ant.* 18.136; it does not appear in the Gospel narratives. However, since this is the name that artists generally use to refer to the dancing girl, I shall refer to her as Salome in this article.

8. Josephus, *Ant.* 18.119: 'Though John, because of Herod's suspicions, was brought in chains to Machaerus...and there put to death, yet the verdict of the Jews was that the destruction visited upon Herod's army was a vindication of John, since God saw fit to inflict such a blow on Herod'.

evangelists. The designation of the girl as a κοράσιον by the two Gospel writers (Mk 6.22; Mt. 14.11) is noteworthy, with the use of the diminutive form indicating a young girl.[9] They clearly portray the girl as a willing accomplice of her mother: she follows Herodias's prompting to request the Baptist's head as the reward for her dance, and symbolically delivers the head to her mother at the conclusion of the episode.

Despite the above similarities, however, there are also significant differences between the Gospel accounts. Most notable is the difference in reporting who desired John the Baptist's death. Mark is at pains to point out that Herodias is the key protagonist in the quest to kill him, but was prevented from achieving her ambition by Herod:

> And Herodias had a grudge against him, and wanted to kill him. But she could not, for Herod feared John, knowing that he was a righteous and holy man, and he protected him. When he heard him, he was greatly perplexed; and yet he liked to listen to him (6.19-20).

In contrast, Matthew omits reference to Herodias's wish to kill John the Baptist and instead attributes this desire to Herod, commenting:

> And though he [Herod] wanted to put him to death, he feared the people, because they held him to be a prophet (14.5).

Matthew's account displays some similarities with Josephus's record, where Herod is said to arrest John the Baptist for reasons of political expediency.[10] But this detail also introduces a tension into the Matthean narrative, since later—in response to the girl's request for the Baptist's head—the evangelist records that 'the king was sorry'. Although this has been interpreted by some scholars as a redactional slip,[11] Matthew's retention of other key Markan details, such as Herodias's role in securing the Baptist's head, suggests that Matthew was not simply attempting to shift the blame from Herodias to Herod, but sees them both as responsible for the death.

Indeed, when assessing the evangelists' respective emphases in apportioning blame for the murder, we should not overlook the political implications of the story. As Ched Myers points out, the narrative functions

9. We might note that Mark uses the same term to refer to Jairus's twelve year old daughter (5.41). In contrast to the age of the girl implied by the Gospels, most artistic representations of Salome portray her as an older figure.

10. Josephus, *Ant.* 18.118: 'Eloquence that had so great an effect on mankind might lead to some form of sedition, for it looked as if they would be guided by John in everything that they did. Herod decided therefore that it would be much better to strike first and be rid of him before his work led to an uprising, than to wait for an upheaval, get involved in a difficult situation and see his mistake'.

11. See Mark Goodacre, 'Fatigue in the Synoptics', *NTS* 44 (1998), pp. 45-58, for the suggestion of narrative fatigue.

as a political parody where 'among all these powerful men a dancing girl determines the fate of John the Baptist...[illustrating] the shameless methods of decision-making among the elite'.[12] So despite Mark's emphasis on Herodias as the prime mover behind the Baptist's death, Herod is still ultimately to be held accountable for the events that transpire.[13]

Reviewing the evangelists' presentations of the Baptist's beheading immediately draws our attention to the incidental place that the girl's dance occupies in the biblical texts. In less than a sentence Mark reports only that 'when Herodias's daughter came in and danced, she pleased Herod and his guests' (6.22).[14] Yet a cursory glance at artistic representations of the story reveals the significant impact that this feature of the narrative has had. This may in part derive from the momentous consequence which the dance achieves, namely the Baptist's death. But the ambiguity of the text concerning the nature of the dance also provides interpreters with the opportunity to fill the gaps with their own contextual imaginings, as illustrated below.

When weighing up the different emphases of the evangelists, two further features of their Gospel accounts should be noted: first, the frequency of references to the head of the Baptist and, second, the repeated mention of the platter, on which the girl asks for the head to be brought. Strikingly, Mark refers to the Baptist's head (κεφαλή) four times (6.24, 25, 27, 28) and includes the unusual verb 'to behead' (ἀπεκεφάλισεν) in 6.27. Despite Matthew's tendency to omit Markan detail, he nevertheless includes two references to the Baptist's head (14.8, 11) and uses the same verb, 'to behead' (14.10). Both evangelists also mention that the head is requested and brought 'on a platter' (Mk 6.25; 6.28; Mt. 14.8; 14.11), a detail added by the girl to her mother's request for the head according to Mark. The prominence of the head and the platter in the biblical narratives is especially noteworthy since some scholars have argued that the focus on these features in artistic representations of the story reflects later historical preoccupations rather than the original narrative.[15]

12. Ched Myers, *Binding the Strong Man: A Political Reading of Mark's Story of Jesus* (Maryknoll, NY: Orbis Books, 1988), p. 216.

13. For further discussion of Herod's responsibility for the Baptist's death, see Jennifer A. Glancy, 'Unveiling Masculinity: The Construction of Gender in Mark 6.17-29', *BibInt* 2 (1994), pp. 42-43. She points out that by framing the narrative as Herod's recollection of events (Mk 6.16) Mark underscores Herod's culpability.

14. There is confusion concerning the girl's identity, since in some important manuscripts (Sinaiticus, Vaticanus and Codex Bezae) she is referred to as 'his [i.e. Herod's] daughter' rather than 'her daughter'. However, I interpret the girl to be Herodias's daughter and Herod's step-daughter, which is supported by the logic of the story.

15. Vander Stichele, 'Capital Re-Visions', p. 82.

In summary, the Gospel accounts of Salome's dance of death reveal considerable ambiguity surrounding the characters involved in the Baptist's beheading. We are given only a passing reference to the girl's dance, in spite of the effusive response this elicits from Herod, with his offer to her of anything she wishes, repeated twice in Mark though partially qualified with the phrase 'even half my kingdom'.[16] Yet both evangelists emphasize the key roles that the dancing girl and Herodias play in the Baptist's death, and both highlight that he is not simply killed in prison, but his head is delivered to the birthday banquet on a platter.

Salome's Dance of Death in Art

A brief survey of biblical commentators reveals the important role that an interpreter's own perspective plays in reading the text. For example, Robert Guelich refers to the girl's dance as 'the dance of prostitutes...in a bawdy setting'.[17] In contrast, Morna Hooker is keen to remind us that 'the dance was not necessarily performed with the eroticism with which later tradition has imbued it'.[18] Both of these commentators show familiarity with the significant impact that later art has had upon scholarly readings of our passage.[19]

The analysis offered here of Salome's dance of death in art will focus in particular upon three representations of different narrative moments: Picasso's twentieth-century dancing Salome; Caravaggio's seventeenth-century depiction of Salome receiving the prize for her dance; and Hinrik Funhof's fifteenth-century altar painting, which concentrates upon the delivery of the Baptist's head to the girl at Herod's birthday banquet. Although two of these images do not depict the dance itself, we will see that the way in which the various artists engage with the character of the girl reveals their understanding of the nature of the dance and its consequences. I begin with the most recent of these three examples, and

16. There is neither space nor necessity to explore here the intertextual implications of this Markan feature, which echoes Esther. See, further, on this theme, Brenda Deen Schildgen, 'A Blind Promise: Mark's Retrieval of Esther', *Poetics Today* 15 (1994), pp. 115-31.

17. Robert A. Guelich, *Mark 1.1–8.26* (Dallas: Word Books, 1989), p. 332.

18. Morna D. Hooker, *The Gospel according to St Mark* (London: A. & C. Black, 1991), p. 161. A similar position is adopted in Michael Hartmann's recent study of Mk 6.14-29, *Der Tod Johannes des Täufers: Eine exegetische und rezeptionsgeschichtliche Studie auf dem Hintergrund narrativer, intertextueller und kulturanthropologischer Zugänge* (Stuttgart: Katholisches Bibelwerk, 2001).

19. See further, Glancy ('Unveiling Masculinity', p. 50), who argues, 'When modern commentators approach this story, they expect to find female characters who are sexually rapacious, and their descriptions of Herodias and her daughter underscore their fears of predatory feminine instincts'.

will then proceed to compare and contrast Picasso's interpretation with those of his predecessors. This will also illustrate that interest in the dancing girl is not simply a reflection of *fin de siècle* fantasies, despite Salome's popularity at the turn of the nineteenth century, but has a much longer history.

Picasso Visualizes Salome's Dance of Death

When we examine artistic representations of the dancing girl we discover that depictions of her vary considerably: is she an innocent victim of her mother's ambitions or a seductive temptress, performing an erotic dance to arouse the guests at Herod's birthday feast? The Gospels are ambiguous, but interpreters—both artists and biblical scholars—have been swift to fill in the gaps in the text to reflect both these positions.[20] We are thereby challenged to adjudicate between competing interpretations of the Gospel narratives.

Pablo Picasso's *Salome* (1905), clearly visualizes the dancing daughter in the second category, portraying her as a seductive temptress (Fig. 1). The artist's interpretation of the biblical narrative shows a gleeful, energetic, nude Salome delighting in the revelation of her genital parts to Herod as she raises her left leg high in the air. Herodias stands behind Herod, averting her gaze both from her daughter's performance and her husband's pleasure in the dance. The severed head of the Baptist has already been secured, and is placed provocatively in the lap of a maidservant who playfully fondles the Baptist's hair while Salome continues dancing. No feast context is represented, nor are any guests present. Rather the image portrays an erotic encounter between the girl and Herod, with Herodias and the maidservant as bystanders in this intimate gathering.

Picasso's depiction of all the biblical characters in the nude is not unusual for this artist; his fascination for nudes is apparent elsewhere in his work.[21] Moreover we should note that his representation of the Gospel narrative is not produced for devotional purposes. Rather, Picasso's etching of the dance reflects a widespread fascination at the end of the nineteenth century with the figure of Salome, whom Dijkstra describes as the 'centrepiece of male masochistic fantasies' during this period.[22]

20. See for example the collection by Hugo Daffner, *Salome: Ihre Gestalt in Geschichte und Kunst* (Munich: H. Schmidt, 1912), which includes over two hundred sculptures, illuminations, engravings and other art based on this story.

21. See further, Diana Widmaier Picasso, *Picasso: Art Can Only Be Erotic* (Munich: Prestel, 2005).

22. Bram Dijkstra, *Idols of Perversity: Fantasies of Feminine Evil in Fin-de-Siècle Culture* (Oxford: Oxford University Press, 1986), p. 379.

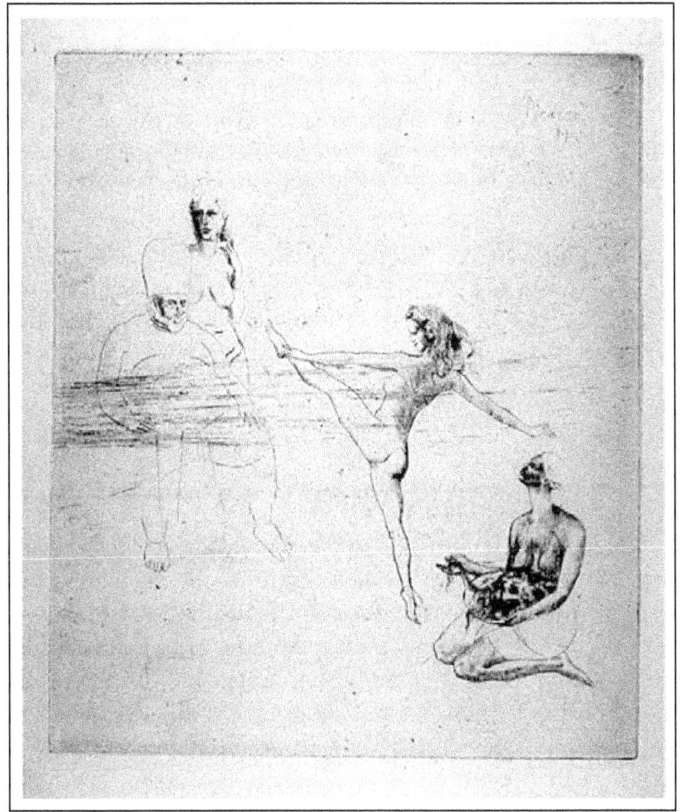

Figure 1. Pablo Picasso, *Salomé* (1905) from *La Suite des Saltimbanques (The Acrobats Set)*. Drypoint on Van Gelder, paper, 40.1 × 34.9 cm. Fine Arts Museums of San Francisco. Museum purchase, M.H. de Young Memorial Museum, 1931. © Succession Picasso/DACS 2007

Gustave Moreau had already brought attention to the erotic potential of the story through his painting *Salome Dancing before Herod*, exhibited in Paris in 1876. Shortly afterwards Flaubert penned his story 'Herodias', in which, perhaps inspired by Moreau's art, he describes the erotic nature of the girl's dance:

> Without bending her knees, she opened her legs and leant over so low that her chin touched the floor. And the nomads inured to abstinence, the Roman soldiers skilled in debauchery, the avaricious publicans, and the old priests soured by controversy all sat there with nostrils distended, quivering with desire.[23]

23. Gustave Flaubert, 'Herodias', in Flaubert, *Three Tales* (London: Penguin, 1961), p. 121.

The imaginative spaces provided by the biblical text are thus vividly filled in with gender constructions that mirror those of the interpreter. As Dijkstra notes:

> In the turn-of-the-century imagination, the figure of Salome epitomized the inherent perversity of women: their eternal circularity and their ability to destroy the male's soul even while they remained nominally chaste in body.[24]

Writers and artists alike portray Salome as a classic example of feminine treachery, or the *femme fatale*, with the girl's acquisition of the Baptist's head seen symbolically to represent castration, thus signifying the triumph of woman over man:

> Symbolic castration, woman's lust for man's severed head, the seat of the brain, that 'great clot of seminal fluid' Ezra Pound would still be talking about in the 1920s, was obviously the supreme act of the male's physical submission to woman's predatory desire.[25]

Indeed, some *fin de siècle* artists went further, and juxtaposed this view of the degeneracy of women with a hostility towards particular racial groups in their representations of the Baptist's beheading. Thus Max Slevogt (*Salome's Dance*, 1895) emphasizes the dancing girl's Semitic origins and depicts a seductive Salome dancing half-naked in the midst of leering Jews and Africans. While Picasso's etching of Salome's dance does not suggest such racial judgement, its representation of an erotic dance, highly charged with sexual significance, reflects similar traits to those adopted by his contemporaries. And in view of the symbolic associations of the severed head, containing vital fluids, Picasso's positioning of the head on the maidservant's lap is also significant.[26] His interpretation of the Baptist's beheading, set against the backdrop of *fin de siècle* fascination with the figure of Salome, reveals the artist's gender construction of woman as dangerous and other.

It is not insignificant that most depictions of Salome were commissioned, executed and paid for by men.[27] In contrast, a strikingly different

24. Dijkstra, *Idols of Perversity*, p. 384.

25. Dijkstra, *Idols of Perversity*, p. 375. Similarly Anderson, 'Feminist Criticism', p. 126; Bach, *Women, Seduction, Betrayal*, p. 259; Julia Kristeva, *Visions capitales* (Paris: Réunion des musées nationaux, 1998), p. 85; Vander Stichele, 'Capital Re-Visions', p. 82.

26. We might compare this with similar representations, for example, Fritz Erler's *Dance Mural* (1898), where the Baptist's head is provocatively positioned between Salome's thighs (reproduced in Dijkstra, *Idols of Perversity*, p. 389).

27. Similarly Glancy ('Unveiling Masculinity', p. 44) comments, 'The familiar, iconic Salome is an invention of men's imaginations'.

perspective was adopted by the few female artists who engaged with the theme during this period, and often sacrificed critical acclaim as a consequence. To take one example:

> Ella Ferris Pell's *Salome* makes a revolutionary statement simply by being nothing but the realistic portrait of a young, strong and radiantly self-possessed woman who looks upon the world around her with confidence, with a touch of arrogance, even—but without any transcendent viciousness.[28]

This highlights that, as with any biblical interpretation where patriarchal frameworks are often tacitly assumed, artistic visualizations of the Bible sometimes reflect androcentric perspectives which can and should be challenged.[29]

While acknowledging the explosion of interest in the figure of Salome at the end of the nineteenth century, and considerable embellishment upon the Gospel narratives as a result, we should nevertheless recognize that portrayals of the girl's dance as evil have a long pedigree which can be traced back to the early Church Fathers. Thus Ambrose comments:

> Is anything so conducive to lust as with unseemly movements thus to expose in nakedness those parts of the body which either nature has hidden or custom has veiled, to sport with the looks, turn the neck, to loosen the hair?[30]

Citing a saying from Cicero ('No-one dances when sober unless he is mad'), Ambrose concludes that the story of John's beheading provides a cautionary lesson about the allures of dancing. Similarly Chrysostom remarks on the beheading narrative, 'For where dancing is, there is the evil one'.[31] Calvin follows this line of interpretation by describing the dance of the girl as a mark of lasciviousness and harlotry.[32] Therefore this theme, which came to prominence at the time when Picasso was working, represents a longstanding strand of the interpretative tradition. Consequently, I would question Caroline Vander Stichele's suggestion that attention to the role of the female characters, the girl's dance and the

28. Dijkstra, *Idols of Perversity*, p. 392. Pell's image is available at http://www.biblical-art.com (accessed 8 August 2006).

29. See further, Anderson, 'Feminist Criticism', pp. 107-108; Glancy, 'Unveiling Masculinity', p. 43.

30. Ambrose, 'Concerning Virgins: Book 3', in *Nicene and Post-Nicene Fathers* (ed. Philip Schaff; Second Series, X; Peabody, MA: Hendrickson, 1994), p. 385.

31. John Chrysostom, 'Homily XLVIII on the Gospel of St Matthew', in *Nicene and Post-Nicene Fathers* (ed. Philip Schaff; First Series, X; Peabody, MA: Hendrickson, 1995), p. 299.

32. John Calvin, *A Harmony of the Gospels Matthew, Mark and Luke*, II (trans. T.H.L. Parker; Edinburgh: Saint Andrew Press, 1972), p. 142.

severed head in the narrative of the Baptist's beheading are to be regarded primarily as features of nineteenth-century decadentism.[33] Rather, these elements, which are found in the biblical narratives themselves, were taken up and commented upon by subsequent interpreters from the early Church onwards, and assumed a new significance in light of the male fear of women's power that developed during the *fin de siècle* period. However, as we shall see below, this understanding of the girl's dance is not the only possible interpretation that can be adopted.

Caravaggio Presents the Baptist's Head to Salome

Our second artistic interpretation of Salome's dance, Caravaggio's *Salome Receives the Head of Saint John the Baptist* (1607–1610), depicts a different narrative moment popular among artists: the presentation of the severed head to the girl (Fig. 2). In contrast to Picasso's interpretation, here we are presented with a fully-clothed girl who turns her head in revulsion when handed the Baptist's head on a platter.

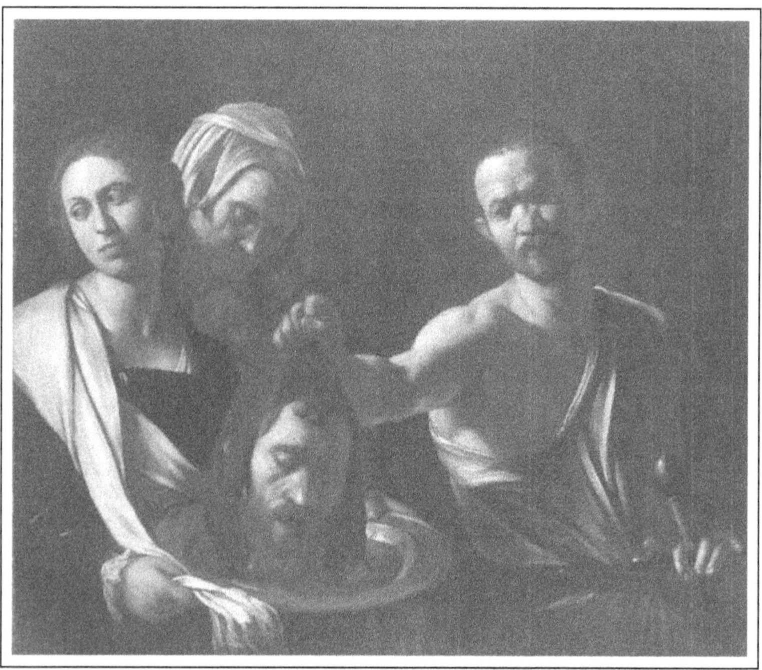

Figure 2. Michelangelo Merisi da Caravaggio, *Salome Receives the Head of Saint John the Baptist*. © The National Gallery, London

33. Vander Stichele, 'Capital Re-Visions', p. 82.

The aversion expressed in Salome's face suggests that the artist regarded her as the tool of her mother's ambitions, obediently complying with Herodias's demand for the Baptist's head, while not desiring this outcome herself. The identity of the second woman in the picture is not clear: Caravaggio presents the heads of the two women very close together, as though emerging from one body, perhaps depicting youth and old age.[34] There is blood on the plate onto which the head is being deposited by the executioner, and the detail of his left hand resting on the sword draws our attention to the weapon used to achieve the beheading.

We can contrast Caravaggio's interpretation of the girl being presented with the head with other representations of Salome holding the platter, where a more triumphant, self-satisfied response to the severed head is apparent. For example, Jacob Cornelisz van Oostsanen's painting *Salome with the Head of John the Baptist* (1524) presents us with a detached figure who seemingly displays no emotional response to the gruesome bloody head on the plate that she clutches, but rather looks askance into the distance.[35] Other artists adopt a different perspective and express neither revulsion nor triumph, but a more compassionate response by Salome. Here I might mention Dürer's woodcut of the Baptist's head being presented to the girl,[36] described by Kristeva as 'almost loving'.[37]

Depictions of a woman holding a man's head are of course not confined to Salome: Judith is frequently represented in art carrying Holofernes' head. But Salome differs from her because, although she demands the head of the Baptist, she does not cut it off herself, as Caravaggio's picture emphasizes. Moreover, the platter often appears to function as the means whereby Salome can keep her hands clean, free of blood, which Caravaggio underscores by the girl's additional use of a scarf to hold the dish. The presence of a platter is usually a distinguishing feature of the Salome narrative, but occasionally some artists, such as Friedrich, depict Salome directly holding the Baptist's head.[38] Equally unusual are those representations of Salome without the head, but simply with an empty plate, awaiting the arrival of her prize.[39]

34. The National Gallery commentary on the picture suggests that the old woman may be Herodias; http://www.nationalgalleryimages.co.uk (accessed 8 August 2006).

35. See http://www.rijksmuseum.nl (accessed 9 August 2006).

36. Albrecht Dürer, *The Beheading of John the Baptist* (1510).

37. Kristeva, *Visions Capitales*, p. 75.

38. Otto Friedrich, *Salome* (c. 1912).

39. See, for example, Henri Regnault, *Salomé* (1870), http://www.metmuseum.org; and Alfred Stevens' *Salome*, http://www.bc.edu/bc_org/avp/cas/fnart/art/19th/salome/salome_stevens_t.jpg (accessed 8 August 2006). Note that in both these

A further feature to note when assessing artistic representations of the Baptist's beheading is the expression on the severed head. Caravaggio's picture presents the Baptist with eyes closed, but mouth open as if still speaking to reproach his murderers. The other three figures in the picture remain silent, with mouths closed. This perhaps corresponds to the interpretative tradition represented in the Church Fathers, which emphasizes that, despite being separated from the body, John's tongue is not deprived of efficacy. Early commentators commonly expressed the view that, although at first sight the wickedness of Herod and Herodias appeared to triumph, at a deeper level they were really defeated, and the Baptist's criticisms could not be silenced.[40]

Caravaggio's depiction of a reluctant and sombre Salome receiving the prize for her dance suggests that this artist regards the girl as an innocent victim of her mother's ambitions, who had charmed Herod without employing sexual antics. Thus by comparing the visualizations of Salome's dance by Caravaggio and Picasso, we are challenged to adjudicate between two very different interpretations. We are thereby also alerted to significant gaps in the biblical narrative.

Funhof at Herod's Birthday Banquet

Finally, we turn to consider Hinrik Funhof's 1483 altar painting, *The Feast of Herod* (Fig. 3), produced for the St Johanniskirche in Lüneburg, Germany, where it can still be found today. The devotional purpose of this work of art should be noted, and can be contrasted with the differing functions of other representations of the Baptist's death which we considered above.

Funhof presents us with a synthesis of narrative moments from the biblical text. He foregrounds two different elements of the beheading episode: the presentation of the Baptist's head to the girl by the executioner on the left-hand side of the altarpiece, and her delivery of the head to her mother, depicted on the right-hand side. The artist also contrasts the beheading episode with other Gospel passages, including the birth of the Baptist and his baptism of Jesus in the background.

Funhof's juxtaposition of different features from the beheading narrative with other Gospel passages highlights a significant contribution of art to biblical exegesis, namely its production of a synchronic dialogue

representations of Salome, the artists include a pearl-handled knife on the platter, highlighting her role in the murder.

40. For example, Ambrose, 'Concerning Virgins: Book 3', p. 386, and Chrysostom, 'Homily XLVIII', p. 300.

between narratives, drawing our attention to intertextual resonances. Thus the association of the beheading incident with the baptism of Jesus prompts the viewer to reflect upon the relationship between these events. However, despite Funhof's synthesis of different narrative moments, the dance of the girl is not represented. This leaves the onlooker to consider how the head ended up on the plate. It also reminds us that noticing what is omitted in a picture is just as significant as analysing what an artist includes.

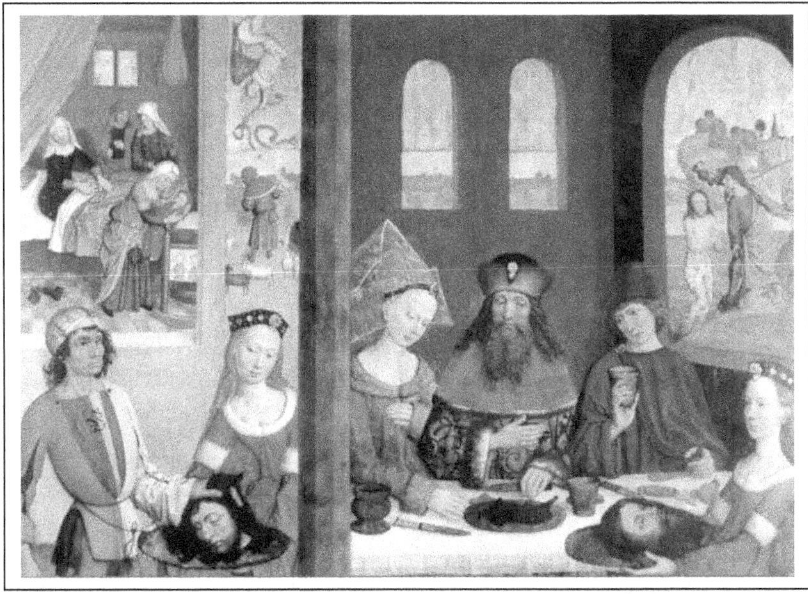

Figure 3. Hinrik Funhof, *The Feast of Herod*, detail from the Altarbild. With permission from St Johanniskirche, Lüneburg

As in the Gospels, Funhof's altarpiece leaves the nature of the dance entirely to the viewer's imagination. The artist focuses rather upon the banquet setting of the narrative, drawing our attention to the food imagery in the story. While biblical commentators have often dismissed the request for the Baptist's head on a platter as a 'macabre detail',[41] Funhof highlights the significance of this feature by drawing a striking parallel between the meat joint on the table and the severed head, which is presented as one of the courses at this royal banquet. Herod holds a knife ready to eat, and Herodias's gaze is directed towards the food on the table as her daughter comes to present her trophy. Funhof's interpretation displays similarities to Rubens's later portrayal of the same event (*The*

41. Hooker, *Gospel according to Mark*, p. 161.

Feast of Herod, 1633), where again the irony of serving up the Baptist's head at a banquet is emphasized, with Herodias lifting her fork ready to savour the Baptist's head.[42]

The feasting imagery in the beheading episode is particularly significant, given that both evangelists place this story immediately before the account of the feeding of the five thousand. This suggests a contrast between the feeding of the multitude—prefiguring the messianic banquet and Jesus' self-sacrifice—and Herod's banquet, where the Baptist's sacrifice is portrayed. The interpretation of the Baptist's death as foreshadowing Jesus' own was well known in the medieval church, with the head on the platter regarded as a symbol of the eucharist. Here we might note, for example, Pseudo-Jerome's suggestion that the plate on which John's head lies is a reminder of the paten used at Mass:

> The body of John is buried, his head is laid on a dish: the letter is covered with earth, the spirit is honoured and received at the altar.[43]

Similarly the late fifteenth-century York breviary reads:

> Caput Johannis in disco: signat corpus Christi: quo pascimur in sancto altari
>
> (St John's head on the dish signifies the body of Christ which feeds us on the holy altar).[44]

Eucharistic interpretation of the Baptist's death was widespread in the medieval period, as evidenced by sculptures, seals, paintings and domestic ornaments of John's head which were produced.[45] This veneration continued throughout the fifteenth and sixteenth centuries, when alabaster tablets depicting the head of John the Baptist on a dish, known as Saint John's heads, were widely circulated. In the light of this cultural situation, we can surmise that Funhof's use of the beheading incident for his altar painting was no coincidence, but rather reflects the eucharistic overtones associated with the story.

As noted above, artistic representations of biblical texts challenge the viewer to consider what characters might look like and to reflect on how they behave in the biblical narrative. Ambiguities in the Gospel accounts

42. I am grateful to John Drury for alerting me to this parallel.

43. Beryl Smalley, *The Study of the Bible in the Middle Ages* (Oxford: Blackwell, 1952), p. 1 n. 3.

44. York Service Book of the Guild of Corpus Christi. Cited by W.H. St John Hope, 'On the Sculptured Alabaster Tablets Called St John's Heads', *Archaeologia* 52 (1890), pp. 669-708 (705).

45. See Hope, 'On the Sculptured Alabaster Tablets', p. 675, who describes the popularity of this image.

concerning the characters of Herod, Herodias and the dancing girl have to be resolved by artists in their visualizations of the text. Funhof's altarpiece seems to portray Herod showing some remorse for the Baptist's death (*contra* Mt. 14.5). He is the only person in the picture to look directly at the severed head, and he does so wistfully. The courtier next to him turns aside and stares into the distance, while the girl holding the platter looks solemnly ahead. Her countenance here is in contrast to the flushed cheeks and wry smile that characterize her response when initially presented with the Baptist's head by the executioner. But perhaps more notably we are drawn to observe the physical similarity between the girl and Herodias, highlighting visually the significance of the mother–daughter relationship in the events which take place.

One further feature to notice is the representation of John the Baptist's head. In contrast to many other representations of the severed head, no blood is apparent, and the plate on which the girl carries the head distances her from the object she transports to her mother. The most striking detail of all is the change of appearance between the two representations of the head: in the depiction on the left hand side of the altar painting, when the executioner presents it to the girl, the Baptist's eyes and mouth are closed, whereas when the head is carried by the girl to Herodias the eyes and mouth are now open. This may reflect the idea that the Baptist's reproach of his murderers continued even after he was beheaded. Later tradition elaborates upon this theme, which is also implied in Mk 6.14, where Herod continues to fear the Baptist after his death, supposing that he had come back to life in Jesus.[46]

Funhof portrays the characters in his painting in typical fifteenth-century attire, reflecting his own cultural context. This reminds us that we are not impartial observers operating in an ahistoric space but need to recognize our own situatedness in a particular time and place when we interpret a biblical text. As Rachel Nicholls points out:

> Understanding involves the interpreter as a person and so involves the context of that person in culture and tradition. This is not just some weary assertion that we can never be free of our own prejudices and limits, it is a positive celebration of our own human identity, our human finitude, as the arena in which we see (and potentially find) understanding.[47]

46. Here we might note, for example, Chrysostom's comments in 'Homily XXIV' and 'Homily XLVIII' on the Gospel of Matthew, pp. 171, 297.

47. Rachel Nicholls, 'Is *Wirkungsgeschichte* (or Reception History) a Kind of Intellectual *Parkour* (or Freerunning)?', at www.bbibcomm.net/news/latest.html, p. 8 (accessed 20 November 2005).

Although Funhof's altarpiece does not directly visualize Salome's dance, the artist's characterisation of the banqueting scene, and his emphasis on the passing on of the severed head to Herodias, suggests an interpretation of the biblical narrative that directs the blame for the Baptist's demise at Herodias. This is also highlighted by the artist's understanding of the sacrificial nature of the Baptist's death, with many details of the picture pointing the viewer towards parallels with Jesus' death. This is the only one of our three examples that explicitly connects the Baptist's beheading with other Gospel passages, thereby giving it a broader contextualization.

The Contribution of Art to Biblical Exegesis

The artistic representations of three different narrative moments from the Gospel accounts of John the Baptist's beheading considered above highlight some key issues for assessing the contribution of art to biblical exegesis.

The Involvement of the Interpreter in the Act of Interpretation

First, all three pictures illustrate the involvement of the interpreter in the process of interpretation. This is exemplified differently by Picasso's etching, Caravaggio's painting and the Funhof altarpiece, but all vividly represent the contextual presuppositions with which artists and biblical interpreters alike 'read' the Gospel narratives.[48] Biblical interpreters often acknowledge in theory the contextual presuppositions that readers bring to the text, but they do not take these seriously in practice. In contrast, art illustrates much more pointedly the contextual nature of biblical interpretation. It thus presents an important challenge to many historical-critical readings of biblical texts, which often assume that neutral and objective interpretations can be attained. Furthermore, as Ulrich Luz notes, the emphasis in art upon context should also alert interpreters to the limitations of our own readings, by reminding us of our own particularity.[49]

Filling the Imaginative Spaces in the Text

By exploring the contrasting ways in which the girl's dance and the request for the head have been presented in art, we are prompted to think

48. On the artist as 'reader' of biblical texts, see further P. Berdini, 'Jacopo Bassani: A Case for Painting as Visual Exegesis', in *Interpreting Christian Art* (ed. H.J. Hornik and M.C. Parsons; Macon, GA: Mercer University Press, 2003), pp. 169-86. See also Bach (*Women, Seduction, Betrayal*, p. 249), who points out, 'A visual image (or images) is in itself a reading, or retelling, not merely an illustration of a reading but a new text in itself'.

49. Ulrich Luz, *Studies in Matthew* (Grand Rapids: Eerdmans, 2005), p. 326.

about the motives, actions and consequences of the characters in the biblical story and to acknowledge the gaps in the text. We are thereby pointed to the dynamic nature of the biblical narrative, which refuses closure and leaves open many avenues for the interpreter to pursue.[50] At the same time we are also alerted to the patriarchal frameworks within which many artists operate, and which need to be exposed. We should not assume that art provides universally 'good' interpretations of the Bible; but artists' visualizations of the story make an important contribution to the broader debate about how to interpret the text. As Cheryl Exum notes, 'We may revise our critical stance toward a biblical text as a result of our encounter with its artistic representation, but even if we do not, our vision has been enlarged'.[51]

Principles of Selection

We have noted different principles of selectivity operating in the visualizations presented by Picasso, Caravaggio and Funhof. What the artists choose to omit is often as significant as what they decide to include in their representations of the biblical narrative. These decisions are sometimes influenced by the purpose for which the work is intended, as is apparent in Funhof's focus on the sacrificial nature of the Baptist's death for his altar painting. Furthermore, Funhof's inclusion of other Gospel events in the background of his painting introduces an intertextual dialogue which also affects our reading of the beheading narrative.

Conclusions

Investigating artists' visualizations of Salome's role in the Baptist's death leads us not only to recognize the diverse cultural impact of the Bible but also to acknowledge a whole realm of new interpretative possibilities. This stimulates the imagination—or as Blake would put it 'rouzes the faculties to act'—challenging us to reflect on what characters might look like and how they behave in the biblical narrative. We are also reminded that understanding a biblical text occurs not simply through elucidation of its statements but by engaging all the senses and involving the whole human

50. As Bach (*Women, Seduction, Betrayal*, p. 249) notes, an analysis of visual representations 'prevents the reader from harmonizing or universalizing characterization—Salomé as loyal daughter and dishonourable Jew, Salomé as virgin or virago—and creates a healthy web of antagonisms among all these cultural representations'.

51. J. Cheryl Exum, 'Beyond the Biblical Horizon: The Bible and the Arts', in *Beyond the Biblical Horizon: The Bible and the Arts* (ed. J. Cheryl Exum; Leiden: E.J. Brill, 1999), p. 2.

being.[52] But, most importantly, the interpretative diversity reflected in art provides a crucial contribution to biblical exegesis. It directs us to the openness of the biblical text which refuses closure, not least because of the gaps in it that biblical scholars habitually fill. In prompting readers to recognize these gaps afresh, art provides an invaluable input for any interpretative endeavour.

BIBLIOGRAPHY

Ambrose, 'Concerning Virgins: Book 3', in *Nicene and Post-Nicene Fathers* (ed. Philip Schaff; First Series, X; Peabody, MA: Hendrickson, 1995).

Anderson, Janice Capel, 'Feminist Criticism: The Dancing Daughter', in *Mark and Method: New Approaches in Biblical Studies* (ed. Janice Capel Anderson and Stephen D. Moore; Minneapolis: Fortress Press, 1992), pp. 103-34.

Bach, Alice, *Women, Seduction, and Betrayal in Biblical Narrative* (Cambridge: Cambridge University Press, 1997).

Berdini, P., 'Jacopo Bassani: A Case for Painting as Visual Exegesis', in *Interpreting Christian Art* (ed. H.J. Hornik and M.C. Parsons; Macon, GA: Mercer University Press, 2003), pp. 169-86.

Callaway, Mary, 'What's the Use of Reception History?', at www.bbibcomm.net/news/latest.html.

Calvin, John, *A Harmony of the Gospels Matthew, Mark and Luke*, II (trans. T.H.L. Parker; Edinburgh: Saint Andrew Press, 1972).

Chrysostom, John, 'Homilies on the Gospel of Saint Matthew', in *Nicene and Post-Nicene Fathers* (ed. Philip Schaff; Second Series, X; Peabody, MA: Hendrickson, 1994).

Daffner, Hugo, *Salome: Ihre Gestalt in Geschichte und Kunst* (Munich: H. Schmidt, 1912).

Dijkstra, Bram, *Idols of Perversity: Fantasies of Feminine Evil in Fin-de-Siècle Culture* (Oxford: Oxford University Press, 1986).

Exum, J. Cheryl, 'Beyond the Biblical Horizon: The Bible and the Arts', in *Beyond the Biblical Horizon: The Bible and the Arts* (ed. J. Cheryl Exum; Leiden: E.J. Brill, 1999).

Flaubert, Gustave, 'Herodias', in Flaubert, *Three Tales* (London: Penguin, 1961).

Glancy, Jennifer, 'Unveiling Masculinity: The Construction of Gender in Mark 6.17-29', *BibInt* 2 (1994), pp. 34-50.

Goodacre, Mark, 'Fatigue in the Synoptics', *NTS* 44 (1998), pp. 45-58.

Guelich, Robert A., *Mark 1.1–8.26* (Dallas: Word Books, 1989).

Hartmann, Michael, *Der Tod Johannes des Täufers: Eine exegetische und rezeptionsgeschichtliche Studie auf dem Hintergrund narrativer, intertextueller und kulturanthropologischer Zugänge* (Stuttgart: Katholisches Bibelwerk, 2001).

Hooker, Morna D., *The Gospel according to St Mark* (London: A. & C. Black, 1991).

52. Similarly, Ulrich Luz, *Matthew 1–7: A Commentary* (trans. Wilhelm C. Linss; Minneapolis: Augsburg, 1989), p. 98.

Hope, W.H. St John, 'On the Sculptured Alabaster Tablets Called St John's Heads', *Archaeologia* 52 (1890), pp. 669-708.

Jensen, Robin M., 'Giving Texts Vision and Images Voice: The Promise and Problems of Interdisciplinary Scholarship', in *Common Life in the Early Church: Essays Honoring Graydon F. Snyder* (ed. Julian V. Hills; Harrisburg, PA: Trinity Press International, 1998), pp. 344-56.

Josephus, Flavius, *Jewish Antiquities* (LCL, 9; trans. L.H. Feldman; Cambridge, MA: Harvard University Press, 1965).

Joynes, Christine E., 'John the Baptist's Death', in *Mark Gospel of Action: Personal and Community Responses* (ed. John Vincent; London: SPCK, 2006), pp. 143-53.

Kovacs, Judith, and Christopher Rowland, *Revelation: The Apocalypse of Jesus Christ* (Oxford: Blackwell, 2004).

Kristeva, Julia, *Visions capitales* (Paris: Réunion des musées nationaux, 1998).

Kuryluk, E., *Salome and Judas in the Cave of Sex: The Grotesque: Origins, Iconography, Techniques* (Evanston, IL: Northwestern University Press, 1987).

Luz, Ulrich, *Matthew 1–7: A Commentary* (trans. Wilhelm C. Linss; Minneapolis: Augsburg, 1989).

—*Studies in Matthew* (Grand Rapids: Eerdmans, 2005).

Myers, Ched, *Binding the Strong Man: A Political Reading of Mark's Story of Jesus* (Maryknoll, NY: Orbis Books, 1988).

Nicholls, Rachel, 'Is *Wirkungsgeschichte* (or Reception History) a Kind of Intellectual *Parkour* (or Freerunning)?', at www.bbibcomm.net/news/latest.html.

Rowland, Christopher, 'Imagining the Apocalypse', *NTS* 51 (2005), pp. 303-27.

Schildgen, Brenda Deen, 'A Blind Promise: Mark's Retrieval of Esther', *Poetics Today* 15 (1994), pp. 115-31.

Smalley, Beryl, *The Study of the Bible in the Middle Ages* (Oxford: Blackwell, 1952).

Vander Stichele, Caroline, 'Capital Re-Visions: The Head of John the Baptist as Object of Art', in *Missing Links: Arts, Religion, Reality* (ed. Jonneke Bekkenkamp; Münster: LIT Verlag, 2000), pp. 71-87.

Widmaier Picasso, Diana, *Picasso: Art Can Only Be Erotic* (Munich: Prestel, 2005).

Zagona, H.G., *The Legend of Salome and the Principle of Art for Art's Sake* (Paris: Librairie Minard, 1960).

The Bible and the Sixteenth-Century Painter: *Nativity*, *Way to Calvary* and *Crucifixion* as Visual Narratives by Michele Tosini

Heidi J. Hornik

The Florentine painter Michele Tosini (1503–1577), better known to his contemporaries as Michele di Ridolfo del Ghirlandaio, incorporated details from specific Gospel narratives into his religious compositions commissioned in and around Florence. Three paintings from diverse periods in the artist's life are studied for their contributions to style and biblical interpretation. Sixteenth-century artists were deliberate in their narrative selection and biblical details that they transfer from the text to the canvas or, in Tosini's case, to the panel. Previous scholarship, with only a few exceptions (namely, Jaroslav Pelikan, Margaret Miles and Paolo Berdini), does not give sufficient attention to researching the precise biblical narrative that becomes the textual inspiration specific to each painting.[1]

A visual tradition was learned and copied, but in some cases this process was not so mundane. By first considering Tosini as the *capo* or head of the most productive workshop in the sixteenth century in Florence (the Ghirlandaio) and then by studying other examples of his work that rely heavily on biblical interpretation, the reader can understand the artist, the Florentine culture and the purpose of the incorporation of the Bible into the painted medium.

The research of the paintings and documents in Italy was facilitated by an Allbritton Grant for Faculty Scholarship 2006–2007, Department of Art, Baylor University.

1. Jaroslav Pelikan, *Jesus through the Centuries* (New Haven: Yale University Press, 1985); *Mary through the Centuries* (New Haven: Yale University Press, 1996); Margaret R. Miles, *Image as Insight: Visual Understanding in Western Christianity and Secular Culture* (Boston: Beacon Press, 1985); Paolo Berdini, *The Religious Art of Jacopo Bassano: Painting as Visual Exegesis* (Cambridge: Cambridge University Press, 1997).

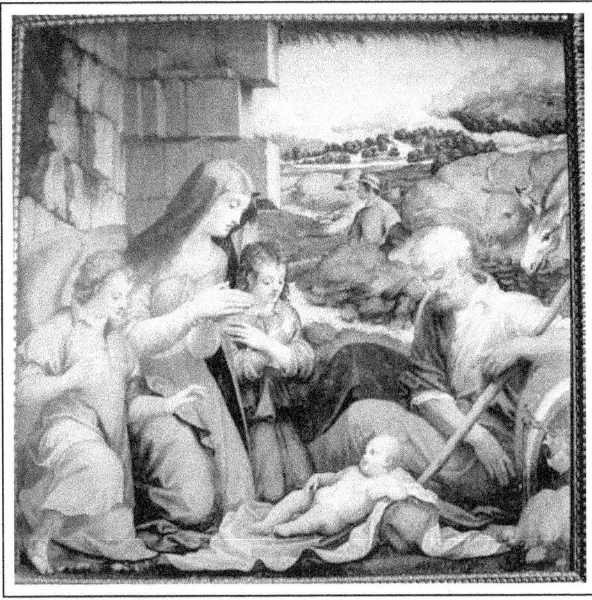

Figure 1. Michele Tosini, *Nativity with the Shepherds*, Cappella di San Michele Arcangelo, Badia di Passignano. Photo: author with permission from the Badia di Passignano

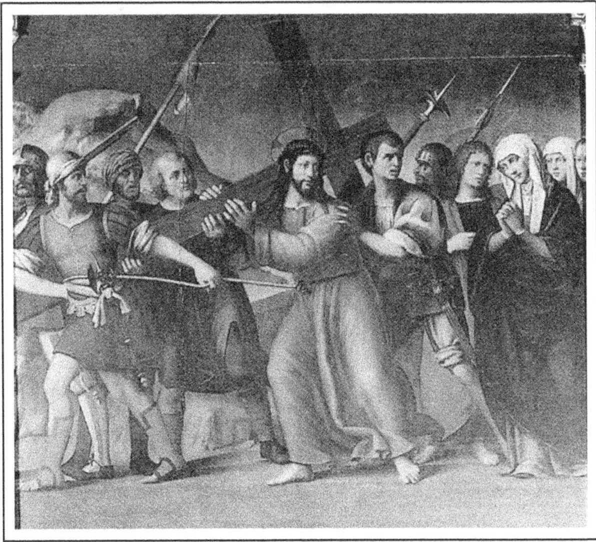

Figure 2. Michele Tosini, *Way to Calvary*, Antinori Chapel, S. Spirito, Florence. Reproduced with permission from Servizio Musei Comunali di Firenze

After a brief introduction to Michele as a painter and teacher, three paintings will be studied in canonical order: *Nativity*, Church of San Michele Arcangelo, Badia di Passignano (Fig. 1); *Way to Calvary*, Antinori Chapel, Santo Spirito, Florence (Fig. 2); *Crucifixion*, Convent of San Vincenzo, Prato (Fig. 3). The canonical order is different from the chronological order in which Tosini painted them. The stylistic analysis will reflect the artist's early style in the *Way to Calvary*, c. 1530–1540, and the mature style in the *Nativity* and *Crucifixion* paintings, 1549–1550 and 1559–1561, respectively. Tosini utilized the various Gospels according to the iconographical significance he employed in a particular painting or fresco cycle.

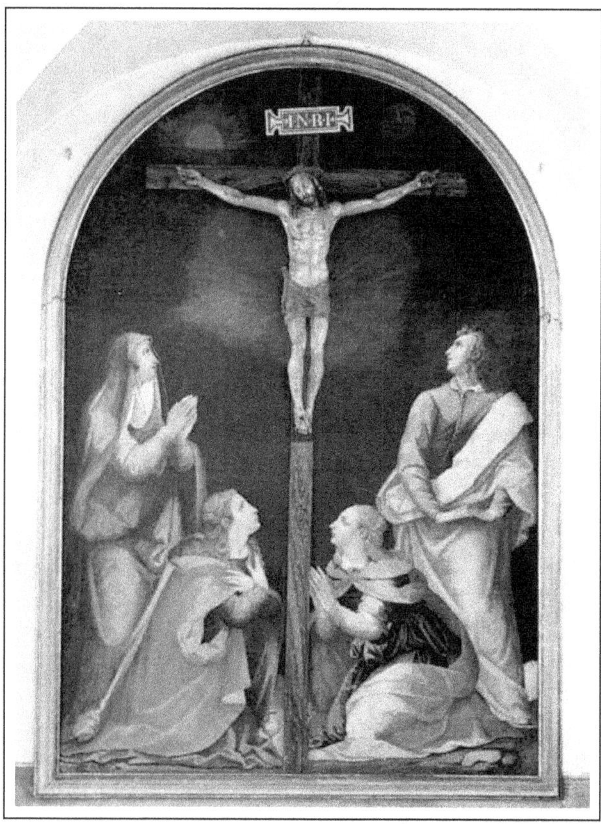

Figure 3. Michele Tosini, *Crucifixion*, Convent of San Vincenzo, Prato. Photo: author with permission from the Convent of San Vincenzo

These three biblical narratives and their painted scenes will be examined, combining biblical and art historical methods. The background for each commission gives the details of how Michele was selected to paint the work. That information is known for two of the paintings. All of the paintings will be discussed in stylistic (Tosini leads the workshop into the 'style of the day' or Mannerist period of art history), historical, and iconographical terms. The method used in this article is a modified version of that implemented in the *Illuminating Luke* volumes that I co-authored with Mikeal C. Parsons.[2] In these volumes we dealt with artists working over a period of four centuries in varied regions of Italy. Here I deal with three paintings by the same artist, all produced in Tuscany during a period of less than forty years. A focus can be maintained to allow the reader to see not only how one master in the Late Renaissance period, known as Mannerism, handled biblical interpretation but also to become familiar with the life of a man deeply involved in shaping Florentine culture through its art.

The work of art historian Paolo Berdini greatly assists this methodology. Berdini understands the interpretation of the text as a 'trajectory of visualization', which he labels 'visual exegesis'. In Berdini's words:

> The painter reads the text and translates his scriptural reading into a problem in representation, to which he offers a solution – the image. In that image the beholder acknowledges, not the text in the abstract, but the painter's reading of the text so that the effect the image has on the beholder is a function of what the painter wants the beholder to experience in the text. This is the trajectory of visualization, and the effect of the text through the image is a form of exegesis. Painting is not the simple visualization of the narrative of the text but an expansion of that text, subject to discursive strategies of various kinds.[3]

This 'visual exegesis' of the paintings intends to contribute a deeper understanding of the relationship between the biblical narratives and their application to sixteenth-century religious painting.

Michele di Ridolfo as Capo della Bottega del Ghirlandaio

Michele di Ridolfo was trained by Domenico Ghirlandaio's son Ridolfo (1483–1561).[4] Ridolfo inheited the Ghirlandaio workshop, or *bottega*,

2. Heidi J. Hornik and Mikeal C. Parsons, *Illuminating Luke: The Infancy Narrative in Italian Renaissance Painting* (Harrisburg, PA: Trinity Press International, 2003); *Illuminating Luke: The Public Ministry of Christ in Italian Renaissance and Baroque Painting* (New York: Continuum, 2005); *Illuminating Luke: The Passion and Resurrection Narratives in Italian Renaissance and Baroque Painting* (New York: T. & T. Clark International, 2007).

3. Berdini, *Religious Art of Jacopo Bassano*, p. 35.

4. Heidi J. Hornik, 'The Testament of Michele Tosini', *Paragone* (1995), pp. 156-67; 'Michele di Ridolfo del Ghirlandaio (1503–1577) and the Reception of Mannerism in Florence' (PhD dissertation, Pennsylvania State University, 1990).

from his father. The *bottega* of the Ghirlandaio was famous for training its artists well. They received numerous commissions because their work was beautifully constructed and expertly painted. The Ghirlandaio artists were known for their creativity and reliable manner. Ridolfo did not have any sons to pass the workshop to and Michele's father, Jacopo, was a messenger and notary for the Signoria, or government officials in Florence, so this student/partner-teacher relationship was beneficial to both men.[5] Michele, who was born in Florence on May 8, 1503, learned how to read and write at a young age because of the importance of that skill to his father and his father's livelihood.[6] Michele was a member of the parish of Santa Maria Novella in Florence when he wrote his testament on 20 March, 1575.[7] This testament revealed information regarding the personal life of the artist. According to the testament, Michele married a woman named Felice and together they had four children.[8] His two sons became painters. The eldest continued the Ghirlandaio workshop into the next generation and the younger son was a Dominican brother in Fiesole. Michele also had two daughters, both of whom became nuns. Dionora (1540–1606) entered the convent of San Vincenzo in Prato on 31 December, 1553.[9] I will return to this event in my discussion of the commission of the *Crucifixion* (Fig. 3).

Michele's artistic training began with Lorenzo di Credi (1459–1537) and continued in the shop of Antonio del Ceraiolo (d. 1525?). The *Way to Calvary* (Fig. 2) is sometimes attributed to Ceraiolo as Michele's early style shows Ceraiolo's influence. This will be discussed further below.[10] Michele's most influential experience came in the workshop of Ridolfo del Ghirlandaio. Ridolfo was known to contemporaries as one of the best draftsman in Florence and was much loved by everyone, particularly by Raphael.[11] Giorgio Vasari (1511–1574) remains the most important

5. Giorgio Vasari, *Le opere di Giorgio Vasari: Le vite de'più eccellenti pittori, scultori ed architettori scritte da Giorgio Vasari pittore Aretino* (ed. Gaetano Milanesi; 9 vols.; 2nd edn, 1568; Florence: Sansoni, 1885), VI, p. 543 n. 3.

6. Hornik, 'The Testament of Michele Tosini', p. 156.

7. It is uncertain when Michele joined the parish or whether he was born there. The baptismal records in the parish of S. Maria Novella have been lost for the year 1503. Recently discovered documents that will be in a forthcoming publication by the author that indicate Michele returned to Santa Maria Novella and worked with his son Baccio on several projects.

8. Hornik, 'The Testament of Michele Tosini', pp. 157, 161 n. 10, 165.

9. Domenico Guglielmo M. Di Agresti, *Santa Caterina de'Ricci: Cronache, diplomatica, lettere varie* (Collana Ricciana; Florence: Olschki, 1969), V, pp. 41-42.

10. The current attribution (14 June, 2006) on the label near the painting in the Church of Santo Spirito is to Antonio Ceraiolo.

11. Vasari, *Le vite*, VI, p. 534.

primary source for Michele today. Michele and Giorgio were friends and colleagues. Vasari often interceded on behalf of Michele as an employment reference for public projects throughout Florence sponsored by Cosimo de'Medici in the mid 1560s. Vasari explained the relationship between Michele and Ridolfo: Michele looked upon 'Ridolfo as a father, and loved him, as one belonging to Ridolfo[;] he has always been and is still known by no other name but Michele di Ridolfo'.[12] Several collaborative works by Michele and Ridolfo during the 1530s and 1540s were reported by Vasari.[13]

Michele's first individual works defined him as a Florentine artist of the sixteenth century with the ability to observe and copy the styles of Agnolo Bronzino, Francesco Salviati and Giorgio Vasari.[14] Tosini's works from 1540–1560 were critical to the dissemination of the styles of the three artists in numerous types of commissions.[15] Michele's strong workshop training, familiarity with the art of his contemporaries, and participation in collaborative projects with Ridolfo del Ghirlandaio secured the foundation necessary for him to progress towards an independent style in the 1550s, to become a participant in the major Florentine public projects of the 1560s, and to receive a broad range of private commissions in the 1560s and 1570s.[16] Michele inherited the workshop from Ridolfo in 1561. According to Vasari and other contemporaries, Michele was well known

12. Vasari, *Le vite*, VI, p. 543. Vasari included Michele in the second edition of *Le vite* in 1568, but does not discuss him in the 1550 edition. See Hornik, 'Michele di Ridolfo', pp. 2-3.

13. Vasari, *Le vite*, VI, pp. 543-47. See Hornik, 'Michele di Ridolfo', pp. 25-56, 196-206, for a discussion of the collaborative works by Ridolfo del Ghirlandaio and Michele Tosini. See also David Franklin, *Painting in Renaissance Florence 1500–1550* (New Haven: Yale University Press, 2001), pp. 103-25; 'Towards a New Chronology for Ridolfo Ghirlandaio and Michele Tosini', *Burlington Magazine* 140 (1998), pp. 445-55, and specifically n. 39, for a useful 'updating' of the works.

14. Heidi J. Hornik, 'Michele Tosini: The Artist, The Oeuvre and The Testament', in *Continuity, Innovation and Connoisseurship: Old Master Paintings at the Palmer Museum of Art* (ed. Mary Jane Harris and Patrick McGrady; University Park, PA: Penn State Press, 2003), pp. 22-37.

15. Michele became so adept at the style of these masters that scholars continue to battle with problems of attribution. Confusion between the hands of Michele, Salviati, and Vasari are most prevalent in portraiture.

16. His public projects included the decoration of the Palazzo Vecchio by Cosimo I de'Medici in 1557, the formation and drafting of the constitution of the Accademia del Disegno (alongside Vasari, the sculptors Montorsoli and Francesco da Sangallo, and the painters Agnolo Bronzino, and Pier Francesco di Sandro Foschi) in 1563, the grand funeral decoration in Florence for Michelangelo in 1564, and the painted decorations for the Medici wedding of Francesco I and Giovanna of Austria in 1565. See Vasari, *Le vite*, VI, pp. 658, 656, 547.

for his ability to attract a large number of talented artists to his shop and to train them well.[17]

The three paintings show Michele di Ridolfo's early, more High Renaissance style in the *Way to Calvary*, c. 1530–40, his mature style from the later 1540s in the *Nativity*, and a truly mannerist style in the *Crucifixion* of 1559–61 in Prato. The private chapel in the Villa Caserotta, a re-discovered private commission completed by Michele Tosini and his workshop in 1561, is critical to our comprehension of Michele's knowledge of the Bible. His interpretative skills created a complex religious iconography that allows him to be classified as an innovator in sixteenth-century Florentine art.[18] These chapel frescoes are in excellent condition and have undergone very little restoration except for some overpainting of the Latin inscriptions. I will use this complex iconographic program to demonstrate Tosini's ability to integrate text and image from canonical and liturgical sources.

Nativity

The Commission and the Badia

The history of the Badia (monastery) is critical to gain an understanding of the connections between Tosini's work and patrons in Florence and those in neighboring towns. The professional relationships that painters and their workshops had with religious orders, wealthy families, and government officials determined which workshop received a new commission. The Ghirlandaio workshop under Domenico, Ridolfo, and Michele maintained its reputation for reliability and creative productivity.

The Badia di Passignano grew out of a movement between the middle of the tenth century and the first thirty years of the eleventh century to reform Benedictine monasticism. The increase of ascetism and an austere lifestyle was believed to be closer to the intentions of Benedict's rules. In 1036 St Giovanni Gualberto founded a monastic congregation at Vallombrosa in the Florentine hills. The lords who possessed the ancient abbey of Passignano donated it to St Giovanni Gualberto in 1049. The restoration began and the abbey gained more prestige in the communities when Gulaberto died and was buried there in 1073.[19] Passignano remained a

17. Vasari, *Le vite*, VI, p. 547.

18. Heidi J. Hornik, 'The Strozzi Chapel by Michele Tosini: A Visual Interpretation of Redemptive Epiphany', *Artibus et Historiae* 46 (2002), pp. 97-118.

19. Ager Clantius, *Badia a Passignano. Collana di Brevi Monografie Chiantigiane* (Florence: Editoriale gli Arci Pressi, 2001), IV, p. 41. The *Nativity* is also illustrated without discussion in *L'organo della Badia di San Michele Arcangelo a Passignano* (Florence: Edizioni Polistampa, 2004), p. 5.

wealthy village and the position of abbot was much sought after throughout the middle ages and Renaissance. The location, just outside Florence, and the desire of both the Guelphs and the Ghibellines to acquire the town, kept the monastery in constant transformation and growth.[20] The Florentine families from the eleventh through the fifteenth centuries also vied for the city. In 1487, Lorenzo il Maginifico de'Medici was able to secure from Pope Innocenzo VIII that the monastery's commendam be awarded to his son Giovanni, who was later to become Pope Leo X.[21]

The renovations of the late fifteenth century included building a refectory and cloister with several works of art.[22] The Romanesque abbey church was modernized and Michele Tosini was brought in to execute the two major paintings on wood panel at the entrance to the choir in the chapel dedicated to St Michael the Archangel. Several other Mannerist painters were chosen to paint the altarpieces for the other smaller chapels in the abbey church. These included Alessandro Allori (1535–1607), who frescoed the tomb of Saint Giovanni in 1581, and Giovanni Butteri (1540–1606), who painted another small chapel in 1600.[23] At this time the abbey became a study center for monks. These friars were learning ancient Greek and Hebrew in order to deepen their understanding of the sacred scriptures as well as the sciences. Galileo Galilei was a teacher at the monastery in 1588.[24]

The *Nativity* (Fig. 1) and its companion piece, *Three Archangels*, executed for the entrance to the *coro* of the abbey church, were first attributed to Michele Tosini by Carlo Gamba (1928), entirely on the basis of style.[25]

20. Guido Carocci, *Il commune di San Casciano in Val di Pesa* (Florence: TIP della Pia Casa di Patronato, 1892), pp. 219-21.

21. Carocci, *Il commune di San Casciano*, p. 42.

22. *La Badia di Passignano* (ed. Monaci Benedettini Vallombrosani del Monastero di Passignano; Bologna: Fotometalgrafica Emiliana, 1989), pp. 17-21.

23. Carocci, *Il commune di San Casciano*, p. 43.

24. Carocci, *Il commune di San Casciano*, p. 43.

25. The *Nativity with the Shepherds* is oil on panel, 135 × 135 cm and is dated 1549–50. See Carlo Gamba, 'Ridolfo e Michele di Ridolfo del Ghirlandaio', *Dedalo* 9 (1928–29), p. 554. For mention of these paintings, see also Bernhard Degenhart, 'Tosini, Michele', in *Allgemeines Lexicon der bildenden Künstler* (ed. U. Thieme and F. Becker; Leipzig: E.A. Seemann, 1939), p. 316; Bernard Berenson, *Italian Pictures of the Renaissance: Florentine School* (London: Phaidon Press, 1963), I, p. 150; II, fig. 1302; Armando Schiavo, 'La Badia di San Michele Arcangelo a Passignano in Val di Pesa', *Benedictina* 7 (1954), pp. 257-88; Armando Schiavo, 'Notizie riguardanti la Badia di Passignano estratte dai fondi dell'Archivio di Stato di Firenze', *Benedictina* 9 (1955), pp. 31-92; Simonetta Prosperi Valenti Rodino, *Dizionario enciclopedico Bolaffi dei pittori e degli incisori italiani* (Turin: Bolaffi, 1974), V, p. 375; Sydney Freedberg, *Painting in Italy 1500–1600* (Baltimore: Penguin Books, 1970), p. 463; *Firenze a la Toscana dei Medici nell'Europa del Cinquecento: Il Primato del disegno* (ed. Paolo Barocchi; Milan: Electa, 1980), p. 146.

There has not been any dispute regarding this attribution, and therefore it has become one of the most securely attributed works in the oeuvre of Tosini.[26] The patron of the two works has been assumed to be Nicolo Ungaro, Prior of the Badia at the time of the renovations and commissioning of these paintings.[27] His family crest appears in the right corner of both panels. This crest was also sculpted on the marble holy water font in the church of Santa Trinità in Florence.[28] Both the church and monastery were under the direction of the order of the Vallombrosan Benedictines. Ridolfo and Michele produced two paintings in the church of Santa Trinità in the 1530s and established their reputation at that time.[29]

Passignano is less than ten miles from the Strozzi Villa Caserotta in Paolini, which contains an entire fresco cycle in the chapel, painted by Michele and the Ghirlandaio workshop in 1561.[30] The chapel cycle emphasized the favorite Florentine feast day of the Epiphany (January 6) through the visual depiction of the two events of that day, the Adoration of the Kings and the Marriage at Cana, and a literal description of the third event, the Baptism of Christ, which appears on the open Gospel book of Mark. The original altar panel is a *Lamentation* that defined the program of the chapel as the full cycle of redemption from the infancy narratives through Christ's sacrifice and death.[31] Redemption in the here and now is emphasized through the repetition of the word *hodie* ('today') in the only three non-biblical inscriptions, and reveals the contemporary liturgical source for the iconography. Liturgically, the Epiphany is the day

26. See also Hornik, 'Michele di Ridolfo', pp. 205, 206, 207, 224. On 10 October, 1810, the Napoleonic invasion ended all monastic activities of Passignano and resulted in the loss of a great part of the monastery's vast archival, bibliographic, and artistic patrimonies. From the Archivio di Stato document ASF. Corporazioni religiose soppresse dal governo-francese. N. 179 it is apparent that large gaps now exist in the historical documents for the Badia di Passignano related to sixteenth-century restorations, so the proof and exact date of this commission will probably never be recovered.

27. Schiavo, 'La Badia di San Michele Arcangelo', pp. 262, 265.

28. For an illustration of the holy water font, see Giuseppe Marchini and Emma Micheletti, *La chiesa di Santa Trinita a Firenze* (Florence: Cassa di Risparmio di Firenze, 1987), p. 243.

29. For a discussion of the *Annunciation* and *St Jerome* paintings by Michele and Ridolfo del Ghirlandaio, see Hornik, 'Michele di Ridolfo', pp. 324-25; Marchini and Micheletti, *La Chiesa di Santa Trinita*, p. 165.

30. Hornik, 'Strozzi Chapel', pp. 97, 118.

31. These inscriptions are painted above the two narrative scenes of the *Adoration of the Magi* and the *Marriage at Cana*, and in a continuous band above the scenes from the childhood of Christ (in *tondi*) that flank the altarpiece depicting the *Lamentation*.

on which the Church is married to Christ.[32] At its Lauds, one of the liturgical hours, the antiphon to the Benedictus, is: '*Today* the Church is joined to her celestial spouse, because in Jordan Christ doth wash her sins; the Magi hasten with gifts to the royal marriage feast, and the guests exult in the water turned to wine'.[33] New beginnings and the emphatic application of this redemption cycle of Christ to the world of the viewer or worshiper significantly contribute to the meaning of this chapel. The nearest church to the Villa is Santa Cecilia in San Casciano. Santa Cecilia was founded by, and remains under, the auspices of the Vallombrosans. It can be assumed that the priest who would serve mass for the Strozzi family in this chapel would have also been Vallombrosan.

The chapel program addresses one of the first objections raised by Martin Luther that served as the basis of Protestantism: *sola scriptura*.[34] Tosini's fresco scenes are entirely biblical. He did not directly draw on apocryphal stories. While he transcribed the biblical passages in the open Gospel books and on the walls of the chapel, they remained secondary to the visual image tradition. This can certainly be understood as a pro-Catholic apologetic in light of the Protestant objections that prompted the Council of Trent's twenty-fifth, and final, session on the invocation, veneration and relics of saints and on sacred images.[35] Tosini incorporated text and image at a critical time in the history of Western civilization, and most definitely did not realize all the potential ramifications for such a combination. In 1561, at age fifty-seven, Michele Tosini was an experienced man, with a mature artistic style. One of his most original contributions and artistic legacies is a small fresco cycle in a private chapel outside of the Florentine metropolis, a cycle which wrestles with some of the same critical issues being discussed in the major cities of London, Geneva, and Trent by some of the greatest theologians of the millennium.[36]

32. *Catholic Encyclopedia* (Encyclopedia Press, 1909), V, p. 506. There was not a specific feast day for the Baptism of Christ in the Roman Church calendar. This event is mentioned, as stated above, in the liturgy for the feast of the Epiphany. For a more recent study of this symbolism, see Rab Hatfield, *Botticelli's Uffizi 'Adoration': A Study in Pictorial Content* (Princeton, NJ: Princeton University Press, 1976), p. 55.

33. *Catholic Encyclopedia*, V, p. 506; see also Hugo Kehrer, *Die heiligen drei Könige in Literatur und Kunst* (Leipzig: A. Seemann, 1908–1909), I, pp. 46-49. Specifically on Augustine's interpretation of the Epiphany, see p. 34.

34. See *Luther's Works* (ed. Jaroslav Pelikan, H.T. Lehman, *et al.*; St Louis, MO: Concordia, 1958), p. 36. In his treatise on *The Babylonian Captivity of the Church* in 1520, Luther stated: 'What is asserted without the Scriptures or proven revelation may be held as an opinion, but need not be believed'.

35. The session was held on 3–4 December, 1563. See *The Council of Trent: Canons and Decrees* (ed. J. Waterworth; Chicago: Christian Symbolic Publication Society, 1848).

36. Hornik, 'Strozzi Chapel', p. 118.

Biblical Narrative as Word into Image

The complex iconographical program of the Strozzi chapel described above revealed the depth of Tosini's understanding of the Bible and his ability to incorporate word and image. Tosini's inspiration for the biblical narrative of the nativity (with the adoration of the shepherds) is told only in the Gospel of Luke. Immediately after the birth of Jesus the angel appears to the shepherds: 'And there were in the same country shepherds watching, and keeping the night watches over their flock. And behold an angel of the Lord stood by them, and the brightness of God shone round about them; and they feared with a great fear. And the angel said to them: fear not; for, behold, I bring you good tidings of great joy, that shall be to all the people: For, this day, is born to you a Saviour, who is Christ the Lord, in the city of David' (Lk. 2.8-11).[37]

The angels describe the scene of the nativity to the shepherds, 'And this shall be a sign unto you. You shall find the infant wrapped in swaddling clothes, and laid in a manager' (Lk. 2.12). In the foreground of the painting, Tosini depicted the visual account of the biblical narrative. The angels have already departed in the Tosini painting. 'And suddenly there was with the angel a multitude of the heavenly army, praising God, and saying: glory to God in the highest; and on earth peace to men of good will' (Lk. 2.13). The whiteness and brightness of the sky can still be seen above the shepherds. Tosini painted the scene as it is happening and as the shepherds have just heard it and are picturing it in their own minds. They are discussing what has just happened to them and deciding what to do about it. 'And it came to pass, after the angels departed from them into heaven, the shepherds said to one another: Let us go over to Bethlehem, and let us see this word that is come to pass, which the Lord hath showed to us' (Lk. 2.15). This event prompts the shepherds to visit the child. 'And they came with haste; and they found Mary and Joseph, and the infant lying in the manger. And seeing, they understood of the word that had been spoken to them concerning this child. And all that heard, wondered: and at those things that were told them by the shepherds. But Mary kept all these words, pondering them in her heart. And the shepherds returned, glorifying and praising God, for all the things they had heard and seen, as it was told unto them' (Lk. 2.16-20).

The foreground shows Mary in prayer over the Christ Child and flanked by two angels. Joseph sleeps just to the right and behind the infant. Tosini combined the biblical source of Mary pondering these thoughts in her heart with the visual tradition of Joseph sleeping. Although the scene went largely overlooked in the visual arts for centuries, eventually this

37. Unless noted, citations from the Bible are from the Douay translation (originally published in 1609–1610).

single verse (Lk. 2.17) served as inspiration for numerous artists to produce the composition known as the Adoration of the Shepherds.[38] This subject was very popular in the region of Europe located north of the Alps, and it was hardly less popular in Italy after the late fifteenth century especially. Domenico Ghirlandaio (1449–1494), working south of the Alps in the city of Florence, painted a major altarpiece depicting the *Nativity and Adoration of the Shepherds* for Francesco Sassetti's sepulchral chapel in Santa Trinita.[39] This painting in some ways typifies the characteristics of the Italian Renaissance (modeling of the figures, local color, anatomical proportion, realistic perspective, use of antiquity) yet it incorporated Northern Renaissance elements in a manner not done earlier and never repeated again.[40]

Tosini and Technique

The typical Tosini use of monumental drapery style can be seen in the Virgin. Once again the draped knees are predominant in both angels and the Virgin. The background scene is reminiscent of numerous works executed by Tosini during his initial training with Ridolfo. The upper portion has a *sfumato* or hazing effect. The Christ Child now appears with bloated abdomen and reclines in an elegant *contrapposto*. The veil of the Virgin falls in the same manner as the Virgin in *Way to Calvary* (Fig. 2). *Changeant* green and brown are visible in the gown of the kneeling angel and on the sleeve of Joseph's robe. Tosini's creativity is demonstrated in a recent article that describes his use of the *carta lucida* technique.[41] The practice of *carta lucida* is the action of tracing by transparency.[42] Leonardo recommended the use of a transparent sheet to trace and then transfer, by

38. See Hornik and Parsons, *Illuminating Luke: The Infancy Narrative*, pp. 98-99, for a discussion of this point.

39. Scholarship on the Sassetti Chapel includes: Marco Chiarini, *Il Ghirlandaio alla Cappella Sassetti in Santa Trinita* (Milan: Silvana Editoriale d'Arte, 1961); Warman Welliver, 'Alterations in Ghirlandaio's S. Trinita Frescoes', *Art Quarterly* 32 (1969), pp. 269-81; Eve Borsook and Johannes Offerhaus, *Francesco Sassetti and Ghirlandaio at Santa Trinita, Florence* (Doornspijk: Dovaco, 1981); Peter Porçal, 'La Cappella Sassetti in S. Trinita a Firenze: osservazioni sull'iconografia', *Antichita viva* 23 (1984), pp. 26-36; Enrica Cassarino, *La cappella Sassetti nella chiesa di Santa Trinita* (Lucca: Pacini Fazzi, 1996).

40. Porçal, 'La Cappella Sassetti', p. 26.

41. Maria Clelia Galassi, 'The Re-use of Design-Models by *Carta Lucida* in the XVth Century Italian Workshops: Written Sources and an Example from Michele di Ridolfo del Ghirlandaio', in *La peinture dans les pays-bas au 16e siècle. Pratiques d'atelier infrarouges et autres méthodes d'investigation* (Leuven: Peeters, 1999), pp. 206-12.

42. Galassi, 'The Re-use of Design Models', p. 205.

pouncing, the image preliminarily observed through a glass sheet and fixed by drawing on that.[43] Students often copied or traced stock figures or single details directly from a painted original by their master rather than from a preparatory cartoon. Galassi employed scientific testing (IRR) to determine that Tosini used the *carta lucida* technique for the Badia *Nativity* and that it is based on a *Nativity* by his teacher, Ridolfo, from the 1520s and today in the Musei Civici, Udine. The figures of the Madonna and two angels are reversed, which is a common benefit of the *carta lucida* method. Both panels present an underdrawing executed with a dry medium, such as charcoal, meaning that Tosini may have copied the stock figures but he was innovative by adding the personal invention of the figure of the sleeping Joseph and the shepherds in the landscape.[44]

Tosini's modifications to the Ridolfo panel are drawn freehand, sometimes with clear *pentimenti* (reworking of the underdrawing) and vigorous strokes. *Pentimenti* is visible in numerous other paintings by Tosini as *disegno*, or draughtsmanship. *Disegno* was an important part of the creative process for Tosini and for some of his friends and contemporaries. In fact, Tosini, along with Bronzino, was asked by Giorgio Vasari, acting on behalf of Cosimo I de'Medici, to form the Accademia del Disegno in 1563 and devise the curriculum for young artists to follow for generations.

Way to Calvary

The patron of the *Way to Calvary* by Michele Tosini is unknown. The altarpiece was originally in the church of the Crocetta in Florence.[45] It was brought to France in 1812. After it had been in Paris for an unknown amount of time, it was returned to Italy and placed in the Antinori Chapel in Santo Spirito where it is located today.

Favoring a Lukan Reading

> And as they led him away, they laid hold of one Simon of Cyrene, coming from the country; and they laid the cross on him to carry after Jesus. And there followed him a great multitude of people, and of women, who bewailed and lamented him. But Jesus turning to them, said: Daughters of Jerusalem, weep not over me; but weep for yourselves and for your children. For behold, the days shall come, wherein they will say: Blessed are the barren, and the wombs that have not borne, and the paps that have

43. Galassi, 'The Re-use of Design Models', p. 206.
44. Galassi, 'The Re-use of Design Models', p. 212.
45. The *Way to Calvary*, 1530–40, is oil on panel that measures 200 × 300 cm. See Géza de Francovich, 'Benedetto Ghirlandaio', *Dedalo* 7 (1925), pp. 708-39 (736).

> not given suck. Then shall they begin to say to the mountains: Fall upon us; and to the hills: Cover us. For if in the green wood they do these things, what shall be done in the dry? (Lk. 23.26-31).

Michele Tosini constructed his composition, *Way to Calvary*, based on several elements found in more than one Gospel. The presence of Simon of Cyrene is one of those characteristics. Simon can be found just to the right of Christ about to take the weight from him. Matthew (27.32), Mark (15.21), and Luke (23.26) all write that Simon carried Jesus' cross while Jesus carries it himself the entire way to Calvary in John 19.17. Simon, being from the country, is barefoot and carries a knife in his belt. A visual parallel is made with Christ, who is the only other figure in the painting portrayed as barefoot.

Joseph of Arimathea is to the left of Christ and behind the cross. The visual tradition occasionally places Joseph in the Way to Calvary compositions as depicted here but usually he is present at the actual descent from the cross or entombment paintings. This is consistent with the Gospel of Mark that describes Joseph as a noble counselor who boldly visited Pilate and begged him for the body of Jesus (15.43). Joseph is depicted wearing finer clothing and shoes. His main role comes after the death of Christ and in preparation for the entombment of Christ. 'And Joseph buying fine linen, and taking him down, wrapped him in the fine linen, and laid him in a sepulcher which was hewed out of a rock. And he rolled a stone to the door of the sepulcher' (Mk 15.46). The role of Joseph in Luke (23.50-53) and Matthew (27.57-60) is very similar to that of Mark. None of the Gospel writers places Joseph on the road to Calvary. In John (19.38-42) Joseph works with Nicodemus in preparing the body and placing it in the tomb. Tosini followed the visual precedents and placed Joseph in the painting of the way to Calvary.

Tosini also followed a visual tradition of having Jesus in a scarlet robe as he walked to Calvary. The basis for this element is in Matthew. Matthew is the only Gospel writer stating that Jesus was wearing a scarlet robe at any time during the trial and crucifixion stories. 'And stripping him, they put a scarlet cloak about him' (Mt. 27.28). Now several verses later, Jesus is put back in his own garments: 'And after they had mocked him, they took off the cloak from him, and put on him his own garments, and led him away to crucify him' (Mt. 27: 31). Nonetheless, for a dramatic visual depiction of the narrative, the scarlet robe is very effective.

The presence of the daughters of Jerusalem to the right of Christ in the painting is distinctively Lukan (Lk. 23.37-31). Christ is speaking to them and delivering the message. Three women are visible with the one in the front clasping or wringing her hands. This is an act of lamentation and sorrow as she listens to Christ's words. There is eye contact between Christ and this woman. The visual tradition allowed this figure to be

Mary, the mother of Jesus. Tosini incorporated the specific narrative of the daughters of Jerusalem and the visual tradition of the presence of Mary along the way to Calvary.[46] This visual tradition included the popular detail of the mother seeing her son carrying his cross to his death. It is an emotionally powerful sentiment to those meditating on the painting and contemplating the Gospel narrative.[47]

Attribution Issues

The attribution has ranged from Michele, the workshop of Michele, and even to Antonio del Ceraiolo, an early teacher of Michele.[48] This painting is similar to, but in no way a copy of, a documented *Way to Calvary* (Fig. 4) by Ridolfo in the National Gallery, London.[49] In 1761, the painting is recorded as a joint work by Michele and Ridolfo and as being located in the Antinori Chapel, Santo Spirito in Florence.[50] The painting has been described as a 'soft and rather feeble production, reminiscent of Raphael's mild, rosy tone, with a touch of Lorenzo di Credi'.[51] In the sixteenth-century Italian Schools catalogue for the National Gallery, the entry for Ridolfo's *Way to Calvary* names two versions.[52] The first version is in the Louvre and is attributed to Benedetto Ghirlandaio (1458–1597), Ridolfo's uncle. The second version is correctly attributed to Michele and is located in Santo Spirito, Florence.[53] The three versions differ considerably and none is in any sense a copy of another, though direct connections are plausible.

46. The presence of Mary on the way to Calvary is continued into contemporary culture in Mel Gibson's film production, *The Passion of the Christ*.

47. For an example of the Pietà, see Michelangelo's work located in St Peter's Basilica, Rome. For the Lamentation, see Raphael's painting in the Borghese Gallery, Rome.

48. Giovanni Richa, *Notizie istoriche delle chiese fiorentine divise ne'suoi quartieri* (Florence, 1761), IX, p. 26 (as Michele and Ridlofo); Joseph Crowe and Giovanni Battista Cavalcaselle, *A New History of Painting in Italy* (New York: E.P. Dutton, 1914), VI, pp. 150-51 (as Michele); Adolfo Venturi, *Storia dell'arte italiana* (Milan,1925), IX, p. 512 (as Michele and Ridolfo); Gamba, 'Ridolfo e Michele', p. 546 (as Michele); Walter and Elisabeth Paatz, *Die Kirchen von Florenz* (Frankfurt am Main: Klostermann, 1940–55), V, pp. 145, 194 n. 196 (as Michele); Berenson, *Italian Pictures*, I, p. 150 (as Michele); Cecil Gould, *National Gallery Catalogues: The Sixteenth Century Italian Schools* (London: National Gallery, 1975), p. 100 (as Michele).

49. Ridolfo's *Way to Calvary*, 1505–10, is oil on panel. See Vasari, *Le vite*, VI, p. 535.

50. Richa, *Notizie istoriche*, IX, p. 26.

51. Crowe and Cavalcaselle, *A New History of Painting*, III, p. 521.

52. Gould, *Sixteenth Century Italian Schools*, p. 100.

53. Gould, *Sixteenth Century Italian Schools*, p. 100.

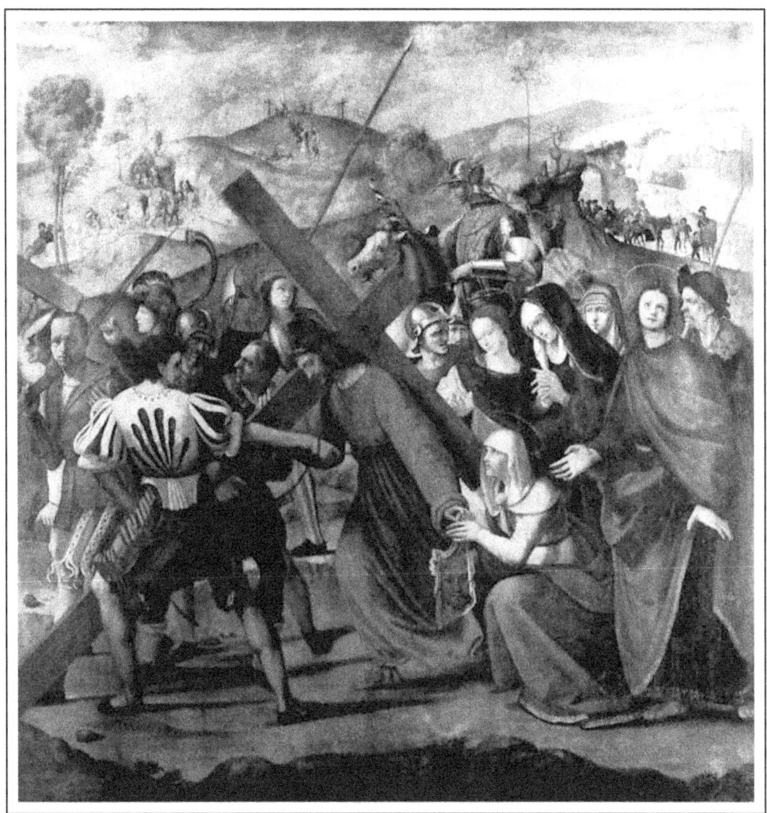

Figure 4. Ridolfo del Ghirlandaio,
Way to Calvary, The National Gallery, London.
Photo: copyright National Gallery, London

A comparison between the Ridolfo (Fig. 4) and Michele (Fig. 2) reveals the differences between master and student. It is also apparent how connoisseurship plays a very important role in making attributions of these early works. The hands of Michele, Ridolfo, Lorenzo di Credi (1459–1537), and Ceraiolo are quite similar. One must reconstruct the oeuvre of each artist to be able to distinguish the hand and the date. The dating of this painting is made according to the style of Tosini's documented works. The 1530–1540 date places the work among the documented altarpanels by Ridolfo and Michele as student/partner and master.[54]

54. The emerging talent of Michele is apparent in the altarpiece executed as a joint work by Michele and Ridolfo (Vasari, *Le vite*, VI, p. 544), commissioned by the Florentine, Leonardo di Giovanni Buonafé (c. 1450–1545), a Carthusian monk for the church of San Jacopo e Lorenzo, Via Ghibellina, Florence. The *Madonna and Child with Sts James, Lawrence, Francis, Claire and Bishop Buonafé* is today located in

Vasari stated that Michele, following in the style of Ridolfo, approached the master so closely that, whereas at the beginning he received from Ridolfo a third of his earnings, they came to execute their works in company, and shared the profits equally.[55] Although Michele's works in the late 1540s and 1550s, unlike Ridolfo's, used the high *maniera* colors of Salviati (1510–1563), both artists continued to use the monumental compositions and figure types of earlier sixteenth-century High Renaissance artists Andrea del Sarto (1486–1530) and Fra Bartolomeo (1473–1517).

Crucifixion

The Commission and La Famiglia Tosini

As stated earlier, Michele Tosini's personal life underwent many changes between 1520 and 1555. He married and all four of his children were born and grew up during these years. Dionora, Michele's eldest daughter, entered the Dominican convent of San Vincenzo, Prato, in December of 1553.[56] Prato is a neighboring city of Florence. Dionora's entrance into the convent was a significant day in the lives of both Dionora and her father. San Vincenzo was most likely chosen by Michele because of its ties with the family parish church of Santa Maria Novella, Florence: both organizations were members of the Dominican order, and many Florentine citizens were present in the convent. The monastery of San Vincenzo in neighboring Prato was founded on 16 May, 1503, under the authority of Pope Julius II, by a Florentine widow and eight women, of whom two were Florentines.[57] From 1507 to 1530 the church and convent were constructed.[58]

the Museo di San Salvi, Florence. New archival information published by Franklin, 'Towards a New Chronology', p. 455, confirms a completion date of 1544. For a discussion of dating works based on the San Jacopo altarpanel, see Hornik, 'Michele Tosini: The Artist, the Oeuvre and the Testament', p. 24.

55. Vasari, *Le vite*, VI, p. 543.

56. Hornik, 'The Testament of Michele Tosini', pp. 158, 164; Domenico Guglielmo M. di Agresti, *Santa Caterina de'Ricci: Cronache, diplomatica, lettere varie* (Collana Ricciana: Florence: Olschki, 1969), V, p. 42; Lodovico Boitel, *S. Caterina de'Ricci, o.p.: Manualetto di pietà per i devoti della santa* (Prato: Stab. Tipo-Litographico G. Rindi, 1946); Florence M. Capes, *St Catherine de'Ricci* (London: Bruns & Oates, 1905).

57. Di Agresti, *Cronache*, p. xx. These nine women were given their vows by the Vicar General of the Congregation of S. Marco in Florence, Brother Francesco Salviati on 29 August, 1503.

58. Di Agresti, *Cronache*, p. xx.

Dionora Tosini was under the direction of Caterina de'Ricci, who had become prioress in 1552. Her uncle and a Domincan, Fra Timoteo, became confessor of the convent of San Vincenzo in 1534 and was made prior of the monastery of San Domenico, Fiesole, in 1549.[59] Dianora's brother, Fra Santi Tosini became a member of the monastery of San Domenico, Fiesole, and painted in the monastery.[60] Timoteo remained in this position until his death on 29 April, 1552. Caterina also had a younger half brother, Giovambattista, from the second marriage of her father.[61] Giovambattista took the same name as his uncle, Fra Timoteo, in 1544.[62] The younger Fra Timoteo was for many years in the parish of Santa Maria della Quercia in Viterbo (outside Rome) where Michele would later receive a major commission.[63]

Caterina is most famous for her ecstasies that began in 1542 when she was twenty years old and continued once a week until 1554.[64] Caterina would lose consciousness at midday every Thursday and only came to herself twenty-eight hours afterwards, at four o'clock on Friday afternoon.[65] The ecstasies attracted curious and devout crowds of people, who interfered with the life of the religious community, and finally in 1554, at the request of Caterina, the nuns prayed to have them cease.[66]

59. Di Agresti, *Cronache*, p. xx. If Fra Santi was older than Dionora, then it is possible he was in the monastery between 1549–1552, when Fra Timoteo was prior.

60. Recent documents discovered by Gianfranco Riccioni confirm that paintings were done by Fra Santi Tosini in the monastery of San Domenico in Fiesole. Further research needs to be done on these documents and paintings attributed to Fra Santi Tosini in the monastery but I thank Dr Riccioni for his collegiality in sharing this information with me.

61. Di Agresti, *Cronache*, p. xxxix.

62. Serafino Razzi, *Vita di S. Caterina de'Ricci, con documenti inediti antecedenti l'edizione* (Collana Ricciana; Florence: Olschki, 1966), III, p. 119.

63. Viterbo. Archivio di S. Maria della Quercia. Libro dei Debitori e dei Creditori, N. 142. Carte 41. Document 27 states that Michele Tosini frescoed the main reliquary under the commission of Fra Timoteo de'Ricci from 1569–1570. See also, Cesare Pinzi, *Memorie e documenti inediti su S. Maria della Quercia* (Rome, 1890), p. 134; Brother Antonio Vittorio of Arezzo, *Libro delle Croniche della Chiesa et Sagrestia et Conv. Quercia*, 1576, Carte 7; and more recently, see Hornik, 'Michele di Ridolfo', pp. 142-151, 207.

64. Razzi, *Vita*, pp. lxiv-lxv.

65. *Butler's Lives of the Saints* (ed. H. Thurston; New York: P.J. Kennedy & Sons, 1956), I, pp. 328-31.

66. Caterina died on 2 February, 1590, at the age of 68 but was not canonized until 13 February, 1747, under Pope Benedict XIV. Benedict, or Prosper Lambertini, had been the 'Promotor of the Faith' when the cause of beatification was brought to the Congregation of Rites.

Upon entering the convent, Dionora Tosini was under the supervision and guidance of St Caterina. From 1552 to 1555, Caterina trained fifteen novices.[67] Dionora, the last novice instructed by Caterina, took her vows on 6 January, 1555, and became known as Sister Michelagnola.[68] She remained in the convent until her death on 17 January, 1606.[69] Dionora lived with and learned from Caterina for seventeen years and was part of the community of San Vincenzo during its most holy and noteworthy period.

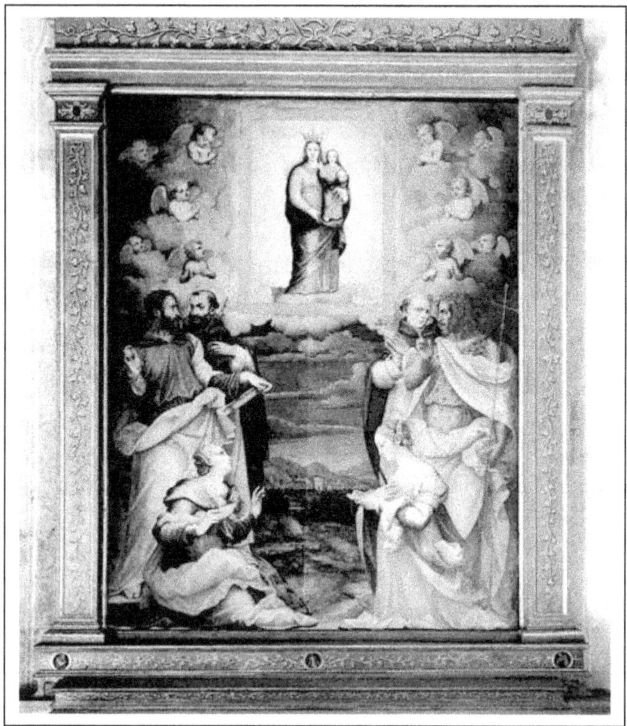

Figure 5. Michele Tosini, *Madonna and Child with Saints Dominic, Luke, Catherine Martyr, Ursula, John the Baptist and Vincent*, Cappella della Madonna di Loreto. Convent of San Vincenzo, Prato. Photo: author with permission from the Convent of San Vincenzo

Michele was commissioned to do the main altarpanel for the Cappella della Madonna di Loreto (Fig. 5) between 1559 and 1561. The chapel is an independent building in the monastery complex of San Vincenzo.

67. Di Agresti, *Cronache*, pp. 41-42.
68. Di Agresti, *Cronache*, p. 42.
69. Di Agresti, *Cronache*, p. 239.

Although documentation for details of the commission for the *Crucifixion* located in the nearby workroom of the convent has not survived, it is a secure attribution based on style and commission opportunity.[70]

The Renaissance Artist, the Crucifixion, and the Gospel of John

> Now there stood by the cross of Jesus, his mother and his mother's sister, Mary of Cleophas, and Mary Magdalen. When Jesus therefore had seen his mother and the disciple standing whom he loved, he saith to his mother: Woman, behold thy son. After that, he saith to the disciple: Behold thy mother. And from that hour, the disciple took her to his own (Jn 19.25-27).

Renaissance artists, and thus the visual tradition, seemed to favor John's account when depicting a crucifixion scene. Matthew (27.55-56) states that Mary Magdalen, Mary the mother of James and Joseph, and the mother of the sons of Zebedee were 'afar off, who had followed' but were not at the foot of the cross. Mark's account (15.40) also states that 'there were also women looking on afar off: among whom was Mary Magdalen, and Mary the mother of James the less and of Joseph, and Salome'. Luke (23.49) does not place anyone at the cross but reports that 'the women that had followed him from Galilee stood far off, beholding these things'. The artist who wanted to include more characters than Christ alone in a Crucifixion scene used the Gospel of John for the literary tradition. The variations on the theme included Mary the mother and John the beloved flanking the cross; Mary the mother, John, and Mary Magdalen; and, more rarely, Jesus, his mother, and some combination of the other three Marys (his mother's sister, Mary of Cleophas, and Mary Magdalen).

High Maniera Style and Johannine Iconography

Tosini, as we have seen in the Strozzi chapel fresco cycle and other paintings from this period, was very aware of the biblical narratives and incorporated, very deliberately, elements from specific Gospels. In this case, he created a balanced and symmetrical composition, with Mary the mother standing next to the kneeling Magdalen on the left side of the cross, while, on the right, one of the other Marys kneels next to a standing John

70. The *Madonna and Child with Saints* (350 × 250 cm) and the *Crucifixion* (c. 250 × 180 cm) can both be dated 1559–61 and are oil on panel. The only two published works (both in 1982) that include the *Crucifixion* attribute the work to Michele Tosini. See Silvestro Bardazzi and Eugenio Castellani, *Il Monastero di San Vincenzo in Prato* (Prato: Cassa di Risparmi e Depositi di Prato, 1982), pp. 271-73; Roberta Roani Villani, 'Contributo a Michele di Ridolfo del Ghirlandaio', *Antichità viva* 21 (1982), pp. 19-22.

the beloved.[71] This characteristic Renaissance style painting, consisting of a balanced and symmetrical composition, is actually more Mannerist in style when studied closely. The figures placed nearest to the cross (Magdalen and a Mary) are not the most important (Mary the mother and John). The gestures of each figure move the viewer's eye around the composition through diagonals and spirals rather than into and out of the background of the picture. As in a typically Mannerist painting, the figures are pushed to the foreground of the painting. The darkened sky of the event becomes the background. The facial features of elongated noses and sunken, beautifully delicate eyes are done in the manner of Vasari. The kneeling Marys are directly related to the kneeling St Ursula in the documented 1559–1561 San Vincenzo altarpiece (Fig. 7). The elaborate hair braids and coiffeurs of the two kneeling Marys were strongly influenced by Bronzino and Vasari, two friends, colleagues, and successful contemporary artists, living and working in Florence with Tosini.

John the beloved, with his clean-shaven face and effeminate curls falling gently on his neck, stands in an exaggerated contrapposto pose. All the draperies are *changeant* or appear as shot silk that reflects the light and color of two or three sumptuous shades of pink, orange, rose, yellow, gold, blue, and green. Tosini learned *changeant* color from studying the paintings of Francesco Salviati in the Sala dei Duecento in the Palazzo Vecchio of Florence during the 1540s. Although Tosini's colors were often deeper than Salviati's pastels, Salviati's influence was strong. Robes are voluminous, but do not overpower the figures by their texture or enormity. Instead, the garments enhance the beauty of the figure and accentuate their gestures of prayer (Mary the mother and the kneeling Mary) or submission (the Magdalen and John). All eyes gaze upwards to the cross and remain focused. The original crucifix by Tosini has been lost and the current one illustrated is attributed to Baccio da Montelupo and dated c. 1700.[72] This work should be dated 1559–1561, when Michele was documented as executing the altarpiece for the chapel.

Conclusion

Michele di Ridolfo del Ghirlandaio succeeded in leading an enormously productive workshop during the sixteenth century in Florence, one of the

71. Bardazzi and Castellani, p. 272, identify the female figure opposite the Magdalen as St Catherine of Alexandria without any explanation. There are no visible attributes to assist a secure identification as St Catherine and, given Tosini's propensity to follow the Gospel narrative, it is more plausible that it is Mary from John's description.

72. Villani, 'Contributo a Michele di Ridolfo', p. 20.

most competitive art markets in the world. A study of the commission details, techniques, and the biblical text as painted subject for these three paintings reveals the stylistic progression from the High Renaissance to Mannerism in the work of Michele Tosini. This brief view into Michele's world shows us that his success was not only based on his ability to train and hire reliable and creative painters and to maintain patronage connections but, more importantly, was based on his knowledge of the Bible and gift for applying the textual narrative to his compositions. Tosini was knowledgeable of the biblical text and of the visual traditions of depicting the text. Patrons in sixteenth-century Florence had many choices and consistently returned to Michele Tosini and the Ghirlandaio workshop for masterful technique and substantive religious iconography. For this Michele Tosini was rewarded with a fine reputation and continued commissions.[73]

BIBLIOGRAPHY

Bardazzi, Silvestro, and Eugenio Castellani, *Il Monastero di San Vincenzo in Prato* (Prato: Cassa di Risparmi e Depositi di Prato, 1982).

Barocchi, Paolo (ed.), *Firenze a la Toscana dei Medici nell'Europa del Cinquecento: Il Primato del disegno* (Milan: Electa, 1980).

Berdini, Paolo, *The Religious Art of Jacopo Bassano: Painting as Visual Exegesis* (Cambridge: Cambridge University Press, 1997).

Berenson, Bernard, *Italian Pictures of the Renaissance: Florentine School* (London: Phaidon Press, 1963).

Boitel, Lodovico, *S. Caterina de'Ricci, o.p.: Manualetto di pietà per i devoti della santa* (Prato: Stab. Tipo-Litographico G. Rindi, 1946).

Borsook, Eve, and Johannes Offerhaus, *Francesco Sassetti and Ghirlandaio at Santa Trinita, Florence* (Doornspijk: Dovaco, 1981).

Capes, Florence M., *St Catherine de'Ricci* (London: Bruns & Oates, 1905).

Carocci, Guido, *Il commune di San Casciano in Val di Pesa* (Florence: TIP della Pia Casa di Patronato, 1892).

Cassarino, Enrica, *La cappella Sassetti nella chiesa di Santa Trinita* (Lucca: Pacini Fazzi, 1996).

Chiarini, Marco, *Il Ghirlandaio alla Cappella Sassetti in Santa Trinita* (Milan: Silvana Editoriale d'Arte, 1961).

Clantius, Ager, *Badia a Passignano. Collana di Brevi Monografie Chiantigiane* (Florence: Editoriale gli Arci Pressi, 2001).

Crowe, Joseph, and Giovanni Battista Cavalcaselle, *A New History of Painting in Italy* (New York: E.P. Dutton, 1914).

73. For additional study on Michele, see Heidi J. Hornik, *Michele Tosini and the Ghirlandaio Workshop in Cinquecento Florence* (Brighton: Sussex Academic Press, forthcoming, 2009).

Degenhart, Bernhard, 'Tosini, Michele', in *Allgemeines Lexicon der bildenden Künstler* (ed. U. Thieme and F. Becker; Leipzig: E.A. Seemann, 1939).

Di Agresti, Domenico Guglielmo, M., *Santa Caterina de'Ricci: Cronache, diplomatica, lettere varie*, V (Collana Ricciana; Florence: Olschki, 1969).

Francovich, Géza de, 'Benedetto Ghirlandaio', *Dedalo* 7 (1925), pp. 708-39.

Franklin, David, *Painting in Renaissance Florence 1500–1550* (New Haven: Yale University Press, 2001).

—'Towards a New Chronology for Ridolfo Ghirlandaio and Michele Tosini', *Burlington Magazine* 140 (1998), pp. 445-55.

Freedberg, Sydney, *Painting in Italy 1500–1600* (Baltimore: Penguin Books, 1970).

Galassi, Maria Clelia, 'The Re-use of Design-Models by *Carta Lucida* in the XVth Century Italian Workshops: Written Sources and an Example from Michele di Ridolfo del Ghirlandaio', in *La peinture dans les pays-bas au 16e siècle. Pratiques d'atelier infrarouges et autres méthodes d'investigation* (Leuven: Peeters, 1999), pp. 206-12.

Gamba, Carlo, 'Ridolfo e Michele di Ridolfo del Ghirlandaio', *Dedalo* 9 (1928–29), p. 554.

Gould, Cecil, *National Gallery Catalogues: The Sixteenth Century Italian Schools* (London: National Gallery, 1975).

Hatfield, Rab, *Botticelli's Uffizi 'Adoration': A Study in Pictorial Content* (Princeton, NJ: Princeton University Press, 1976).

Hornik, Heidi J., 'Michele di Ridolfo del Ghirlandaio (1503–1577) and the Reception of Mannerism in Florence' (PhD dissertation, Pennsylvania State University, 1990).

—*Michele Tosini and the Ghirlandaio Workshop in Cinquecento Florence* (Brighton: Sussex Academic Press, forthcoming, 2009).

—'Michele Tosini: The Artist, The Oeuvre and The Testament', in *Continuity, Innovation and Connoisseurship: Old Master Paintings at the Palmer Museum of Art* (ed. Mary Jane Harris and Patrick McGrady; University Park, PA: Penn State Press, 2003), pp. 22-37.

—'The Strozzi Chapel by Michele Tosini: A Visual Interpretation of Redemptive Epiphany', *Artibus et Historiae* 46 (2002), pp. 97-118.

—'The Testament of Michele Tosini', *Paragone* (1995), pp. 156-67.

Hornik, Heidi J., and Mikeal C. Parsons, *Illuminating Luke: The Infancy Narrative in Italian Renaissance Painting* (Harrisburg, PA: Trinity Press International, 2003).

—*Illuminating Luke: The Public Ministry of Christ in Italian Renaissance and Baroque Painting* (New York: Continuum, 2005).

—*Illuminating Luke: The Passion and Resurrection Narratives in Italian Renaissance and Baroque Painting* (New York and London: T. & T. Clark International, 2007).

Kehrer, Hugo, *Die heiligen drei Könige in Literatur und Kunst* (Leipzig: A. Seemann, 1908–1909).

Marchini, Giuseppe, and Emma Micheletti, *La chiesa di Santa Trinita a Firenze* (Florence: Cassa di Risparmio di Firenze, 1987).

Miles, Margaret R., *Image as Insight: Visual Understanding in Western Christianity and Secular Culture* (Boston: Beacon Press, 1985).

Paatz, Walter, and Elisabeth Paatz, *Die Kirchen von Florenz* (Frankfurt am Main: Klostermann, 1940–55).

Pelikan, Jaroslav, *Jesus through the Centuries* (New Haven: Yale University Press, 1985).
—*Mary through the Centuries* (New Haven: Yale University Press, 1996).
Pelikan, Jaroslav, H.T. Lehman, *et al.* (eds.), *Luther's Works* (St Louis, MO; Concordia, 1958).
Porçal, Peter, 'La Cappella Sassetti in S. Trinita a Firenze: osservazioni sull'iconografia', *Antichita viva* 23 (1984), pp. 26-36.
Razzi, Serafino, *Vita di S. Caterina de'Ricci, con documenti inediti antecedenti l'edizione*, III (Collana Ricciana; Florence: Olschki, 1966).
Richa, Giovanni, *Notizie istoriche delle chiese fiorentine divise ne'suoi quartieri* (Florence: P.G. Viviani, 1761).
Rodino, Simonetta Prosperi Valenti, *Dizionario enciclopedico Bolaffi dei pittori e degli incisori italiani* (Turin: Bolaffi, 1974).
Schiavo, Armando, 'La Badia di San Michele Arcangelo a Passignano in Val di Pesa', *Benedictina* 7 (1954), pp. 257-88.
—'Notizie riguardanti la Badia di Passignano estratte dai fondi dell'Archivio di Stato di Firenze', *Benedictina* 9 (1955), pp. 31-92.
Thurston, H. (ed.), *Butler's Lives of the Saints* (New York: P.J. Kennedy & Sons, 1956).
Vallombrosani del Monastero di Passignano, Monaci Benedettini (ed.), *La Badia di Passignano* (Bologna: Fotometalgrafica Emiliana, 1989).
Vasari, Giorgio, *Le opere di Giorgio Vasari: Le vite de'più eccellenti pittori, scultori ed architettori scritte da Giorgio Vasari pittore Aretino* (ed. Gaetano Milanesi; 9 vols.; 2nd edn, 1568; Florence: Sansoni, 1885).
Venturi, Adolfo, *Storia dell'arte italiana* (Milan: Hoepli, 1925).
Villani, Roberta Roani, 'Contributo a Michele di Ridolfo del Ghirlandaio', *Antichità viva* 21 (1982), pp. 19-22.
Waterworth, J. (ed.), *The Council of Trent: Canons and Decrees* (Chicago: Christian Symbolic Publication Society, 1848).
Welliver, Warman, 'Alterations in Ghirlandaio's S. Trinita Frescoes', *Art Quarterly* 32 (1969), pp. 269-81.

PAINTING THE GOSPEL: HENRY OSSAWA TANNER'S *THE ANNUNCIATION* AND *NICODEMUS*

Kelly J. Baker

In 1924, Jessie Fauset, a writer for *The Crisis*, interviewed Henry Ossawa Tanner (1859–1937), and she asked him about a particular story involving a conversation between the artist and his father. The story revolved around his father and the bishop's desire for his son to be a minister, and Tanner's supposed reply was, 'No, father, you preach from the pulpit and I will preach with my brush'. When asked if this event had occurred, the artist replied, 'My answer was: That's a pretty story—I won't destroy it'. When Fauset asked him again about the story in her interview, he gave her an answer, and she responded, 'For the first time in my life I resemble a great artist. I won't destroy a pretty story.'[1] Fauset's fascination with whether or not Tanner preached with his brush characterizes the response of audiences, journalists, art historians, and other scholars to the art of Henry Tanner. Whether Tanner preached with his brush is a question worth exploring, but the religious experience portrayed in his paintings is hard to deny. Tanner, an artist of the late nineteenth and early twentieth centuries, portrayed dramatic biblical paintings on canvas. In describing the motivations behind his art, he wrote:

> I paint things that I see and believe...I believe in my religion. I have chosen the character of my art because it conveys my message and tells what I want to tell my own generation and leave to the future.[2]

In a world seemingly divided by race, he chose to paint biblical narratives because they represented the God of his beliefs. Tanner, the 'dean of American painters',[3] was an African-American artist of international

1. Jessie Fauset, 'Henry Ossawa Tanner', *The Crisis* 27 (1924), p. 258.
2. H.O. Tanner, 'The Artist's Autobiography', *The Advance* 20 (1913), p. 14, quoted in Marcus Bruce, *Henry Ossawa Tanner: A Spiritual Biography* (New York: Crossroad, 2002), p. 120.
3. James Weldon Johnson, *Black Manhattan* (Salem: Ayer Company, 1990), p. 279.

acclaim, and his work ranged from seascapes to landscapes to black genre to the grand religious paintings that compose the majority of his œuvre. The white press and academy initially labeled Tanner as a Negro artist, based on his race rather than his work, which offended the artist because his artistic merit was ignored in favor of his racial heritage.[4] African-American intellectuals like W.E.B. Du Bois, Booker T. Washington, and Alain Locke agreed with this label for Tanner, but for different and complicated reasons. Tanner was the first African-American painter of international acclaim, and, during his lifetime, he was thought to be one of the greatest painters America had produced. Thus for black intellectuals, he became representative of the potential of people with African ancestry and a symbol, at least for Du Bois, of the 'Talented Tenth', 'the gifted role models standing as irrefutable evidence against racist claims of inferiority and destined to guide and inspire the rest'.[5] This artist became a beacon of what the race could achieve. Tanner's art and life have been and continue to be the grounds for cultural contestation, but his rendering of religion requires much more analysis and reflection.[6] Examination of his religious art and his commentary about his religion highlight the importance of Protestant Christianity in the life of the artist and demonstrate how Tanner visually crafted the world as he hoped it could be.

Tanner's biblical scenes presented a utopian rendering of the world in which the divine intervened in human affairs. These narratives verified his unwavering faith in a God of possibility. For Tanner, the Bible was both domestic and ordinary. It provided countless examples of relationship between the divinity and humanity, but, more importantly, his paintings served as a possible venue for the viewer's interaction with God.

4. To stay true to the sentiment of his contemporaries, I refer to Tanner as a Negro artist because it was the term used to describe him in his lifetime. When I refer to more recent scholarship, I will use the term 'African-American artist'.

5. Albert Boime, 'Henry Ossawa Tanner's Subversion of Genre', *Art Bulletin* 75 (1993), pp. 415-41 (438).

6. For biographies of Tanner, see Marcia Mathews, *Henry Ossawa Tanner: American Artist* (Chicago: University of Chicago Press, 1969; repr. 1994) and Bruce, *Henry Ossawa Tanner*. For reflections on his works, see Dewey F. Mosby and Darrel Sewell, *Henry Ossawa Tanner* (New York: Rizzoli, 1991); Naurice Frank Woods, 'Lending Color to Canvas: Henry O. Tanner's African-American Themes', *American Visions* 6 (1991), pp. 14-20; Boime, 'Henry Ossawa Tanner's Subversion of Genre'; Brooks Adams, 'Tanner's Odyssey', *Art in America* 79 (1991), pp. 93, 108-12; Sharon Kay Skeel, 'Black American in the Paris Salon', *American Heritage* 42 (1991), pp. 77-83; Jennifer J. Harper, 'The Early Religious Painting of Henry Ossawa Tanner: A Study of the Influences of Church, Family, and Era', *American Art* 6 (1992), pp. 69-85; Judith Wilson, 'Lifting the "Veil": Henry O. Tanner's *The Banjo Lesson* and *The Thankful Poor*', in *Critical Issues in American Art: A Book of Readings* (Boulder, CO: Westview Press, 1998), pp. 199-219.

Tanner's work, specifically *The Annunciation* (1898) and *Nicodemus* (1899), represent the artist's desires to make biblical narratives 'real' to viewers, and these paintings are Tanner's visual exegesis about the potential for a hope-filled world in which the divine intervenes on behalf of humanity. His exaltation of the sacred in the ordinary confirmed that God was present in the most unexpected places.

'It is not by accident that I have chosen to be a religious painter'

In 1856, John Brown, supposed anti-slavery advocate, with his men attacked the small town of Osawatomie, Kansas, and killed five slavery supporters. In 1859, Henry, the first of Benjamin Tucker (B.T.) and Sarah Tanner's seven children, was born in Pittsburgh. Though these two events might appear unrelated, a spirit of reform and justice connects them. B.T. Tanner, an African-American minister, chose to honor John Brown's abolitionist sentiments and actions by naming his son Henry 'Ossawa' Tanner. Ossawa was a veiled reference to the attack on Osawatomie that protested the institution of slavery, and the elder Tanner desired to pass on to his son the magnitude of the race's struggle against oppression and enslavement, hope for emancipation and true freedom, and moral values. Thus early on, Henry Ossawa Tanner was marked by his father's lifelong activism and passion for social justice. Both parents influenced his life and work with their intellectual and spiritual strivings.

B.T. Tanner was born in Pittsburgh in 1835, and he had the advantage that many African Americans of the time period did not, growing up free in a slave society. He began his career as a barber to pay for his education and eventually became a minister, an editor of *The Christian Recorder*, a board member of Howard University and other African-American educational institutions, and, above all, an activist for the African Methodist Episcopal (A.M.E.) Church. The ministry was not a route to preach for B.T. Tanner, but instead a method to pursue religious scholarship and to act as an advocate for the race. In 1860, he became an 'official' advocate for the denomination as well as for African Americans, when he was given his pastoral certificate, which began his career as a minister and as a theologian. He published several theological treatises, ranging from his description of the African Methodist Episcopal Church, *An Apology for African Methodism* (1867), to *The Color of Solomon—What?* (1895) and *Theological Lectures* (1894), all of which were explorations of race in the Bible. Additionally, B.T. Tanner viewed Methodism, his religious tradition, as a mechanism for social justice. He stated, 'Methodism, in short, is an uprising of the religious manhood of the Christian world against the slights and negligences, the oppressions and burden-some rituals of its religious teachers—it is a living protest against priestly injustice and disobedience'.[7] Methodism was a vehicle in which the oppressed could protest their oppression, racial or otherwise, and this emphasis on the power of the religious to overcome injustice would prove valuable to the younger Tanner.[8]

Sarah, Henry's mother, was a strong influence on her son, and her encounters with racism affected the young Henry deeply. Unlike her husband, Sarah Elizabeth Miller Tanner was not born free but into slavery, in Virginia, on 18 May, 1840. She was the daughter of a slave woman, Elizabeth, who bore twelve children, six with the master of her plantation and six with Charles Miller.[9] Elizabeth was unable to acquire the freedom of her children, and thus, with the help of the Underground Railroad and abolitionists, she obtained the means for their escape to Pennsylvania.[10] Sarah was quite the opposite of her fiery and opinionated husband. She was known for her quiet reassurance and her teaching skills. Tanner's parents helped those marginalized by slavery attain education, and Sarah managed a neighborhood school in her Pittsburgh home to provide a route to education for the disenfranchised.[11]

When the artist was thirteen, his family moved permanently to Philadelphia, where he attended Robert Vaux Grammar School, which was one of the most prestigious schools in the city. He graduated in 1877 as valedictorian of his class and delivered an address on the importance of education. However, Tanner did not seek further educational instruction, but, instead, he decided to pursue an art career. With his choice of vocation, Tanner faced prejudice from a white-dominated art world and an America in which race profoundly mattered. Tanner gained entrance to the Pennsylvania Academy of the Fine Arts in 1879, where he studied

7. Benjamin Tucker Tanner, *An Apology for African Methodism* (Baltimore, 1867), p. 78, located at the University of North Carolina, Chapel Hill, Documenting the American South Project, http://docsouth/unc.edu/church/tanner/tanner.html.

8. For more on Tanner's relationship to the AME, see Kristin Schwain, 'Figuring Belief: American Art and Modern Religious Experience' (PhD dissertation, Stanford University, 2001).

9. Bruce, *Henry Ossawa Tanner*, p. 28.

10. Marcia Matthews promoted the story that Charles Miller took his family to freedom in an oxcart, but it is believed that she obtained this 'sanitized' version of the story from Henry O. Tanner's son, Jesse. For Matthews's discussion, see Matthews, *Henry Ossawa Tanner*, p. 6. For discussion of how the story became 'sanitized', see William Seraile, *Fire in His Heart: Bishop Benjamin Tucker Tanner and the* A.M.E. *Church* (Knoxville: University of Tennessee Press, 1998), p. 5.

11. See Lynda Roscoe Hartigan, *Sharing Traditions: Five Black Artists in Nineteenth-Century America* (Washington, DC: Smithsonian Institution Press, 1985), pp. 99-100.

intermittently under the guidance of Thomas Eakins. Eakins provided Tanner with a realistic style that focused on the use of light. Tanner was the first African-American student to attend the Pennsylvania Academy full-time, but the artist remained suspiciously quiet about his time at the academy.[12]

However, another student at the academy, Joseph Pennell, who became a 'great American illustrator', remarked upon Tanner's presence at the academy. In his memoirs in a chapter labeled 'The Coming of the Nigger', Pennell described Tanner as 'an octoroon, very well dressed, far better than most of us...and he drew very well'.[13] At beginning of his tenure at the academy, Tanner went unnoticed by the students until he started 'wanting things'. Pennell reported an incident in which several students 'crucified' Tanner by loosely tying his hands and feet to his own easel in the middle of Broad Street. Pennell remarked further 'there has never been a great Negro or Jew artist in the history of the world'.[14] Pennell wrote his memoirs during a time in which Tanner had been acclaimed in Paris, and it could be likely that he wanted to injure Tanner's reputation. Pennell's racist recollections highlight the impact of racism on Tanner and explain why Tanner permanently settled in Europe.

In 1891, Tanner left America to study in Europe. He set sail for Rome with stops along the way in London, then Paris, and finally Rome. Rome, however, was not fortune's fate for Henry Tanner. Once he arrived in Paris, he 'completely forgot' his plans to study in Rome, and, instead, decided to study in Paris at the Académie Julian. At the Académie Julian, Tanner had several teachers who instructed him and influenced his work, including Jean Joseph Benjamin-Constant, Jean-Paul Laurens, and Gérôme. These teachers were known for not forcing their own artistic styles on their students, and Benjamin-Constant was fond of Tanner's paintings and sketches. Benjamin-Constant and Laurens were both widely known for their genre, historical, and biblical scenes, which relied on the realism and 'sharp' colors of 'French academic painting'.[15] Due to illness, Tanner returned to America for a couple of years, but he returned to France in 1894. After 1894, he would travel to his home country only a few more times, and France became his permanent residence.[16] In 1895, Tanner officially turned to biblical paintings with the production of *Daniel and the Lion's Den*, which won an honorable mention in the Salon of 1896.

12. Bruce, *Henry Ossawa Tanner*, p. 55.

13. Joseph Pennell, *The Adventure of an Illustrator* (Boston: Little, Brown & Company, 1925), p. 53.

14. Pennell, *The Adventure of an Illustrator*, p. 54.

15. Hartigan, *Sharing Traditions*, p. 103.

16. Boime, 'Henry Ossawa Tanner's Subversion of Genre', p. 418.

Christianity and its narratives appealed to the artist. He painted biblical themes to express how the world could be. The religious figures that Tanner depicted were spared from the mouths of lions, resurrected from the dead, and enlightened about the kingdom of God. The divine appeared in the lion's den, in one's home, or on a rooftop to guide humanity. Tanner's biblical realm was a realm of possibility, and his spiritual upbringing by his parents influenced his depictions. The imperfect world marred by racism also led Tanner to approach the biblical narrative as a design for a better world. He strived to capture its essence and detail with his brush. Tanner stated:

> It is not by accident that I have chosen to be a religious painter. I have no doubt of an inheritance of religious feeling, and for this I am glad, but I have also decided [for]...an intelligent religious faith not due to inheritance but my own conviction. I believe my religion. I have chosen the character of my art because it conveys my message and tells what I want to tell my own generation and leave to the future.[17]

His religious faith permeated his canvases and reflected his spiritual heritage. He admitted that he did inherit his father's religious feeling and denominational background, but it was his own religious conviction that guided him into the arena of religious painting. His new themes were an outpouring of his religious faith, and he conveyed his faith along with a message of universal humanity to his viewers.

As his life progressed, Tanner became 'unorthodox' in his beliefs and shed the denominational strictures of the A.M.E. His faith became more spiritual and more concerned with universal themes in Christianity, which directed another biographer to describe him as a mystic. Tanner 'believed in God and the revelations of the Bible' yet he also thought that an open mind 'made humans more receptive to an encounter with the divine', and he wanted his paintings to provide a place where this interaction could occur.[18] God and humanity needed this communication, and Tanner sought for his paintings to provide a venue for this connection. He chose to paint religious scenes because they conveyed his message of interaction between humanity and divinity, and he desired future generations to have access to this through his paintings. Tanner hoped this message would remind viewers of his paintings of the presence of God, and that they, too, could rely on the divine in periods of struggle like the figures in his art.

17. Tanner, 'The Artist's Autobiography', p. 14, quoted in Bruce, *Henry Ossawa Tanner*, p. 120.

18. Bruce, *Henry Ossawa Tanner*, p. 15.

'There was race in it'

Before we delve into the work of Henry Tanner, I should mention that my approach is quite unconventional in contrast to previous scholarship on Tanner. My approach challenges both the artist's contemporaries and previous scholarship that privileged racial interpretations of his biblical art. Several of Tanner's religious paintings have been identified using biblical narratives as code for racialized narratives. These biblical paintings, then, are not simply biblical paintings, but, instead, they are symbolic forms of African-American life, culture, and history. Scholars note that Tanner's religious paintings are an extension of his previous genre paintings, which impart the dignity of African Americans.[19] For some, these works are a further outpouring of racial identity in a different visual rendering. Some assume that, since there was a historical process of creative identification and interpretation of the Bible by African Americans, Tanner also participated in this process. The composition of the paintings contained racial subtexts represented by familiar biblical narratives that resonated with the history of Africans in America. In other words, the religious became the metaphor for the racial. The artist portrayed African-American history and experiences to African Americans who viewed his paintings.

Tanner's contemporaries also recognized the racial in these religious works. In 1908, W.S. Scarborough suggested that two of Tanner's paintings could express race. Scarborough saw Tanner's paintings as not only a reflection of biblical stories but as important communicators of African-American experience. The narratives that Tanner chose were narratives that Africans in America used to interpret their shared history as enslaved peoples. He commented, 'Of this picture [*The Resurrection of Lazarus*] there could be said what was said of "Daniel"—"there was race in it", a quality that one critic avers to be new to Biblical painting. Be that as it may, Mr. Tanner studied to put "race in it"'.[20] Scarborough's statement

19. The following scholars note that Tanner's shift to religious paintings did not mean that he was casting aside his racial identity, but he found a new way to communicate this identity using his religious themes: Dewey F. Mosby, *Across Continents and Cultures: The Art and Life of Henry Ossawa Tanner* (Kansas City: The Nelson-Atkins Museum of Art, 1995), pp. 1-40; Mosby, 'Paris, Racial Awareness, and Success: 1891–1897', in Mosby and Sewell, *Henry Ossawa Tanner*, pp. 86-146; Romare Bearden and Harry Henderson, *A History of African American Artists: From 1792 to the Present* (New York: Pantheon Books, 1992), pp. 95-110; Albert Boime, 'Henry Ossawa Tanner's Subversion of Genre', pp. 415-41; and Harper, 'The Early Religious Paintings of Henry Ossawa Tanner'.

20. W.S. Scarborough, 'Henry Ossian [*sic*] Tanner', *Southern Workman* 31 (1902), pp. 661-70 (666). Scarborough was a friend of Bishop Tanner and the Tanner family. He was also Vice-President of Wilberforce University.

was echoed not only by other contemporaries but also by later scholars of Tanner's work. For instance, art historian Dewey F. Mosby proposed that there was a universality of themes along with racial connotations of the scenes portrayed. Mosby noted that *Daniel and the Lion's Den* (1895), one of Tanner's most recognizable paintings, encapsulated themes of slavery, false accusation, execution, and martyrdom. He argued that, since the African experience in America was characterized by struggle, oppression, and slavery, the prophet Daniel became a symbol of the struggles of the enslaved. The painting was Tanner's homage to this struggle. Another critic, Jennifer Harper, suggested there was a connotation of freedom and emancipation for blacks in Tanner's work. Daniel's redemption and 'subsequent emancipation' could be linked to the Emancipation Proclamation[21] and the hope of freedom that this biblical narrative communicated to African-American believers.

Scarborough's commentary informed these scholars' discussions of the connection of biblical themes to racial issues of the day. It is possible that Scarborough's words were taken out of context because it seems that he was referring to the Jewish figuration instead of racial context. Scarborough stated that Tanner 'studied to put "race" in' the paintings but race came from the 'fruit of originality' to use 'the lowly people of Palestine for his types' and 'he has succeeded admirably...in showing us the Jew as he must have lived and looked nearly twenty centuries ago'.[22] The racial context of the paintings could have referred to Tanner's careful depiction of the figures in each of the works as 'authentically' Jewish. Art historian Albert Boime noted that Afrocentric readings of Tanner's work often assert connections between the African and the Jew, and some have even proposed that the portrayal of the Jews in Tanner's paintings were representative of the A.M.E. From his commentary, it is hard to determine if Scarborough actually meant that the artist was portraying the African race or the ethnicity of the biblical figures. The ambiguity of Scarborough's statements should not lead us to dismiss scholarly interpretations that use his commentary to interpret Tanner's work. Boime, additionally, noted that Tanner's religious works were 'transformed into a site for contestation between competing and differing ideologies' because 'various groups had designs on his African-American person and intellectual talents...to fulfill a particular role in support of their respective agendas'.[23]

Tanner was more ambivalent about his racial heritage than his contemporaries suggest. In fact, Tanner objected being labeled as a Negro

21. Harper, 'The Early Religious Paintings', p. 74.
22. Scarborough, 'Henry Ossian [*sic*] Tanner', p. 666.
23. Boime, 'Henry Ossawa Tanner's Subversion of Genre', p. 438.

because he wanted to be judged on his artistic merit instead of his cultural heritage. In a letter to Eunice Tietjens, written in 1914, Tanner stated:

> Now am I a Negro? Does not 3/4 of the English blood in my veins which when it flowed in 'pure' Anglo-Saxon veins and which has done in the past effective and distinguished work—does this not count for anything? Does the 1/4 or 1/8 of 'pure' Negro blood count for all? I believe it (the Negro blood) counts and counts to my advantage—though it has caused me at times a life of great humiliation and great sorrow...And that it is the source of my talents (if I have any) I do not believe, any more than I believe all errors [come] from my English ancestors.[24]

Obviously, the artist was pained by his constant identification as a Negro artist and the assumption that his talent came from his racial experiences. The artist, like his father, preferred to be referred to as 'American' because, unlike the appellation 'Negro', it was not a designation that had been imposed on African Americans.[25] He had experienced the benefits and the painful barriers that were attached to the term 'Negro'. Newspaper articles were preoccupied with identifying Tanner as a Negro artist and usually provided a physical description of him as well. An article in *Alexander's Magazine* described him as having 'little or no trace nor suggestion of African ancestry'; instead he appeared 'Latin... rather than types of tropical origin'.[26] Another critic stated, 'Altho[ugh] his paintings exhibit that full-blooded sense of rhythm and color which gives peculiar charm to the art productions of his race, Tanner's work is above all racial distinctions'.[27] This author attempted to remove racial stereotyping while reinforcing racial classification. Obviously, journalists were aware of the barriers that race caused for the artist. Leading black

24. From Henry Tanner's draft of a letter to Eunice Tietjens, 25 May, 1914, in the Henry Ossawa Tanner papers, 1850–1978 (bulk 1890–1920), Archives of American Art, Smithsonian Institution, Washington, DC, reel D306, C3. Eunice Tietjens was an art critic who was writing an article on Tanner's life and career. Tanner was offended by her reference to his African-American heritage as the source of his artistic talent. He fought friends and critics alike throughout his life to make them view his artistic talent without reference to race.

25. Seraile, *Fire in his Heart*, p. 176.

26. William R. Lester, 'Henry O. Tanner, Exile for Art's Sake', *Alexander's Magazine* 7 (1908), pp. 69-73 (70). See also Elbert Francis Baldwin, 'A Negro Artist of Unique Power', *Outlook* 64 (1900), pp. 793-96. This article described Tanner as having '[N]egro blood' and as 'not resembl[ing] a too-often-accepted type' because there were only 'hints of African descent'.

27. Anonymous, 'An Afro-American Painter Who Has Become Famous in Paris', *Current Literature* 45 (1908), pp. 405-408 (405). The author also suggested that Tanner should be considered as a great American painter despite the author's initial racial distinctions and qualifications.

intellectual Booker T. Washington also commented on Tanner's race from a different position: 'Tanner is proud of his race. He feels deeply representative of his people...'[28] Washington also noted that Tanner was attempting to establish the place of African Americans in the realm of art. Tanner was proud of his race, but Washington's assertion that the artist thought of himself as representative of the race might be more hope than fact. Washington wanted Tanner to be representative of the race, yet Tanner's position remains ambiguous at best.

Racial interpretations are not as clear as some would like to suggest, and they obfuscate our understandings of the artist's work and their religious value. Rather than qualifying Tanner's religious works as symbols for racial sub-texts, I examine Tanner's work in his own terms and through the eyes of his contemporaries to find his conceptions of the Bible. Tanner described his paintings as intended to show his belief. His paintings do not just confirm the interaction between human and divine but rather provide a place for others to see the presence of God in the human arena. He painted the gospel to convey a Bible filled with domesticity, humanity, and an unwavering faith in God.

'My effort has been to not only put the Biblical incident in the original setting'

For Tanner, painting the gospel was an arduous task because of the serious content portrayed. Previous religious paintings of other artists did not convey the true religious sentiment that he believed they should nor did they allow for a communication of a religious message. To the artist, religious sentiment belonged in religious art. Religious art without this true sentiment disturbed him. His religious emotions about the divine, then, became the message he conveyed in his art to show his relationship with God. Tanner's intent for his paintings was to make the Bible 'real' to his viewers and demonstrate that God interacted with humanity in his time as well as biblical times. He stated:

> My effort has been to not only put the Biblical incident in the original setting...but at the same time give the human touch 'which makes the whole world kin' and which ever remains the same. While giving the truth of detail not to lose sight of more important matter, by this I mean that color and design should be as carefully thought out as if the subject had only these qualities. To me it seems no handicap to have a subject of nobility worthy of one's best continued effort. There is but one thing more important than these qualities and that is to try and convey to your public the

28. Washington, quoted in Anonymous, 'An Afro-American Painter', p. 405.

> reverence and elevation these subjects impart to you, which is the primary cause of their choice.[29]

His commentary characterized the significance of his religious subjects to him, but also his desire to impart this 'reverence' to the audiences of his paintings. The relationship between humanity and God should have made 'the whole world kin', but Tanner realized that many did not recognize the humanity of all races and peoples. His art was a medium to show that all had the similar struggles, joys, and the potential for a relationship with God. His work emphasized themes of hope, struggle, sacrifice, rebirth, and unwavering faith in God that supplied his biblical figures with the ability to persevere. According to biographer Marcus Bruce, the artist 'infused' common scenes 'with a set of questions and ideas that they otherwise might not have', which meant that Tanner's paintings motivated the viewer to examine his or her own life and self.[30] Tanner demonstrated that those involved in these often miraculous moments were above all human and ordinary, which implied that each human had the power to interact with and have faith in the divine. In *The Annunciation* (1898) and *Nicodemus* (1899), Tanner depicted the interaction between the divine and the human in midst of domesticity and ordinary moments of human life.

The Annunciation (Fig. 1) is one of Tanner's most famous religious paintings; it depicts the moment that Mary learns from the angel Gabriel that she will give birth to the son of God. The description of this momentous event is in the Gospel of Luke:

> In the sixth month the angel Gabriel was sent by God to a town in Galilee called Nazareth, to a virgin engaged to a man whose name was Joseph… The virgin's name was Mary. And he came to her and said, 'Greetings, favored one! The Lord is with you.' But she was much perplexed by his words and pondered what sort greeting this might be. The angel said to her, 'Do not be afraid, Mary, for you have found favor with God. And now, you will conceive in your womb and bear a son, and you will name him Jesus' (Lk. 1.26-31, NRSV).

This large painting (57 by 71¼ inches) presents a young, vulnerable Mary and a beam of light as Gabriel. The room is constructed of light gray stone, and a red drapery frames Mary, who appears small and delicate. She is located in her sleeping quarters with blankets disheveled and drooping onto the floor. Mary is dressed in loose, neutral-toned robes that flow off her lap into a pool of fabric on a slightly rumpled rug. Her bare foot peeks

29. Henry O. Tanner, 'Effort', statement published in 'Exhibition of Religious Paintings by H.O. Tanner', checklist of an exhibition at Grand Central Art Galleries, New York, 1924, n.p., as quoted in Hartigan, *Sharing Traditions*, pp. 106-107.

30. Bruce, *Henry Ossawa Tanner*, pp. 111.

out from under her robes. To her left, a small lamp burns, emitting a faint amount of light. Gabriel appears as a bright infusion of light that dominates the left of the painting. This golden warm light erases the details of the rest of the room. Tanner conveys a sense that the light was blinding yet compelling. Unlike previous paintings of the same subject, the artist relies upon simplicity of scene instead of a grandiose recreation (e.g. Fra Angelico's *The Annunciation*). A contemporary of Tanner described the painting's novelty, albeit unintentionally:

> ...the young Jewish peasant sitting on the edge of the couch wearing the common striped cotton of the Eastern women of the poorer class, a costume which they have kept to the present day, no halo or celestial attributes about her, and only the flood of golden light to herald the approach of the angel. It was decidedly an unconventional treatment of the subject.[31]

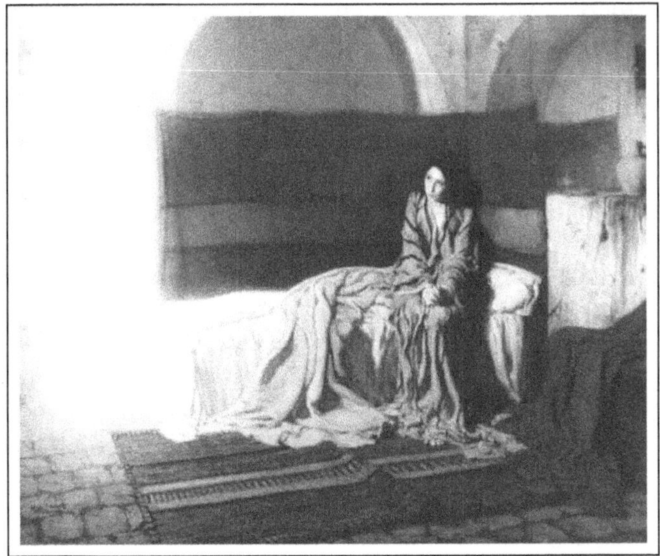

Figure 1. Henry Ossawa Tanner, *The Annunciation*. Courtesy of the Philadelphia Museum of Art, the W.P. Wilstach Fund

In Tanner's composition, the mundane is exalted. His attention to detail uplifts the simple adornments of this room. Objects like the askew rug and disheveled bed and blankets reflect the confusion and drama of the moment. The fabrics appear almost liquid in their creases and in the way they flow onto the rug and stone floor. These objects show how abruptly the messenger of God awakened Mary, a young Jewish girl,

31. Helen Cole, 'Henry O. Tanner, Painter', *Brush & Pencil* 6 (1900), pp. 101-102.

without halo to indicate her sacred status. She appears sleepy and pensive rather than accepting or gracious. Her confusion signals that she is thinking about this unexpected task with which she has been presented. Her hands are folded tightly together, perhaps because of her anxiety. Mary appears as one might expect her to be: nervous, wary, and startled rather than calmly celestial. Gabriel appears as a infusion of light that penetrates the room with its glow. Tanner's Mary is not celestial or divinely beautiful but remarkably average. Above all, she is awkwardly human. She struggles to comprehend Gabriel's message, and she listens with her head tilted ever so slightly as she considers this messenger. Her eyes are riveted upon him, and her lips are pursed. She watches the celestial light with confusion as she ponders her great responsibility. Tanner's emphasis on Mary's humanity makes it possible for the viewer to relate to her as a person instead of seeing her in the elevated position as the mother of Jesus. Whereas Mary is substantial, Gabriel is immaterial. Tanner captures what the experience might have felt like for this situation, and the ordinary nature of this event makes this rendering exceptional.

By portraying Mary as ordinary, Tanner shows the potential for all humans to have this intimate relationship with the divine. In his rendering, the divine is intrusive and insistent. In Tanner's visual exegesis, Gabriel's command to the young May not to be afraid makes sense because Gabriel appears in a form that would inspire fear, formless and light rather than human. This portrayal of the angel as radical Other makes this presentation more compelling by demonstrating the stark difference between humanity and divinity. Mary is flesh, and the angel is fleshless and formless. This divine beacon overshadows her small lamp. Humanity is dwarfed in the presence of the divine's magnitude. Tanner makes this young woman's awe and fear awe-filled and awful, palpable to the viewers of the painting. In the ordinary, disheveled world, Tanner shows the intrusion of the divine. The mundane has the potential to invite the sacred.

As in other paintings, Tanner depicts God and messengers of God in the form of light, which reveals their divine status to contrast to their human counterparts. A *New York Times* art critic proposed that Tanner was 'pantheistic' in his paintings because he revered everything and light was his way to express love. Light 'is always a source of goodness' and 'even touched by it, people are safe'.[32] Light was Tanner's expression of God, so illumination in his paintings showed God's guidance and comfort for humanity. Tanner bathes his painting of the annunciation in a warm light that signals that a miracle just occurred. Tanner used light as a

32. Michael Brenson, 'For Tanner, Light Was Love', *New York Times* (17 February, 1991), p. H33.

metaphor for his creation of his works as well. For him, 'brilliant ideas' were a pleasure to work with, but some times these ideas did not last.

> Then one by one the great hopes you have vanish, the various qualities you knew you were going to get fail to materialize, the lights go out—what misery—then it is determination to succeed has to be evoked...but again light begins to appear and with it a picture, something quite a little different in details from your original idea, but one which work is a pleasure.[33]

Light, then, for Tanner became his much-needed inspiration that possibly was derived from his relationship with God. His reliance upon light as an analogy for the divine in his paintings resonates with the way he described his life and viewed God's interaction in his own life. When art became a drudge, Tanner sought light, which inspired and motivated him to paint. Light was a metaphor for his painting and in his life.

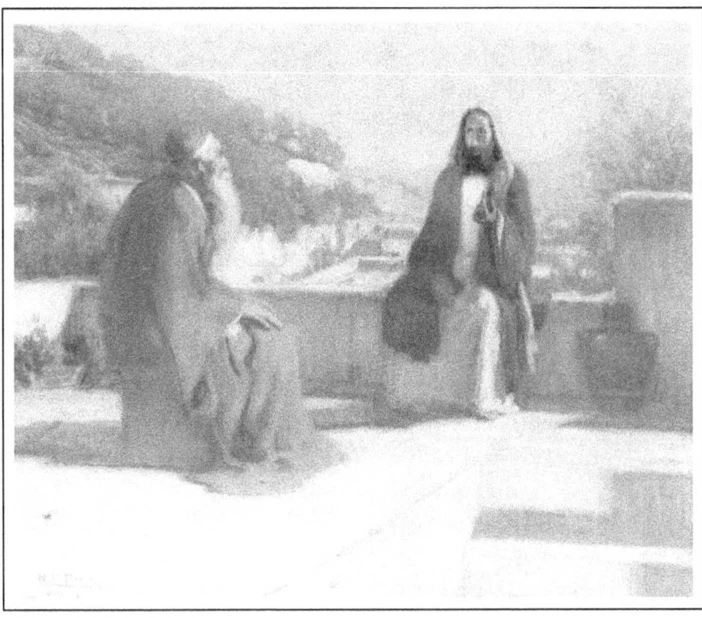

Figure 2. Henry Ossawa Tanner, *Nicodemus*. Courtesy of the Pennsylvania Academy of Fine Arts, Philadelphia, Joseph E. Temple Fund

Another painting, *Nicodemus*, the winner of the Lippincott Prize, is a quite different composition from *The Annunciation*. *Nicodemus* (Fig. 2) depicts Jesus' meeting with the Pharisee, Nicodemus, in which they discuss Jesus' revolutionary teachings. It portrays Nicodemus's desire to learn

33. H.O. Tanner, 'The Story of an Artist's Life II', *The World's Work* 18 (1909), p. 11775.

from Christ, but it also reflects the need to meet in secrecy for both participants because of the danger involved. The encounter is described in the Gospel of John:

> Now there was a Pharisee named Nicodemus, a leader of the Jews. He came to Jesus by night and said to him, 'Rabbi, we know that you are a teacher who has come from God; for no one can do these signs that you do apart from the presence of God'. Jesus answered him, 'Very truly, I tell you, no one can see the kingdom of God without being born from above. (Jn. 3.1-3, NRSV).

The passage reflects on the necessity of rebirth to be part of the kingdom of God, a theme that also appeared in Tanner's earlier painting, *The Resurrection of Lazarus* (1897). *Lazarus* was painted after Tanner had toured Palestine, and the artist had already been commended for his depictions of 'the Orient'.[34] In the painting, Jesus is engaged in an avid conversation with Nicodemus on a stone rooftop during the night. Unlike *The Annunciation*, which has warm colors, *Nicodemus* has a cooler palette of blues and greens. The night sky is a darker blue, and the rugged hillside is visible in the background. Nicodemus is a wizened figure with a long gray beard and dark clothing. His back is hunched and his hands rest firmly on his knees. He blends into the stone rooftop, yet Tanner captures his rapt attention, which reflects the desire to learn from Christ. His robes flow, which again demonstrates Tanner's fascination with garments. The rendering of Jesus with dark skin and hair is unique. As Jesus shares his wisdom, a warm yellow light, coming from the stairwell, illuminates his face partially. Jesus appears pensive as he gestures to Nicodemus while speaking. Jesus is the central focus of the work, and he appears more real than Nicodemus, who appears to be an extension of the foreground. Jesus' presence is warm and life-like, and he provides a stark contrast to the gray figure, who appears more fixture than person.

Tanner covers the figures with the shroud of night. Scholars who noted the use of religion 'as' the metaphor for African-American history and culture in Tanner's paintings found an implicit subtext, or 'hidden transcript', in *Nicodemus*. They noted the correlation between the secrecy involved in Nicodemus' visit and the secrecy of worship among slaves and ex-slaves, who also had their meetings at night for the protection and cover of darkness.[35] The story of Nicodemus would thus reflect the

34. Alan C. Braddock, 'Painting the World's Christ: Tanner, Hybridity, and the Blood of the Holy Land', *NCAW* 3 (2004), at http://19thc-artworldwide.org/autumn_04/articles.

35. Mosby, 'Paris, Racial Awareness, and Success: 1891–1897', p. 135. James Scott proposed the idea of hidden transcripts as a method that oppressed peoples use to express their resistance. It seems to apply to Mosby's characterization of Tanner's

African-American experience of secrecy in the early history of their religious experiences. Race would be an obvious component of Tanner's paintings for African-American audiences, who could note the 'hidden' theme because of Tanner's appropriations of biblical narratives that were important for African-American history. Tanner would be communicating a racial message and a commentary on social justice despite his representation of white characters in his biblical paintings.

In contrast to racial interpretations, I would argue that Tanner's painting of the conversation between Jesus and Nicodemus could be understood as another artistic attempt to show the connection between the human and the divine. As in *The Annunciation*, the divine communicates with the human. Jesus converses and gestures to an attentive Nicodemus, yet he does not appear as a divine figure but rather as a universal figure. In an earlier sketch, Tanner portrayed Jesus with a halo, but in the painting, the halo is gone. Jesus is ordinary and human, even though the Gospel of John has Nicodemus asserting that Jesus must have come from God. Jesus and Nicodemus become the pictorial assertion of the connection between human and divine in mundane places. As in Tanner's other paintings, warm light again signals the presence of God, since Jesus appears luminous. Jesus' divinity is apparent in his luminosity. Moreover, Alan Braddock argues that Tanner portrays Christ as racially mixed in order to present a universal savior rather than one who belongs to a particular race.[36] Tanner's Jesus has dark skin and dark hair, which was an unconventional presentation of Jesus. According to Braddock, Tanner's portrayal of the universality of Christ served as a critique of racism. This portrayal of Christ transcended racial barriers and highlighted the arbitrary nature of racial classification. Braddock also noted that *Nicodemus* articulated a 'utopian' vision of Christianity in which race did not

use of subtext as a way to communicate with African Americans, yet still make his paintings marketable to white buyers. Bearden and Henderson see the exchange between Christ and Nicodemus as parallel to the secret exchange between abolitionists and slaves, which converted slaves to the cause of abolitionism. It is important to note that this painting is often associated with the secrecy involved with slavery and religion. See Bearden and Henderson, *A History of African American Artists*, p. 95; James C. Scott, *Domination and the Arts of Resistance: Hidden Transcripts* (New Haven: Yale University Press, 1990), pp. 1-16. In his first chapter, Scott explores how oppressed people express their autonomy through a hidden transcript that is communicable to others in the same positions. To apply Scott's ideas to Tanner's work, I think, would demonstrate that Tanner was expressing racial subtexts of struggle and oppression to African-American viewers of his paintings. The addition of Scott's theory to previous scholarship on Tanner would enhance the argument about the racial subtexts of Tanner's religious paintings.

36. Braddock, 'Painting the World's Christ'.

influence the realm of faith. Tanner portrays Christianity as a universal faith with a racially ambiguous savior, who inhabited the most mundane of spaces. *Nicodemus* is another attempt by Tanner to show that God is present in the domesticity of everyday life. For Braddock, 'Tanner's biblical pictures may not allegorize African-American identity so much as offer a utopian vision of *world* community to which he thought the United States ought to aspire'.[37]

Tanner's Jesus was a hybrid savior, who was not bound by the dictates of racial classification but was present for all of humanity. Tanner's rendering of Jesus illuminated both the extraordinary, raising people from the dead, and the ordinary, conversing with religious leaders, and Tanner's savior was the intrusion of the divine in the realm of humanity. Yet, as in *The Annunciation*, the divine's messenger, or the divine messenger, does not present a clear message. Just as both Mary and Nicodemus attempt to understand what they are presented with, the viewers wrestle with obscured messengers, a beam of light and a Jesus whose face is partially hidden in darkness. Tanner's paintings force the viewer to ponder these biblical events and what they mean about our world. The viewer must study the painting to find the message about the place of the divine in our universe and the implications of the role of divinity for humanity. What is obvious is that for Tanner the divine inhabited the mundane to guide humanity. His paintings again and again focus on divine presence, often in the form of absence or in the form of Jesus. For Tanner, God was always present. In the vision of the world Tanner created, God and humanity communicate, and race is an arbitrary category that even God's son defies.

In *Nicodemus*, light again warmly glows with the presence of God. Here a warm orange light, rather than a dramatic refiguration of divine presence in the immaterial form of Gabriel, illuminates Jesus' face. After all, Jesus was both human and divine, and Tanner tempered Jesus' light to reflect his hybridity. Light reveals Jesus' divinity, while Nicodemus remains in shadow. In a conversation with Hale Woodruff, Tanner remarked, 'I see light chiefly as a means of achieving luminosity... There should be a glow which indeed consumes the theme or subject. Still, a light-glow which rises and falls in intensity as it moves through the painting.'[38] For Tanner, light proved to be a crucial element of his work, and he manipulated light to invigorate his paintings in a way similar to the way he felt God reinvigorated his life and the lives of the biblical figures. God's presence and the human connection to God were the universal truths of Christianity and suggested the kinship of all humanity. By

37. Braddock, 'Painting the World's Christ', emphasis original.

38. Hale Woodruff, 'My Meeting with Henry O. Tanner', *The Crisis* 77 (1970), pp. 7-12 (11).

showering the painting with light or presenting a faint glow, Tanner made God's presence known in the most average of places. The artist's son, Jesse Tanner, explained his father's faith and the message that his paintings communicated:

> Though my father felt that the presence of God stretches out through the cosmos and his love extends to other worlds than our own, he also felt that man has an active role to play and should not submit passively to his fate. Christ watches over his flock...but evil is a tangible thing and *God needs us* to help fight with him against evil and *we need God* to guide us. (We all have a little of God in us).[39]

Jesse Tanner captured the essence of Tanner's belief and the core of the religious paintings. Tanner desired the viewers of his paintings to be cognizant of the interaction between God and humanity and not to be passive, and his paintings were an example of the potential for interaction. His art was also demonstrative of the omnipresence of God in the universe and of God's presence inside all people.

'Hence every picture is instinct with religious emotion'

It is obvious why art critics and viewers of his paintings constantly mention the emotion that exudes from Tanner's paintings. The artist's illustration of emotion, religious or otherwise, was a different approach to painting the human figure.[40] This emotion was a reflection of Tanner's own feelings toward divinity that he captured on canvas. His works

39. Jesse Ossawa Tanner, 'Introduction', in Matthews, *Henry Ossawa Tanner*, p. xiii. Emphasis original.

40. During Tanner's career, portraiture was popular in America and Europe, and it was a style of painting that guaranteed the monetary success of artists. Between 1825–1870, portraiture dominated the art world in two styles, 'blatant realism', which rivaled photography, and romantic sentimentality. The figures of both of these styles were stiff and often they lacked any form of emotion, and they were noted for their plainness. Female figures often had a slight smile, but male figures were painted with harsh realism that did not idealize. One art historian, Fredrick Hartt, classified the realism of this time period as an 'almost puritanical concentration on fact instead of fancy'. From 1870–1900, portraiture changed slightly, with artists usually illustrating the quiet introspection of the figures. Winslow Homer painted 'stoic' confrontations of human and nature, despite the high drama of these situations, and Thomas Eakins, Tanner's mentor, focused on introspection. The lack of emotion and the themes of introspection are quite the opposite of Tanner's paintings, which were filled with a sense of religious emotion ranging from awe to disbelief to the artist's own form of quiet reverie. See Wayne Craven, *American Art: Culture and History* (New York: Harry N. Abrams, 1994), especially pp. 231, 341; and Frederick Hartt, *Art: A History of Painting, Sculpture, Architecture* (New York: Harry N. Abrams, 2nd edn, 1985), especially p. 823.

mirrored his deep religious feelings for God. The emotion that washed over the audiences of his paintings echoed his own responses to God: awe, shock, reverence, and joy. As Oscar L. Joseph of *The Epworth Herald* observed about Tanner:

> He is also expressing his own experiences. What he has seen and heard with confidence he paints. Hence every picture is instinct with religious emotion. And this is of such a nature that it thrills also the spectator and rouses within him the faith, hope, and love which were first kindled in the heart of the artist. If 'the end of art is to deepen and intensify the sense of life', that purpose is here fully realized.[41]

Joseph poetically describes his experience of Tanner's religious paintings in a way that emphasizes their messages of faith and the religious emotion that is present on the canvases. To Joseph, Tanner not only demonstrated hope and faith, but his art 'deepened the sense of life' because of his display of his personal religious experience and the potential of others to gain this awareness from Tanner's work. Another art critic, Elbert Baldwin, felt that Tanner's representations of Christ as human appealed to viewers, yet the longer one studied Tanner's Christ the more god-like he became.[42] Baldwin approached the painting as Tanner had intended, with reflection and repeated study, in order to understand the nuance of the subject. Baldwin went beyond Joseph's commentary by suggesting not only religious feeling but also inspiration from God because of the art's impact on the viewer.

Even Eunice Tietjens, who focused on the artist's race, described his canvases as having a 'rich simplicity of color and a quiet restfulness of mass', and she also noticed the inspiration or 'spell' of the Tanner's work. She observed, 'Perhaps their strongest charm lies in the fact that their interest increases with time till [*sic*] at last in some subtle fashion a very real spell is woven which [one] felt can never be quite lost again'.[43] Tietjens approached the painting in much the same manner as Baldwin, by studying it carefully, and she was drawn to Tanner's paintings in an almost magical way because of the artist's inspiration and profound renderings of humanity and divinity. Another critic, William E. Barton, commented that the 'French government had thrown off religion', but even in their irreligious state, they were buying religion in the form of

41. Oscar L. Joseph, 'Henry O. Tanner's Religious Paintings', *The Epworth Herald* (6 March, 1909), pp. 1042-43, located in the Henry Ossawa Tanner Papers, Archives of American Art, Smithsonian Institution, Washington, DC, reel D307.

42. Baldwin, 'A Negro Artist of Unique Power', p. 793.

43. Draft of Eunice Tietjens's article on Henry Tanner, 1914, located in the Henry Ossawa Tanner papers 1850–1978 (bulk 1890–1920), Archives of American Art, Smithsonian Institution, Washington, DC, reel D 307.

Tanner's paintings because of the impact of his work.[44] The French government bought both *The Resurrection of Lazarus* and *Christ at Emmaus*, a rare honor for an American artist. Tanner was in Jerusalem when *Lazarus* was purchased, and a friend wrote to him, 'Come home, Tanner, to see the crowds before your picture'.[45] The presence of religion could not be denied in Tanner's works even in the discussions of his paintings by scholars. Lynda Hartigan classified his paintings as genuinely spiritual and proposed that this 'spirituality' led to Tanner's wide public reception and recognition. She commented that Tanner 'saw his painting as his mission —a culmination rather than an initiation of a tradition'.[46] She recognized Tanner's devotion to his painting and his message. Hartigan also noticed the spirituality of his work that other critics as well deemed a unique element.

The most recent biographer of Tanner describes his work as spiritual and even biblical. Marcus Bruce states that the artist's paintings are 'his autobiography and, more importantly, his Bible. Each is a testament, a Bible-like chronicle of the struggles, triumph, failures, resources and revelations of an African-American painter living and working in America and France.'[47] Tanner's work was his own Bible as well as a representation of the Bible, and he relied on what he believed to be the essence of Christianity, the interaction between human and divine, as a way to depict the biblical text. His imagery has power because it depicts the struggles and the joys humanity faces and the presence of God in human affairs no matter what the situation. The viewer can relate to the figures in the paintings and then 'see' how the divine interacted in his or her life as well. Many critics observed the spirituality in Tanner's art, and some affirmed its power to leave one spellbound or with a deeper sense of being, of life. It appears that the artist was successful in his desire to show his personal relationship with the divine and to encourage others (through his paintings) to interact with God as well. A goal of his art was to show the connection, and he hoped his paintings would help 'make the whole world kin'.

> For comfort and understanding, the artist turned to his personal relationship with God. Tanner felt the presence of God, and, in his work, depicted prophets and ordinary men and women who were aware of it as well.

44. William E. Barton, 'An American Painter of the Resurrection: Henry Ossawa Tanner', *The Advance* 20 (1913), p. 11, located in the Henry Ossawa Tanner papers, Archives of American Art, Smithsonian Institution, Washington, DC, reel D 307.

45. H.O. Tanner, 'The Story of an Artist's Life I', *The World's Work* 18 (1909), p. 11773 (Tanner speaks of himself in the third person in this article).

46. Hartigan, *Sharing Traditions*, p. 114.

47. Bruce, *Henry Ossawa Tanner*, p. 15.

> Tanner observed God's presence in all of the events in his life, and he believed that 'it was good God who opened the way and gave me good friends, thus filling me with confidence in the future, which never deserted me in those darkest days'.[48]

Tanner's art expresses again and again what the world should be: a utopian world above the barriers of race. He strove to make the Bible 'real' for his viewers, so that they could see for themselves the presence of God. A contemporary of Tanner, William R. Lester, noted the 'glow of reverent devotion' and 'intensity of spiritual expression' in Tanner's art and classified the artist as a 'practical believer', who painted 'dramatic portrayals of moving Scriptural scenes' that were reminiscent 'of those earlier days when immortal masters pictured on the walls or canvas with earnest faith and profound soul experiences of humanity'.[49] Lester felt the spiritual intensity of Tanner's paintings and saw the 'glow' of the artist's personal devotion.

Tanner's images have a power to communicate the authenticity of God's relationship with biblical figures and with the artist himself. Tanner painted what he learned from the biblical narratives and from his faith in God, so that he could convince the audiences of his paintings of God's presence in the universe. Painting was not just a career choice to Henry Tanner but also devotion, religious experience, and practice. The artist believed that divinity existed in even the most ordinary places, and he painted the presence of divinity in the human arena in order to convince his viewers of this truth. Both *The Annunciation* and *Nicodemus* presented the power and the presence of the divine. Tanner communicated with his brush an understanding of the beauty of the biblical narrative and the power of the divine that exuded from the Bible's pages. His son, Jesse, believed that:

> A Tanner can do more than give you enjoyment, it can come to your rescue, it can reaffirm your confidence in man and his destiny, it can help you surmount your difficulties or console you in your distress. A picture by Tanner is really a part of the artist himself, a mystic whose visions are deeply personal yet universal in significance.[50]

48. Tanner, 'The Story of an Artist's Life I', p. 11664.

49. William R. Lester, 'Henry O. Tanner: Exile for Art's Sake', *Alexander's Magazine* 7 (1908), p. 72.

50. Tanner, 'Introduction', pp. xii-xiii.

BIBLIOGRAPHY

Adams, Brooks, 'Tanner's Odyssey', *Art in America* 79 (1991), pp. 108-12, 93.

Anonymous, 'An Afro-American Painter Who Has Become Famous in Paris', *Current Literature* 45 (1908), pp. 405-408.

Baldwin, Elbert Francis, 'A Negro Artist of Unique Power', *The Outlook* 64 (1900), pp. 793-96.

Barton, William E., 'An American Painter of the Resurrection: Henry Ossawa Tanner', *The Advance* 20 (1913), p. 11.

Bearden, Romare, and Harry Henderson, *A History of African-American Artists: From 1792 to the Present* (New York: Pantheon Books, 1993).

Boime, Albert, 'Henry Ossawa Tanner's Subversion of Genre', *Art Bulletin* 75 (1993), pp. 415-41.

Braddock, Alan, 'Painting the World's Christ: Tanner, Hybridity, and the Blood of the Holy Land', *NWAC* 3 (2004), at http://19thc-artworldwide.org/autumn_04/articles.

Brenson, Michael, 'For Tanner, Light Was Love', *The New York Times* 140 (17 February, 1991), pp. H33, 35.

Bruce, Marcus C., *Henry Ossawa Tanner: A Spiritual Biography* (New York: Crossroad, 2002).

Cole, Helen, 'Henry O. Tanner, Painter', *Brush and Pencil* 6 (1900), pp. 97-107.

Craven, Wayne, *American Art: Culture and History* (New York: Harry N. Abrams, 1994).

Dubois, W.E.B., 'The Criteria of Negro Art', *The Crisis* 32 (1926), pp. 290-97.

Fauset, Jessie, 'Henry Ossawa Tanner', *The Crisis* 27 (1924), pp. 255-58.

Harper, Jennifer, 'The Early Religious Paintings of Henry Ossawa Tanner: A Study of the Influences of Church, Family, and Era', *American Art* 6 (1992), pp. 68-85.

Hartigan, Lynda Roscoe, *Sharing Traditions: Five Black Artists in Nineteenth-Century America* (Washington, DC: Smithsonian Institution Press, 1985).

Hartt, Frederick, *Art: A History of Painting, Sculpture, Architecture* (New York: Harry N. Abrams, 2nd edn, 1985).

Johnson, James Weldon, *Black Manhattan* (Salem: Ayer Company, 1990).

Lester, William R., 'Henry O. Tanner, Exile for Art's Sake', *Alexander's Magazine* 7 (1908), pp. 69-73.

Locke, Alain, *The Negro and His Music. Negro Art: Past and Present* (repr. New York, Arno Press, 1969 [1936]).

—*The New Negro* (New York: Albert & Charles Boni, 1927; repr. New York: Atheneum, 1980).

Matthews, Marcia, *Henry Ossawa Tanner: American Artist* (Chicago: University of Chicago Press, 1969 [repr. 1994]).

Mosby, Dewey F., *Across Continents and Cultures: The Art and Life of Henry Ossawa Tanner* (Kansas City: The Nelson-Atkins Museum of Art, 1995).

Mosby, Dewey F., and Darrel Sewell, *Henry Ossawa Tanner* (New York: Rizzoli International, 1991).

Pennell, Joseph, *The Adventure of an Illustrator* (Boston: Little, Brown & Company, 1925).

Scarborough, W.S., 'Henry Ossian [sic] Tanner', *Southern Workman* 31 (1902), pp. 661-70.

Schwain, Kristin Ann, 'Figuring Belief: American Art and Modern Religious Experience' (PhD dissertation, Stanford University, 2001).

Scott, James C., *Domination and the Arts of Resistance: Hidden Transcripts* (New Haven: Yale University Press, 1990).

Seraile, William, *Fire in His Heart: Bishop Benjamin Tucker Tanner and the A.M.E. Church* (Knoxville: University of Tennessee Press, 1998).

Skeel, Sharon Kay, 'Black American in the Paris Salon', *American Heritage* 42 (1991), pp. 77-83.

Tanner, Benjamin Tucker, *An Apology for African Methodism* (Baltimore, 1867), located at the University of North Carolina, Chapel Hill, Documenting the American South Project, http://docsouth/unc.edu/church/tanner/tanner.html.

Tanner, Henry Ossawa, 'Henry Ossawa Tanner Papers, 1850–1978 (bulk 1890–1920)' (Washington, DC: Archives of American Art, Smithsonian Institution).

—'The Story of an Artist's Life I', *The World's Work* 18 (1909), pp. 11661-66.

—'The Story of an Artist's Life II', *The World's Work* 18 (1909), pp. 11769-75.

Wilson, Judith, 'Lifting the "Veil": Henry O. Tanner's The Banjo Lesson and The Thankful Poor', in *Critical Issues in American Art: A Book of Readings* (ed. Mary Ann Calo; Boulder, CO: Westview Press, 1998), pp. 199-219.

Woodruff, Hale, 'My Meeting with Henry O. Tanner', *The Crisis* 77 (1970), pp. 7-12.

Woods, Naurice, Jr, 'Insuperable Obstacles: The Impact of Racism on Creative and Personal Development of Four 19th Century African American Artists' (PhD dissertation, The Union Institute Graduate School, 1993).

—'Lending Color to Canvas: Henry O. Tanner's African-American Themes', *American Visions* 6 (1991), pp. 14-20.

WILLIAM BLAKE AND THE NEW TESTAMENT: THE PERSPECTIVE OF THE PICTURES

Christopher Rowland

The most famous words of William Blake, thoroughly part of English culture, are saturated with biblical allusions. They reflect a sophisticated and complex engagement with the Bible, the interpretation of which is an ongoing challenge for the biblical scholar:

And did those feet in ancient time.
Walk upon Englands mountains, green:
And was the holy Lamb of God.
On Englands pleasant pastures seen!

And did the Countenance Divine.
Shine forth upon our clouded hills?
And was Jerusalem builded here.
Among these dark Satanic Mills?

Bring me my Bow of burning gold:
Bring me my Arrows of desire:
Bring me my Spear: O clouds unfold:
Bring me my Chariot of fire!

I will not cease from Mental Fight.
Nor shall my Sword sleep in my hand:
Till we have built Jerusalem,
In Englands green & pleasant Land.

Would to God that all the Lords people
were Prophets (*Numbers xi. ch. 29V*).

In the immediately preceding context of what we now know as 'Jerusalem' are indications of what Blake considered to be some of the major obstacles to the use of Scripture. Chief among these were rote learning and the dulling effects of memory as opposed to imagination. Blake protests at the way in which the writings of classical antiquity are given prominence over those of the Bible. The effects of reading the Bible in the light of such texts is to quench the spirit of imagination. Blake wants to lead a movement of protest. He writes, 'We do not want either Greek or Roman models if we are but just & true to our own Imaginations, those Worlds of Eternity in which we shall live for ever in Jesus our Lord'.[1]

The pictures included with this article are produced with the permission of the National Trust and the Philadelphia Museum of Art. Website references are offered where some of the pictures discussed in this article were to be found in June 2006.

1. William Blake, 'Preface', *Milton: A Poem in Two Books*, in *Blake: Complete Writings* (ed. G. Keynes; Oxford: Clarendon Press, 1966), p. 480. See also R. Essick and J. Viscomi, *Milton, A Poem*(London: Blake Trust/Tate Gallery, 1998), p. 94.

This famous poetic passage brings together several important themes. First and foremost it is written by a man without any formal education, whose wisdom is that of the streets, of popular culture, and the conventional arts of the apprentice. Secondly, we can see some of the recurring themes of Blake's writing: his campaign against an education based solely on memory rather than inspiration, and his conviction that the domination of classical culture had quenched the vitality of biblical inspiration. Thirdly, the allusions to the Scriptures give a distinctive flavour to his interpretation. The New Jerusalem is not something remote or far off but a possibility, something which may be built in England's green and pleasant land. There is also no disjunction between human activity and divine activity, nothing here about 'leaving it all to God', for the simple reason that God is involved through the imaginative and creative work of the artist. Elijah's chariot is not just part of past history, or even future expectation, but something which can be the inspiration of the poet. Here a new Elijah comes on the scene, condemning the idolatries of Ahab and Jezebel, and offering an alternative to the Baalism of a contemporary culture which, according to Blake, had led to the capitulation of Christianity to a religion of virtues, rules, and the acceptance of war and violence. The spirit and power of Elijah were ever available for those who would exercise their imagination by contemplative thought. Prophecy likewise is not just a thing of the past. It is the vocation of all people. The vision of the New Jerusalem is one that is open to all and the task of building belongs to all.

Any discussion of William Blake's poetry, art and writing about any part of the Bible cannot hope to do anything more than scratch the surface. Yet it is an important subject and one which has been somewhat marginal to Blake studies over recent decades. There have, of course, been exceptions. Nearly sixty years ago, John Davies studied Blake's theology in his Oxford doctorate. The book it produced is full of insight, but concentrates too much on the written words, attempts too much systematisation, and leaves the pictures largely unconsidered.[2] Leslie Tannenbaum's book, meanwhile, does an excellent job of locating Blake within the context of emerging historical scholarship in the eighteenth century (as does the study by Prickett and Strathman) but is unsatisfactory when it comes to looking at the sweep of Blake's biblical hermeneutics.[3]

2. J.G. Davies, *The Theology of William Blake* (Oxford: Clarendon Press, 1948).

3. L. Tannenbaum, *Biblical Tradition in Blake's Early Prophecies: The Great Code of Art* (Princeton, NJ: Princeton University Press, 1982); S. Prickett and C. Strathman, 'Blake and the Bible', in *Palgrave Advances in William Blake Studies* (ed. Nicholas Williams; London: Palgrave Macmillan, 2005), pp. 109-31

Jon Mee's book on late eighteenth-century millenarianism is a necessary corrective to the view that Blake was idiosyncratic in his self-understanding.[4] In the world of Joanna Southcott and Richard Brothers, with their prophetic ministries and millenarian hopes, William Blake's work is very much at home, whatever differences we may want to note between them.[5] Both Chris Burdon's and Morton Paley's study of the Apocalypse in English literature remind us that Blake, like his contemporaries Wordsworth, Coleridge and Shelley, found themselves inspired by the book of Revelation, its images and its genre.[6] Burdon's book is a major and timely contribution by a biblical theologian, demonstrating the importance of Blake within emerging historical scholarship generally, and in a vibrant interpretative apocalyptic culture at the end of the eighteenth century. There is a growing appreciation of the importance of religion for the Romantic Movement, as Robert Ryan's book reminds us.[7] Some of Blake's most explicit statements about the Bible are found in marginal notes he made to the response of Bishop Watson to Tom Paine.[8]

William Blake came from an artisan background and was apprenticed to an engraver in London. His expertise in this craft was fundamental to his art. He so refined and perfected his skill that he evolved a way of producing the exercise of his own imagination in his own unique method of engraving. If Joseph Viscomi is to be believed, the engraving technique he perfected enabled him to translate the fruits of his inspiration immediately onto copper plates.[9] Thereby inspiration and execution came to be united in a way with few parallels in the history of artistic production. In his work, Blake was able to develop his own mythology, rooted in the symbols and images of the biblical prophecies and apocalypses, to challenge the domination of deference to the old words and phrases. He was an implacable enemy of devotion to 'memory' (tradition) at the expense of inspiration or imagination. For Blake, the Bible pre-eminently stimulated the imagination, that privileged space where human and divine could find communion. Blake would have sympathized with Coleridge's

4. Jon Mee, *Dangerous Enthusiasm* (Oxford: Clarendon Press, 1992).

5. E.P. Thompson, *Witness against the Beast* (Cambridge: Cambridge University Press, 1993).

6. C. Burdon *The Apocalypse in England: Revelation Unravelling, 1700–1834* (London: Macmillan, 1997); Morton Paley, *Apocalypse and Millennium in English Romantic Poetry* (Oxford: Clarendon Press, 1999).

7. R. Ryan, *The Romantic Reformation: Religious Politics in English Literature 1789–1824* (Cambridge: Cambridge University Press, 1997).

8. Blake, 'Marginal Notes on Watson's Apology' (*Blake: Complete Writings*, pp. 390-95), well surveyed in Prickett and Strathman, 'Blake and the Bible'.

9. J. Viscomi, *Blake and the Idea of the Book* (Princeton, NJ: Princeton University Press, 1993).

statement that 'in the Bible there is more that finds me than I have experienced in all other books put together'.

In the last year of his life, Blake described the Bible as 'the Great Code of Art' (as he describes it in one of his aphorisms in his *Laocöon* engraving).[10] It is unlikely, in the light of all that we know of Blake's work, that he meant that he saw the Bible as an elaborate code, the cracking of which was the task of the interpreter, whether writer or artist. Perhaps the closest we can get to an explanation might be to use the analogy of the code which unlocks doors in modern buildings thereby giving access to another space. Also possible, in the light of the way in which the word 'code' is used in writing at the time of Blake, is to see it as a system, or collection, of rules or regulations.[11] It would not be inappropriate, therefore, to see his words here as indicating that the Bible offered, in its variety and totality, the prime hermeneutical collection, or aesthetic guide, full of interpretative potential, in the sense that its surface meaning opened up infinite imaginative possibilities, rather than functioning as a system demanding one definitive solution from an enlightened interpreter. In this sense, therefore, and notwithstanding some of the other things he wrote about the interpretation of the Bible, Blake's hermeneutic is in key respects traditional, harking back to aspects of patristic biblical interpretation in its desire to move from the literal sense to other levels of meaning. Indeed, the ways in which Blake, seemingly deliberately, sets difficulties in his texts, most obviously in the ways in which pictures do not relate, and indeed sometimes bear no relationship, to the text, resembles what Origen describes as the *proskommata* placed in the text by the Holy Spirit to 'trip up' and thereby enliven the readings and be an antidote to complacency. That contrasts with the emerging historicism which fascinated contemporary interpreters like Coleridge, not to mention the dismissive attitude taken to patristic and medieval interpretation by earlier English writers like William Tyndale in *The Obedience of the Christian Man*.[12]

Blake's relationship with the Bible is a complex one, and it would be possible to devote this article entirely to what Blake wrote *about* the Bible. But, as Jean Hagstrum has aptly remarked, Blake read the Bible, but he also *saw* it: the white page came stained with colour and scored

10. See online: Laocöon:http://www.ucalgary.ca/~eslinger/img/content.gifs/laoc/Laocoon.html.

11. In the Oxford English Dictionary a code is 'a collection of writings forming a book, such as the Old or the New Testament'. Thus in 1794 William Paley (*Evid.* I.I.ix. §3) wrote: 'The Christian Scriptures were divided into two codes or volumes' and 'Intending by the one a code or collection of Christian sacred writings, as the other expressed the code or collection of Jewish sacred writings'.

12. W. Tyndale, *The Obedience of a Christian Man* (ed. and with an Introduction and Notes by David Daniell; London: Penguin, 2000).

with line.[13] This view echoes that of John Ruskin, who, in *The Modern Painters*, famously wrote of sight: 'to see clearly is poetry, prophecy and religion, all in one'.[14] For Blake (as for Wordsworth) seeing with the imaginative eye was just on a par with physical sight.[15] In the reader's engagement with his texts, word and image jostle with each other on the page. Blake demands the involvement of the reader/spectator in creating meaning from poems in which there is no definitive meaning waiting to be discovered. Rather, on almost every page Blake's books summon those who engage with them to participate in the exegetical task. The often indeterminate relationship between text and image similarly demands that the reader engage with the text; their own imagination thus contributes to making sense of the relationship, sometimes the gap, between the two.

The kind of interpretative process set up by Blake is illustrated by a passage from one of his letters, which offers a way of understanding the heart of Blake's hermeneutics. Here, Blake comes as close as anywhere to describing what is going on in his work, and it is an emphasis on the effects of the text, making Blake something of a pioneer of *Wirkungsgeschichte*. It is in a letter where Blake is asked precisely for a code to help the reader/viewer understand his work:

> You say that I want somebody to Elucidate my Ideas. But you ought to know that What is Grand is necessarily obscure to Weak men. That which can be made Explicit to the Idiot is not worth my care. The wisest of the Ancients consider'd what is not too Explicit as the fittest for Instruction, because it rouzes the faculties to act. I name Moses, Solomon, Esop, Homer, Plato... Why is the Bible more Entertaining & Instructive than any other book? Is it not because they [*sic*] are addressed to the Imagination, which is Spiritual Sensation & but mediately to the Understanding or Reason...[16]

In 'mediately to the understanding or reason' Blake stresses the importance of reason as a secondary, intermediary, agent in the direct encounter which takes place between the imagination and biblical text, in which process the Bible proves to be such a paradigmatic means of engagement.

13. J.H. Hagstrum, 'Blake and the Sister-Arts Tradition', in *Blake's Visionary Forms Dramatic* (ed. D. Erdman and J. Grant; Princeton: Princeton University Press, 1970), pp. 82-91.

14. J. Ruskin, *Modern Painters* (London: Smith, 1846), V, p. 333.

15. Cf. 'We are led to Believe a Lie When we see not Thro the Eye' and 'I question not my Corporeal or Vegetative Eye any more than I would Question a Window concerning a Sight I look thro it & not with it' (Blake, *Blake: Complete Writings*, pp. 433, 617). See, further, M.H. Abrams, *Natural Supernaturalism: Tradition and Revolution in Romantic Literature* (New York: W.W. Norton, 1971), pp. 263-64.

16. 'Letter to Trusler', in Blake, *Blake: Complete Writings*, pp. 793-94.

The reference to reason in the context of his reply to Dr Trusler reminds us that throughout his work Blake challenged the hegemony of reason. In so doing he used three major English intellectuals to epitomize the tradition against which he was protesting: the philosopher Francis Bacon (1561–1626), the mathematician Isaac Newton (1642–1727) and the philosopher John Locke (1632–1704). Blake often grouped them together.[17] While he recognised their creativity, Blake saw in their work a displacement of the imagination by reason and a reduction of all things to material causes. In Blake's view, empiricism allows only one type of evidence (sense-data), and, therefore, one type of cognitive experience. Such a position represents, for Blake, a contraction of the variety and complexity of human experience, as it effectively excludes inspiration, emotion, art and religion as valid sources of knowledge, as well as the recognition of what he terms 'minute particulars'. It was this restricted prioritization in the use of reason, not reason itself, that Blake considered problematic. Indeed, at the climax of his final redemptive epic, 'Jerusalem', the hitherto infernal trinity of Newton, Bacon and Locke are caught up in the 'Chariots of the Almighty' to take their rightful place in a dialectic with imagination, and other facets of human intellectual life. The hegemonic intellectual culture which Newton, Bacon and Locke represented, Blake considered as the spirit of his age, and it was with this that he struggled throughout his life. He protested against the exercise of reason which tended to disallow personal interpretative engagement.

While there can be few writers and artists whose work is so permeated with biblical themes, Blake is at the same time one of the Bible's fiercest critics, not least in the way he inveighed against a theology which viewed God as a remote monarch and lawgiver, as well as the preoccupation with the words of the text. Throughout his life the Bible dominated Blake's imaginative world, even in the early period when he was more critical. This is no better exemplified than in the 1790s Urizen books, where Blake very deliberately parodies the book of Genesis and, to a lesser extent, Exodus. The rewritten creation story is clearly intended to challenge the normative role this story had in the moral ordering of society. Recent Blake criticism on his early work has stressed the way in which Blake's own production of variant versions of his manuscripts, especially in the Urizen books, subverted the notion of an authoritative text. Even though he set great store by the effectiveness of his illuminated texts, Blake was very conscious of his own writing as potentially itself an authoritative text, and made strenuous attempts to problematize his own text: he issued

17. I am grateful to Dr Jonathan Roberts of the University of Liverpool for his comments on Blake and empiricism; see now J. Roberts, *William Blake's Poetry: A Reader's Guide* (London: Continuum, 2007).

differing versions, varying both the order and the colour of the illuminations, as well, of course, as using the juxtaposition of text and image as a way of enhancing and problematizing the other. It is important to remember this when we wrestle with the conundrum that the great deconstructor of the supremacy of writing was himself not only dependent on it but published written texts which were no ordinary or ephemeral productions but themselves prophetic and authoritative.

Arguably, Blake's portrayal of Urizen, the god of law and hierarchy, a picture which has uncanny resemblances to aspects of the Old Testament divinity, is a deity in diabolical guise. Blake's theology is not merely a re-run of gnostic theology, which is itself a complex exploration of the contradictions of the Bible and the tensions that exist in relating the different aspects of the divine character.[18] Rather, it is a heuristic device to illuminate the fragmentation evident in the human personality and to challenge hegemonic readings which used the Bible as a means of enforcing state religion and an understanding of religion which sees it as primarily about 'Moral Virtue'. The heavily ironic tone of *The Marriage of Heaven and Hell* exemplifies the antinomian streak in Blake's work. The oft-repeated denunciation of the religion of 'thou shalt not' scattered through the early prophetic books is the hallmark of the religion he sought to challenge. For Blake the key to religion was mutual forgiveness of sins rather than the inculcation of Moral Virtue, using the Bible as its foundation.

There is a change in Blake's writings with regard to the Bible, between the 1780s and 1790s and the last decades of his life (suggested by letters of 22 November 1802).[19] The attitude of the 1790s is exemplified by the marginal notes which Blake made on 'Watson's Apology'. The latter was an attempt by the Bishop of Llandaff to answer Tom Paine's searching critique of the Bible. Blake's comments reflect many of the reservations which are now commonplace in modern biblical criticism. Thus, he is outspokenly dismissive of what he considers the primitive tribal legends of the Old Testament which justify the slaughter of whole tribes and nations. Nevertheless, while his political sympathies seem to lie with Paine, the marginal notes found in Blake's copy of the text indicate that Blake was not in sympathy with Paine and his Deism or rationalism.

The change in Blake's attitude to the Bible after the French Revolution and the period of repression in 1790s England is most marked in the

18. Cf. A.D. Nuttall, *The Alternative Trinity: Gnostic Heresy in Marlowe, Milton & Blake* (Oxford: Clarendon Press, 1998).

19. Blake, *Blake: Complete Writings*, pp. 19-811. See J.H. Hagstrum, 'The Wrath of the Lamb: A Study of William Blake's Conversions', in *From Sensibility to Romanticism* (ed. F. Hilles and H. Bloom; Oxford: Oxford University Press, 1965), pp. 311-30.

famous added Preface to 'Milton', where Blake rejects the hegemony of classical learning and pleads for a return to the Bible as the prime hermeneutical inspiration. Thereafter, in his art and his illuminated books, there is a more positive engagement with the Bible as the prime source of his inspiration and the principal hermeneutical gateway, though, it should be added, only if it is appropriately read. After 1800, as Blake develops further his complex myth of human individual and social redemption, there is a sense in which his prime inspiration moves from the particularities of society, which he sees in the streets of London, to the Bible, from text serving the 'minute particulars' of life[20] to the inner life becoming intertwined with the textual exposition of a redemptive myth. This is the case in a work like *Jerusalem*, which becomes the way of interpreting the contingent experiences of different circumstances. In addition, the prophet becomes more didactic as his books become a key to human liberation.

Nevertheless, significant continuities remain between the strong assertion of the priority of the Bible after 1800 and what Blake was writing and depicting in the 1780s and 1790s. Thus, in the *Job* engravings, completed shortly before his death, there is once again the depiction of false religion as one which is in thrall to the dominance of book religion and not of visionary immediacy infused with the divine spirit. The *Job* sequence reflects Blake's major theological concerns throughout his life, therefore, and is consistent with other texts and images produced in the last years of his life.

There are numerous verbal allusions to Revelation throughout the illuminated books, particularly in *Jerusalem*. Some are quite explicit, but the link with the biblical book is, seemingly, rarely deliberate and not at a self-conscious level. Thus, Wesley and Whitefield are the two witnesses of Revelation 11 in *Milton* 21(20).55. The dragon red and the hidden harlot recur throughout the late prophetic books, especially *Jerusalem* (plate 66 has allusions to plague and war and there is a reference to the descent of the New Jerusalem in plate 86). Blake was no commentator on Revelation, as he believes himself to be a prophet like John. In his own prophecy, Revelation is woven into the fabric of his own prophetic vision. Indeed, Blake explicitly traces a continuity between his own imaginative creation of his mythical world and the vision seen by John on Patmos. So, Blake sees himself as in continuity with the prophets of old and recognizes them, perhaps somewhat tongue in cheek in 'The Marriage of Heaven and Hell', as the kind of people he might dine with, and who might be quizzed about their prophecies. His own prophecies also mimic their style. The style of biblical prophecy had been the subject of detailed

20. Thompson, *Witness against the Beast*, pp. 179-94.

examination by Robert Lowth in his *Lectures on the Sacred Poetry of the Hebrews*. This book had a far-reaching impact on late eighteenth-century authors, probably including Blake.[21] When Lowth writes of Isaiah's 'prophetic impulse, which bears away the mind with irresistible violence, and frequently in rapid transitions from near to remote objects, from human to divine', he could have been writing of the character, and confusion, of some of Blake's prophetic texts.[22]

So much then by way of introduction to Blake and the Bible. Let us now turn to the pictures. The images considered below come from all periods of Blake's life and include one which was left unfinished at his death. The sequence starts with the *Job* engravings, the culmination of a long interpretative fascination of Blake with the book of Job, starting with the watercolours, originally done for Thomas Butts.[23] It is some of the late Job engravings of 1825 which we shall be considering, which give us a significant insight into Blake's understanding of the Bible. Next come pictures of the Nativity, the Transfiguration and the Conversion of Saul, which give us a flavour of Blake's understanding of the relationship between heaven and earth. This will be followed by a focus on the book of Revelation and related visionary depictions. The final picture to be considered is one of the extant versions of the Last Judgment, which Blake painted on several occasions, though the largest of these is now lost. The one considered here is still in the home of its original patron, Petworth House, and has an accompanying commentary by Blake. If the emphasis in the selection tends to be on the visionary texts in the Bible, that should not be taken to indicate the overall range of subjects treated by Blake in the biblical paintings. Blake in no way concentrated on the visionary passages of the Bible in the paintings he did for Butts, and one or two non-visionary depictions are discussed. Nevertheless it is fair to say that the illustrations of Revelation, or Ezekiel's vision, seem to evoke in Blake an originality that is often not so prominent in his illustrations of other biblical passages.

The Job *Sequence as a Guide to Blake's Hermeneutics*

The importance of the *Job* paintings and engravings as a guide to Blake's understanding of the Bible, and his hermeneutic more generally, is widely

21. Prickett and Strathman, 'Blake and the Bible', pp. 109-31.

22. Robert Lowth, *Lectures on the Sacred Poetry of the Hebrews* (London: Routledge, 1995), pp. 85-86; Tannenbaum, *Biblical Tradition in Blake's Early Prophecies*, p. 27.

23. Blake also painted scores of temperas on biblical subjects for Thomas Butts between 1799 to 1803. Butts became a great supporter and friend of Blake.

recognized.[24] Blake's exegesis of Job is a version of *Sachkritik*, in which a reading of a text is offered in the light of what its interpreter deems to be its essential subject matter. There are centrally placed references to 2 Cor. 3.6 and Heb. 10.6 on plates 1 and 21.[25] These suggest that the story is about Job's conversion from a religion of the letter and of sacrifice to the immediacy of vision (42.5), when he sees God face to face. In seeing God, he recognizes the divine in his likeness, and the demonstration of this conversion comes only when Job practices the forgiveness of sins.[26]

In interpreting the divine theophany (chs. 38–41), Blake interprets the vision of God in the whirlwind as a vision of Jesus Christ.[27] Job's understanding of God changes from transcendent monarch to immanent divine presence, epitomized by the words quoted on plate 17: 'At that day ye shall know that I am in my Father, and ye in me, and I in you. If ye loved me, ye would rejoice because I said I go to the Father' (Jn 14.20). Other Johannine texts quoted here are 10.30; 14.9, 15 and 28. This is the moment when the contents of the books are actually seen by the reader (hitherto we have seen them on the lap of God or Job and his wife). The first book quotation relates to Job's experience of God, the divine in human. There is the proper ordering of text and image, perhaps even of imagination and reason. Blake's hermeneutic resembles a familiar interpretative approach in early Christian writings, where theophanies in the Hebrew Bible are interpreted as visions of Christ. In so far as it is appropriate to pigeon-hole Blake's theology, Blake's rewritten Lord's Prayer of 1827, in which he paraphrases the opening 'Jesus, our Father, who art in thy heaven call'd by thy Name the Holy Ghost', seems to be a form of modalism, a view which may well be a relic from his Swedenborgian days (cf. 'God blessing the Seventh Day' and Jerusalem plates 96, 99).

The Nativity *and Blake's Mystical Theology*[28]

This scene has Joseph and Mary on the left with what I assume are Elizabeth and the infant John. Between them is a celestial Christ, cruciform in shape. Behind them is a window through which there is a heavenly,

24. B. Lindberg, *William Blake's Illustrations to the Book of Job* (Abo: Abo Akademi, 1973); K. Raine, *The Human Face of God: Blake and the Book of Job* (London: Thames & Hudson, 1982); H. Fisch, *The Biblical Presence in Shakespeare, Milton and Blake* (Oxford: Clarendon Press, 1999).

25. Job's initial state: http://life.fhl.net/Art/main03/images/FIG26.jpg; Job and family restored: http://collection.aucklandartgallery.govt.nz/images/display/19711980/1980_10_21.jpg.

26. Job prays for his friends: http://www2.ku.edu/~sma/blake/prb0018x.jpg.

27. Vision of Christ: http://www.glencairnmuseum.org/NewChurchArt.html.

28. Nativity: http://life.fhl.net/Art/main03/images/FIG40.jpg.

cross-shaped light, perhaps the star of Bethlehem. A very different reading is offered by David Bindman who suggests that 'the Christ child apparently springs from the Virgin's womb in a radiance of light, to be caught by Anne's, Mary's mother, outstretched hands'.[29] Indeed, Mary looks like Blake's depiction of *The Woman Clothed in the Sun* as well as Jerusalem (especially plate 26). The swooning woman is a feature of some aspects of Gothic art. The Nativity scene and the infant on the lap of the old woman make it more likely that we have Lk. 2.16 woven together with the theme of the Visitation (Lk. 1.39-44). What is striking about this picture is the way in which two women are given a prominent place, in comparison with other nativity scenes, which are dominated by men.

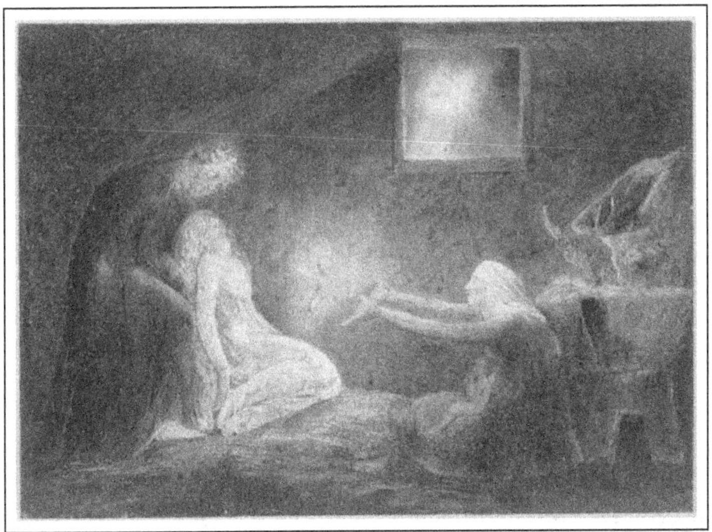

Figure 1. William Blake, *The Nativity*

Alternatively, one might see this as a merging of two biblical scenes, the Nativity (Lk. 2.6-7) and the Presentation of Christ in the Temple (Lk. 2.25-38, the Lucan version of the Epiphany to the gentiles, 2.32). So, the woman with the child on the right is the prophet Anna, who along with Simeon hails the infant Christ (now a little bigger than the celestial child and more 'flesh and blood'). This is the child who would be a light to lighten the Gentiles, about whom Anna began to speak to all who were looking for the redemption of Jerusalem (Lk. 2.35-36).

The complexity of the picture may indeed be even greater. Mary swooning may not be so much at the birth but at the moment of the

29. David Bindman, 'Blake as Painter', in *The Cambridge Companion to William Blake* (ed. Morris Eaves; Cambridge: Cambridge University Press, 2003), p. 97.

Annunciation. After all, the moment of conception is sometimes depicted in the form of this 'laser beam' moment, and it may be this to which Mary reacts. If so, that would mean that the scene could be a complex overlapping depiction of Nativity, Annunciation, Visitation, and Presentation.

Is the light coming through the window a star or a cross? Or is there a figure, or even a face with eyes? Even a close examination of the original in Philadelphia still makes it difficult to decide. Whichever it may be, it suggests the Eternal Word is linked here with what Blake terms the 'minute particular' of the Word become flesh in Jesus of Nazareth. There is a direct line between that heavenly light and the babe, suggesting that the babe comes, as it were, direct from heaven. That being said, the main scene has its own source of light, and is not dependent on that coming through the window/picture. Nevertheless the direct beam, laser-like, parallel to earlier depictions of the Annunciation rather than the Nativity, suggests a close link between the heavenly, outside the confines of the stable, and the celestial child within.

Whatever the identity of the second child, its ruddy features are in stark contrast with the rather ethereal air-borne child between the two women. If it is John the Baptist, a text like Lk. 7.28 may indicate that this one, so clearly 'born of women', contrasts with the Son of God descending from the world above.

The extraordinary air-borne position of the celestial child reminds one of some lines from Blake's earlier poem, 'Infant Sorrow', from *Songs of Experience*: 'My mother groan'd! My father wept, Into the dangerous world I leapt; Helpless, naked, piping loud, Like a fiend hid in a cloud.' Those last words coincide with my view that this looks like a celestial, rather than mundane, birth. There is a passage in the early Christian apocalypse, *The Ascension of Isaiah*, where the 'unnatural' character of Christ's birth is stressed, and the true celestial nature of the Saviour hidden from the eyes of those who saw it. In *The Ascension of Isaiah* 11.7-14, we read that, after a short pregnancy, Mary suddenly looks in astonishment and sees a small baby before her. A voice comes to Mary and Joseph telling them to share this vision with no one else. In keeping with the theme of the hiddenness of the glory of the celestial Christ evident in the rest of the work, no one is able to understand whence he had come.

> And after two months while Joseph was in his house, and Mary his wife, but both alone, it came to pass that when they were alone that Mary straightway looked with her eyes and saw a small babe, and she was astonished. And after she had been astonished, her womb was found as formerly before she had conceived. And when her husband Joseph said unto her: 'What has astonished thee?' his eyes were opened and he saw the infant and praised God, because into his portion God had come. And a voice came to them: 'Tell this vision to no one'. And the story regarding the infant was noised broad in Bethlehem. Some said: 'The Virgin Mary hath borne a child, before

> she was married two months'. And many said: 'She has not borne a child, nor has a midwife gone up (to her), nor have we heard the cries of (labour) pains'. And they were all blinded respecting Him and they all knew regarding Him, though they knew not whence He was.

The focus of attention on the celestial Christ makes one wonder whether Blake's Christology reflects one of the features of earlier radical Christology, the celestial flesh of Jesus. Influential among early Anabaptist groups in the sixteenth century, Melchior Hoffman viewed Christ as the possessor of celestial flesh (a view, incidentally, which was inherited by Menno Simons and early Mennonites). This affected some Baptist circles in the late seventeenth century in England.[30] There is some suggestion that Moravian Christology may have leaned towards the docetic also.

What we may have here is an emanation from Mary of the indwelling Christ who exists in every person. Mary gives birth to the cosmic Christ, indwelling her as he does every person. That Christ becomes a mediator between Mary and (presumably) the aged Elizabeth with John the Baptist on her knee. Christ then is the means of linking people, for he embodies the fibres of love which bind the two women. In *Jerusalem* 4.7-8, the fibres of love are identical with Christ. Indeed, at the start of *Jerusalem*, Christ addresses the poet in words which conflate Eph. 5.14 and Jn 14.10, the last of which pervades the *Job* theophany engraving: 'Awake! Awake O sleeper of the land of shadows, wake! Expand! I am in you and you in me, mutual in love divine, Fibres of love from man to man thro' Albion's pleasant land'.

Blake's Christology is complex. He can be found making surprisingly radical statements about the Jesus of history and the miraculous: 'Christ died as an Unbeliever'.[31] Also, in the early *Marriage of Heaven and Hell*, Jesus is viewed as the supreme antinomian who 'was all virtue, and acted from impulse, not from rules'.[32] In *The Everlasting Gospel*, Blake could read the Gospel narratives like his contemporary Reimarus, and regard Jesus as

30. Professor John Briggs of Regent's Park College, Oxford, in private correspondence writes: 'The principal advocate of the Melchiorite position had been Matthew Caffyn, a leader of the Kent and Sussex General Baptists (1628–1715). Ernest Payne suggests Blake's father was a dissenting minister, possibly Baptist, but advances no evidence'. It is worth noting that the spiritual birth of the messiah was a feature of beliefs of the followers of Joanna Southcott, who explained her pregnancy as the giving birth to the messiah who was then snatched up to heaven after a spiritual birth (Rev. 12.5). See John F.C. Harrison, *The Second Coming: Popular Millenarianism 1780–1850* (London: Routledge & Kegan Paul, 1979). The link between millenarianism and docetism in Christian theology is a subject requiring further examination.

31. Blake, 'Marginal Notes on Watson's Apology', in *Blake: Complete Writings*, p. 387.

32. Blake, *The Marriage of Heaven and Hell*, in *Blake: Complete Writings*, p. 24.

the leader of a revolution that seemed to fail. But it seems to me that such a view does not do justice to the totality, and even heterodoxy, of Blake's later christological concerns, which are better characterized as Pauline, particularly in the vein of Ephesians and Colossians. This is unsurprising since the Bible is not a mere history book, for 'the Hebrew Bible and the Gospel of Jesus are… Eternal Vision or Imagination of all that exists' (*A Vision of the Last Judgment*). In later works like *Jerusalem*, as well as being the Word made flesh, Christ becomes a kind of space wherein one discovers the way of redemption. In particular, mutual forgiveness and the forsaking of what Blake describes as 'religion hid in war' are the keys to true existence. Thus, Blake's understanding of a supra-individual Christ resembles some interpretations of the Pauline *en Christo*, in which humans inhabit a Christ-informed, salvific, space characterised by mutual forgiveness. In this vision of the cosmic Christ, the historical specificity of the life of the historical Jesus is left behind.

The Depiction of Biblical Visionary Accounts

Annunciation to the Shepherds[33]

In this image, the angels have the circular motion of the angelic host praising God. The wheel shape evokes Ezekiel's wheels. The circular movement of the angels is a depiction of angels which Blake uses elsewhere, for example, in 'God on the Seventh Day'. The divine presence in the incarnate Christ is recognised by the tabernacle or church-like quality of the shelter given to the infant Jesus. In keeping with Blake's non-conformity, the divine presence is not to be found especially in buildings but wherever the divine image is to be found, whether in Christ or in humans who reflect the divine image, though it would seem that in *Jerusalem* the stones and the appurtenances shine with the glory of the divine vision (plates 12 and 79). The birth of Jesus in this church-like shelter is one of several similar scenes. One of the most distinctive, however, is the way in which the birth is juxtaposed with the image of the beast from the sea (and is that the harlot on the left of the seven-headed beast?). This illustrates a theme of Milton's 'Ode on the Morning of Christ's Nativity'.[34] This depiction not only resembles other depictions of the beast of Revelation 17 but also echoes Revelation 12 and the birth of the messiah to the woman, who is being pursued by the dragon. This is most clearly seen in the tail of the dragon, which drags down the stars from heaven

33. Annunciation to the Shepherds: http://www.biblical-art.com/B%5Cblake%5Cblake0261.jpg.

34. Milton's 'Ode on the Morning of Christ's Nativity': http://photos1.blogger.com/img/149/1934/1024/Blake_%20Milton_On%20the%20Morning%20of_fmlac10549_26a.jpg

(Rev. 12.4). In this picture, however, the beast is on his way to the abyss (cf. Rev. 11.7; cf 13.1). So, Rev. 19.20 appears to be taking place at the moment of Jesus' birth, as is suggested by Milton's poem (xviii: 'The Old Dragon under ground, in straiter limits bound').

The Baptism[35]

This is a commentary on the opening of *Paradise Regained*, when the Spirit descends as a dove on Jesus. It puts together several themes in the opening fifty lines, reflecting the description of the event as a very public one ('to his great baptism flocked With awe the regions round'). Blake makes the celestial conversation that Milton describes there into a more public scene. Blake captures the moment when, at the baptism, Satan flees from the scene:

> ...in likeness of a Dove The Spirit descended, while the Father's voice From Heaven pronounced him his beloved Son. That heard the Adversary, who, roving still About the world, at that assembly fame Would not be last, and, with the voice divine Nigh thunder-struck, the exalted man to whom Such high attest was given a while surveyed With wonder; then, with envy fraught and rage, Flies to his place, nor rests, but in mid air To council summons all his mighty Peers, Within thick clouds and dark tenfold involved, A gloomy consistory.

The theology is similar to that found in the image discussed below where the defeat of Satan and his hosts is linked with aspects of the incarnate life of Christ.

Transfiguration[36]

Here, there is a sharing of the divine glory, as the disciples are wrapped around with the hem of Jesus' garment. Behind are the patriarchs/heavenly host. Are the figures the heavenly alter egos of Moses and Elijah?[37]

Conversion of Saul[38]

Blake informs us that this image is a commentary on Acts 9.6: 'Rise and enter the city and you will be told what you are to do'. It is similar to 'Transfiguration' in that Saul is wrapped up in the glory of the visionary person he sees. Christ is surrounded in a whirl of light by other figures: are

35. Baptism: http://www.biblical-art.com/B%5Cblake%5Cblake0263.jpg.

36. Transfiguration: http://www.biblical-art.com/B%5Cblake%5Cblake0189.jpg.

37. Cf. Blake's 'Epitome of James Harvey's Meditations' where the transfiguration replaces the cross, and scenes of forgiveness are featured instead of the divine fury. See M. Butlin, *Paintings and Drawings of William Blake* (New Haven: Yale University Press, 1981), p. 967.

38. Conversion of Saul: http://www.biblical-art.com/B%5Cblake%5Cblake0216.jpg.

they the heavenly host like Isaiah 6 and Revelation 4–5 or the Christians with whom Christ is linked, whom Saul is persecuting? Perhaps the former.

The Agony in the Garden[39]
In this depiction of Lk. 22.43, Blake makes the event less a strengthening of Jesus in the light of the torment which is about to come as, seemingly, a moment of rescue. The disciples are mingled with their shady environment (clearly so despite the deterioration in the quality of the picture because of the media used). The angel appears to be rescuing Jesus, as it were, from a sea or morass, removing him from suffering rather than strengthening him for it (it is very similar to Blake's 'The Reunion of Soul and Body', from his illustrations to Blair's 'The Grave'). This is almost literally a moment of rapture (though it does need to be set alongside the following picture which does not suggest an escape from suffering). One might almost want to assert that it resembles a Cerinthian Christology (Irenaeus, *Adv. Haer.* I.26.1; cf. III.3.4) and may parallel the kind of docetism we see in 'The Nativity'.

Albion Meets the Crucified Jesus[40]
The grasp that Blake had of Johannine theology is nowhere better seen than in plate 76 of his last (and longest) illuminated book, *Jerusalem*. Here Albion (Britain) and Jesus are brought face to face. The links between them are indicated by the similarity of colour. Here Albion imitates the crucified Jesus. Christ, in being crucified on a tree, suggests the human Christ linked with the 'vegative state' which he would put off, in a manner akin to that described in Colossians, where Christ on the cross puts off the body of flesh (Col. 2.14-15). But the radiance proceeding from the crucified one depicts the glory which is linked with being lifted up on the cross in the Gospel of John (especially 3.14 and 12.32).

Blake as an Interpreter of the Detail of Scripture: Capturing Particular Moments in the Bible

The Woman taken in Adultery[41]
Here, Blake captures the moment in Jn 8.10 between Jesus stooping to the ground and writing in the dust and his words to the woman, when he

39. Angel strengthens Jesus: http://www.tate.org.uk/collection/N/N05/N05894_8.jpg.

40. Glory of crucified Jesus: http://membres.lycos.fr/gabriellesegui/hpbimg/blake-Jerusalem%20.jpeg.

41. Woman taken in adultery: http://38.114.160.229/fif=fpx/sc6/SC687.fpx&obj=iip,1.0&wid=120&cvt=jpeg.

is left alone with the woman as the accusers flee. My guess is that Blake would have wanted to capture this moment before the final words of Jesus, 'Sin no more'. This would parallel what he does in the *Job* depiction when he has Job's words, 'Now my eye hath seen thee', without 'therefore I repent in dust and ashes'. Blake would not have wanted to subscribe to traditional morality, and this avoidance is captured in this painting. Jesus is not given the last word, therefore. His fingers point to nothing at all on the earth. There is, therefore, no condemnation, not even a final admonitory 'you must do better next time'.[42]

The Triumphal Entry[43]

What is depicted is Matthew's version of the event. This can be seen by the prominent place given in the picture to children (Mt. 21.15). As we know, in Matthew's version it is the children, along with the impaired, who greet Christ in the Temple. Here Blake has this event taking place on the entry into Jerusalem, seen in the far distance. The preference for Matthew's version coincides with Blake's conviction that knowledge and insight are something innate and not learned. This picks up an important contrast which Blake makes frequently between 'memory' and 'inspiration', for example, in the famous prelude to *Milton* (quoted at the beginning of this article).

Elsewhere, in response to the learned enquirer mentioned earlier, who wanted Blake to explain his pictures, Blake saw children as possessing particular insight:

> But I am happy to find a Great Majority of Fellow Mortals who can Elucidate My Visions, & Particularly they have been Elucidated by Children, who have taken a greater delight in contemplating my Pictures than I even hoped. Neither Youth nor Childhood is Folly or Incapacity. Some Children are Fools & so are some Old Men. But There is a vast Majority on the side of Imagination or Spiritual Sensation.[44]

In this he echoes their importance in the Synoptic Gospels, especially, of course, the Gospel of Matthew (11.25; 18.2-3, 10; 19.13-15).

The Wise and Foolish Virgins[45]

In this image, Blake links Mt. 25.1-13 with the distinctive Matthean eschatological symbol of the angelic trumpet in Mt. 24.31.

42. See further, J. Moskal, *Blake, Ethics, and Forgiveness* (Tuscaloosa: University of Alabama Press, 1994), pp. 32-35.

43. Triumphal entry into Jerusalem: http://images.scran.ac.uk/RB/images/thumb/0155/01550345.jpg.

44. 'Letter to Trusler' in Blake, *Blake: Complete Writings*, pp. 793-94.

45. Wise and Foolish Virgins: http://www.metmuseum.org/special/William_ Blake/images/17.R.jpg.

The Interpretation of the Apocalypse

Four and Twenty Elders[46]
This picture combines Revelation 4 and 5, with the rainbow, eyes and the sealed scroll. The lamb in this picture is curiously passive and anonymous. Ezekiel 1 lies at the base of Blake's depiction of John's vision in these chapters.[47]

Ezekiel's Wheels[48]
What is striking about this picture is the prominence of the human figure among the four creatures (man, lion, ox and eagle) which surround the divine throne/chariot. In Jewish interpretations (*Ber. R.* 47.6; 69.3; 82.6; Targumim on Gen. 28.12; *The Prayer of Joseph*), the figure of a man was linked with ancestors like Jacob or Abraham, and in early Christian use of this passage the human figure was linked with Christ (Jn 12.41; Justin, *Dial.* 126). The link between humanity and divinity is hinted at in the painting. Blake evokes the amber (the *hashmal*) and blue of Ezekiel 1, which are part of the reception history of this important chapter.[49]

The Unfinished Sketches of 1 Enoch[50]
At the end of his life Blake was engaged in illustrations of the book of Genesis, with which the opening chapters of the *Apocalypse of Enoch* (also known as *1 Enoch*) have a close relationship. *1 Enoch* offers a very different understanding of the origin of evil in the world (cf. Gen. 6.4): evil comes into the world as the result of the acts of the fallen angels and their seduction of women on earth. Laurence's English translation of *1 Enoch* was published in 1822, five years before Blake's death. Nevertheless Blake may have known about *Enoch* before 1822. As early as 1773, the book of Enoch was discussed at the Society of Antiquaries, and an excerpt was published in *The Monthly Magazine* in 1801.[51] In one of the sketches we

46. 24 elders http://www.tate.org.uk/collection/N/N05/N05897_8.jpg.

47. On Blake and Ezekiel's *merkabah*, see Harold Bloom, *Ringers in the Tower: Studies in Romantic Tradition* (Chicago and London: University of Chicago Press, 1971), pp. 65-80.

48. Ezekiel's wheels http://www.biblical-art.com/B%5Cblake%5Cblake0186.jpg.

49. Bloom, *Ringers in the Tower*, pp. 65-80; Christopher Rowland 'Ezekiel's Merkavah in the Work of William Blake and Christian Art', in *The Reception History of Ezekiel* (ed. H. de Jonge; London: Ashgate, 2007), pp. 182-97.

50. J. Beer, 'Blake's Changing View of History: The Impact of the Book of Enoch', in *Historicizing Blake* (ed. S. Clark and D. Worrall; Basingstoke: Macmillan, 1994), pp. 159-78.

51. Beer, 'Blake's Changing View of History'; G.E. Bentley, 'A Jewel in an Ethiop's Ear', in *Blake in His Time* (ed. R. Essick and D. Pearce; Bloomington: University of Indiana Press, 1978), pp. 213-40.

have the vision of the Great Glory (*1 En.* 14.8-24) with a canopy similar to what we find not only in 'The Twenty Four Elders' but also in the opening *Job* engraving. There are also hints of the rivers of fire.

The Whore of Babylon[52]

Here, Babylon points with her finger to the stream pouring forth from the cup in her right hand, which turns out to be full of violence and beings with bowls and trumpets.[53] The angels hold both bowls *and trumpets*. Thus, the pouring and the trumpet blasts take place simultaneously as war rages. There are close links between the iniquity of Babylon and the death and destruction described in the previous chapters of Revelation, especially the trumpet (chs. 8–11) and bowl (ch. 16) sequences. Thus, the sequence of disasters which have been described by John earlier in the vision is linked with the political violence caused by the culture of Babylon and outlined in chs. 17–19.[54]

Edward Young's Night Thoughts[55]

This picture of Babylon glosses 'Virtue's Apology, or, the Man of the World Answer'd, in which are considered, the Love of this Life, the ambition and Pleasure, with the wit and Wisdom of the World'. These words prompt Blake to understand this socially and politically, and not just in terms of personal morals. At the time he painted this picture, Blake was acutely aware of the culture of repression in war-torn England. It was a situation in which, to quote his own words written at the time, 'The Beast and the Whore rule without control' ('Annotations to Watson's Apology'). As in Revelation 13, the vision is interpreted synchronically rather than diachronically. It is not a succession of empires, therefore, but a sevenfold, contemporary, imperial and cultural oppression. Blake very pointedly depicts the heads of the beast as contemporary military, royal, legal and ecclesiastical powers. He took the opportunity of

52. The Whore of Babylon 2: http://www.apocalyptic-teories.com/gallery/whoreofbabylon/blakewhorebg.jpg.

53. Cf. G.E. Bentley, *The Stranger from Paradise: A Biography of William Blake* (New Haven: Yale University Press, 2001), plate 75: 'The Whore is directing wine-bearing and trumpeting spirits from her Cup of Abominations to incite the iron-clad warriors who are being devoured by the Beast'.

54. Bentley, *Stranger from Paradise*, plates 74a and 75, notes that there is 'a disconcerting but slight and probably coincidental similarity between the portrait of Betsy Butts and the Whore of Babylon painted for Thomas Butts in the same year' [1809].

55. The Whore of Babylon 1: http://library.uncg.edu/depts/speccoll/exhibits/Blake/Nighttp.jpg.

this commission to insert his protest against the political repression in the England of the 1790s. There is a long tradition of political interpretation of apocalyptic images, rooted in Daniel and the Apocalypse, going back to the radicalism of mid-seventeenth-century England. In it, the heads of the beasts function as a way of understanding political oppression, and do not refer just to eschatological prediction. The following quotation, from a seventeenth-century political activist whose self-understanding was infused with images from the Apocalypse, interprets the beasts of Daniel in a way similar to the way in which the heads of the beast are interpreted by Blake in the *Night Thoughts* illustration:

> These four powers are the four beasts, which Daniel saw rise up out of the sea... And this Sea is the bulk and body of mankind...for out of Mankind arises all that darkness and tyranny that oppresses itself... The first Beast which Daniel saw rise up out of the deceived heart of mankind, was like a lion; and had eagles' wings: And this is kingly power, which takes the sword, and makes way to rule over others thereby, dividing the creation, one part from another; setting up the conqueror to rule, making the conquered a slave; giving the earth to some, denying the earth to others...The second Beast was like a bear; And this is the power of the selfish laws, which is full of covetousness...the power of prisons...the power of whipping, banishment, and confiscation of goods...the power of hanging, pressing, burning, martyring...take these three ribs out of the mouth of the law, or Inns of Court trade, and that beast hath no power but dies... The third Beast was like a leopard...this is the thieving art of buying and selling the earth with her fruits one to another...this beast had four wings: policy; hypocrisy; self-love and hardness of heart; for this beast is a true self-lover, to get the earth to himself, to lock it up in chests and barns, though others starve for want... The fourth Beast is the imaginary clergy-power, which indeed is Judas; and this more terrible and dreadful than the rest... When Christ the Anointing spirit rises up, and enlightens mankind, then in his light, they shall see the deceit and falsehood of this beast, that hath deceived all the world; and shall fall off from him, and leave him naked and bare; and if he will teach and rule, let him shew his power over the beasts; for the people will all look up to God, to be taught and governed by him.[56]

The representation of Babylon is, for Blake, curiously literal for one who was suspicious of literal interpretations of Scripture. Blake was usually extraordinarily sensitive to issues of economic oppression and race, but less often to issues of gender. Perhaps in the context of illustrating another's book he dared not risk too much of a departure from the Bible.

56. Gerrard Winstanley, 'The Fire in the Bush', in *Radical Christian Writings: A Reader* (ed. A. Bradstock and C. Rowland; Oxford: Blackwell, 2002), pp. 120-37 (132-34).

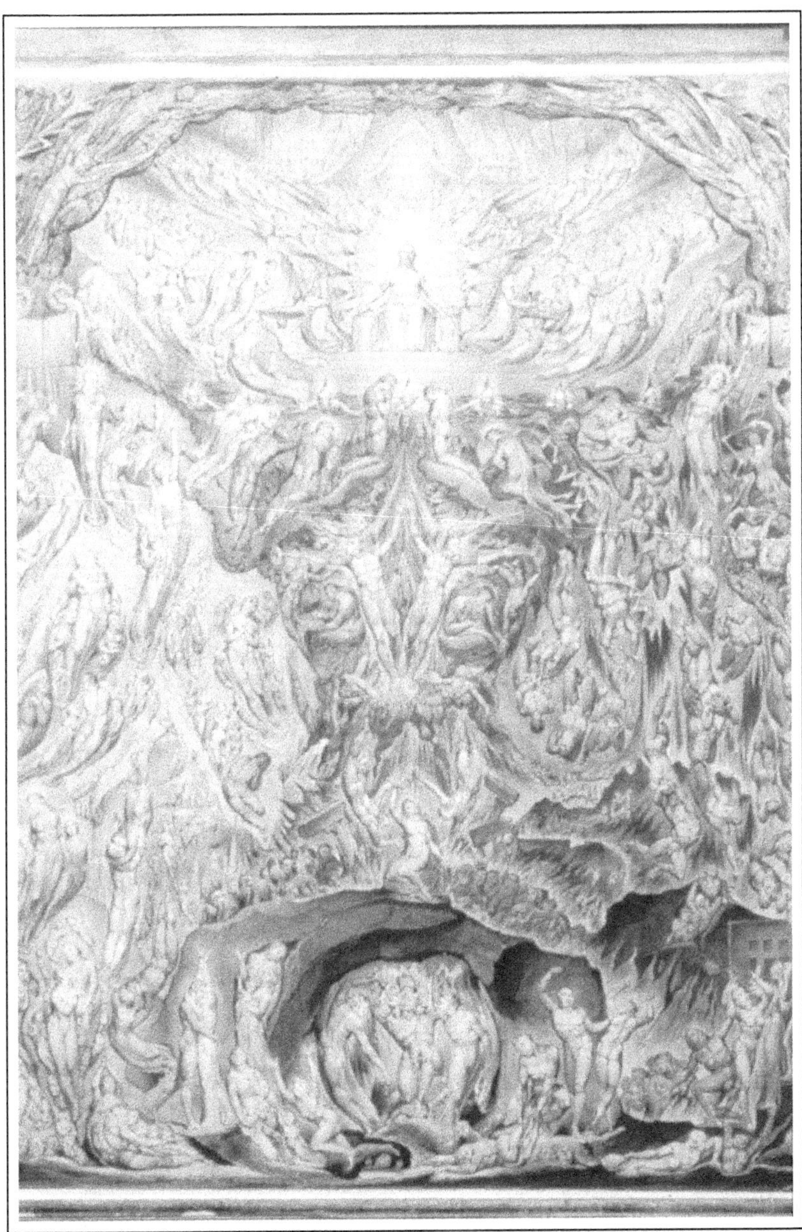

Figure 2. William Blake, *The Last Judgement*

The Last Judgement *as a Guide to Blake's Soteriology*[57]

Unusually, Blake wrote at length about *The Last Judgement* and a commentary is extant on this picture.[58] In the picture, there is movement

57. Last Judgement: http://biblia.com/images/judgement-blake2c.jpg.

58. The Design of The Last Judgment which I have completed by your recommendation [under a fortunate star] for the Countess of Egremont [by a happy accident] it is necessary to give some account of: & its various parts ought to be described, for the accomodation [*sic*] of those who give it the honour of attention.

Christ seated on the Throne of judgment: [The Heavens in Clouds rolling before him & around him] before his feet & around him the heavens in clouds are rolling like a scroll ready to be consumed in the fires of the Angels; who descend [before his feet] with the[ir] Four Trumpets sounding to the four Winds

Beneath; [the] Earth is convulsed with the labours of the Resurrection--in the Caverns of the Earth is the Dragon with Seven heads & ten Horns, Chained by two Angels & above his Cavern[s] on the Earth's Surface is the Harlot also siezed & bound by two Angels with chains while her Palaces are falling [in] into ruins & her Councellors [*sic*] & Warriors are descending into the Abyss in wailing & despair.

Hell opens beneath the Harlots seat on the left hand into which the Wicked are descending [while others rise from their Graves on the brink of the Pit].

The right hand of the Design is appropriated to the Resurrection of The Just; the left hand of the Design is appropriated to the Resurrection & Fall of the Wicked.

Immediately before the Throne of Christ is Adam & Eve, kneeling in humiliation, as representatives of the whole Human Race; Abraham & Moses kneel on each side beneath them; from the cloud on which Eve kneels [& beneath Moses & from the Tables of Stone which utter lightnings] is seen Satan wound round by the Serpent & falling headlong; the Pharisees appear on the left hand pleading their own righteousness before the Throne of Christ; & before the Book of Death which is opend on clouds by two Angels & many groupes of Figures are falling from before the Throne & from before the Sea of Fire which flows before the steps of the Throne on which [are] is seen the seven Lamps of the Almighty burning before the Throne: many Figures chained & bound together in various attitudes of Despair & Horror fall thro the air & some are scourged by Spirits with flames of fire into the Abyss of Hell which opens [to recieve (*sic*) them] beneath on the left hand of the Harlots Seat, where others are howling & [descending into the flames & in the act of] dragging each other into Hell & [of] contending in fighting with each other on the [very] brink of Perdition.

Before the Throne of Christ on the Right hand the Just in humiliation & in exultation rise thro the Air with their Children & Families: some of whom are bowing before the Book of Life which is opend on clouds by two Angels; many groupes arise [with] Exultation [in Joy]; among them is a Figure crownd with Stars & the Moon beneath her feet with six infants around her. She represents the Christian Church. [The] Green hills appear beneath: with the Graves of the Blessed which are seen bursting with their births of immortality; Parents & Children Wives & Husbands embrace & arise together & in exulting attitudes of great joy tell each other that The New Jerusalem is ready to descend upon Earth; they arise upon the air rejoicing: others newly awakend from the Grave stand upon the Earth embracing & shouting to the Lamb who cometh in the Clouds in Power & great Glory

clockwise indicated by the direction of the bodies and the change in the colours from dark to light. Christ is the point around which the whole picture moves. He sits impassively, in contrast with the more active (and threatening) Christ in judgment of Michelangelo's Sistine Chapel depiction, which may indeed have been an inspiration for Blake's own work. It is commonplace in Blake's work for the fire of judgment to be purgative, for example, *Jerusalem* 96:35, where the lake of fire becomes the living waters. At the end of 'Ninth Night' of *Four Zoas* there is talk about passing through fire and not being consumed (9:844).

Elsewhere, Blake hopes viewers of the picture will identify with its details, thus in writing about *The Last Judgement*:

> If the Spectator could enter into these Images in his Imagination, approaching them on the Fiery Chariot of his Contemplative Thought, if he could enter into Noah's Rainbow or into his Bosom, or could make a Friend & Companion of one of these images of wonder, which always intreats him to leave mortal things (as he must know), then would he arise from his Grave, then would he meet the Lord in the Air & then he would be happy.[59]

It is this process which is depicted in this picture. Judgment is always happening with eternity always ready and available. This is in line with Johannine eschatology: 'He that heareth my word and believeth in him that sent me hath everlasting life and shall not come into condemnation but passeth from death to life' (Jn 5.24).

The Whole upper part of the Design is a View of Heaven opened: around the Throne of Christ in the Cloud which rolls away are the Four Living Creatures filled with Eyes, attended by Seven Angels with the Seven Vials of the Wrath of God & above these [there are] Seven Angels with the Seven Trumpets compose [composing] the Cloud, which by its rolling away displays the opening Seats of the Blessed, on the right & left of which are seen the Four & Twenty Elders seated on Thrones to Judge the Dead. Behind the Seat & Throne of Christ [appears] appear the Tabernacle with its Veil opened: [&] the Candlestick on the right: the Table with Shew bread on the left, [&] in [the] midst, the Cross in place of the Ark [with the two] Cherubim bowing over it.

On the Right hand of the Throne of Christ is Baptism. On [his] the left is the Lords Supper: the two introducers into Eternal Life. Women with Infants approach the Figure of an aged Apostle which represents Baptism; & on the left hand the Lords Supper is administerd by Angels, from the hands of another [aged] Apostle; these Kneel on each side of the Throne which is surrounded by a glory, [in the glory] many Infants appear in the Glory representing [the] Eternal Creation flowing from the Divine Humanity in Jesus: who opens the Scroll of Judgment upon his knees before the Living & the Dead

Such is the Design which you, my Dear Sir, have been the cause of my producing & which but for you might have slept till the Last Judgment.

WILLIAM BLAKE [18 January 1808] Feby 1808.

59. Blake, *Blake: Complete Writings*, p. 611.

One of the interesting things about Blake's detailed textual commentary on the picture is that it is at odds with what we found expressed earlier by Blake with regard to his hermeneutical method: 'The wisest of the ancients consider'd what is not too explicit as the fittest for instruction, because it rouzes the faculties to act'. Blake seems not to be allowing the faculties to act here, except in a very passive way. One can only assume that this represents the kind of compromise he felt he had to make in order to accommodate his patron, though the existence of another lengthy written commentary on *The Last Judgement* suggests that he was prepared to adopt a more explicitly didactic mode later in his life than seems to be the case in the pre-1800 illuminated books.

Elsewhere in his commentary on the picture, Blake writes of the tabernacle above the enthroned Christ. That is open and empty. There is no access to God, therefore, except through the enthroned Christ. Blake's emphasis on Jn 1.18 and Col. 1.15 as the key to theological understanding is a prominent feature of his theology, especially in the last years of his life. As we have seen, in the *Job* sequence, Christ is the one who makes the Father known. In his version of the Lord's Prayer, Father and Son are equated ('Jesus, our Father, who art in thy heaven call'd by thy Name the Holy Ghost'), and Blake comes very close to a form of modalism in his trinitarianism. This may be a relic of his Swedenborgianism, for Swedenborg identified Christ with the Old Testament God.

Steve Goldsmith writes perceptively of this drawing:

> The Last Judgement picture suggests not asceticism but freedom from sexual restraint. The fiery gulph that defines the primary axis in the Last Judgement series is distinctly vaginal...most clearly pronounced in the Petworth figure, the arrangement of trumpeting angels suggests the labia. The Logos and Babylon are positioned at two ends of the vulva.[60]

There is a similarity to the fiery ball in which Satan descends in the *Job* engravings (plate 16). There it would appear to be a one-off event (cf. Lk. 10.18; Jn 12.31; Rev. 12.8: Isa. 14.12). More likely, however, the conversion of Job and the fall of Satan are a repeated experience in life, when the descent into the abyss is a prelude to catharsis and the rising up to glory to be with Christ symbolizes the reordering of theological and ethical priorities.

Lest we think that such an interpretation is merely the product of a post-Freudian age, a copy of a medieval woodcut, which served to offer a series of mnemonics about the interpretation of the Gospel of John (symbolised by the eagle), indicates that others made this kind of connection. Mary Carruthers has pointed out how in a medieval block book known as

60. S. Goldsmith, *Unbuilding Jerusalem: Apocalypse and Romantic Representation* (Ithaca, NY: Cornell University Press, 1993), pp. 147-48.

the *Ars memorandi*, which may have been intended to help the cleric, or interested layperson, remember in order the contents of each chapter in the four Gospels, the prompt for John 3 shows a vulva cut into the body of the Johannine eagle to recall the words Jesus addresses to Nicodemus, 'unless a person be born again'.[61] So, when an individual embraces truth, the last judgment happens and a new birth takes place. That is the way into the kingdom of God. That link of new birth and eschatology is there in Mt. 19.28 as well as Jn 3.5. Of course, John 3 has Nicodemus misunderstanding Jesus' words about rebirth when he responds, 'How can anyone be born after having grown old? Can one enter a second time into the mother's womb and be born?' The medieval woodcut is based on Nicodemus's misunderstanding, which talks of the impossibility of entering into one's mother's womb. But the rebirth is not literal but spiritual. It is that rebirth which Blake seeks to portray in his *Last Judgement* picture.

Possible links between Blake and the Moravians via his mother, Catherine, may explain the connection to the German medieval text. This may offer a plausible contact between Blake and the religious symbolism linked with the vulva and so explain the image at the centre of *The Last Judgement*.[62] In Moravian piety both the circumcision and the final wound, in which the lance pierces Jesus' side (Jn 19.34) are given a sexual/theological explanation. The Moravian leader, Nicolaus Ludwig von Zinzendorf (1700–1760), exhorted his followers to become like children and imagine 'the hole' in the side of Jesus as a place into which they might feel drawn, where they might bathe in the blood and the womb-like warmth. An examples of a Moravian hymn illustrates this:

> What Pleasure doth a heart perceive, that rests in the precious Hole, lives there, loves and sports, works and praises the little Lamb, and tho' it storms and blusters without, feels nothing of it within his dwelling… My heart dwells in Jesus' side… I lay myself in the Hole made by the Spear… I have licked all over that Rock Salt! O how well did it taste, on that moment my little Soul is transported into the little Side-Hole.[63]

The womb into which one entered was seen as 'a little model chapel of God', a notion that appears to be reflected in one of the drawings which accompany Blake's *The Four Zoas*. Here Blake sketched a naked woman whose womb has been changed into a shrine with, penis-like, a statue at its centre. So, the vaginal symbolism of the hole in Jesus' side in

61. I am grateful to Mary Carruthers of New York University, who drew this to my attention and from whose book, *The Medieval Craft of Memory* (Philadelphia: University of Pennsylvania Press, 2002), p. 259, this image comes.

62. Marsha Keith Suchard, *Why Mrs Blake Cried: William Blake and the Sexual Basis of Spiritual Vision* (London: Century, 2006), pp. 36-42.

63. Quoted in Keith Suchard, *Why Mrs Blake Cried*, p. 39.

Moravian piety may well be the mediating link with the use of the image of the vulva in the medieval material. Of course, the way in which Blake uses the imagery is not explicitly linked with John 19. Nevertheless what is of importance here is the similar hermeneutical model, which is common to both Moravian piety and Blake's imagery in the *Last Judgement*, in which entry through the vagina into the womb is used as an imaginative means of understanding the saving process.[64] The entry of the 'Spectator...into these Images in his Imagination' is exactly what we find Zinzendorf commending to his followers.

Concluding Comments

What has been offered here is a survey of aspects of Blake's biblical hermeneutic in his pictures and engravings. They offer some examples of the extraordinary creativity that is evident in his depiction of biblical images. We can see how throughout his life Blake was wrestling with the interpretation of the Bible and expressing his deep sense of prophetic vocation. Blake seems something of a religious and artistic 'maverick', but recent study has suggested that this is not the case. His life coincides with an extraordinary outburst of prophetic activity in late eighteenth-century and early nineteenth-century England. Blake is part of a rich prophetic environment and offers a unique way into the prophetic imagination, difficult as it is sometimes for the normal canons of rationality to comprehend. His understanding of prophecy is not as transparent as that of some of his contemporaries. It is more obscure and, in some sense, self-aware in its complexity. Indeed, in Blake's work there is a grasp of human psychology, which complexifies the steps which are needed to achieve redemption. Throughout his artistic career, Blake problematized the reading of texts and the authority given to sacred Scripture as representing the unambiguous directive of Almighty God by the juxtaposition of text and image. It is less stark in the later work, but still very much present, as the *Job* sequence indicates. The material surveyed in this article reminds us why Blake is a subject worthy of study in theology and biblical studies.

BIBLIOGRAPHY

Abrams, M.H., *Natural Supernaturalism: Tradition and Revolution in Romantic Literature* (New York: W.W. Norton, 1973).

Beer, J., 'Blake's Changing View of History: The Impact of the Book of Enoch', in *Historicizing Blake* (ed. S. Clark and D. Worrall; Basingstoke: Macmillan, 1994), pp. 159-78.

64. I am grateful to Dr Lutz Doering of King's College, London, for the initial suggestion about a Moravian background for this imagery.

Bentley, G.E., 'A Jewel in an Ethiop's Ear', in *Blake in His Time* (ed. R. Essick and D. Pearce; Bloomington: University of Indiana, 1978), pp. 213-40.

—*The Stranger from Paradise: A Biography of William Blake* (New Haven: Yale University Press, 2001).

Blake, W., *Blake: Complete Writings* (ed. G. Keynes; Oxford: Clarendon Press, 1966).

—*William Blake's Illuminated Books* (ed. D. Bindman; 6 vols.; London: Tate Gallery Publications/William Blake Trust, 1991–95).

—*William Blake's Illustrations for the Book of Job* (New York: Dover, 1995).

—*William Blake: The Complete Illuminated Books* (ed. D. Bindman; London: Thames & Hudson, 2000).

Bloom, H., *Blake's Apocalypse: A Study in Poetic Argument* (Ithaca, NY: Cornell University Press, 1970).

—*Ringers in the Tower: Studies in Romantic Tradition* (Chicago: University of Chicago Press, 1971).

Bradstock A., and C. Rowland, *Radical Christian Writings: A Reader* (Oxford: Blackwell, 2002).

Brown, D., *Discipleship and Imagination: Christian Tradition and Truth* (Oxford: Oxford University Press, 2000).

Burdon, C., *The Apocalypse in England: Revelation Unravelling, 1700–1834* (London: Macmillan, 1997).

Butler, M., *Romantics, Rebels and Reactionaries* (Oxford: Clarendon Press, 1981).

Butlin, M., *The Paintings and Drawings of William Blake* (New Haven: Yale University Press, 1981).

Carruthers, M., *The Medieval Craft of Memory* (Philadelphia: University of Pennsylvania Press, 2002).

Davies, J.G., *The Theology of William Blake* (Oxford: Clarendon Press, 1948).

Eaves, M., *The Cambridge Companion to William Blake* (Cambridge: Cambridge University Press, 2003).

Erdman, D.V. (ed.), *Blake: Prophet against Empire* (Princeton, NJ: Princeton University Press, 1977).

Essick, R., and J. Viscomi, *Milton, A Poem* (London: Blake Trust/Tate Gallery, 1998).

Fisch, H., *The Biblical Presence in Shakespeare, Milton and Blake* (Oxford: Clarendon Press, 1999).

Frye, N., *Fearful Symmetry* (Princeton, NJ: Princeton University Press, 1947).

Glen, H., *Vision and Disenchantment* (Cambridge: Cambridge University Press, 1983).

Goldsmith, S., *Unbuilding Jerusalem: Apocalypse and Romantic Representation* (Ithaca, NY: Cornell University Press, 1993).

Hagstrum, J.H., 'Blake and the Sister-Arts Tradition', in *Blake's Visionary Forms Dramatic* (ed. D. Erdman and J. Grant; Princeton: Princeton University Press, 1970), pp. 82-91

—'The Wrath of the Lamb: A Study of William Blake's Conversions', in *From Sensibility to Romanticism* (ed. F. Hilles and H. Bloom; Oxford: Oxford University Press, 1965), pp. 311-30.

Harrison, J.F.C., *The Second Coming: Popular Millenarianism 1780–1850* (London: Routledge & Kegan Paul, 1979).

Keith Suchard, M., *Why Mrs Blake Cried: William Blake and the Sexual Basis of Spiritual Vision* (London: Century, 2006).

Lindberg, B., *William Blake's Illustrations to the Book of Job* (Abo: Abo Akademi, 1973).

Lowth, Robert, *Lectures on the Sacred Poetry of the Hebrews* (London: Routledge, 1995).
McGann, J.J., 'The Idea of the Indeterminate Text: Blake's Bible of Hell and Dr Alexander Geddes', *Studies in Romanticism* 25 (1986), pp. 303-24.
Mee, J., *Dangerous Enthusiasm* (Oxford: Clarendon Press, 1992).
Mitchell, W.J.T., *Iconology: Image, Text, Ideology* (Chicago: Chicago University Press, 1986).
Moskal, J., *Blake, Ethics, and Forgiveness* (Tuscaloosa: University of Alabama Press, 1994).
Nuttall, A.D., *The Alternative Trinity: Gnostic Heresy in Marlowe, Milton and Blake* (Oxford: Clarendon Press, 1998).
Paley, M.D., *Apocalypse and Millennium in English Romantic Poetry* (Oxford: Clarendon Press, 1999).
—*The Apocalyptic Sublime* (New Haven: Yale University Press, 1986).
Prickett S., and C. Strathman, 'Blake and the Bible', in *Palgrave Advances in William Blake Studies* (ed. Nicholas Williams; London: Palgrave Macmillan, 2005), pp. 109-31.
Priestman, M., *Romantic Atheism: Poetry and Free Thought, 1780–1830* (Cambridge: Cambridge University Press, 1999).
Raine, K., *The Human Face of God: Blake and the Book of Job* (London: Thames & Hudson, 1982).
Roberts, J., *William Blake's Poetry: A Reader's Guide* (London: Continuum, 2007).
Rowland, C., 'Blake and the Bible: Biblical Exegesis in the Work of William Blake', in *Biblical Interpretation: The Meanings of Scripture—Past and Present* (ed. John Court; London: T. & T. Clark International, 2003), pp. 168-84.
—'Blake and the Bible: Biblical Exegesis in the Work of William Blake', *International Journal of Systematic Theology* 7 (2005), pp. 142-55.
—'Ezekiel's Merkavah in the Work of William Blake and Christian Art', in *The Reception History of Ezekiel* (ed. H. de Jonge; London: Ashgate, 2007), pp. 182-97.
Ruskin, J., *Modern Painters* (London: Smith, 1846).
Ryan, R., *The Romantic Reformation: Religious Politics in English Literature 1789–1824* (Cambridge: Cambridge University Press, 1997).
Tannenbaum, L., *Biblical Tradition in Blake's Early Prophecies: The Great Code of Art* (Princeton, NJ: Princeton University Press, 1982).
Thompson, E.P., *Witness against the Beast* (Cambridge: Cambridge University Press, 1993).
Tyndale, W., *The Obedience of a Christian Man* (ed. and with an Introduction and Notes by David Daniell; London: Penguin, 2000).
Viscomi, J., *Blake and the Idea of the Book* (Princeton, NJ: Princeton University Press, 1993).
Winstanley, Gerrard, 'The Fire in the Bush', in *Radical Christian Writings: A Reader* (ed. A. Bradstock and C. Rowland; Oxford: Blackwell, 2002), pp. 120-37.

INDEXES

INDEX OF REFERENCES

Index of Authors

www.ingramcontent.com/pod-product-compliance
Lightning Source LLC
LaVergne TN
LVHW020051110826
845155LV00021B/64

* 9 7 8 1 9 0 6 0 5 5 9 1 2 *